DICTIONARY OF
DAILY LIFE
OF INDIANS
OF THE AMERICAS

DICTIONARY OF
DAILY LIFE
OF INDIANS
OF THE AMERICAS

VOLUME TWO

AMERICAN INDIAN PUBLISHERS, INC.
177 F Riverside Avenue
Newport Beach, California

Library of Congress Cataloging in Publication Data
Main entry under title:

Dictionary of daily life of Indians of the Americas.

Includes index.
1. Indians--Dictionaries and encyclopedias.
E54.5.D53   306'.08997   82-1761
ISBN 0-937862-26-6   AACR2

Much of the material included in this edition also appears in the twenty volume Encyclopedia of Indians of the Americas and is used with permission of the publishers.

GOUGE is a chisel-like instrument with a curved or hollowed blade, used in many parts of aboriginal North America primarily for working wood and stone. Indians in some areas where maple sap was collected reportedly used gouge-like instruments for tapping the trees. Most gouges were of stone or bone, but some were of shell, antler, or copper. Many are hard to distinguish from adze and scraper blades unless they were supplied with a handle which is still intact. A gouge used by the Eskimos and Indians of the Eastern Woodlands consisted of a wooden handle with a beaver tooth set in one or both ends.

GOURDS are fruits that were widely employed for vessels as well as in a number of other ways by the Indians of the Americas. Before the invention of pottery these plants must have been particularly valuable to man, and their use continued after the arrival of pottery, as it does today in many parts of the Americas. The fruits of both plants have been called both gourds and calabashes and sometimes the distinction between them is not made. However, the plants producing them are very different. One, usually called the *bottle gourd,* comes from a cucurbit *(Lagenaria siceraria)* whereas the other, the tree gourd, comes from a bignoniaceous plant *(Crescentia cujete).* The latter is a small tree, widespread in the American tropics, whereas the former is a large vine, also widespread in the tropics but whose cultivation extended into the temperate zone as well. It is generally agreed that the bottle gourd is native to Africa, but it is found in Mexico at 7000 BC and nearly as early in Peru. Thus it appears to be one of the oldest domesticated plants in the Americas, and how it arrived here has been the subject of much discussion. Some have held that it must have been carried by man, whereas others believe that the fruits must have floated across the Atlantic. Since the fruit has been shown to float for long periods in salt water without losing seed viability, the latter view is quite plausible.

GRASSWORK was used for ornamental, utilitarian, and ceremonial purposes among various tribes.

Indians of the South, the Hopi and Pima of the Southwest, the Tlingit of the Northwest Coast, and Eskimos sometimes wove grass into their baskets. Some tribes used polished white and yellow grass stems as basket decoration. The Hupa of Northwest California used stems as fringe on clothing. Flat grass stems, sometimes dyed, were sewn onto dressed skins as decoration in a manner similar to that used with porcupine quills.

In the Midwest the Wichita and Caddo Indians made loose grass into domed, thatched houses in which several families lived. Grass was used for bedding, fiber for cord, perfume, and tinder. The Cheyenne burned grass to make paint of the ashes mixed with blood and tallow. Pueblo Indians tied stiff stems into bundles for use as hairbrushes.

Grass was used in ceremonies by several tribes. Some Plains Indians burned grass for lighting the pipe in rituals. Some placed balls of grass into the eye sockets and nose of sacred buffalo skin in the belief grass would make it live. The Pawnee used sod in a ritual as a symbol of life and growth.

GRINDING STONE is any of a wide variety of hard abrasive stones used universally from earliest times in North America for grinding stone, bone, ivory, wood, shell, and metal in the shaping, sharpening, and polishing of a side range of tools, weapons, and other objects. Any hard, gritty rock was used such as diorite, quartzite, or granite. Grinding stones varied in size from those easily held in one hand to large exposed surfaces of rock. They are often distinguishable from ordinary rocks only by signs of wear such as narrow grooves left from sharpening projectile and other points or broad channels made in shaping larger implements.

Grinding, as well as being an important means of shaping softer materials, was one of the principle methods of working stone, for which it was usually

the youth, encouraging initiative in war, hunting, and other activities. It was believed that the guardian spirit would protect from almost any predicament. A vision quest for a guardian spirit was part of the process of acquiring the mark of maturity. Throughout the Great Lakes area and the Mississippi Valley the vision of a guardian spirit was a necessary part of growing up and the first religious retreat, or "hambeday," marked an important event in the life of a youth that could be compared to confirmation in Christian terms. The spirits sometimes were given names such as Canoe People or War Spirit. In some areas important spirits came only to chiefs or shamans. Commoners had less powerful guardian spirits. Among the hunter-gatherers, visions and the friendly help of guardian spirits were available to the average tribesman. The spirit could be contacted only through a vision that was reached after strenuous effort, but when reached he was sure to promise good luck throughout life.

South America

Shamans derived their power from their association with spirits whom they could summon at will to assist them in their many functions. As a rule, ordinary men did not enjoy any companionship with the super-naturals and, therefore, were obliged to resort to shamans when they needed the spirits' assistance. Nevertheless, the notion of the guardian spirit is not entirely lacking in South America; some references occur in the literature, but apparently the concept never was so clearly defined as among North American Indians.

The best instance of the quest for a guardian spirit in the North American manner occurs among the *Charrua* of Uruguay.

Some men went on top of a solitary hill where there was a pile of stones to fast in order to find a companion. There they inflicted on themselves many wounds and suffered a rigorous penance until in their mind they saw a living being whom they invoked in times of peril as their guardian angel.

Witoto myths collected by Preuss contain frequent

allusions to protecting animal spirits captured during a hunting party. They advised their master when he was in danger and ran errands for him. There is also an allusion to a guardian spirit in a *Taulipang* myth in which a mutilated man sends his spirit in the guise of a bird to warn his wife.

A statement about the beliefs of the *Island Carib* may be construed as a reference to guardian spirits.

They believe that these good spirits, or gods, are many and every person believes that among them he has one all to himself; this is his particular spirit, his own familiar.

Yet spirits were invoked only through shamans, so that it seems these familiars were not guardian spirits in the strict sense of the word.

Every *Yahgan* was under the protection of a diminutive spirit assigned to him at his birth by a shaman.

The notion of the guardian spirit may perhaps throw some light on the nature of the mystic relationship between the *Inca* and his Wauki, or supernatural guardian, with whom he was united by a fraternal bond. The supernatural brother was represented by a statue. Still, there is little evidence that the belief in a personal guardian was widespread in Peru and even less that it was the soul of some ayllu ancestor.

GUMS AND RESINS. From humble beginnings, the chewing-gum industry has become big business, built on *chicle* (chee-klay). This principal ingredient of "gum" is from a tree, also named chicle, that yields one of the finest white resins in the world. This is in Middle America, where, during the rainy season, the Indians extract the resin by a process similar to that for obtaining rubber. The Indian name in the Nahuatl language is *chictle*.

Incidentally, the wood of the tree is of remarkable value. The Maya carved logs of it into beams for their vast temples, where it has withstood the ravages of time for a thousand years.

GUNS, primarily shoulder weapons, were first acquired by Indians on the North Atlantic Coast in the seventeenth century through trade with the French, English, and Dutch. As guns diffused along with the migration of whites throughout the rest of North America during the next two centuries, they became a significant factor in the drastic enviromental, cultural, and economic changes experienced by the Indians during those times.

The early smooth-bore muzzle-loading muskets were not immediately adopted by the Indians in preference to traditional weapons. Compared to the bow and arrow they were more awkward and time consuming to load and less dependable. Gradually, however, improved forms of the musket and later the rifle were developed until in the nineteenth century the breech-loading rifle, cartridge ammunition, and finally the repeating rifle came into use. In hunting and warfare the improved guns, for Indians who could obtain them, rendered the bow and arrow and the lance largely obsolete.

In warfare the use of rifles and cannon by whites put Indians using native weapons at a tremendous disadvantage. The use of guns in war was one of the major factors contributing to a much higher proportion of combatants killed than generally had occurred in earlier traditional forms of Indian warfare.

Hunting by the Indians before aquisition of guns had been primarily for subsistence purposes. It had been a limiting factor on the animal populations hunted but generally had not seriously depleted them or threatened the survival of any species. The efficiency of the gun coupled with the tremendous growth of the fur trade was a major factor in producing excessive hunting pressure by both Indians and whites. The diffusion of guns throughout North America was repeatedly followed by serious depletion of game populations on which most Indians depended to a significant extent for food. Probably the most well known example is that of the buffalo on the Plains, where the use of the gun and horse made possible the reduction of a population ranging from Canada to Mexico to near extinction within about eighty years.

H

HABITATIONS. *See* DWELLINGS.

HACIENDAS. Although, in time, the *encomienda* and the *hacienda* became confused, at the start, there were radical differences between the two institutions in Latin America. In general, these lay in (1) form of ownership, (2) labor employed, and (3) type of production.

With respect to the first, ownership of the *encomienda* was insecure, whereas that of the *hacienda* was definitive; that is to say, the latter might be bequeathed, transferred, or sold, without restriction.

The second difference also was fundamental. Whereas the *encomendero* had forced native labor at his disposition, the *hacendado* was obliged to hire help—although, upon occasion, the Indians might give him manual labor by means of a *repartimiento*. The *hacienda* gave rise to a new social stratum: the peon, composed in part of Indians and in part of imported Negro workmen.

The third distinction lay in the fact that the *encomienda* tended, as a rule, to preserve ancient crops and ancient methods of cultivation, whereas, under the *hacienda,* a different type of economic activity generally was developed—in Totonacapan, particularly stock raising and sugar cane production.

Late sixteenth-century records mention numerous authorizations for Spanish colonists to establish ranches *(estancias)*. Undoubtedly, the lands were indigenous property, either abandoned by the occupants or taken from them. At the time of the Discovery the great Totonac center of "Cempoala" is credited by one source with between 20,000 and 30,000 *vecinos* (heads of families) by another with "more than twenty thousand houses." But by the end of the sixteenth century, it was reduced to 12 taxable individuals and a few years later, to 8 heads of families (*indios casados*). The greater part of its lands were converted into cattle ranches and stock raising became of considerable importance.

Haciendas dedicated to sugar cane and its elaboration also flourished, contributing to the reduction in numbers and to the dispersal of the native population, and at the same time stimulating the introduction of Negro slaves.

HAIR AND HAIRWORK made from animal, and occasionally human hair were widely used as textile material. Animals which provided hair were the horse, deer, moose, buffalo, mountain goat, sheep, dog, rabbit, beaver, and others.

Hair was used as decoration in many areas. Indians of the Eastern Woodlands embroidered moose hair onto a deerskin, cloth, or birchbark base which they made into garments, pouches, and moccasins. They frequently dyed the deerskin black to contrast with the soft colors of the vegetable dyed moose hair. Midwest Indians wove spun buffalo hair into pouches which were used to store medicine bundles or were presented as gifts. By the middle of the 19th century they used commercial yarn instead of buffalo hair. Fringe made of dyed deer hair decorated these bags. Plains Indians decorated hides of deer, elk, or buffalo, which were sometimes painted, with dyed horsehair or porcupine quills. In the Southwest, horsehair was used on Kachina masks and dolls by the Hopi and Zuni Indians. In the 20th century Papagos have made miniature baskets of horsehair. Among the Northwest Coast tribes the Tlingit wove goat hair into abstract animal designs on a cedar bark base to make clothing such as shirts and shoulder blankets, which were worn by the wealthy.

Hair was used not only for decoration but also for utilitarian purposes. It was sometimes braided into

BRAIDS

Utes, Hualpai Taos

**LOOSE HAIR
(WITH BANGS)**
Cocopah, Havasupai, others

HAIR KNOT
Havasupai, Papago

BRAID-DOUBLE CHONGO
Pueblos

**LOOSE HAIR
(WITHOUT BANGS)**
Yuma, Maricopa Mohave

**LOOSE HAIR
(WITHOUT BANGS)**
Apache, Papazo, others

LOW KNOT
Pima

BRAIDS
Plains Indians
(note scalp lock)

cord and used as rope. Horsehair has been used as stuffing for items such as pillows, dolls, and drumsticks. Some Plains Indians used cowskin pads stuffed with animal hair instead of saddles. Hair was sometimes combined with other fibers in weaving textiles and baskets.

HAMMER is an ancient and common tool fashioned with a wide variety of forms and purposes by the North American aborigines. Hammers ranged in size from small finger-held stones to large sledges. They were either hafted or unhafted, and the heads were made primarily of stone, but also of bone, ivory, shell, antler, and copper. Wooden mallets were probably used to some extent from ancient times but are difficult to detect archaeologically.

The most simple, common, and ancient hammers were unhafted stones having little or no shaping. They ranged from the size of walnuts to large rocks requiring two hands to lift. These hammerstones are often nearly indistinguishable from ordinary stones except for signs of wear, but some were fashioned in a thick discoidal shape with shallow depressions in each side for gripping. As well as being of general utility, hammerstones were commonly used for pecking and flaking in fashioning other stone implements.

Pounding tools with both a head and handle fashioned from a single piece of stone were widely distributed. They are of a wide range of craftsmanship and variety of forms, and their history is not well known. The majority are in the shape of large pestles consisting of a heavy base with a curved or flat bottom face, and of a thinner upper section, sometimes knobbed or ridged, for the handle.

HAMMOCK, an Indian invention, has wide distribution, with concentration in the Orinoco-Amazon region of South America.

Hammock materials are chiefly leaf fibers, bast, and cotton. Inner barks are pulled off, split into small strands and dried (*Tule*); pinnate leaflets of the tucum palm are shredded with thumb and forefingers. Thigh spinning combines singles into double-ply cord (*Witoto, Tucano, Yagua*).. Palm fiber is commonly used for hammocks throughout the Guiana region, and balls of spun fiber are an important trade item in some districts (*Tucano*); caraguata fibers (*Bromelia*) are used by the *Lengua*; maguey (*Agave americana*) by tribes in Central America. Smaller *Carib* hammocks are sometimes made of aeta palm wraps and cotton wefts; similar combinations are reported from the *Aueto, Mojo,* and some *Arawak*-speaking tribes on the upper Xingu. The idea of using cotton has spread among bast using tribes (*Guianas, Bacairi, Chane*) chiefly through the *Carib* and *Guarani*. Tribes that have not completely substituted cotton for bast still use both materials. Cotton hammock cord must be strong. Ordinarily, two or more spinnings are given to reduce the size and make the strand more uniform (*Tule*). The *Arecuna* grow, spin, and distribute spun cotton in a district where hammock making is very important. Twine is offered for sale or exchange in big balls of sufficient size to complete one hammock. The *Paressi* and *Mundurucu* also make fine cotton hammock twine. Among the *Central Arawak* there is much trade in hammocks with the whites; the makers vary the sizes, textures, and qualities. Provisional hammocks were fashioned by Guiana Indians from bush rope and lianas; the *Apinaye, Eastern Timbira,* and *Sherente* make only this type by plaiting together tips of buriti palm leaflets. The hammock length includes that of the bed plus the length of suspension cords. Guiana Indians set their poles from 5 to 7 feet apart; bamboo supporting frames may be from over 6 to nearly 10 feet in size (lower Xingu); the ordinary *Paressi* hammocks are often more than 10 by 4 feet; the regulation length of hammocks on the Rio Negro reaches 15 feet.

Hammock techniques include the following:

(1) True weaving by interlacing warp and weft elements as in cloth making. *Tule* and *Cuna* weave on a frame of poles bound together with vines. Each *Tule* village has several of these, communally owned. There is no heddle arrangement: weft is put through with the

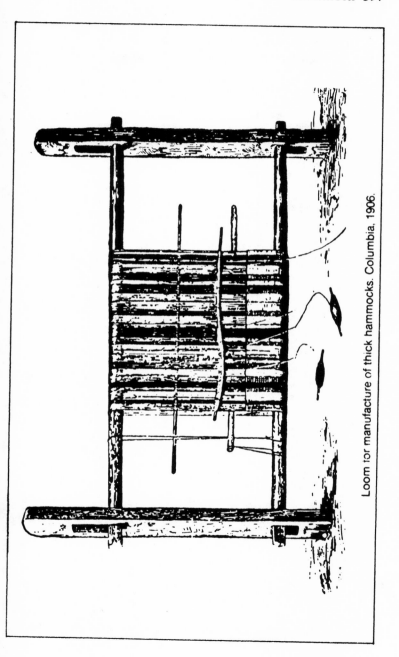

Loom for manufacture of thick hammocks. Columbia, 1906.

fingers; the battening sword is the only tool. Thick clothlike hammocks are made among tribes in Venezuela and Columbia; in northwest Brazil they are woven on *Arawak* looms equipped with shed roll and heddle stick with pendent loops. The weaver has bobbins and a weaving sword. Although there is some doubt regarding the technique employed by lower Xingu tribes, their hammocks are clothlike in texture.

(2) In the Guiana region hammocks with twined "bars" are made on frames consisting of two upright poles sunk in the ground, on upright frames without or with head sticks like the ordinary *Arawak* loom, and on special contrivances for holding warps taut (*Cubeo*). Warping is done by different methods; women in some Guiana tribes walk around and around two poles carrying big balls of cotton string in their hands. Warps are spaced and slack is eliminated as work proceeds.

The warp skein in barred hammocks is crossed at regular intervals by two twining weft elements or by two pairs of countertwined weft elements. Wooden gages maintain uniform distances between the bars. The side of the *Paressi* hammock edges are broken by small tassels formed by knotting the ends of the weft elements.

Simple twining appears in hammocks from *Tupi* groups, from *Mojo, Chiriguano, Bacairi,* the Guapore River, etc.

(3) *Cayapa* hammocks are netted with coarse pita string. No mesh gage is used, since the meshes are from 4 to 6 inches on a side. The term netting may have been used more often to indicate appearance than technique. The *Warrau* make "purse net" hammocks on square wooden frames raised up from the ground; the hammock cord is a continuous length. Held in a long skein, it is stretched to make a warp element between the end-bars, then is returned to enclose it and the previously stretched warp in a wrapping coil. *Witoto* procedures cross strings "knotted" from one edge string to that on the opposite side. The hammock frame consists of two posts driven into the hut floor; the only tools are the women's fingers. Finely netted bases of palm string are characteristic of the feather-decorated hammocks of northwest Amazon tribes; *Tupi-Cawahib*

net small hammocks. Women on the upper Xingu in netting hammocks use a wooden needle. "Looped" bast-fiber hammocks are reported from the *Tule* and *Choco;* "coiled netting" for the *Guaymi.*

Guiana tribes use three shuttles to enclose each long hammock warp in a unit of three-strand braid; cross bars are spaced.

Men and women make hammocks. The latter frequently make the bed, and men add the heavier suspension cords, which are adjusted to make the hammock hang evenly. Men and women work on the same hammock in Guiana tribes; among the *Bora* it is woman's "light work."

Hammocks are colored in various ways: by painting while yet on the loom (Guianas), and by striping with colored string prepared before the fabrication is commenced. The *Aueto* alternate dark blue and white bands of cotton weft on tucum warp; the *Tucano* set up blue, yellow, and red stripes; the *Arekena* set up multicolored stripe patterns.

HARPOON is a spear with one or two detachable heads to which a retrieving line is connected, used by many North American aborigines for hunting fish, aquatic mammals, and sea turtles. Its primary advantage was that once the point was embedded, the line was much more effective than a spear shaft for holding, playing, and retrieving the prey, especially larger species. Harpoons were used throughout most of the Arctic, eastern and western Subarctic, Great Lakes region, Northwest Coast, southern California, and in parts of the Plateau, Great Basin, northeastern United States, and possibly on the east coast of Florida. They are still an important hunting weapon of the Eskimos.

Before iron and steel were readily available, harpoons were made of wood, bone, ivory, shell, stone, sinew, and hide. The detachable harpoon heads were of two general types: a barbed head with the line attached near its butt end, the barbs serving to hold it fast in the prey; a toggle-head, which was slightly

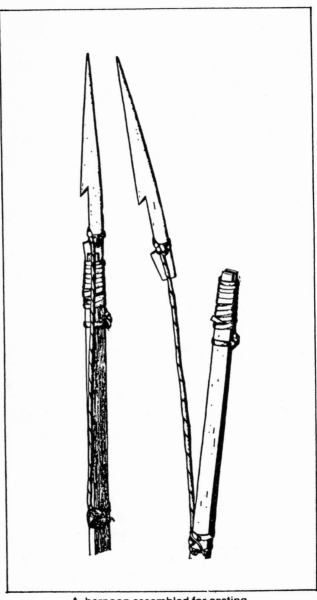

A harpoon assembled for casting.

HIDES AND SKINS were one of the most important and versatile natural materials utilized by North American Indians. They were used to some extent by all tribes but most commonly in the Arctic, Subarctic, northeastern United States, Prairies, and Plains, where tribes depended primarily on hunting for their subsistence.

Among hunting tribes, tanned hide was the commonest material used for clothing. Buckskin, because of its softness and pliability, was favored for articles worn next to the skin. Other hides, such as those of the Plains. It was the most common covering for dwellings, used either alone or in combination with other materials, in most of the Arctic, Subarctic, Prairies, and parts of the Northwest Coast, Plateau, Great Basin, and Southwest. Many storage and transport containers were made of hide, which was one of the most practical materials for this purpose among nomadic tribes. The Eskimos used seal or other skin as the covering for the kayak and umiak, and other hide boats were used in parts of the eastern and western Subarctic, Northwest Coast, Plains, Great Lakes region, and Southeast. Hide was also one of the most widely used materials for defensive armor. The most common shield was a circular hide type characteristic of the Plains and several other areas. Hide was the material most frequently used for body armor, the commonest form consisting simply of an untailored hide wrapped around the body under one arm and tied over the opposite shoulder. One of the most indispensable and universal uses of hide was for lashing, either alone or in combination with natural cements, in the construction of boats, dwellings, tools, weapons, religious objects, and many other articles.

Colonists and early Anglo-American frontiersmen often adopted Indian methods of utilizing hides and skins. The growth of the fur trade and the introduction of the gun and steel trap, however, eventually led to serious depletion of game populations. Game shortages and introduction of mass-produced textiles and other European materials and technology largely eliminated the role of hides and skins in Indian culture.

HIEROGLYPHICS. A postclassic phase of Mayan civilization flourished in Yucatan, heavily influenced by contact with Mexican (i.e. Aztec and Toltec) culture, until the Spanish conquest. Major sites include Chichen Itza and Uxmal. At the time of the arrival of the Spaniards, this civilization was still partly alive, and a system of hieroglyphic writing, on bark paper and in stone, was still in use. This writing, and the religious and calendrical systems represented by means of it, must rank among the highest cultural artistic, and intellectual achievements of aboriginal America. The decipherment of the writing system began in the latter part of the last century, and relied at first especially on materials from Yucatan, including the three surviving Mayan codices, painted in many colors on bark paper, and pleated accordion-fashion. These codices, known as the Dresden, the Madrid, and the Paris, for the libraries where the originals are kept, were interpreted with the help of a document prepared by the first Bishop of Yucatan, Diego de Landa (1524-1579) containing much information on the knowledge and practices of the Yucatec Mayas which the Spanish were then energetically suppressing. An edition of this document, *Landa's Relacion de las cosas de Yucatan,* translated into English and heavily annotated by A. M. Tozzer, remains an excellent source of information on the culture of Yucatan at this period, and contains precious information on the writing system given to Landa by Mayas who still knew it. The system consists of several hundred signs, some used as word signs, some used as syllable signs, to "spell out" or to remind the reader of pronunciations, and some used as "affixes" in a variety of ways in combination with main signs. The interpretation of the arithmetic and calendrical signs, explained more fully in Landa, is essentially complete, and most signs for deities have been reasonably well identified. Landa was less helpful with the textual uses of the glyphs, however, since he seems to have considered the system

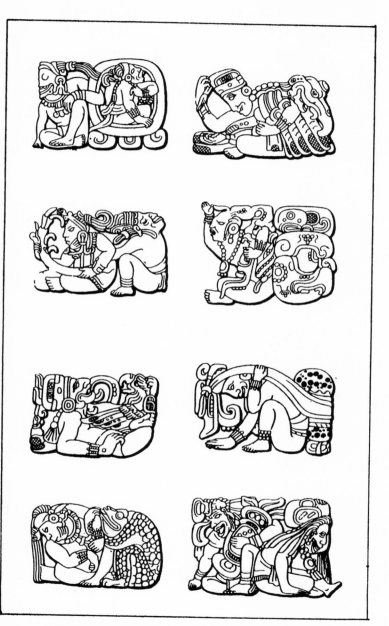

Maya Hieroglyphs (carved on stone stela).

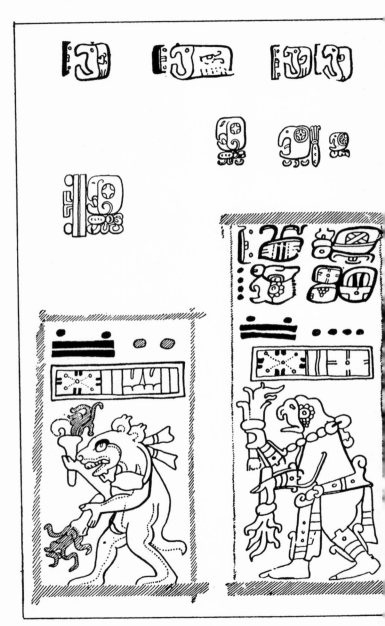

Glyphs of the month Kayab and turtle figures.

Glyphs and diety figures from the Maya codices.

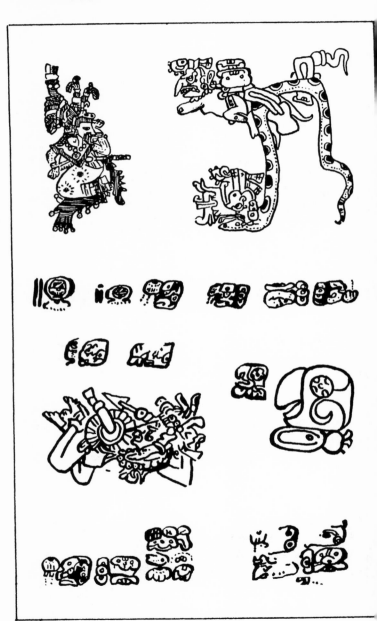

Glyphs and diety figures from the Maya codices.

as alphabetic in principle, which it certainly is not. With the aid of studies of earlier inscriptions, however, the content of textual passages is slowly becoming clearer, though much remains to be learned.

HORSE. The wild horse roamed over North America in late Pleistocene times; it became extinct less than 10,000 years ago. It was associated with the ancestors of the Indians as demonstrated in cave deposits in southern Chile; but Indians living in the New World have traditions of such an animal. The Spanish expeditions and settlements brought horses into the country during the 16th century.

The first horses seen by the Indians were those of the Spanish invaders of Mexico. A few years later De Soto brought the horse into Florida and westward to the Mississippi, while Coronado, on his march to Quivira in 1541, introduced it to the Indians of the Great Plains. When the Aztec saw the mounted men of Cortes they supposed horse and man to be one.

It was worshiped by the Aztec, and by most of the tribe was considered to have a mysterious or sacred character. Its origin was explained by myths representing horses to have come out of the earth through lakes and springs or from the sun. When Antonio de Espejo visited the Hopi of Arizona in 1583, the Indians spread cotton scarfs or kilts on the ground for the horses to walk on, believing it to be sacred. This sacred character is sometimes shown in the names given to the horse, as the Dakota *sunka wakan,* 'mysterious dog.' Its use in transportation accounts for the term 'dog' often applied to it, as the Siksika *ponokamita,* 'elk dog;' Cree *mistatim,* 'big dog;' Shawnee *mishawa* 'elk.'

The Indians of the forests learned to use them sparingly, but the Natives of Mexico and southwestern United States took them readily, especially the Apache, Navajo and others. From here horses spread rapidly northward by trade and theft. Lewis and Clark found Indians using them in Washington and parts of Oregon. They were not adopted by the Indians of

California and Nevada; but along the main range of the Rocky Mountains and eastward to the Mississippi all of the tribes soon became horse Indians, turning more nomadic. The Kiowa, for example, ranged more than 1000 miles in a summer. Some eastern forest tribes, formerly partially agricultural, moved out into the grassland, acquired horses and lived as hunting nomads, adopting the culture of the horse Indians.

Culture

The possession of the horse had an important influence on the culture of the Indians and changed the mode of life of many tribes. Before they had horses the Indians were footmen, making short journeys and transporting their possessions mostly on their backs. The hunting Indians possessed an insignificant amount of property, since the quantity that they could carry was small. All this was changed. An animal had been found which could carry burdens and drag loads. The Indians soon realized that the possession of such an animal would increase their freedom of movement and enable them to increase their property, since one horse could carry the load of several men. Besides this, it insured a food supply and made the moving of camps easy and swift and long journeys possible. In addition to the use of the horse as a burden bearer and as a means of moving rapidly from place to place, it was used as a medium of exchange.

The introduction of the horse led to new intertribal relations; systematic war parties were sent forth.

The horse was usually killed at the grave of its owner, just as his arms were buried with him, in order that he might be equipped for the journey that he was about to take. A number of Plains tribes practiced a horse dance. There were songs about horses, and prayers were made in their behalf. On the whole, however, the horse's place in ceremony was only incidental. On the occasion of great gatherings horses were led into the circle of the dancers and there given away, the donor counting a coup as he passed over the gift to the recipient.

Among some tribes a father gave away a horse when

his son killed his first big game or on other important family occasions. In the dances of the soldier-band societies of most tribes 2,4, or 6 chosen men ride horses during the dance. Their horses were painted, the tails were tied up as for war, hawk or owl feathers were tied to the forelock or tail, and frequently a scalp, or something representing it, hung from the lower jaw. The painting represents wounds received by the rider's horse, or often there is painted the print of a hand on either side of the neck to show that an enemy on foot had been ridden down. In preparing to go into a formal battle the horse as well as his rider received protective treatment. It was ceremonially painted and adorned, as described above, and certain herbs and medicines were rubbed or blown over it to give it endurance and strength.

Among some of the Plains tribes there was a guild of horse doctors who devoted themselves especially to protecting and healing horses. They doctored horses before going into battle or to the buffalo hunt, so that they should not fall, and doctored those wounded in battle or on the hunt, as well as the men hurt in the hunt. In intertribal horse races they "doctored" in behalf of the horses of their own tribe and against those of their rivals.

HOUSES. *See* DWELLINGS.

HUNTING. Indians were keen naturalists. They knew the life-histories of the animals they hunted, the different stages of their growth, their seasonal movements and hibernation haunts, and the various foods they sought for sustenance. Difficulties of observation naturally prevented them from gaining as complete a knowledge of the habits of the fish, but they recognized every stage of the salmon from the egg to the adult, and the Nootka of Vancouver island artificially stocked their rivers by transporting salmon ova from one stream to another. Nor were the Indians less observant of the flora of their territories, noting not only the edible plants, and those that were useful for tools, weapons, and various household appliances, but many inconspicuous varieties that apparently served no useful purpose whatever. Their interest in their environment, and eagerness to experiment, led to their discovering the medical properties of many plants, and Indian simples gained a deservedly high repute among the early colonists. Several of them, indeed, have found a place in our culture, and others fail to appear there only because modern science has found better sources elsewhere for the same remedies.

Nowhere was the Indian's keenness of observation more displayed than in hunting. Few have equalled them in these pursuits, except when superior equipment has given them an initial advantage; for the aborigines employed practically every method that was known to the white man, and others that were unknown. All tribes were not equally proficient in both pursuits; some excelled in hunting, others in fishing; and there were poor hunters, and poor fishermen, in every community. The Cree, who were among the most skillful hunters on the continent, regarded fishing as an occupation worthy only of women, and scorned their Chipewayan neighbours, who were keener fishermen but less proficient in hunting moose and caribou. Generally speaking, however, the average Indian, whatever his tribe, possessed more ability in both pursuits than the average white man, because from his earliest childhood he was trained to give the closest attention and study to every outdoor phenomenon.

Among all the methods of securing game, the still-hunt offers perhaps the greatest scope for individual skill. To the experienced Indian a turned leaf, a broken twig, a slight scraping of a tree, a faint track in the moss, each told a story. In the treeless Arctic the Eskimo who sighted a caribou tested the direction of the air-current by tossing up a shred of down or fur, or by moistening his finger to discover which side felt the cooler; then, if the topography of the ground prevented him from approaching his quarry under cover, he would wait in hiding for several hours, or he would imitate its actions and gait, and boldly advancing into the open, lure it within range of his arrows. Similarly, the Prairie Indian often masked himself under a buffalo hide and approached the buffalo herds unsuspected. Many of the natives could imitate the calls of various birds and animals; and the "moose-call" of the Algonquin tribes, usually performed with a roll of birch-bark, has been passed on to Europeans. The explorer Thompson, himself no mean hunter, pays tribute to the skill of one of his Cree. "An Indian came to hunt for us," he says, "and on looking about thought the ground good for moose, and told us to make no noise; he was told no noise would be made except the falling of the trees, this he said the moose did not mind; when he returned, he told us he had seen the place a doe moose had been feeding in the beginning of May; in two days more he had unravelled her feeding places to the beginning of September. One evening he

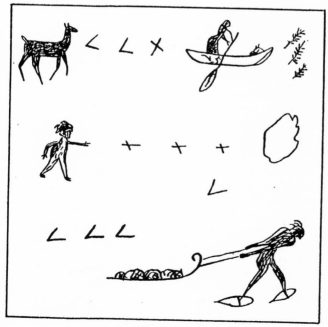

Hunting notices.

remarked to us, that he had been so near to her that he could proceed no nearer, unless it blew a gale of wind, when this took place he set off early, and shot the moose deer. This took place in the very early part of October.''

Most Indian tribes employed dogs for bringing to bay their game, especially moose, bear, and caribou; they then attacked the quarry with spears rather than with bows and arrows, which often failed to take effect. The Eskimo dog was strong and hardy, and, though not a match for the Arctic wolf, fierce enough to check the progress of a polar bear; but the dogs possessed by the Indians were in gereral small and ill-nourished.

Until the Indians obtained firearms, however, and even after they secured flintlock guns that required reloading after each shot, the still-hunt, whether with or without dogs, was less effective against animals that wandered in herds, such as the deer, caribou, musk-oxen, and buffalo, than the community hunt in which a large body of men participated, often aided by women and children. This community hunt corresponded in many ways to the ''beating'' of tigers and leopards in the Asiatic jungles, and the rounding up of ostriches by the Bushmen of South Africa. It was indeed an ancient method, successfully employed by men of the Old Stone Age in Europe, thousands of years before the Christian era, in hunting the wild reindeer, mammoths, and other animals that in those days migrated back and forth across the Carpathian mountains. The Salish Indians of the Columbia river practised it in a very simple form; they merely surrounded a herd of antelope in a plain and shot down a small proportion before the remainder broke through the circle and escaped. The Plains Indians, the Iroquoians and other Eastern Woodland tribes, and the Indians of the Mackenzie River Basin adopted a more complex method; they drove or lured the buffalo, caribou, or deer into some kind of trap, usually an enclosed pound, and shot down entire herds. The old explorer Henry has left an excellent description of the

the buffalo from taking a wrong direction. There they lie down between fascines and cross-sticks, and if the buffalo attempt to break through, the people wave their robes, which causes the herd to keep on, or turn to the opposite side, where other persons do the same. When the buffalo have been thus directed to the entrance of the pound, the Indian who leads them rushes into it and out at the other side, either by jumping over the enclosure or creeping through an opening left for that purpose. The buffalo tumble in pell-mell at his heels, almost exhausted, but keep moving around the inclosure from east to west, and never in a direction against the sun. What appeared extraordinary to me on those occasions, was that when word was given to the camp of the near approach of the buffalo, the dogs would skulk away from the pound, and not approach until the herd entered. Many buffaloes break their legs, and some their necks, in jumping into the pound, as the descent is generally six or eight feet and stumps are left standing there. The buffalo being caught, the men assemble at the inclosure, armed with bows and arrows; every arrow has a particular mark of the owner, and they fly until the whole herd is killed.''

Buffalo were occasionally driven over precipices instead of into a pound; and their bones may still be recovered in large numbers from certain ravines on the prairies. The northern Indians, who saw no buffalo, but who impounded caribou during the winter months, often set hedges and snares inside their enclosures, which were built only of saplings and brush. In summer they adopted the same methods as the Eskimo, forcing the caribou into lakes and rivers to spear them from canoes, or else driving them against a line of archers concealed in shallow pits. The Nootka Indians similarly drove the black-tailed deer into bays and fiords, and the Algonquian Indians speared the moose as it swam from one bank or headland to another.

Steel traps for the capture of fur-bearing game originated, of course, with whites, but Indians had long employed both dead-falls and snares, the former mainly for carnivorous animals, the latter for herbivorous. Dead-falls, operated by some kind of trigger, were especially common in British Columbia, where the Carrier Indians alone constructed at least four varieties. Most of the Athapaskan tribes in the north depended largely on snares for the capture of caribou and moose, and everywhere this was the accepted method for small animals like rabbits, hares, and marmots, and for birds like grouse and ptarmigan. Both snares and dead-falls required the exercise of much ingenuity and woodcraft, and all the Indians were skilful trappers centuries before there were any trading posts where their furs could find a market.

Along with the more standard arrowheads the Indians designed several other point varieties primarily for hunting small game. Multiple-pointed arrows were used throughout the Arctic and Northwest Coast down to the Columbia River and by a few tribes in northern California, the Plateau, and the Southwest. Blunt or knobbed arrowheads were in widespread use. They had the advantages of greater durability and a smaller probability of sticking in trees if a shot was missed. A crossed-stick variety was made of from one to four small sticks, slightly larger than a match, glued or bound across the arrow shaft near its point. This type was used in the Southwest, Great Basin, and California, and in some parts of the Plateau and Northwest Coast. In the Arctic, multiple barbs or prongs were sometimes tied pointing forward near the middle of the arrow shaft. These afforded an additional chance of wounding small game if the arrow narrowly missed or glanced off.

The arrow shaft was usually of reed, cane, or stems or strips of wood. The Eskimo often used driftwood or pieces of bone lashed together. For durability, foreshafts of a harder material or grade of wood were often added.

The atlatl, also called spear thrower, throwing stick, throwing board, or dart sling, was a device for giving additional force and accuracy in throwing a dart, spear, or harpoon. It consisted of a shaft about one to two feet long with one end fashioned as a grip and the other notched to fit the trailing end of the spear. It was sometimes grooved lengthwise to accomodate the shaft of the spear. Some atlatls were apparently equipped with a stone weight or balance attached part way up the shaft for increased effectiveness.

The device was used in prehistoric times in the Great Basin, Southwest, Southeast, and southern Florida. It was used in both prehistoric and historic times by all Eskimo tribes, by the Tlingit on the Northwest Coast, in Baja California, and on the Mississippi Delta.

The atlatl appears to have lost much of its importance with the adoption of the bow and arrow.

I

INSTITUTE OF AMERICAN INDIAN ARTS
is a national institution for training in the arts directed to the special needs of Native Americans — the Indians, Eskimos, and Aleuts of the United States.

Creation of the Institute was recommended in 1960 by the Indian Arts and Crafts Board of the United States Department of the Interior. Founded in 1962 by the Bureau of Indian Affairs, USDI, the school is adminstered by the Bureau's Branch of Education. The Indian Arts and Crafts Board continues to serve as advisors for the development of the Institute.

Located in Santa Fe, New Mexico, the Institute is situated in the heart of the historic Pueblo Indian settlements clustered along the Rio Grande. As the focus of commerce and communication in the area since its founding about 1600, the city of Santa Fe has been intimately associated with Indian arts of the Southwest for more than three and a half centuries.

In the early 1930s the Bureau of Indian Affairs first centered specialized art training — primarily painting — at the Santa Fe Indian Boarding School. This school was one of the first to focus national attention on the potentials of specialized art education for Native American youth.

The facilities of the Santa Fe Indian Boarding School were remodeled in the early 1960s to accommodate the expanded concepts of the Institute of American Indian Arts.

Directed to Native American youth from all areas of the United States who are interested in a career in the arts, the Institute offers training in virtually every field of the arts — painting, graphics, sculpture, ceramics, textiles, exhibition arts, photography, as well as drama, music, the dance, creative writing, and a limited offering in commerical art.

Institute students, at both the high school and post-graduate levels, are provided the tools, leadership and freedom for exploration in a broad scope of contemporary disciplines, in combination with the encouragement of an appreciation and knowledge of historic Native American aesthetics. The Institute's educational program, administered by a highly qualified professional staff, is dedicated to offering the opportunity for today's Native American youth to make a significant and distinctive contribution to modern American culture.

J

JADE was commonly used by the Aztecs and other Mexican tribes, the Mayas, all Indians of Central America, the West Indians and the Peruvians; it was also used less commonly by the Eskimo and British Columbia Indians, the Mount Builders, the Pueblos, and the peoples of British Guiana, Ecuador, and Brazil. Nephrite, a variety of jade, was commonly used and highly prized by the Eskimo and the Indians of British Columbia, Venezuela, Colombia, Ecuador, and Brazil; it was also known to the Indians of Oregon and Washington, the Pueblos, the Aztecs, Mayas, the ancient Costa Ricans, and the Indians of Montserrat Island, Cuba, and the Lesser Antilles, and of Argentina and Chile. The single occurrence known among the Peruvian Indians is reported in the Ica Valley. It was also probably known to the Haitian Indians.

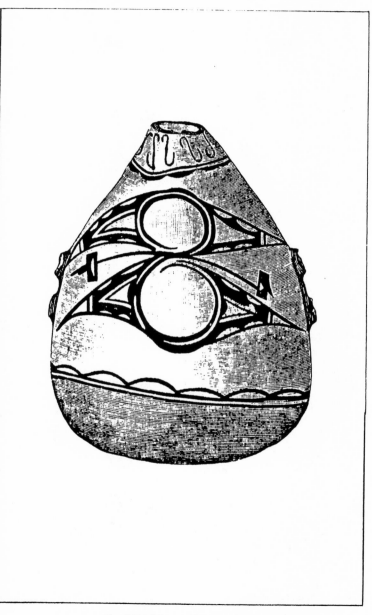

Zuni Pueblo ceremonial jar.

Wolpi water jars.

tribes. Their weight and bulk, and especially the fragility of clay jars, discouraged their use among more nomadic tribes who preferred lighter, more resiliant containers. Jars were of special value for the vital function of the protection and storage of food, especially seed and other plant foods, for winter or other periods of food scarcity.

In areas where bark or basketry containers were commonly used, these were sometimes made in semi-rigid watertight forms which approximated jars. Gourds, where they were cultivated in the Southwest, Prairies, Eastern Woodlands and Southeast, were frequently used to make jars. Specimens carved from soapstone have

Inca jar.

been found in some of the many areas north of Mexico where this material was used.

Thoughout much of the United States, southern Canada, and Alaska where clay utensils were in general use, baked clay jars were the most common type and were often decorated with incising or engraving. The fashioning of jars was most advanced and their use most prevalent where pottery was highly developed in parts of the Southwest and in the mound provinces of the Mississippi valley and the Gulf States. In these areas jars were made from a wide range of colored clays and were sometimes shaped and decorated for exclusively ornamental and ceremonial purposes.

JEWELRY served Indians throughout the Americas, as body decoration, indication of rank or wealth, and ceremonial regalia. Jewelry was crafter from bone, metals, seeds, wood, and whatever other materials were available.

Copper was widely traded from plentiful sources near the Great Lakes, in Alaska, and the Arctic, where it was picked up or gained from shallow excavations in nearly pure form. Copper beads, earrings, bracelets, and anklets were hammered out of the cold metal. But in Mexico, copper was melted and cast into bells by the lost-wax method. Prehistoric wood and shell jewelry has been found covered with thin sheets of copper overlay.

Shell was especially used as jewelry, being traded inland from both coasts and taken from rivers. Small shells were used as beads and strung into necklaces. Large pieces of shell were cut from clam, conch, and abalone, and were highly polished and decorated for use as ear pendants and gorgets. Small discs were cut out of shell, about the size and shape of a faucet washer, and strung together or used with other materials, for example, a prehistoric necklace from the Southwest that alternated discs of shell and turquoise. A circle was cut from the center of one valve of a clam shell, leaving the rim as a bracelet; small versions were finger rings.

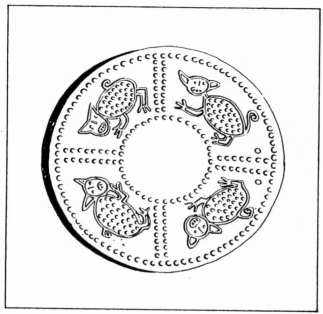

Breastplate.

Turquoise was quarried in the Southwest, and was the gem used most north of Mexico, but agate and other semi-precious stones were also employed. In pre-European Mexico, the gem galaxy was greater, including amber, rock crystal, onyx, and jade. Jade was more precious than gold to the Aztecs and was used only by the nobility. Jade pendants, bracelets, anklets, and figures were sometimes believed to hold magic charms.

Stone and bone beads were drilled, then carved into many shapes, polished, incised, and inlaid. Stone, bone, and metal were formed into labrets, nose ornaments, and earrings. Animal teeth and claws, such as seal teeth among the Eskimos and bear claws on the Plains, were turned into jewelry. Seeds and bark were used, too, and vegetable fibers were wound around leather, woven and braided to become bracelets, necklaces, and other ornaments.

Gold was probably unknown north of the Rio

Grande, but was beautifully worked and elaborately cast in ancient Mexico, especially by Mayan (*c.* A.D. 300–900) and later by Mixtec and Zapotec artists in Oaxaca. Their works in gold included necklaces, bracelets, labrets, finger rings, breastplates, and masks.

In the late 19th century, first the Navajo and then the Pueblo Indians learned to work metal. Navajo craftsmen began absorbing this skill in the 1850s by watching Mexican metal workers and U.S. army smiths. The confinement of over 8,000 Navajo at Fort Sumner from 1864 to 1868 was punitive instruction against stealing

Inca arm band.

sheep, but a so gave the Indians experience in metal working. Re urning to a homeland reservation Navajo smiths beca.ne professionals specializing in working silver, "the metal of the moon." White traders saw a profit here, and brought Mexican silversmiths to be teachers. The traders also provided a supply of silver — first from silver dollars, then Mexican pesos, and finally directly from California mines. Craftsmen at Zuni, Hopi, and the other Pueblos learned from the Navajo.

"The silversmith among either Pueblos or Navajos is a person of mighty influence," wrote an American traveler in the 1880s. The silversmith was something of a banker, each year turning about a third of the silver money that came to the tribes through trade into jewelry. The jewelry was prized aesthetically, as a status symbol, and was also a savings account.

Navajo beadmaking began in the 1870s, and about 1878–80, the first tone was set in silver, linking silver and turquoise. Silver ornaments were soldered onto other jewelry in a technique called *applique. Repoussage*, hammering the design outward from underneath, was practiced at the turn of the century. Elaborate bracelets were cast in carved-stone molds; the mold generally was used only once. Another bracelet style was called "stones-all-around," with usually seven matched stones wreathed in silver settings.

In 1881, a U.S. army lieutenant reported that the Navajo possessed abundant silver earrings and bracelets, and, "they make it into fantastic necklaces." The *naja*, a crescent-shaped ornament was a favorite pendant, as was the cross that may have been used first. The "squash blossom" motif in cast silver combined with turquoise was derived from a Spanish pomegranate design. Zuni developed a glowing mosaic form with the stones set between strands of silver to make abstract or figurative designs.

The classic period of Southwestern jewelry making (1889–1900) when Navajo smiths like Slender Maker of Silver turned the European craft into their own monumental art form, was followed by commercialization and curioism. But in the 1970s, artists like Charles Loloma, Hopi, created jewelry from the old materials

— silver, gold, ironwood, turquoise, coral, leather, and feathers — that was contemporary sculpture, but, in Loloma's words, "Reflects who I am, where I come from — everything becomes a part of it."

NANCY FINKE

K

KNIFE is an instrument with a sharpened edge for cutting, which the American aboriginese used universally from earliest times and fashioned in a variety of forms. Most knives were made from ground slate or chipped igneous stone, though wood, reed, bone, antler, shell, ivory, and animal teeth were also used. Copper blades have been found in the Great Lakes region and adjoining areas and on the Northwest Coast. Iron and steel, after their introduction, rapidly replaced the earlier materials in most forms. Knives ranged in size from small chips to two or three foot blades and often were hafted by cementing or lashing to a wood, bone, or ivory handle and carried on the person in sheaths. They were the Indian's most common sidearm and one of his most valuable implements in war, hunting, skinning and skin dressing, preparing and serving food, working wood, bark, hide, and other materials, and in surgery and ceremonial activities.

The earliest knives were crude chipped stone blades made from flakes of stone with or without secondary chipping of the edges. From this early type, knife blades differentiated into a wide variety of forms of which three general types can be roughly distinguished: the standard elongated blade, the wide or crescent-shaped blade, and the oblique or razor-like blade. The elongated form consisted of fairly blunt to long and slender blades a great number of which were similar to lance heads or projectile points, from which they often cannot be distinguished unless a haft is still intact. They were beveled on one or both edges and generally hafted.

Most were straight, but afew were bent or sickle-
shaped. The wide blades were flat and rectangular-,
crescent-, wide-leaf-, or similunar-shaped, and many
were provided with pads or handles on the back made of
leather, wood, bone, or ivory. They were generally used
for chopping food, skinning, and fleshing hides. The
third type consisted of a small point or razor edge
embedded in a bone, antler, ivory, or wooden handle
and served for delicate cutting purposes. Draw knives,
consisting of a blade with a handle at each end, were

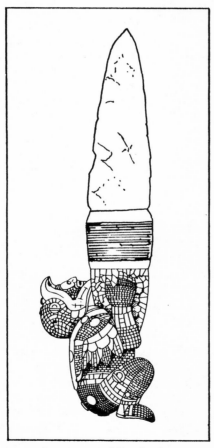

A ceremonial flint knife.

Flakes from black jasper pebbles specialized for use as knives or scrapers.

commonly used in some areas for shaving wood or other materials. Combined forms of these types of blade and hafting were common.

In a class all its own is the Eskimo snow knife. It is an elongated bone or ivory blade roughly two or three feet long and is generally slightly curved and wider near the point. It has been used from prehistoric times to the present to cut out and shape blocks of snow in the construction of snow dwellings, or igloos.

L

LABRET, is a somewhat spool-shaped ornament worn in a hole pierced through the lip, or a flat piece extending the lip outward from the face. This type of ornament had its most constant and general use among Northwest Coast and Arctic tribes. The most recent labrets worn, around the turn of the century, were small silver studs pierced through the lip. Earlier labrets were made of shell, wood, bone, stone, ivory, and jade. They were often carved or inlaid. A labret was a mark of high status for Haida, Tsimshian, Tlingit, and Heiltsuk women who wore one labret in the center of the lower lip. If Aleut and Eskimo men had their lips pierced, it was at puberty with one hole below each side of the mouth. A plug was inserted in

LANGUAGE. Before discussing the extent to which we may reconstruct the history of languages, it seems necessary to describe briefly the essential traits of human speech.

In our present discussion we do not deal with gesture-language or musical means of communication, but confine ourselves to the discussion of articulate speech; that is, to communication by means of groups of sounds produced by the articulating organs—the larynx, oral cavity, tongue, lips, and nose.

Character of Phonetics

Speech consists of groups of sounds produced by the articulating organs, partly noises made by opening and closing certain places in the larynx, pharynx, mouth, or nose, or by restricting certain parts of the passage of the breath; partly resonant sounds produced by the vocal chords.

Number of Sounds Unlimited

The number of sounds that may be produced in this manner is unlimited. In our own language we select only a limited number of all possible sounds; for instance, some sounds, like *p*, are produced by the closing and a sudden opening of the lips; others, like *t*, by bringing the tip of the tongue into contact with the anterior portion of the palate, by producing a closure a. this point, and by suddenly expelling the air. On the other hand, a sound might be produced by placing the tip of the tongue between the lips, making a closure in this manner, and by expelling the air suddenly. This sound would to our ear partake of the character of both our *t* and our *p*, while it would correspond to neither of these. A comparison of the sounds of the well-known European languages—like English, French, and German; or even of the different dialects of the same languages, like those of Scotch and of the various English dialects—reveals the fact that considerable variation occurs in the manner of producing sounds, and that each dialect has its own characteristic phonetic system, in which each sound is nearly fixed, although subject to slight modifications which are due to accident or to the effects of surrounding sounds.

Each Language Uses a Limited Number of Sounds

One of the most important facts relating to the phonetics of human speech is, that every single language has a definite and limited group of sounds, and that the number of those used in any particular dialect is never excessively large.

It would seem that this limitation in the use of sounds is necessary in order to make possible rapid communication. If the number of sounds that are used in any particular language were unlimited, the accuracy with which the movements of the complicated mechanism required for producing the sounds are performed would presumably be lacking, and consequently rapidity and accuracy of pronunciation, and with them the possibility of accurate interpretation of the sounds heard, would be difficult, or even impossible. On the other hand, limitation of the number of sounds brings it about that the movements required in the production of each become automatic, that the association between the sound heard and the muscular movements, and that between the auditory impression and the muscular sensation of the articulation, become firmly fixed. Thus it would seem that limited phonetic resources are necessary for easy communication.

Alleged Lack of Differentiation of Sounds in Primitive Languages

It has been maintained that this is not a characteristic found in more primitive types of languages, and particularly, examples of American languages have often been brought forward to show that the accuracy of their pronunciation is much less than that found in the languages of the civilized world.

It would seem that this view is based largely on the fact that certain sounds that occur in American languages are interpreted by observers sometimes as one European sound, sometimes as another. Thus the

Pawnee language contains a sound which may be heard more or less distinctly sometimes as an *l*, sometimes an *r*, sometimes as *n*, and again as *d*, which, however, without any doubt, is throughout the same sound, although modified to a certain extent by its position in the word and by surrounding sounds. It is an exceedingly weak *r*, made by trilling with the tip of the tongue at a point a little behind the roots of the incisors, and in which the tongue hardly leaves the palate, the trill being produced by the lateral part of the tongue adjoining the tip. As soon as the trill is heard more strongly, we receive the impression of an *r*. When the lateral movement prevails and the tip of the tongue does not seem to leave the palate, the impression of an *l* is strongest, while when the trill is almost suppressed and a sudden release of the tongue from the palate takes place, the impression of the *d* is given. The impression of an *n* is produced because the sound is often accompanied by an audible breathing through the nose. This peculiar sound is, of course, entirely foreign to our phonetic system; but its variations are not greater than those of the English *r* in various combinations, as in *broth, mother, where*. The different impression is brought about by the fact that the sound, according to its prevailing character, associates itself either with our *l*, or our *r*, *n*, or *d*.

Other examples are quite common. Thus, the lower Chinook has a sound which is readily perceived as a *b*, *m*, or *w*. As a matter of fact, it is a *b* sound, produced by a very weak closure of the lips and with open nose, the breath passing weakly both through the mouth and through the nose, and accompanied by a faint intonation of the vocal chords. This sound associates itself with our *b*, which is produced by a moderately weak release of the lips; with our *m*, which is a free breath through the nose with closed lips; with our *w*, which is a breath through the lips, which are almost closed, all accompanied by a faint intonation of the vocal chords. The association of this sound with *w*, is particularly marked when it appears in combination with a *u* vowel, which imitates the characteristic *u* tinge of our *w*. Still another example is the *b* sound, which is produced with half-closed nose by the Indians of the Strait of Fuca, in the State of Washington. In this case the characteristic trait of the sound is a semiclosure of the nose, similar to the effect produced by a cold in the head. Not less common are sounds intermediate between our vowels. Thus we seem to find in a number of Indian languages a vowel which is sometimes perceived as *o*, sometimes as *u* (continental pronunciation), and which is in reality pronounced in a position intermediate between these two sounds.

The correctness of this interpretation of Indian phonetics is perhaps best proved by the fact that observers belonging to different nationalities readily perceive the sounds in accordance with the system of sounds with which they are familiar. Often it is not difficult to recognize the nationality of a recorder from the system selected by him for the rendering of sounds.

Still another proof of the correctness of this view of Indian phonetics is given by the fact that, wherever there is a greater number of Indian sounds of a class represented by a single sound in English, our own sounds are misinterpreted in similar manner. Thus, for instance, the Indians of the North Pacific coast have a series of *l* sounds, which may be roughly compared to our sounds *tl, cl, gl*. Consequently, a word like *close* is heard by the Indians sometimes one way, sometimes another; our *cl* is for them an intermediate sound, in the same way as some Indian sounds are intermediate sounds to our ears. The alternation of the sounds is clearly an effect of perception through the medium of a foreign system of phonetics, not that of a greater variability of pronunciation than the one that is characteristic of our own sounds.

While the phonetic system of each language is limited and fixed, the sounds selected in different types of languages show great differences, and it seems necessary to compare groups of languages from the point of view of their constituent phonetic elements.

Brief Description of Phonetics

A complete discussion of this subject can not be given at this place; but a brief statement of the characteristics of articulate sounds, and the manner of rendering them by means of symbols, seems necessary.

All articulate sounds are produced by the vibrations of the articulating organs, which are set in motion by breathing. In the vast majority of cases it is the outgoing breath which causes the vibrations; while in a few languages, as in those of South Africa, the breath, while being drawn in, is used for producing the sound.

One group of sounds is produced by the vibration of the vocal chords, and is characterized by the form given to the cavities of mouth and nose. These are the vowels. When the nose is closed, we have pure vowels; when the posterior-part of the nose is more or less open, more or less nasalized vowels. The character of the vowel depends upon the form given to the oral cavity. The timbre of the vowels changes according to the degree to which the larynx is raised; the epiglottis lowered or raised; the tongue retracted or brought forward and its back rounded or flattened; and the lips rounded and brought forward, or an elongated opening of the mouth produced by retracting the corners of the mouth. With open lips and the tongue and pharynx at rest, but the soft palate (velum) raised, we have the pure vowel *a*, similar to the *a* in *father*. From this sound the vowels vary in two principal directions. The one extreme is *u* (like *oo* in English *fool*), with small round opening of the protruding lips, tongue retracted, and round opening between tongue and palate, and large opening between larynx and pharynx, the larynx still being almost at rest. The transitional sounds pass through *a* (*aw* in English *law*) and *o* (as in *most*), but the range of intermediate positions is continuous. In another direction the vowels pass from *a* through *e* (*a* in English *mane*) to *i* (*ee* in *fleet*). The *i* is pronounced with extreme retraction of the corners of the mouth and elongated opening of the lips, with very narrow flat opening between tongue and palate, and the posterior part of the tongue brought forward, so that there is a wide opening in the back part of the mouth, the larynx being raised at the same time.

Variations of vowels may be produced by a different grouping of the movements of the articulating organs. Thus, when the lips are in *i* position, the tongue and pharynx and larynx in *u* position, we have the sound *u*, which is connected with the *a* by a series passing through *o*. These sounds are similar to the German umlaut.

Other combinations of positions of the tongue and of the lips occur, although the ones here described seem to be the most frequent vowel-sounds. All vowels may become very much weakened in strength of articulation, and dwindle down to a slight intonation of the vocal chords, although retaining the peculiar vowel timbre, which depends upon the position of mouth, nose, and lips. When this articulation becomes very weak, all the vowels tend to become quite similar in character, or may be influenced in their timbre by neighboring consonants, as will be described later.

All sounds produced by vibrations in any part of the articulating organs other than the vocal chords are consonants. These vibrations may be produced either by closing the air-passages completely and then suddenly opening the closure, or by producing a narrowing of stricture at any point. The former series of sounds are called "stops" (like our *p, t, k*). In all of these there is a complete closure before the air is expelled. The latter are called "spirants" or "continued" (like our *s* and *f*), in which there is a continuous escape of breath. When a stop is made and is followed by a breathing through a stricture at the same place, sounds develop like our *ts*. These are called "affricatives." When the mouth is completely stopped, and the air escapes through the nose, the sound is called a "nasal consonant" (like our *m* and *n*). There may also be stricture and nasal opening. A rapidly repeated series of stops, a trill, as represented by our *r*. The character of the sound depends on upon the parts of the articulating organs that produce the closure or stricture, and upon the place where these occur. Closure or stricture may be made by the lips, lips and tongue, lips and teeth, tongue and teeth, tongue and hard palate, tongue and soft plate (velum), by the vocal chords, and in the nose.

In the following table, only the principal groups of consonants are described. Rare sounds are omitted. According to what has been said before, it will be recognized that here also the total number of possible sounds is infinitely large.

Bilabial stop . . . . .p
Linguo-palatal stops:
    Apical (dental, alveolar, post-alveolar) . . . . . . .t
    Cerebral (produced with the tip of the tongue
      turned backward) . . . . .t
    Dorsal:
      Anterior palatal . . . . .k
      Medial . . . . .k
      Velar . . . . .q
Glottal (a stop produced with the vocal chords) . . . .[3]
Nasal . . . . .N

Almost all these stops may be modified by giving to the closure a different degree of stress. In English we have two principal degrees of stress, represented, for instance, by our *b* and *p* or *d* and *t*. In many languages, as, for instance, in Sioux and in the languages of the Pacific coast, there are three degrees of stress that may be readily differentiated. The strongest of these we call the "fortis," and indicate it by following the consonant by an ! (*p!, t!*).

When these steps are not accompanied by any kind of vibration of the vocal chords, they are called "surds."

It is, of course, also possible that more than one stop may be made at one time. Thus it might be possible to close at the same time the lips and the posterior part of the mouth with the tongue. This type of combination is, however, rare; but we find very frequently articulation of the vocal chords with stops. This results in the voiced consonants, or sonants. In English we find that almost always the stress of articulation of the voiced sound is less than the stress of articulation of the unvoiced sound, or surd; but this correlation is not necessary. In American languages particularly, we find very commonly the same degree of stress used with voicing and without voicing, which brings it about that to the European ear the surd and sonant are difficult to distinguish.

A third modification of the consonants is brought about by the strength of breathing accompanying the release of the closure. In a sound like *t*, for instance, the sound may be simply produced by closing the mouth, by laying the tip of the tongue firmly against the palate, producing a slightly increased amount of air-pressure behind the tongue, and then releasing the closure. On the other hand, the sound may be produced by bringing about the closure and combining the release with the expiration of a full breath. Sounds which are accompanied by this full breathing may be called "aspirates," and we will designate the aspiration by , the symbol of the Greek spiritus asper. This full breathing may follow the stop, or may begin even before the completion of the closure. With the increased stress of the posterior part of the tongue, so that only the air that has been poured into the vocal cavity is expelled.

In the case of voiced consonants, the voicing may either be entirely synchronous with the consonant, or it may slightly precede or follow it. In both of these cases we may get the impression of a preceeding or following exceedingly weak vowel, the timbre of which will depend essentially upon the accompanying consonant. When the timbre is very indefinite, we write this vowel *E*; when it is more definite, *A, I, O, U*, etc. In other cases, where the release at the closure is made without a full breath going out, and simply by compressing the air slightly in the space behind the closure,

free breathing *h,* which, in its most characteristic form, is produced by the expiration of the breath with all the articulating organs at rest.

In tabular form we obtain thus the following series of the most important consonantic sounds:

The vocalic tinge of consonants is expressed by superior vowels following them: ᵃ ᵉ ⁱ ᵒ ᵘ The series of affricatives which begin with a stop and end with a continued sound have been omitted from this table.

It will be noticed that in the preceding table the same symbols are used in several columns. This is done, because, ordinarily, only one, or at most two, series of these groups occur in one language, so that these differences can be expressed in each special case by diacritical marks. Attempts have been made by other authors to give a general system of sound representation. For any particular language, these are liable to become cumbersome, and are therefore not used in the sketches contained in this volume.

Unconsciousness of Phonetic Elements

In the preceding pages we have briefly discussed the results of an analysis of the phonetic elements of human speech. It must, however, be remembered that the single sound as such has no independent existence, that it never enters into the consciousness of the speaker, but that it exists only as a part of a sound-complex which conveys a definite meaning. This will be easily recognized, if we consider for a moment grammatical forms in the English language in which the modification of the idea is expressed by a single sound. In the word *hills,* the terminal *s* does not enter our consciousness as a separate element with separate significance, expressing the idea of plurality,—except, perhaps, in so far as our grammatical training has taught us the fact that plurals may be formed by the use of a terminal *s,*—but the word forms a firm unit, which conveys a meaning only as a whole. The variety of uses of the terminal *s* as a plural, possessive, and third person singular of the verb, and the strong effort required to recognize the phonetic identity of these terminal elements, may be adduced as a further proof of the fact that the single phonetic elements become conscious to us only as a single sound, like *mail* and *nail, snake* and *stake,* makes it also clear that the isolation of sounds is a result of secondary analysis.

Grammatical Categories

Differences in Categories of Different Languages

In all articulate speech the groups of sounds which are uttered serve to convey ideas, and each group of sounds has a fixed meaning. Languages differ not only in the character of their constituent phonetic elements and sound-clusters, but also in the groups of ideas that find expression in fixed phonetic groups.

Limitation of the Number of Phonetic Groups Expressing Ideas

The total number of possible combinations of phonetic elements is also unlimited; but only a limited number are used to express ideas. This implies that the total number of ideas that are expressed by distinct phonetic groups is limited in number.

Since the total range of personal experience which language serves to express is infinitely varied, and its whole scope must be expressed by a limited number of phonetic groups, it is obvious that an extended classification of experiences must underlie all articulate speech.

This coincides with a fundmental trait of human thought. In our actual experience no two sense-impression or emotional states are identical. Nevertheless we classify them, according to their similarities, in wider or narrower groups the limits of which may be determined from a variety of points of view. Notwithstanding their individual differences, we recognize in our experiences common elements, and consider them as related or even as the same, provided a sufficient number of characteristic traits belong to them in common. Thus the limitation of the number of phonetic groups expressing distinct ideas is an expres-

As an example of the manner in which terms that we express by independent words are grouped together under one concept, the Dakota language may be selected. The terms *naxta'ka* TO KICK, *paxta'ka* TO BIND IN BUNDLES, *yaxta'ka* TO BITE, *ic'a'xtaka* TO BE NEAR TO, *boxta'ka* TO POUND, are all derived from the common element *xtaka* TO GRIP, which holds them together, while we use distinct words for expressing the various ideas.

It seems fairly evident that the selection of such simple terms must to a certain extent depend upon the chief interests of a people; and where it is necessary to distinguish a certain phenomenon in many aspects, which in the life of the people play each an entirely independent role, may independent words may develop, while in other cases modifications of a single term may suffice.

Thus it happens that each language, from the point of view of another language, may be arbitrary in its classifications; that what appears as a single simple idea in one language may be characterized by a series of distinct phonetic groups in another.

The tendency of a language to express a complex idea by a single term has been styled "holophrasis," and it appears therefore that every language may be holophastic from the point of view of another language. Holophrasis can hardly be taken as a fundamental characteristic of primitive languages.

We have seen before that some kind of classification of expression must be found in every language. This classification of ideas into groups, each of which is expressed by an independent phonetic group, makes it necessary that concepts which are not readily rendered by a single one among the available sound-complexes should be expressed by combinations or by modifications of what might be called the elementary phonetic groups, in accordance with the elementary ideas to which the particular idea is reduced.

This classification, and the necessity of expressing certain experiences by means of other related ones, which by limiting one another define the special idea to be expressed, entail the presence of certain formal elements which determine the relations of the single phonetic groups. If each idea could be expressed by a single phonetic group, languages without form would be possible. Since, however, ideas must be expressed by being reduced to a number of related ideas, the kinds of relation become important elements in articulate speech; and it follows that all languages must contain formal elements, and that their number must be the greater, the fewer the elementary phonetic groups that define special ideas. In a language which commands a very large, fixed vocabulary, the number of formal elements may become quite small.

Grammatical Processes

It is important to note that, in the languages of the world, the number of processes which are utilized to express the relations of terms is limited. Presumably this is due to the general characteristics of articulate speech. The only methods that are available for expressing the relations between definite phonetic groups are their composition in definite order, which may be combined with a mutual phonetic influence of the component elements upon one another, and inner modification of the phonetic groups themselves. Both these methods are found in a great many languages, but sometimes only the method of composition occurs.

Word and Sentence

In order to understand the significance of the ideas expressed by independent phonetic groups and of the elements expressing their mutual relations, we have to discuss here the question, What forms the unit of speech? It has been pointed out before that the phonetic elements as such can be isolated only by analysis, and that they occur in speech only in combinations which are the equivalents of definite concepts.

Since all speech is intended to serve for the communication of ideas, the natural unit of expression is

sometimes to designate a certain unit as a word, sometimes to deny its independent existence. We shall see later on, in the discussion of American languages, that this practical difficulty confronts us many times, and that it is not possible to decide with objective certainty whether it is justifiable to consider a certain phonetic groups as an independent word or as a subordinate part of a word.

Nevertheless there are certain elements contained in our definition which seem to be essential for the interpretation of a sound-complex as an independent word. From the point of view of grammatical form, the least important; from the point of view of phonetics, however, the most fundamental, is the phonetic independence of the element in question. It has been pointed out before how difficult it is to conceive the independence of the English *s,* which expresses the plural, the possessive, and the third person singular of the verb. This is largely due to the phonetic weakness of this grammatical element. If the idea of plurality were expressed by an element as strong phonetically as the word *many;* the possessive part of the word, by an element as strong as the preposition *of;* and the third person singular, by an element like *he*—we might, perhaps, be much more ready to recognize the character of these elements as independent words, and we actually do so. For example, *stones, John's, loves,* are single words; while *many sheep, of stone, he went,* are considered as two words. Difficulties of this kind . are met with constantly in American languages. Thus we find in a language like the Chinook that modifying elements are expressed by single sounds which phonetically enter into clusters which are pronounced without any break. To give an example: the word *ania'lot* I GIVE HIM TO HER may be analyzed into the following elements: *a* (tense), *n* I, *i* HIM, *a* HER, *l* TO, *o* (direction away, *t* TO GIVE. Here, again, the weakness of the component elements and their close phonetic association forbid us to consider them independent words; while the whole expression appears to us as a firm unit.

Whenever we are guided by this principle alone, the limitation of the word unit appears naturally ex-ceedingly uncertain, on account of the difference in impression of the phonetic strength of the component elements.

It also happens that certain elements appear sometimes with such phonetic weakness that they can not possibly be considered as independent units of the sentence, while closely related forms, or even the same forms in other combinations, may gain the strength which they are lacking in other cases. As an example of this kind may be given the Kwakiutl, in which many of the pronominal forms appear as exceedingly weak phonetic elements. Thus the expression HE STRIKES HIM WITH IT is rendered by *mix i dɛqs,* in which the two ter-minal elements mean: *q* HIM, *s* WITH IT. When, however, substantives are introduced in this expression for ob-ject and instrument, the *q* assumes the fuller form *xa,* and the *s* the fuller form *sa,* which we might quite readily write as independent words analogous to our articles.

I doubt very much whether an investigator who would record French in the same way as we do the un-written American languages would be inclined to write the pronominal elements which enter into the tran-sitive verb as independent words, at least not when recording the indicative forms of a positive verb. He might be induced to do so on discovering their freedom of position which appears in the negative and in some interrogative forms.

The determining influence of the freedom of posi-tion of a phonetically fixed part of the sentence makes it necessary to included it in our definition of the word.

Whenever a certain phonetic group appears in a variety of positions in a sentence, and always in the same form, without any, or at least without material, modifications, we readily recognize its individuality, and in an analysis of the language we are inclined to consider it as a separate word. These conditions are fully realized only in cases in which the sound-complex

slightest doubt as to what constitutes the word in our ordinary sense of the term. The same is true in many cases in Iroquois, a language in which conditions quite similar to those in the Inuit prevail. Here an example may given from the Oneida dialect. *Watgajijanegale* THE FLOWER BREAKS OPEN consists of the formal elements *wa-*, *-t-*, and *-g-*, which are temporal, modal, and pronominal in character; the vowel *-a-*, which is the character of the stem *-jija* FLOWER, which never occurs alone; and the stem *-negale* TO BREAK OPEN, which also has no independent existence.

In all these cases the elements possess great clearness of significance, but the lack of permanence of form compels us to consider them as parts of a longer word.

While in some languages this gives us the impression of an adequate criterion for the separation of words, there are other cases in which certain parts of the sentence may be thus isolated, while the others retain their independent form. In American languages this is particularly the case when nouns enter the verbal complex without any modification of their component elements. This is the case, for instance, in Pawnee: *ta takᵘt* I HAVE CUT IT FOR THEE, and *riks* ARROW, combine into *tatu rikskᵘt* I CUT THY ARROW. The closeness of connection of these forms is even clearer in cases in which far-reaching phonetic modifications occur. Thus the elements *ta-t-ru n* combine into *ta hu n* I MAKE (because *tr* in a word changes to *h*); and *ta-t-riks-ru n* becomes *tahikstu n* I MAKE AN ARROW (because *r* after *s* changes to *t*). At the same time *riks* ARROW occurs as an independent word.

If we follow the principle laid down in the preceding remarks, it will readily be seen that the same element may appear at one time as an independent noun, then again as a part of a word, the rest of which has all the characteristics before described, and which for this reason we are not inclined to consider as a complex of independent elements.

Ambiguity in regard to the independence of parts of the sentence may also arise either when in their significance they become dependent upon other parts of the sentence, or when their meaning is so vague and weak as compared to the other parts of the sentence that we are led to regard them as subordinate parts. Words of this kind, when phonetically strong, will generally be considered as independent particles; when, on the other hand, they are phonetically weak, they will generally be considered as modifying parts of other words. A good example of this kind is contained in the Ponca texts by the Rev. James Owen Dorsey, in which the same elements are often treated as independent particles, while in other cases they appear as subordinate parts of words. Thus we find *ceama* THESE but *jabe ama* THE BEAVER.

The same is true in regard to the treatment of the grammar of the Sioux by the Rev. S. R. Riggs. We find in this case, for instance, the element *pi* always treated as the ending of a word, probably owing to the fact that it represents the plural, which in the Indo-European languages is almost always expressed by a modification of the word to which it applies. On the other other hand, elements like *kta* and *sni,* signifying the future and negation respectively, are treated as independent words, although they appear in exactly the same form as the *pi* mentioned before.

Other examples of this kind are the modifying elements in Tsimshian, a language in which innumerable adverbial elements are expressed by fairly weak phonetic groups which have a definite position. Here, also, it seems entirely arbitrary whether these phonetic groups are considered as separate words, or whether they are combined with the verbal expressions into a single word. In these cases the independent existence of the word to which such particles are joined without any modification will generally determine us to consider these elements as independent particles, provided they are phonetically strong enough; while whenever the verbal expression to which they are joined is modified either by the insertion of these elements between its component parts, or in some other way, we are inclined to consider them as parts of the word.

It seemed important to discuss somewhat fully the concept of the word in its relation to the whole sentence, because in the morphological treatment of American languages this question plays an important role.

Stem and Affix

The analytic treatment of languages results in the separation of a number of different groups of the elements of speech. When we arrange these according to their functions, it appears that certain elements recur in every single sentence. These are, for instance, the forms indicating subject and predicate, or, in modern European languages, forms indicating number, tense, and person. Others, like terms expressing demonstrative ideas, may or may not occur in a sentence, These and many others are treated in our grammars. According to the character of these elements, they seem to modify the material contents of the sentence; as, for instance, in the English sentences *he strikes him,* and *I struck thee,* where the idea of striking somebody appears as the content of the communication; while the ideas *he, present, him,* and *I, past, thee,* appear as modifications.

It is of fundamental importance to note that this separation of the ideas contained in a sentence into material contents and formal modifications is an arbitrary one, brought about, presumably, first of all, by the great variety of ideas which may be expressed in the same formal manner by the same pronominal and tense elements. In other words, the material contents of the sentence may be represented by subjects and predicates expressing an unlimited number of ideas, while the modifying elements—here the pronouns and tenses—comprise, comparatively speaking, a very small number of ideas. In the discussion of a language, the parts expressing the material contents of sentences appear to us as the subject-matter of lexicography; parts expressing the modifying relations, as the subject-matter of grammar. In modern Indo-European languages the number of ideas which are expressed by subordinate elements is, on the whole, limited, and for this reason the dividing-line between grammar and dictionary appears perfectly clear and well drawn. In a wider sense, however, all etymological processes and word compositions must be considered as parts of the grammar; and, if we include those, we find that, even in Indo-European languages, the number of classifying ideas is quite large.

In American languages the distinction between grammar and lexicography often becomes quite obscure, owing to the fact that the number of elements which enter into formal compositions becomes very large. It seems necessary to explain this somewhat more fully by examples. In the Tsimshian language we find a very great number of adverbial elements which can not be considered as entirely independent, and which, without doubt, must be considered as elements modifying verbal ideas. On account of the very large number of these elements, the total number of verbs of motion seems to be somewhat restricted, although the total number of verbs that may be combined with these adverbial ideas is much larger than the total number of the adverbial ideas themselves. Thus, the number of adverbs appears to be fixed, while the number of verbs appears unlimited; and consequently we have the impression that the former are modifying elements, and that their discussion belongs to the grammar of the language, while the latter are words, and thier discussion belongs to the lexicography of the language. The number of such modifying elements in Inuit is even larger; and here the impression that the discussion of these elements belongs to the grammar of the language is increased by the fact that they can never take an initial position, and that they are not placed following a complete word, but are added to an element which, if pronounced by itself, would not give any sense.

Now, it is important to note that, in a number of languages, the number of the modifying elements may increase so much that it may become doubtful which

look for a number of fundamental categories. In most Indo-European languages, nouns are classified according to gender, they are modified by forms expressing singular and plural, and they also appear in syntactic combinations as cases. None of these apparently fundamental aspects of the noun are necessary, elements of articulate speech.

GENDER

The history of the English language shows clearly that the gender of a noun may practically be suppressed without interfering with the clearness of expression. While we still find traces of gender in English, practically all inanimate objects have come to belong to one single gender. It is interesting to note that, in the languages of the world, gender is not by any means a fundamental category, and that nouns may not be divided into classes at all, or the point of view of classification may be an entirely different one. Thus the Bantu languages of Africa classify words into a great many distinct groups the significance of most of which is not by any means clear. The Algonquian of North America classify nouns as animate and inanimate, without, however, adhering strictly to the natural classification implied in these terms. Thus the small animals may be classified as inanimate, while certain plants may appear as animate. Some of the Siouan languages classify nouns by means of articles, and strict distinctions are made between animate moving and animate at rest, inaminate long, inanimate round, inanimate high, and inanimate collective objects. The Iroquois distinguish strictly between nouns designating men and other nouns. The latter may again be subdivided into a definite and indefinite group. The Uchee distinguish between members of the tribe and other human beings. In America, true gender is on the whole rare; it is found, perhaps, among a few of the languages of the lower Mississippi; it occurs in the same way as in most Indo-European languages in the Chinook of Columbia river, and to a more limited extent among some of the languages of the state of

Washington and of British Columbia. Among North American languages, the Inuit and Athapascan have no trace of a classifaction of nouns. The examples here given show clearly that the sex principle. which underlies the classification of nouns in European languages, is merely one of a great many possible classifications of this kind.

PLURAL

Of a somewhat different character is the plural of Indo-European nouns. Beccause, for the purpose of clear expression, each noun must be expressed either as a singular or as a plural, it might seem that this classification is almost indispensable; but it is not difficult to show, by means of sentences, that, even in English, the distinction is not always made. For instance, in the sentence *The wolf has devoured the sheep,* it is not clear whether a single sheep is meant, or a plurality of sheep are referred to. Nevertheless, this would not, on the whole, be felt as an inconvenience, since either the context would show whether singular or plural is meant, or an added adjective would give the desired information.

While, according to the structure of our European languages, we always tend to look for the expression of singularity or plurality for the sake of clearness of expression, there are other languages that are entirely indifferent towards this distinction. A good example of this kind is the Kwakiutl. It is entirely immaterial to the Kwakiutl whether he says, *There is a house* or *There are houses.* The same form is used for expressing both ideas, and the idea of singularity and plurality must be understood either by the context or by the addition of a special adjective. Similar conditions prevail in the Athapascan languages and in Haida. In Siouan, also, a distinction between singularity and plurality is made only in the case of animate objects. It would seem that, on the whole, American languages are rather indifferent in regard to the clear expression of plurality, but that they tend to express much more rigidly the ideas of collectivity or distribution. Thus the Kwakiutl, who are rather indifferent to the expression of plurality, are very particular in denoting whether the objects spoken of are distributed here or there. When this is the case, the distribution is carefully expressed. In the same way, when speaking of fish, they express by the same term a single fish and a quantity of fish. When, however, they desire to say that these fish belong to different species, a distributive form expressing this idea is made use of. A similar indifference to the idea of singular and plural may be observed in the pronouns of several languages, and will be noted later on.

On the other hand, the idea of number may be much more strongly emphasized that it is in the modern languages of Europe. The dual, as in Greek, is of common occurrence the world over; but it happens also that a trialis and paucalis—expressions for *three* and *a few* —are distinguished.

CASE

What is true of number is no less true of case. Psychologically, the substitution of prepositional expressions for cases would hardly represent a complete absence of the concept of cases. This is rather found in those languages in which the whole group of relations of the nouns of a sentence is expressed in the verb. When, for instance, in Chinook, we find expressions like *he her it with cut, man, woman, knife,* meaning *The man cut the woman with the knife,* we may safely say that the nouns themselves appear without any trace of case-relationship, merely as appositions to a number of pronouns. It is true that in this case a distinction is made in the pronoun between subject an object, and that, in tha sense, cases are found, although not as nominal cases, but still as pronominal cases. The case-relation, however, is confined to the two forms of subject and object, since the oblique cases are expressed by pronominal objects, while the characteristic of each particular oblique relation is expressed by adverbial elements. In the same language, the genitive relation is eliminated by substituting for it possessive expressions, like, for instance, *the man, his house,* instead of *the man's house.* While, therefore, case-expressions are not entirely eliminated, their number, which in some European languages is considerable, may be largely reduced.

Thus we find that some of our nominal categories either do not occur at all, or occur only in very much reduced forms. On the other hand, we must recognize that other new categories may occur which are entirely foreign to our European languages. Classifications like those referred to before—such as animate and inanimate, or of nouns designating men, and other nouns; and, further, of nouns according to form—are rather foreign to us, although, in the connection of verb and noun, form-classifications occur. Thus we do not say, *a tree is somewhere,* but *a tree stands:* not, *the river is in New York,* but, *the river flows through New York.*

TENSE

Tense classes of nouns are not rare in American languages. As we may speak of *a future husband* of *our late friend,* thus many Indian languages express in every noun its existence in presence, past, or future, which they require as much for clearness of expression as we require the distinction of singular and plural.

PERSONAL PRONOUNS

The same lack of conformity in the principles of classification may be found in the pronouns. We are accustomed to speak of three persons of the pronoun, which occur both in the singular and in the plural. Although we make a distinction of gender for the third person of the pronoun, we do not carry out this principle of classification consistently in the other persons. The first and second persons and the third person plural have the same form for masculine, feminine, and neuter. A more rigid application of the sex system is made, for instance, in the language of the Hottentots of South Africa, in which sex is

not only the ideas corresponding to the three personal pronouns occur, but also those of position in space in relation to the speaker,—which are specified in seven directions: as, center, above, below, in front, behind, right, left,—and expressing points of the compass in relation to the position of the speaker.

It must be borne in mind that the divisions which are mentioned here are all *necessary* parts of clear expression in the languages mentioned. For instance, in Kwakiutl it would be inconceivable to use an expression like our *that house,* which means in English *the single house away from the speaker.* The Kwakiutl must express this idea in one of the following six forms:

The (singular or plural) house visible near me
   invisible near me
   visible near thee
   invisible near thee
   visible near him
   invisible near him

while the Inuit would express a term like *this man* as

This man near me
   near him
   behind me
   in front of me
   to the right of me
   to the left of me
   above me
   below me, etc.

Verbal Categories

We can follow out similar differences in the verb. In our Indo-European languages we have expressions signifying persons, tenses, moods, and voices. The ideas represented by these groups are quite unevenly developed in various languages. In a great many cases the forms expressing the persons are expressed simply by a combination of the personal pronoun and the verb; while in other cases the phonetic complexes expressing personal relations are developed in an astonishing manner. Thus the Algonquian and the

Inuit possess special phonetic groups expressing definite relations between the subject and object which occur in transitive verbs. For example, in sentences like *I strike thee,* or *They strike me,* the combination of the pronouns *I—thee,* and *they—me,* are expressed by special phonetic equivalents. There are even cases in which the indirect objects (as in the sentence, *I send him to you)* may be expressed by a single form. The characteristic trait of the forms here referred to is, that the combined pronoun can not be reduced to its constituent elements, although historically it may have originated from combinations of separate forms. It is obvious that in cases in which the development of the pronoun is as weak as in the Siouan languages, to which I have referred before, the definiteness of the pronominal forms of the verb, to which I have referred before, the definiteness of the pronominal forms of the verb, to which we are accustomed, is entirely lost. Thus it happens that in the Sioux the verb alone may be used as well for the more or less abstract idea of verbal action as for the third person of the indicative.

Much more fundamental are the existing differences in regard to the occurrence of tenses and modes. We are accustomed to verbal forms in which the tense is always expressed with perfect definiteness. In the sentence *The man is sick* we really express the idea, *The single definite man is sick at the present time.* This strict expression of the time relation of the occurrence is missing in many languages. The Inuit, for instance, in expressing the same idea, will simply say, *single man sick,* leaving the question entirely open whether the man was sick at a previous time, is sick at the present time, or is going to be sick in the future. The condition here is similar to the one described before in relation to plurality. The Inuit can, of course, express whether the man is sick at the present time, was sick, or is going to be sick, but the grammatical form of his sentences does not *require* the expression of the tense relation. In other cases the temporal ideas may be expressed with much greater nicety than we find in our familiar grammars. Generally, languages in which a multi-

sick, or whether he has dreamed it. It seems, however, better not to complicate our present discusion by taking into consideration the possibilities of exact expression that may be required in idiomatic forms of speech, but rather to consider only those parts of the sentence which, according to the morphology of the language, *must* be expressed.

We conclude from the examples here given that in a discussion of the characteristics of various languages different fundamental categories will be found, and that in a comparison of different languages it will be necessary to compare as well the phonetic characteristics as the characteristics of the vocabulary and those of the grammatical concepts in order to give each language its proper place.

III. CLASSIFICATION OF LANGUAGES
Origin of Dialects

In many cases the determination of the genetic relationship of languages is perfectly simple. Wherever we find close similarities in phonetics, in vocabularies, and in details of grammar, there can not be the slightest doubt that the languages that are being studied are varieties of the same ancestral form.

To a certain extent the differentiation of a single language into a number of dialects is spontaneous. When communication between peoples speaking the same tongue ceases, peculiarities of pronunciation will readily manifest themselves in one region or the other and may become permanent. In some cases these modifications of pronunciation may gradually increase and may become so radical that several quite different forms of the original language develop. At the same time words readily assume a new significance, and if the separation of the people should be accompanied by a differentiation of culture, these changes may proceed at a very rapid rate.

In cases of such phonetic changes and of modifications in the significance of words, a certain degree of regularity may always be observed, and for this reason the historical relationship between the new dialects and the older forms can always be readily established and may be compared to the modifications that take place in a series of generations of living beings.

Another form of modification may occur that is also analogous to biological transformations. We must recognize that the origin of language must be looked for in human faculties that have once been active, but which have disappeared. As a matter of fact, new additions to linguistic devices and to linguistic material are constantly being made. Such spontaneous additions to a language may occur in one of the new dialects, while they do not occur in the other. These, although related to the structure of the older language, will be so entirely new in their character that they can not be directly related to the ancestral language.

It must also be considered that each of these dialects may incorporate new material. Nevertheless in all cases where the older material constitutes the bulk of the material of the language, its close relationship to the ancestral tongue will readily be recognized. In all these cases, phonetics, details of grammatical structure, and vocabulary will show far-reaching similarities.

Comparison of Distinct Languages

The problem becomes much more difficult when the similarities in any of these traits become less pronounced. With the extension of our knowledge of primitive languages, it has been found that cases are not rare in which languages spoken in certain continuous areas show radical differences in vocabulary and in grammatical form, but close similarity in their phonetic elements. In other cases the similarity of phonetic elements may be less pronounced, but there may exist a close similarity in structural details. Again, many investigators have pointed out peculiar analogies in certain words without being able to show that grammatical form and general phonetic character coincide.

Many examples of such conditions may be given. In America, for instance, the phonetic similarity of the languages spoken between the coast of Oregon and Mount St. Elias is quite striking. All these languages are characterized by the occurrence of a great many peculiar *k* sounds and peculiar *l* sounds, and by their tendency towards great stress of articulation, and, in most cases, towards a clustering of consonants. Consequently to our ear these languages sound rough and harsh. Notwithstanding these similarities, the grammatical forms and the vocabularies are so utterly distinct that a common origin of the languages of this area seems entirely out of the question. A similar example may be given from South Africa, where the Bantu negroes, Bushmen, and Hottentots utilize some peculiar sounds which are produced by inspiration—by drawing in the breath, not by expelling it—and which are ordinarily called "clicks." Notwithstanding this very peculiar common trait in their languages, there is no similarity in grammar and hardly any in vocabulary.

We might also give the example of the Siouan and the Iroquois languages of North America, two stocks that have been in proximity, and which are characterized by the occurrence of numerous nasalized vowels; or the phonetic characteristics of Californian languages, which sound to our ear euphonious, and are in strong contrast to the languages of the North Pacific coasts.

It must be said that, on the whole, such phonetic characteristics of a limited area appear in their most pronounced form when we compare the whole region with the neighboring districts. They form a unit rather by contrast with foreign phonetics that when compared among themselves, each language having its own peculiar characteristics in a group of this kind. Thus, the Tlingit of the North Pacific coast differs very much from the Chinook of Columbia river. Nevertheless, when both languages are compared to a language of southern California, the Sioux or the Algonquian, traits that are common to both of them appear to quite a marked degree.

What is true of phonetics is also true of grammatical form, and that is evidently a characteristic trait of the languages of the whole world. In North America particularly such groups of languages can be readily recognized. A more detailed discussion of this problem will be given in another place, and it will be sufficient to state here, that languages—like, for instance, the Athapascan, Tlingit, and Haida—which are spoken in one continuous area on the northwest coast of our continent show certain common characteristics when compared with neighboring languages like the Inuit, Algonquian, and Tsimshian. In a similar way, a number of Californian languages, or languages of southern British Columbia, and languages like the Pawnee and Iroquois, each form a group characterized by certain traits which are not found in other languages.

In cases where such morphological similarities occur without a corresponding similarity of vocabulary, it becomes exceedingly difficult to determine whether these languages may be considered as descendants of one parent language; and there are numerous cases in which our judgment must be suspended, because, on the one hand, these similarities are far-reaching, while, on the other hand, such radical differences are found that we can not account for them without assuming the introduction of an entirely foreign element.

Similar phenomena have recently induced P.W. Schmidt to consider the languages of Farther India and of Malaysia as related; and the same problem has been discussed by Lepsius, and again by Meinhoff, in reference to the relation of the languages of the Hottentot to a number of east African languages and to the languages of the Hamitic peoples of North Africa.

Difficulties also arise in cases where a considerable number of similar words are found without a corresponding similarity of grammatical forms, so that we may be reluctant to combine two such languages, notwithstanding their similarities of vocabulary.

The comparison of vocabularies offers peculiar difficulties in American languages. Unfortunately, our knowledge of American is very limited, and in many cases we are confined to collections of a few hundred words, without any information in regard to grammatical forms. Owing to the strong tendency of many American languages to form compound words or derivatives of various kinds, it is very difficult in vocabularies of this kind to recognize the component elements of words, and often accidental similarities may obtrude themselves which a thorough knowledge of the languages would prove to be of no significance whatever.

Setting aside this practical difficulty, it may happen quite often that in neighboring languages the same term is used to designate the same object, owing, not to the relationship of the languages, but to the fact that the word may be a loan word in several of them. Since the vocabularies which are ordinarily collected embrace terms for objects found in most common use, it seems most likely that among these a number of loan words may occur.

Even when the available material is fuller and more thoroughly analyzed, doubt may arise regarding the significance of the apparent similarities of vocabularly.

Mutual Influences of Languages

In all these cases the final decision will depend upon the answer to the questions in how far distinct languages may influence one another, and in how far a language without being subject to foreign influences may deviate from the parental type. While it seems that the time has hardly come when it is possible to answer these questions in a definite manner, the evidence seems to be in favor of the existence of far-reaching influences of this kind.

Phonetic Influences

This is perhaps most clearly evident in the case of phonetics. It is hardly conceivable why languages spoken in continuous areas, and entirely distinct in vocabulary and in grammatical structure, should partake of the same phonetic characteristics, unless, by imitation, certain phonetic traits may be carried beyond a single linguistic stock. While I do not know that historical evidence of such occurrences has been definitely given, the phenomenon as it occurs in South Africa, among the Bantu and Hottentot, admits of hardly any other explanation. And the same is true, to a more or less pronounced extent, among other distinct but neighboring languages.

The possibility of such a transfer of sounds can not be denied. Among the American Indians, for instance —where intermarriages between individuals belonging to different tribes are frequent; where slave women raise their own and their masters' children; and where, owing to a small number of individuals constituting the tribe, individuals who have mastered several distinct languages are not by any means rare—ample opportunity is given for one language to exert its phonetic influence over another. Whether this explanation is adequate, is a question that remains to be decided by further historical studies.

Grammatical Influences

Influence of the syntax of one language upon another, and even, to a certain extent, of the morphology of one language upon another, is also probable. The study of the languages of Europe has proved clearly the deep influence exerted by Latin upon the syntax of all the modern European languages. We can also recognize how certain syntactic forms of expression occur in neighboring languages on our American continent. To give an instance of this kind, we find that, in the most diverse languages of the North Pacific coast, commands are given in the periphrastic form, *It would be good if you did so and so;* and in many cases this periphrastic form has been substituted entirely for the ordinary imperative. Thus it may well be that groups of psychological concepts which are expressed by means of grammatical forms have developed in one language under the influence of another; and it is difficult to say, if we once admit such influence, where the limit may be to the modifications caused by such processes.

On the other hand, its seems exceedingly difficult to understand why the most fundamental morphological traits of a language should disappear under the influence of another form of thought as exhibited in another language. This would mean that the greater number of grammatical forms would disappear, and entirely new categories develop. It certainly can not be denied that far-reaching modifications of this kind are possible, but it will require the most cautious proof in every single case before their existence can be accepted.

Cases of the introduction of new suffixes in European languages are not by any means rare. Thus, the ending *-able* of French words has been adopted so frequently into English that the ending itself has attained a certain independence, and we can form words like *eatable*, or even *get-at-able*, in which the ending, which was originally French, is added to an English word. In a similar way the French verbal ending *-ir*, combined with the German infinitive ending in *-en*, is used in a large number of German words as though it were a purely German ending. I do not know, however, of any observations which would point to a radical modification of the morphological traits of a language through the influence of another language.

Lexicographic Influences

While the phonetic influence of distinct languages upon one another and the modification of morphological traits in different languages are still obscure, the borrowing of words is very common and sometimes reaches to an enormous extent. The vocabulary of English is an excellent example of such extensive amalgamation of the vocabularies of quite distinct languages, and the manner by which it has been attained is instructive. It is not only that Anglo-Saxon adopted large parts of the vocabulary of the Norman conquerors, that it took over a few terms of the older Celtic languages, and adopted some words from the Norse invaders; but we find also, later, introductions from Latin and Greek, which were introduced through the progress of the arts and sciences, and which filtered down from the educated to the uneducated classes. Furthermore, numerous terms were adopted from the less civilized peoples with whom the English-speaking people came into contact in different parts of the world. Thus, the Australian and the Indian-English have each adopted a great many native terms, quite a number of which have found their way into colloquial and written modern English. This phenomenon is so common, and the processes by which new words enter into a language are so obvious, that a full discussion is not required. Another example that may be mentioned here is that of the Turkish language, which has adopted a very large number of Arab words.

In such a transfer of the vocabulary of one language into another, words undergo, of course, far-reaching changes. these may be partly due to phonetic difficulties, and consist in the adaptation of an unfamiliar group of sounds to the familiar similar sounds of the language by which the word has been adopted. There may be assimilations by which the grammatical form of a word is made similar to more familiar forms. Futhermore, changes in the significance of the word are common, and new derivations may be formed from the word after it has once become entirely familiar, like other native words.

In this respect a number of American languages seem to behave curiously when compared with European languages. Borrowing of words in Europe is particularly common when a new object is first introduced. In almost all these cases the foreign designation is taken over with more or less fundamental phonetic modifications. Examples of this kind are the words *tobacco, canoe, maize, chocolate*—to take as illustration a few words borrowed from American languages. American natives, on the other hand, do not commonly adopt words in this manner, but much more frequently invent descriptive words by which the new object is designated. Thus the Tsimshian of British Columbia designate rice by a term meaning *looking like maggots*. The Kwakiùtl call a steamboat *fire on its back moving on the water*. The Inuit call cut tobacco *being blown upon*. Words of this type are in wide use; nevertheless, loan words taken from English are not be any means rare. The terms *biscuit, dollar, coffee, tea,* are found in a great many Indian languages. The probable reason why descriptive words are more common in American languages than in European languages lies in the frequent occurrence of descriptive nouns.

We find, therefore, that there are two sets of phenomena which must be considered in the classification of the languages: (1) differences which can easily be proved to be derived from modifications of a single ancestral language; and (2) similarities which can not be thus explained, and some of which may be due to the effects of mixture.

Origin of Similarities; by Dissemination or by Parallel Development

Before we proceed with this consideration, we have to discuss the two logical possibilities for such similarities. Either they may be due to dissemination from a common source, so that they originated only a single time, and were diffused by the influence of one people upon another; or it may be that they are due to an independent origin in many parts of the world.

This alternative is present in the explanation of all ethnic phenomena, and is one of the fundamental questions in regard to which the ethnologist, as well as the investigator of languages, must be clear. In the older considerations of the position of the American race among the races of man, for instance, it has always been assumed ·that occurrence of similar phenomena among the peoples of the Old World and of the New proved genetic relationship. It is obvious that this method of proving relationship assumes that, wherever similarities occur, they must have been carried by the same people over different parts of the world, and that therefore they may be considered as proof of common descent. The method thus applied does not take into consideration the possibility of a gradual diffusion of cultural elements from one people to another, and the other more fundamental one of a parallel but independent development of similar phenomena among different races in remote parts of the world. Since such development is a logical possibility, proofs of genetic relationship must be based on the occurrence of sporadic resemblances alone.

A final decision of this vexed problem can be given only by historical evidence, which is hardly ever available, and for this reason the systematic treatment of the question must always proceed with the greatest caution.

The cases in which isolated similarities of ethnic phenomena in remote parts of the world have been recorded are numerous, and many of these are of such a character that transmission cannot be proved at all. If, for instance, the Indians of South America use sacred musical instruments, which must not be seen by women, and if apparently the same custom prevails among the Australian aborigines, it is inadmissible to assume the occurrence of what seems to be the same custom in these two remote districts as due to transmission. It is perfectly intelligible that the custom may have developed independently in each continent. On the other hand, there are many cases in which certain peculiar and complex customs are distributed over large continuous areas, and where transmission over large portions of this area is plausible. In this case, even if independent origin had taken place in different parts of the district in question, the present distribution is fully explained by the assumption of extended dissemination.

It is true, for instance, in the case of similar traditions which are found distributed over large districts. An example of this is the story of two girls who noticed two stars, a bright one and a small one, and wished these stars for their husbands. The following morning they found themselves in the sky, married to the stars, and later on tried to return to the earth by letting themselves down through a hole in the sky. This rather complex tale is found distributed over the American continent in an area extending from Nova Scotia to the mouth of the Mississippi river and westward to the Rocky mountains, and in places even on the Pacific ocean, for instance, in Alaska and in the state of Washington. It would seem difficult to assume, in a case of this kind, the possibility of an independent invention of the tale at a number of distinct points; but it must be assumed that, after the tale had once attained its present form, it spread by dissemination over that part of the continent where it is now found.

In extreme cases the conclusions drawn from these two types of explanation seem quite unassailable; but there are naturally a very large number of others in which the phenomenon in question is neither sufficiently complex, nor distributed over a sufficiently large continuous area, to lead with certainty to the conclusion of an origin by dissemination; and there are others where the sporadic distributions seem curiously arranged, and where vague possibilities of contact occur. Thus it happens often that a satisfactory conclusion cannot be reached.

We must also bear in mind that in many cases a continuous distribution may once have existed, but may have become discontinuous, owing to the disappearance of the phenomena in question in intermediate regions. If, however, we want to follow a safe method, we must not admit such causes for sporadic distribution, unless they can be definitely proved by other evidence; otherwise, the way is open to attempts to bring into contact practically every part of the world with all others.

The general occurrence of similar ethnic phenomena in remote parts of the world admits also of the explanation of the existence of a certain number of customs and habits that were common to large parts of mankind at a very early period, and which have maintained themselves here and there up to the present time. It can not be denied that this point of view has certain elements in its favor; but in the present state of our knowledge we can hardly say that it would be possible to prove or disprove it.

We meet the same fundamental problem in connection with similarities of languages which are too vague to be considered as proofs of genetic relationship. That these exist is obvious. Here we have not only the common characteristics of all human language, which have been discussed in the preceding chapter, but also certain other similarities which must here be considered.

Influence of Environment on Language

It has often been suggested that similarities of neighboring languages and customs may be explained by the influence of environment. The leading thought in this theory is, that the human mind, under the stress of similar conditions, will produce the same results; that consequently, if the members of the same race live in the same surroundings, they will produce, for instance, in their articulate speech, the same kind of phonetics, differing perhaps in detail according to the variations of environment, but the same in their essential traits. Thus it has been claimed that the moist and stormy climate of the North Pacific coast caused a chronic catarrhal condition among the inhabitants, and that to this condition is due the guttural pronunciation and harshness of their languages; while, on the other hand, the mildness of the California climate has been made responsible for the euphonious character of the languages of that district.

I do not believe that detailed investigations in any part of the world would sustain this theory. We might demand proof that the same language, when distributed over different climates, should produce the same kind of modifications as those here exemplified; and we might further demand that, wherever similar climates are found, at least a certain approach to similarity in the phonetics of the languages should occur. It would be difficult to prove that this is the case, even if we should admit the excuse that modifying influences have obscured the original similarity of phonetic character. Taking for instance, the arctic people of the Old and New Worlds as a unit, we find fundamentally different traits in the phonetics of the Inuit, of the Chukchee of eastern Siberia, and of other arctic Asiatic and European peoples. The phonetics of the deserts of Asia and South Africa and of southwestern North America are not by any means the same. The prairie tribes of North America, although living in nearly the same climate, over a considerable area, show remarkable differences in the phonetics of their languages; and, on the other hand, the tribes belonging to the Salish family who live east of the Rocky mountains, in the interior of British Columbia, speak a language that is not less harsh that that of their congeners on the northern coast of the state of Washington. In any attempt at arranging phonetics in accordance with climate, the discrepancies would be so numerous, that an attempt to carry out the theory would lead to the necessity of explaining exceptions rather than examples corroborating its correctness.

What is true in regard to phonetics is no less true in regard to morphology and vocabulary. I do not think that it has ever been claimed that similar words must necessarily originate under the stress of the same conditions, although, if we admit the correctness of the principle, there is no reason for making an exception in regard to the vocabulary.

I think this theory can be sustained even less in the field of linguistics than in the field of ethnology. It is certainly true that each people accommodates itself to a certain extent to its surroundings, and that it even may make the best possible use of its surroundings in accordance with the fundamental traits of its culture, but I do not believe that in any single case it will be possible to explain the culture of a people as due to the influence of its surroundings. It is self-evident that the Inuit of northern arctic America do not make extended use of wood, a substance which is very rare in those parts of the world, and that the Indians of the woodlands of Brazil are not familiar with the uses to which snow may be put. We may even go further, and acknowledge that, after the usefulness of certain substances, plants, and animals—like bamboo in the tropics, or the cedar on the North Pacific coast of America, or ivory in the arctic regions, or the buffalo on the plains of North America—has once been recognized, they will find the most extended use, and that numerous inventions will be made to expand their usefulness. We may also recognize that the distribution of the produce of a country, the difficulties and ease of travel, the necessity of reaching certain points, may deeply influence the habits of the people. But with all this, to geographical conditions cannot be ascribed more than a modifying influence upon the fundamental traits of culture. If this were not true, the peculiar facts of distribution of inventions, of beliefs, of habits, and of other ethnological phenomena, would be unintelligible.

For instance, the use of the underground house is distributed, in America and Asia, over the northern parts of the plateaus to parts of the Great Plains, northward into the arctic region; and crossing Bering strait we find it in use along the Pacific coast of Asia and as far south as northern Japan, not to speak of the subterranean dwellings of Europe and North Africa. The climate of this district shows very considerable differences, and the climatic necessity for underground habitations does not exist by any means in many parts of the area where they occur.

In a similar area we find the custom of increasing the elasticity of the bow by overlaying it with sinew. While this procedure may be quite necessary in the arctic regions, where no elastic wood is available, it is certainly not necessary in the more southern parts of the Rocky mountains, or along the east coast of Asia, where a great many varieties of strong elastic wood are available. Nevertheless the usefulness of the invention seems to have led to its general application over an extended district.

We might also give numerous examples which would illustrate that the adaption of a people to their surroundings is not by any means perfect. How, for instance, can we explain the fact that the Inuit, not withstanding their inventiveness, have never thought of domesticating the caribou, while the Chukchee have acquired large reinder-herds? Why, on the other hand, should the Chukchee, who are compelled to travel about with their reindeer-herds, use a tent which is so cumbersome that a train of many sledges is required to move it, while the Inuit have reduced the frame of their tents to such a degree that a single sledge can be used for conveying it from place to place?

Other examples of a similar kind are the difference in the habitations of the arctic Athapascan tribes and those of the Inuit. Notwithstanding the rigor of the climate, the former live in light skin tents, while the Inuit have succeeded in protecting themselves efficiently against the gales and snows of winter.

What acutally seems to take place in the movements of peoples is, that a people who settle in a new environment will first of all cling to their old habits and only modify them as much as is absolutely necessary in order to live fairly comfortable, the comfort of life being generally of secondary importance to the inertia or conservatism which prevents a people from changing their settled habits, that have become customary to such an extent that they are more or less automatic, and that a change would be felt as something decidedly unusual.

Even when a people remain located in the same place, it would seem that historical influences are much stronger than geographical influences. I am inclined, for instance, to explain in this manner the differences between the cultures of the tribes of arctic Asia and of arctic America, and the difference in the habits of the tribes of the southern plateaus of North America when compared with those of the northern plateaus of North America. In the southern regions the influence of the Pueblos has made itself felt, while farther to the north the simpler culture of the Mackenzie basin gives the essential tone to the culture of the people.

While fully acknowledging the importance of geographical conditions upon life, I do not believe that they can be given a place at all comparable to that of culture as handed down, and to that of the historical influence exerted by the cultures of surrounding tribes; and it seems likely that the less direct the influence of the surroundings is, the less also can it be used for accounting for peculiar ethnological traits.

So far as language is concerned, the influence of geographical surroundings and of climate seems to be exceedingly remote; and as long as we are not even able to prove that the whole organism of man, and with it the articulating organs, are directly influenced by geographical environment, I do not think we are justified in considering this element as an essential trait in the formation or modification of human speech, much less as a cause which can be used to account for the similarities of human speech in neighboring areas.

Influence of Common Psychic Traits

Equally uncertain seems to be the resort to the assumption of peculiar psychic traits that are common to geographical divisions of the same race. It may be claimed, for instance, that the languages of the Athapascan, Tlingit, and Haida, which were referred to before as similar in certain fundamental morphological traits, are alike, for the reason that these three peoples have certain psychical traits in common which are not shared in by other American tribes.

It seems certainly admissible to assume slight differences in the psychical make-up among groups of a race which are different in regard to their physical type. If we can prove by means of anatomical investigations that the bodily form, and with it the nervous system and the brain of one part of a race show differences from the analogous traits of another part of the race, it seems justifiable to conclude that the physical differentiation may be accompanied by psychic differences. It must, however, be borne in mind that the extent of physical difference is always exceedingly slight, and that, within the limits of each geographical type, variations are found which are great as compared to the total differences between the averages of the types. To use a diagram:

If *a* represents the middle point of one type and *b* and *c* its extremes, *a'* the average of another type and *b'* and *c'* its extremes, and if these types are so placed, one over the other, that types in the second series correspond to those in the first series vertically over them, then it will be seen that the bulk of the population of the two types will very well coincide, while only the extremes will be more frequent in the one group than in the other. That is to say, the physical difference is not a difference in kind, but a difference more or less in degree, and a considerable overlapping of the types necessarily takes place.

If this is true in regard to the physical type, and if, furthermore, the difference in psychical types is inferred only from the observed differences of the physical types, then we must assume that the same kind of overlapping will take place in the psychical types. The differences with which we are dealing can, therefore, be only very slight, and it seems hardly likely that these slight differences could lead to radically diverse results.

As a matter of fact, the proof which has been given before, that the same languages may be spoken by entirely distinct types, shows clearly how slight the effect of difference in anatomical type upon language is at the present time, and there is no reason to presume that it has ever been greater. Viewing the matter from this standpoint, the hereditary mental differences of various groups of mankind, particularly within the same race, seem to be so slight that it would be very difficult to believe that they account in any way for the fundamental differences in the traits of distinct languages.

Uncertainty of Definition of Linguistic Families

The problem thus remains unsolved how to interpret the similarities of distinct languages in cases where the similarities are no longer sufficient to prove genetic relationship. From what has been said we may conclude that, even in languages which can easily be proved to be genetically related, independent elements may be found in various divisions. Such independent elements may be due partly to new tendencies which develop in one or the other of the dialects, or to foreign influence. It is quite conceivable that such new tendencies and foreign influences may attain such importance that the new language may still be considered as historically related to the ancestral family, but that its deviations, due to elements that are not found in the ancestral language, have become so important that it can no longer be considered as a branch of the older family.

Thus it will be seen that the concept of a linguistic family cannot be sharply defined; that even among the dialects of one linguistic family, more or less foreign material may be present, and that in this sense the languages, as has been pointed out by Paul, are not, in the strict sense of the term, descendants of a single ancestral family.

Thus the whole problem of the final classification of languages in linguistic families that are without doubt related, seems destined to remain open until our knowledge of the processes by which distinct languages are developed shall have become much more thorough than it is at the present time. Under these circumstances we must confine ourselves to classifying American languages in those linguistic families for which we can give a proof of relationship that cannot possibly be challenged. Beyond this point we can do no more than give certain definite classifications in which the traits common to certain groups of languages are pointed out, while the decision as to the significance of these common traits must be left to later times.

IV. LINGUISTICS AND ETHNOLOGY

It seems desirable to say a few words on the function of linguistic researches in the study of the ethnography of the Indians.

Practical Need of Linguistic Studies for Ethnological Purposes

First of all, the purely practical aspect of this question may be considered. Ordinarily, the investigator who visits an Indian tribe is not able to converse with the natives themselves and to obtain his information first-hand, but he is obliged to rely more or less on data transmitted by interpreters, or at least by the help of interpreters. He may ask his question through an interpreter, and receive again through his mouth the answer given by the Indians. It is obvious that this is an unsatisfactory method, even when the interpreters are good; but, as a rule, the available men are either not sufficiently familiar with the English language, or they are so entirely out of sympathy with the Indian point of view, and understand the need of accuracy on the part of the investigator so little, that information furnished by them can be used only with a considerable degree of caution. At the present time it is possible to get along in many parts of America without interpreters, by means of the trade-jargons that have developed everywhere in the intercourse between the whites and the Indians. These, however, are also a very unsatisfactory means of inquiring into the customs of the natives, because, in some cases, the vocabulary of the trade-languages is extremely limited, and it is almost impossible to convey information relating to the religious and philosophic ideas or to the higher aspects of native art, all of which play so important a part in Indian life. Another difficulty which often develops whenever the investigator works with a particularly intelligent interpreter is, that the interpreter imbibes too readily the views of the investigator, and that his information, for this reason, is strongly biased, because he is not so well able to withstand the influence of formative theories as the trained investigator ought to be. Anyone who has carried on work with intelligent Indians will recall instances of this kind, where the interpreter may have formulated a theory based on the questions that have been put through him, and has interpreted his answers under the guidance of his preconceived notions. All this is so obvious that it hardly requires a full discussion. Our needs become particularly apparent when we compare the methods that we expect from any investigator of cultures of the Old World with those of the ethnologist who is studying primitive tribes. Nobody would expect authoritative accounts of the civilization of China or of Japan from a man who does not speak the languages readily, and who has not mastered their literatures. The student of antiquity is expected to have a thorough mastery of the ancient languages. A student of Mohammedan life in Arabia or Turkey would hardly be considered a serious investigator if all his knowledge had to be derived from second-hand accounts. The ethnologist, on the other hand, undertakes in the majority of cases to elucidate the innermost thoughts and feelings of a people without so much as a smattering of knowledge of their language.

It is true that the American ethnologist is confronted with a serious practical difficulty, for, in the present state of American society, by far the greater number of customs and practices have gone out of existence, and the investigator is compelled to rely upon accounts of customs of former times recorded from the mouths of the old generation who, when young, still took part in these performances. Added to this he is confronted with the difficulty that the number of trained investigators is very small, and the number of American languages that are mutually unintelligible exceedingly large, probably exceeding 300 in number. Our investigating ethnologists are also denied opportunity to spend long continuous periods with any partricular tribe, so that the practical difficulties in the way of acquiring languages are almost insuperable. Nevertheless, we must insist that a command of the language is an indispensable means of obtaining accurate and thorough knowledge, because much information can be gained by listening to conversations of the natives and by taking part in their daily life, which, to the observer who has no command of the language, will remain entirely inaccessible.

It must be admitted that this ideal aim is, under present conditions, entirely beyond our reach. It is, however, quite possible for the ethnographer to obtain a theoretical knowledge of native languages that will enable him to collect at least part of the information that could be best obtained by a practical knowledge of the language. Fortunately, the Indian is easily misled, by the ability of the observer to read his language, into thinking that he is also able to understand what he reads. Thus, in taking down tales or other records in the native language, and reading them to the Indians, the Indian always believes that the reader also understand what he pronounces, because it is quite inconceivable to him that a person can freely utter the sentences in his language without clearly grasping their meaning. This fact facilitates the initial stages of ethnographic information in the native languages, because, on the whole, the northern Indians are eager to be put on record in regard to questions that are of supreme interest to them. If the observer is capable of grasping by a rapid analysis the significance of what is dictated to him, even without being able to express himself freely in the native language, he is in a position to obtain much information that otherwise would be entirely unobtainable. Although this is wholly a makeshift, still it puts the observer in an infinitely better position than that in which he would be without any knowledge whatever of the language. First of all, he can get the information from the Indians first-hand, without employing an interpreter, who may mislead him. Furthermore, the range of subjects on which he can get information is considerably increased because the limitations of the linguistic knowledge of the interpreter, or those of the trade-language are eliminated. It would seem, therefore, that under present conditions we are more or less compelled to rely upon an extended series of texts as the safest means of obtaining information from the Indians. A general review of our ethnographic literature shows clearly how much better is the information obtained by observers who have command of the language, and who are on terms of intimate friendship with the natives, than that obtained through the medium of interpreters.

The best material we possess is perhaps contained in the naive outpourings of the Inuit, which they write and print themselves, and distribute as a newspaper, intended to inform the people of all the events that are of interest. These used to contain much mythological matter and much that related to the mode of life of the people. Other material of similar character is furnished by the large text collections of the Ponca, published by the late James Owen Dorsey; although many of these are influenced by the changed conditions under which the people now live. Some older records on the Iroquois, written by prominent members of the tribe, also deserve attention; and among the most recent literature the descriptions of the Sauk and Fox by Dr. William Jones are remarkable on account of the thorough understanding that the author has reached, owing to his mastery of the language. Similar in character, although rendered entirely in English, are the observations of Mr. James Teit on the Thompson Indians.

In some cases it has been possible to interest educated natives in the study of their own tribes and to induce them to write down in their own language their observations. These, also, are much superior to English records, in which the natives are generally hampered by the lack of mastery of the foreign language.

While in all these cases a collector thoroughly familiar with the Indian language and with English might give us the results of his studies without using the native language in his publications, this is quite indispensable when we try to investigate the deeper problems of ethnology. A few examples will show clearly what is meant. When the question arises, for instance, of investigating the poetry of the Indians, no translation can possibly be considered as an adequate substitute for the original. The form of rhythm, the treatment of the language, the adjustment of text to music, the imagery, the use of metaphors, and all the numerous problems involved in any thorough investigation of the style of poetry, can be interpreted only by the investigator who has equal command of the ethnographical traits of the tribe and of their language. The same is true in the investigation of rituals, with their set, more or less poetic phrases, or in the investigation of prayers and incantations. The oratory of the Indians, a subject that has received much attention by ethnologists, is not adequately known, because only a very few speeches have been handed down in the original. Here, also, an accurate investigation of the method of composition and of the devices used to reach oratorical effect, requires the preservation of speeches as rendered in the original language.

There are also numerous other features of the life of the Indians which can not be adequately presented without linguistic investigation. To these belong, for instance, the discussion of personal, tribal, and local names. The translations of Indian names which are popularly known—like Sitting-Bull, Afraid-Of-His-Horse, etc.—indicate that names possess a deeper significance. The translations, however, are so difficult that a thorough linguistic knowledge is required in order to explain the significance adequately.

In all the subjects mentioned heretofore, a knowledge of Indian languages serves as an important adjunct to a full understanding of the customs and beliefs of the people whom we are studying. But in all these cases the service which language lends us is first of all a practical one—a means to a clearer understanding of ethnological phenomena which in themselves have nothing to do with linguistic problems.

Theoretical Importance of Linguistic Studies
Language a Part of Ethnological Phenomena
in General

It seems, however, that a theoretical study of Indian languages is not less important than a practical knowledge of them; that the purely linguistic inquiry is part and parcel of a thorough investigation of the psychology of the peoples of the world. If ethnology is understood as the science dealing with the mental phenomena of the life of the peoples of this world, human language, one of the most important manifestations of mental life, would seem to belong naturally to the field of work of ethnology, unless special reasons can be adduced why it should not be so considered. It is true that a practical reason of this kind exists, namely, the specialization which has taken place in the methods of philological research, which has progressed to such an extent that philology and comparative linguistics are sciences which require the utmost attention, and do not allow the student to devote much of his time to other fields that require different methods of study. This, however, is no reason for believing that the results of inguistic inquiry are unimportant to the ethnologist. There are other fields of ethnological investigation which have come to be more or less specialized, and which require for their successful treatment peculiar specialization. This is true, for instance, of the study of primitive music, of primitive art, and, to a certain extent, of primitive law. Nevertheless, these subjects continue to form an important part of ethnological science.

If the phenomena of human speech seem to form in a way a subject by itself, this is perhaps largely due to the fact that the laws of language remain entirely unknown to the speakers, that linguistic phenomena never rise into the consciousness of primitive man, while all other ethnological phenomena are more or less clearly subjects of conscious thought.

The question of the relation of linguistic phenomena to ethnological phenomena, in the narrower sense of the term, deserves, therefore, special discussion.

Language and Thought

First of all, it may be well to discuss the relation between language and thought. It has been claimed that the conciseness and clearness of thought of a people depend to a great extent upon their language. The ease with which in our modern European languages we express wide abstract ideas by a single term, and the facility with which wide generalizations are cast into the frame of a simple sentence, have been claimed to be one of the fundamental conditions of the clearness of our concepts, the logical force of our thought, and the precision with which we eliminate in our thoughts irrelevant details. Apparently this view has much in its favor. When we compare modern English with some of those Indian languages which are most concrete in their formative expression, the contrast is striking. When we say *The eye is the organ of sight,* the Indian may not be able to form the expression *the eye,* but may have to define that the eye of a person or of an animal is meant. Neither may the Indian be able to generalize readily the abstract idea of an eye as the representative of the whole class of objects, but may have to specialize by an expression like *this eye here*. Neither may he be able to express by a single term the idea of *organ*, but may have to specify it by an expression like *instrument of seeing*, so that the whole sentence might assume a form like *An indefinite person's eye is his means of seeing*. Still, it will be recognized that in this more specific form the general idea may be well expressed. It seems very questionable in how far the restriction of the use of certain grammatical forms can really be conceived as a hindrance in the formulation of generalized ideas. It seems much more likely that the lack of these forms is due to the lack of their need. Primitive man, when conversing with his fellowman, is not in the habit of discussing abstract ideas. His interests center around the occupations of his daily life; and where philosophic problems are touched upon, they appear either in relation to definite individuals or in the more or less anthropomorphic forms of religious beliefs. Discourses on qualities without connection with the object to which the qualities belong, or of activities or states disconnected from the idea of the actor or the subject being in a certain state, will hardly occur in primitive speech. Thus the Indian will not speak of goodness as such, although he may very well speak of the goodness of a person. He will not speak of a state of bliss apart from the person who is in such a state. He will not refer to the power of seeing without designating an individual who has such power. Thus it happens that in languages in which the idea of possession is expressed by elements subordinated to nouns, all abstract terms appear always with possessive elements. It is, however, perfectly conceivable that an Indian trained in philosphic thought would proceed to free the underlying nominal forms from the possessive elements, and thus reach abstract forms strictly corresponding to the abstract forms of our modern languages. I have made this experiment, for instance, with the Kwakiutl language of Vancouver Island, in which no abstract term ever occurs without its possessive elements. After some discussion, I found it perfectly easy to develop the idea of the abstract term in the mind of the Indian, who will state that the word without a possessive pronoun gives a sense, although it is not used idiomatically. I succeeded, for instance, in this manner, in isolating the terms for *love* and *pity,* which ordinarily occur only in possessive forms, like *his love for him or my pity for you.* That this view is correct may also be observed in languages in which possessive elements appear as independent forms, as, for instance, in the Siouan languages. In these, pure abstract terms are quite common.

There is also evidence that other specializing elements, which are so characteristic of many Indian languages, may be dispensed with when, for one reason or another, it seems desirable to generalize a term. To use the example of the Kwakiutl language, the idea *to be seated* is almost always expressed with an inseparable suffix expessing the place in which a person is seated, as *seated on the floor of the house, on the ground, on the beach, on a pile of things,* or *on a round thing,* etc. When, however, for some reason, the idea of the state of sitting is to be emphasized, a form may be used which expresses simply *being in a sitting posture.* In this case, also, the device for generalized expression is present, but the opportunity for its application arises seldom, or perhaps never. I think what is true in these cases is true of the structure of every single language. The fact that generalized forms of expression are not used does not prove inability to form them, but it merely proves that the mode of life of the people is such that they are not required; that they would, however, develop just as soon as needed.

This point of view is also corroborated by a study of the numeral systems of primitive languages. As is well known, many languages exist in which the numerals do not exceed two or three. It has been inferred from this that the people speaking these languages are not capable of forming the concept of higher numbers. I think this interpretation of the existing conditions is quite erroneous. People like the South American Indians (among whom these defective numeral systems are found), or like the Inuit (whose old system of numbers probably did not exceed ten), are presumably not in need of higher numerical expressions, because there are not many objects that they have to count. On the other hand, just as soon as these same people find themselves in contact with civilization, and when they acquire standards of value that have to be counted, they adopt with perfect ease higher numerals from other languages and develop a more or less perfect system of counting. This does not mean that every individual who in the course of his life has never made use of higher numerals would acquire more complex systems readily, but the tribe as a whole seems always to be capable of adjusting itself to the needs of counting. It must be borne in mind that counting does not become necessary until objects are considered in such generalized form that their individualities are entirely lost sight of. For this reason it is possible that even a person who has a flock of domesticated animals may know them by name and by their characteristics without ever desiring to count them. Members of a war expedition may be known by name and may not be counted. In short, there is no proof that the lack of the use of numerals is in any way connected with the inability to form the concepts of higher numbers.

If we want to form a correct judgment of the influence that language exerts over thought, we ought to bear in mind that our European languages as found at the present time have been moulded to a great extent by the abstract thought of philosophers. Terms like *essence* and *existence*, many of which are now commonly used, are by origin artificial devices for expressing the results of abstract thought. In this they would resemble the artificial, unidiomatic abstract terms that may be formed in primitive languages.

Thus it would seem that the obstacles to generalized thought inherent in the form of a language are of minor importance only, and that presumably the language alone would not prevent a people from advancing to more generalized forms of thinking if the general state of their culture should require expression of such thought; that under these conditions the language would be moulded rather by the cultural state. It does not seem likely, therefore, that there is any direct relation between the culture of a tribe and the language they speak, except in so far as the form of the language will be moulded by the state of the culture, but not in so far as a certain state of culture is conditioned by morphological traits of the language.

Unconscious Character of Linguistic Phenomena

Of greater positive importance is the question of the relation of the unconscious character of linguistic phenomena to the more conscious ethnological phenomena. It seems to my mind that this contrast is only apparent, and that the very fact of the unconsciousness of linguistic processes helps us to gain a clearer understanding of the ethnological phenomena, a point the importance of which can not be underrated. It has been mentioned before that in all languages certain classifications of concepts occur. To mention only a few: we find objects classified according to sex, or as animate and inanimate, or according to form. We find actions determined according to time and place, etc. The behavior of primitive man makes it perfectly clear that all these concepts, although they are in constant use, have never risen into consciousness, and that consequently their origin must be sought, not in rational, but in entirely unconscious, we may perhaps say instinctive, processes of the mind. They must be due to a grouping of sense-impressions and of concepts which is not in any sense of the term voluntary, but which develops from quite different psychological causes. It would seem that the essential difference between linguistic phenomena and other ethnological phenomena is, that the linguistic classifications never rise into consciousness, while in other ethnological phenomena, although the same unconscious origin prevails, these often rise into consciousness, and thus give rise to secondary reasoning and to re-interpretations. It would, for instance, seem very plausible that the fundamental religious notions—like the idea of the voluntary power of inanimate objects, or of the anthropomorphic character of animals, or of the existence of powers that are superior to the mental and physical powers of man—are in their origin just as little conscious as are the fundamental ideas of language. While, however, the use of language is so automatic that the opportunity never arises for the fundamental notions to emerge into consciousness, this happens very frequently in all phenomena relating to religion. It would seem that there is no tribe in the world in which the religious activities have not come to be a subject of thought. While the religious activities may have been performed before the reason for performing them had become a subject of thought, they attained at an early time such importance that man asked himself the reason why he performed these actions. With this moment speculation in regard to religious activities arose, and the whole series of secondary explanations which form so vast a field of ethnological phenomena came into existence.

It is difficult to give a definite proof of the unconscious origin of ethnic phenomena, because so many of them are, or have come to be, subjects of thought. The best evidence that can be given for their unconscious origin must be taken from our own experience, and I think it is not difficult to show that certain groups of our activities, whatever the history of their earlier development may have been, develop at present in each individual and in the whole people entirely sub-consciously, and nevertheless are most potent in the formation of our opinions and actions. Simple examples of this kind are actions which we consider as proper and improper, and which may be found in great numbers in what we call good manners. Thus table manners, which on the whole are impressed vigorously upon the child while it is still young, have a very fixed form. Smacking of the lips and bringing the plate up to the mouth would not be tolerated, although no esthetic or other reason could be given for their rigid exclusion; and it is instructive to know that among a tribe like the Omaha it is considered as bad taste, when invited to eat, not to smack one's lips, because this is a sign of appreciation of the meal. I think it will readily be recognized that the simple fact that these habits are customary, while others are not, is sufficient reason for eliminating those acts that are not customary, and that the idea of propriety simply arises from the continuity and automatic repetition of these acts, which brings about the notion that manners contrary to custom are unusual, and therefore not proper manners. It may be observed in this connection that bad manners are always accompanied by rather intense feelings of displeasure, the psychological reason for which can be found only in the fact that the actions in question are contrary to those which have become habitual. It is fairly evident that in our table manners this strong feeling of propriety is associated with the familiar modes of eating. When a new kind of food is presented, the proper manner of eating which is not known, practically any habit that is not in absolute conflict with the common habits may readily establish itself.

The example of table manners gives also a fairly good instance of secondary explanation. It is not customary to bring the knife to the mouth, and very readily the feeling arises, that the knife is not used in this manner because in eating thus one would easily cut the lips. The lateness of the invention of the fork, and the fact that in many countries dull knives are used and that a similar danger exists of pricking the tongue or the lips with the sharp-pointed steel fork which is commonly used in Europe, show readily, that this explanation is only a secondary rationalistic attempt to explain a custom that otherwise would remain unexplained.

If we are to draw a parallel to linguistic phenomena in this case, it would appear that the grouping of a number of unrelated actions in one group, for the reason that they cause a feeling of disgust, is brought about without any reasoning, and still sets off these actions clearly and definitely in a group by themselves.

On account of the importance of this question, it seems desirable to give another example, and one that seems to be more deeply seated than the one given before. A case of this kind is presented in the group of acts which we characterize as modest. It requires very little thought to see that, while the feelings of modesty are fundamental, the particular acts which are considered modest or immodest show immense variation, and are determined entirely by habits that develop unconsciously so far as their relation to modesty is concerned, and which may have their ultimate origin in causes of an entirely different character. A study of the history of costume proves at once that at different times and in different parts of the world it has been considered immodest to bare certain parts of the body. What parts of the body these are, is to a great extent a matter of accident. Even at the present time, and within a rather narrow range, great variations in this respect may be found. Examples are the use of the veil in Turkey, the more or less rigid use of the glove in our own society, and the difference between street costume and evening dress. A lady in full evening dress in a streetcar, during the daytime, would hardly appear in place.

We all are at once conscious of the intensity of these feelings of modesty, and of the extreme repugnance of the individual to any act that goes counter to the customary concepts of modesty. In a number of cases the origin of a costume can readily be traced, and in its development no considerations of modesty exert any influence. It is therefore evident that in this respect the grouping-together of certain customs again develops entirely unconsciously, but that, nevertheless, they stand out as a group set apart from others with great clearness as soon as our attention is directed toward the feelings of modesty.

To draw a parallel again between this ethnological phenomenon and linguistic phenomena, it would seem that the common feature of both is the grouping-together of a considerable number of activities under the form of a single idea, without the necessity of this idea itself entering into consciousness. The difference, again, would lie in the fact that the idea of modesty is easily isolated from other concepts, and that then secondary explanations are given of what is considered modest and what not. I believe that the unconscious formation of these categories is one of the fundamental traits of ethnic life, and that it even manifests itself in many of its more complex aspects; that many of our religious views and activities, of our ethical concepts, and even our scientific views, which are apparently based entirely on conscious reasoning, are affected by this tendency of distinct activities to associate themselves under the influence of strong emotions. It has been recognized before that this is one of the fundamental causes of error and of the diversity of opinion.

It seems necessary to dwell upon the analogy of ethnology and language in this respect, because, if we adopt this point of view, language seems to be one of the most instructive fields of inquiry in an investigation of the formation of the fundamental ethnic ideas. The great advantage that linguistics offer in this respect is the fact that, on the whole, the categories which are formed always remain unconscious, and that for this reason the processes which lead to their formation can be followed without the misleading and disturbing factors of secondary explanations, which are so common in ethnology, so much so that they generally obscure the real history of the development of ideas entirely.

Cases are rare in which a people have begun to speculate about linguistic categories, and these speculatioi s are almost always so clearly affected by the faulty reasoning that has led to secondary explanations, that they are readily recognized as such, and can not disturb the clear view of the history of linguistic processes. In America we find this tendency, for instance, among the Pawnee, who seem to have been led to several of their religious opinions by linguistic similarities. Incidentally such cases occur also in other languages, as, for instance, in Chinook mythology, where the Culture Hero discovers a man in a canoe who obtains fish by dancing, and tells him that he must not do so, but must catch fish with the net, a tale which is entirely based on the identity of the two words for *dancing*, and *catching with a net*. These are cases which show that Max Muller's theory of the influence of etymology upon religious concepts explains some of the religious phenomena, although, of course, it can be held to account for only a very small portion.

Judging the importance of linguistic studies from this point of view, it seems well worth while to subject the whole range of linguistic concepts to a searching analysis, and to seek in the peculiarities of the grouping of ideas in different languages an important characteristic in the history of the mental development of the various branches of mankind. From this point of view, the occurence of the most fundamental grammatical concepts in all languages must be considered as proof of the unity of fundamental psychological processes. The characteristic groupings of concepts in American languages will be treated more fully in the discussion of the single linguistic stocks. The ethnological significance of these studies lies in the clear definition of the groupings of ideas which are brought out by the objective study of language.

There is still another theoretical aspect that deserves special attention. When we try to think at all clearly, we think, on the whole, in words; and it is well known that, even in the advancement of science, inaccuracy of vocabulary has often been a stumbling-block which has made it difficult to reach accurate conclusions. The same words may be used with different significance, and by assuming the word to have the same significance always, erroneous conclusions may be reached. It may also be that the word expresses only part of an idea, so that owing to its use the full range of the subject-matter discussed may not be recognized. In the same manner the words may be too wide in their significance, including a number of distinct ideas the differences of which in the course of the development of the language were not recognized. Furthermore, we find that, among more primitive tribes, similarities of sound are misunderstood, and that ideas expressed by similar words are considered as similar or identical, and that descriptive terms are misunderstood as expressing an identity, or at least close relationship, between the object described and the group of ideas contained in the description.

All these traits of human thought, which are known to influence the history of science and which play a more or less important role in the general history of civilization, occur with equal frequency in the thoughts of primitive man. It will be sufficient to give a few examples of these cases.

One of the most common cases of a group of views due to failure to notice that the same word may signify diverse objects, is that based on the belief of the identity of persons bearing the same name. Generally the interpretation is given that a child receives the name of an ancestor because he is believed to be a re-incarnation of the individuality of the ancestor. It seems, however, much more likely that this is not the real reason for the views connected with this custom, which seems due to the fact that no distinction is made between the name and the personality known under the name. The association established between name and individual is so close that the two seem almost inseparable; and when a name is mentioned, not only the name itself, but also the personality of its bearer, appears before the mind of the speaker.

Inferences based on peculiar forms of classification of ideas, and due to the fact that a whole group of distinct ideas are expressed by a single term, occur commonly in the terms of relationship of various languages; as, for instance, in our term *uncle*, which means the two distinct classes of father's brother and mother's brother. Here, also, it is commonly assumed that the linguistic expression is a secondary reflex of the customs of the people; but the question is quite open in how far the one phenomenon is the primary one and the other the secondary one, and whether the customs of the people have not rather developed from the unconsciously developed terminology.

Finally, a few examples may be given of cases in which the use of descriptive terms for certain concepts, or the metaphorical use of terms, has led to peculiar views or customs. It seems plausible to my mind, for instance, that the terms of relationship by which some of the eastern Indian tribes designate one another were originally nothing but a metaphorical use of these terms, and that the further elaboration of the social relations of the tribes may have been largely determined by transferring the ideas accompanying these terms into practice.

More convincing are examples taken from the use of metaphorical terms in poetry, which, in rituals, are taken literally, and are made the basis of certain rites. I am inclined to believe, for instance, that the frequently occurring image of *the devouring of wealth* has a close relation to the detailed form of the winter ritual among the Indians of the North Pacific coast, and that the poetical simile in which the chief is called the *support of the sky* has to a certain extent been taken literally in the elaboration of mythological ideas.

Thus it appears that from practical, as well as from theoretical, points of view, the study of language must be considered as one of the most important branches of ethnological study, because, on the one hand, a thorough insight into ethnology can not be gained without practical knowledge of language, and, on the other hand, the fundamental concepts illustrated by human languages are not distinct in kind from ethnological phenomena; and because, furthermore, the peculiar characteristics of languages are clearly reflected in the views and customs of the peoples of the world.

V. CHARACTERISTICS OF NORTH AMERICAN LANGUAGES

In older treatises of the languages of the world, languages have often been classified as isolating, agglutinating, polysynthetic, and inflecting languages. Chinese is generally given as an example of an isolating language. The agglutinating languages are represented by the Ural-Altaic languages of northern Asia; polysynthetic languages, by the languages of America; and inflecting languages, by the Indo-European and Semitic languages. The essential traits of these four groups are: That in the first, sentences are expressed solely by the juxtaposition of unchangeable elements; in the agglutinating languages, a single stem is modified by the attachment of numerous formative elements which modify the fundamental idea of the stem; in polysynthetic languages, a large number of distinct ideas are amalgamated by grammatical processes and form a single word, without any morphological distinction between the formal elements in the sentence and the contents of the sentence; and in the inflecting languages, on the other hand, a sharp distinction is made between formal elements and the material contents -of the sentence, and stems are modified solely according to the logical forms in which they appear in the sentence.

An example of what is meant by polysynthetic is given, for instance, in the following Inuit word: *takusariartorumagaluarnerpa?* "DO YOU THINK HE REALLY INTENDS TO GO TO LOOK AFTER IT? *(takusar[pa]* he looks after it; *-iartor[poq]* he goes to; *-uma[voq]* he intends to; *-[g]aluar[poq]* he does so—but; *-ner[poq]* do you think he—; *-a*, interrogation, third person.) It will be recognized here, that there is no correspondence between the suffixed elements of the fundamental stem and the formal elements that appear in the Indo-European languages, but that a great variety of ideas are expressed by the long series of suffixes. Another example of similar kind is the Tsimshian word *t-yuk-ligi-lo-ɛp-daʟɛt* "HE BEGAN TO PUT IT DOWN SOMEWHERE IN-SIDE (*t*, he; *yuk* to begin; *ligi* somewhere; *lo* in; *d'ɛp* down; *daʟ* to put down; *-t* it).

American languages have also been designated as in-corporating languages, by which is meant a tendency to incorporate the object of the sentence, either nominal or pronominal, in the verbal expression. Ex-amples of this tendency are the Mexican *ni-petla-twiwa* "I MAKE MATS" (*petla-tl* mat); or the Pawnee *ta-t-i'tka'wit* "I DIG DIRT" (*ta* indicative; *t-* I; *i'tkarᵘ* dirt; *-pit* to dig *[rp* in contact, form *'w]*); or the Oneida *g-nagla'-sl-i-ẓak-s* "I SEARCH FOR A VILLAGE" (*g-* I; *-nagla'* to live; *-sl-* abstract noun; *-i-* verbal character; *-ẓak* to search; *-s* continuative).

A more thorough knowledge of the structure of many American languages shows that the general designation of all these languages as polysynthetic and incorporating is not tenable. We have in America a sufficiently large number of cases of languages in which the pronouns are not incorporated, but joined loosely to the verb, and we also have numerous languages in which the incorporation of many elements into a single word hardly occurs at all. Among the languages treated here, the Chinook may be given as an example of lack of polysynthesis. There are very few, if any, cases in which a single Chinook word expresses an extended complex of ideas, and we notice particularly that there are no large classes of ideas which are expressed in such form that they may be considered as subordinate. An examination of the structure of the Chinook grammar will show that each verbal stem appears modified only by pronominal and a few adverbial elements, and that nouns show hardly any tendency to incorporate new ideas such as are expressed by our adjectives. On the other hand, the Athapascan and the Haida and Tlingit may be taken as examples of languages which, though polysynthetic in the sense here described, do not readily incorporate the object, but treat both pronominal subject and pronominal object as independent elements. Among the languages of northern North America, the Iroquois alone has so strong a tendency to incorporate the nominal object into the verb, and at the same time to modify so much its independent form, that it can be considered as one of the characteristic languages that incorporate the object. To a lesser extent this trait belongs also to the Tsimshian, Kutenai, and Shoshone. It is strongly developed in the Caddoan languages. All the other incorporating languages treated here, like the Inuit, Algonquian, and Kwakiutl, confine themselves to a more or less close incorporation of the pronominal object. In Shoshone, the incorporation of the pronominal object and of the nominal object is so weak that it is almost arbitrary whether we consider these forms as incorporated or not. If we extend our view over other parts of America, the same facts appear clearly, and it is not possible to consider these two traits as characteristics of all American languages.

On the other hand, there are certain traits that, although not common to all American languages, are at least frequent, and which are not less characteristic than the tendency to objective incorporation and to polysynthesis. The most important of these is the tendency to divide the verb sharply into an active and a neutral class, one of which is closely related to the possessive forms of the noun, while the other is treated as a true verb. We might perhaps say that American languages have a strong tendency to draw the dividing line between denominating terms and predicative terms, not in the same way that we are accustomed to do. In American languages many of our predicative terms are closely related to nominal terms, most frequently the neutral verbs expressing a state, like *to sit, to stand*. These, also, often include a considerable number of adjectives. On the other hand, terms expressing activities—like *to sing, to eat, to kill*—are treated as true predicative terms. The differentiation of these two classes is generally expressed by the occurence of an entirely or partially separated set of pronouns for the predicative terms.

Beyond these extremely vague points, there are hardly any characteristics that are common to many American languages. A number of traits, however, may be enumerated which occur with considerable frequency in many parts of America.

The phonetic systems of American languages differ very considerably, but we find with remarkable frequency a peculiar differentiation of voiced and unvoiced stops,—corresponding to our *b, p; d,/t; g, k,*—which differ in principle from the classification of the corresponding sounds in most of the European languages. An examination of American vocabularies and texts shows very clearly that all observers have had more or less difficulty in differentiating these sounds. Although there is not the slightest doubt that they differ in character, it would seem that there is almost everywhere a tendency to pronounce the voiced and unvoiced sounds with very nearly equal stress of articulation, not as in European languages, where the unvoiced sound is generally pronounced with greater stress. This equality of stress of the two sounds brings it about that their differences appear rather slight. On the other hand, there are frequently sounds, particularly in the languages of the Pacific coast, in which a stress of articulation is used which is considerably greater than any stresses occurring in the languages with which we are familiar. These sounds are generally unvoiced; but a high air-pressure in the oral cavity is secured by closing the glottis and nares, or by closing the posterior part of the mouth with the base of the tongue. The release at the point of articulation lets out the small amount of strongly compressed air, and the subsequent opening of glottis and nares or base of tongue produces a break in the continuity of sound.

We find also with particular frequency the occurrence of a number of lingual stops corresponding more or less strictly to our *k* sounds which, however, are more finely differentiated than our *k* sounds. Thus the velar *k,* which is so characteristic of Semitic languages, occurs with great frequency in America. On the other hand, the labio-dental *f* seems to be rather rare, and where a similar sound occurs it is often the bilabial sound.

The same may be said of the *r*, which on the whole is a rare sound in American languages, and the trill of which is almost always so weak that it merges into the *d, n, l,* or *y,* as the case may be.

On the whole, the system of consonants of American languages is well developed, particularly owing to the occurrence of the three stresses to which I referred before, instead of the two with which we are more familiar. In some groups of languages we have also a quite distinct set of stops accompanied by full breathing, which correspond to the English surds. Furthermore, a peculiar break, produced by closing the vocal cords, occurs quite commonly, not only in connection with sonants, but also following or preceding vowels or affricative consonants. This intonation is sometimes quite audible, and sometimes merely a break or hiatus in the continuity of pronunciation. Sometimes it seems related to the pronunciation of a voiced consonant in which the voicing is preceded by a closure of the vocal chords. In other cases it seems related to the production of the great stress of articulation to which I referred before. For instance, in a strong *t* the tongue may be pressed so firmly against the palate that all the articulating organs, including the vocal chords, take part in the tension, and that the sudden expulsion of the air is accompanied also by a sudden relaxation of the vocal chords, so that for this reason the strong, exploded sound appears to be accompanied by an intonation of the vocal chords.

As stated before, these traits are not by any means common to all American languages, but they are sufficiently frequent to deserve mention in a generalized discussion of the subject.

On the other hand, there are languages which are exceedingly deficient in their phonetic system. Among these may be mentioned, for instance, the Iroquois, which possesses not a single true labial consonant; or the Haida, in which the labials are confined to a few sounds, which are rather rare.

The vocalic systems of the northern languages seem peculiarly uncertain. The cases are very numerous in which obscure vowels occur, which are evidently related to fuller vowels, but whole affiliations often can not be determined. It would seem that in the southern languages these weak vowels are not so prominent. We also find very frequently a lack of clear distinction between *o* and *u* on the one hand, and *e* and *i* on the other. Although the variability of vowels in some of the languages seems beyond doubt, there are others in which the vocalic system is very definite and in which distinctions are expressed, not only by the timbre of the vowel, but also by its rising or falling tone. Among these may be mentioned the Pawnee and the Takelma. The Pawnee seems to have at least two tones, a sinking tone and a rising tone, while in Takelma there seem to be three tones. Nasalized vowels are very common in some languages, and entirely absent in others. This nasalization occurs both with open lips and with closed lips. An example of the latter is the Iroquois u^m.

It is not possible to give any general characterization of American languages with regard to the grouping of sounds. While in some languages consonantic clusters of incredible complexity are formed, others avoid such clusters altogether. There is, however, a habit of pronunciation which deserves attention, and which is found very widely distributed. This is the slurring of the ends of words, which is sometimes so pronounced, that, in an attempt to write the words, the terminations, grammatical or other, may become entirely inaudible. The simplest form in which this tendency expresses itself is in the suppression of terminal consonants, which are only articulated, but not pronounced. In the Nass river dialect of the Tsimshian, for instance, the terminal *n* of the word *gan* "TREE" is indicated by the position of the tongue, but is entirely inaudible, unless the word is followed by other words belonging to the same sentence. In that language the same is true of the sounds *l* and *m*. Vowels are suppressed in a similar manner by being only indicated by the position of the mouth, without being articulated. This happens frequently to the *u* following a *k*, or with an *i* in the same position. Thus the Kwakiutl pronounce *wa'Dɛkⁿ*. If, however, another vowel follows, the *u* which is not articulated appears as a *w*, as in the form *wa'dɛkwa*.

The slurring, however, extends over whole syllables, which in these cases may appear highly modified. Thus, in the Oneida dialect of the Iroquois, a peculiar *l* sound is heard, which presumably occurs only in such slurred syllables. It is very remarkable that the Indians of all tribes are perfectly conscious of the phonetic elements which has thus been suppressed, and can, when pressed to do so, pronounce the words with their full endings.

Another trait that is characteristic of many American languages, and that deserves mention, is the tendency of various parts of the population to modify the pronunciation of sounds. Thus we find that among some Inuit tribes the men pronounce the terminal *p*, *t*, *k*, and *q* distinctly, while the women always transform these sounds into *m*, *n*, *n*, and *n*. In some dialects the men have also adopted this manner of pronouncing, so that the pronunciation has become uniform again. Such mannerisms, that are peculiar to certain social groups, are of course not entirely foreign to us, but they are seldom developed in so striking a manner as in a few of the Indian languages.

In many American languages we find highly developed laws of euphony,—laws by which, automatically, one sound in a sentence requires certain other sounds either to precede or to follow it. In the majority of cases these laws of euphony seem to act forward in a manner that may be compared to the laws of vowel harmony in the Ural-Altaic languages. Particularly remarkable among these laws is the influence of the *o* upon following vowels, which occurs in a few languages of the Pacific coast. In these, the vowels following an *o* in the same word must, under certain conditions, be transformed into *o* vowels, or at least be modified by the addition of a *w*. Quite different in character are the numerous influences of contact of sounds, which are very pronounced in the Siouan languages, and occur again in a quite different form in the Pawnee. It may be well to give an example of these also. Thus, in Dakota, words ending with an *a* and followed by a word beginning with a *k* transform the former into *e*, the latter into *c*. In Pawnee, on the other hand, the combination *tr* is always transformed into an *h*; *b* following an *i* is generally changed into a *w*; *rp* becomes *hw*, etc. While in some languages these phonetic changes do not occupy a prominent place, they are exceedingly important in others. They correspond in a way to the laws of euphony of Sanskrit.

Just as much variety as is shown in phonetic systems is found in the use of grammatical devices. In discussing the definition of the word, it has been pointed out that in some American languages the word-unit seems to be perfectly clear and consistent, while in others the structure of the sentence would seem to justify us in considering it as composed of a number of independent elements combined by juxtaposition. Thus, languages which have a polysynthetic character have the tendency to form firmly knit word-units, which may be predicative sentences, but may also be used for denominative purposes. For example, the Chinook may say, *He runs into the water,* and may designate by this term *the mink*; or the Hupa may say *They have been laid together,* meaning by this term *a fire.* On the other hand, there are innumerable languages in America in which expressions of this kind are entirely impossible.

In forming words and sentences, affixes are used extensively, and we find prefixes, as well as suffixes and infixes. It is not absolutely certain that cases occur in America where true infixing into a stem takes place, and where it might not be better explained as an insertion of the apparently infixed element into a compound stem, or as due to secondary phonetic phenomena, like those of metathesis; but in the Siouan languages at least, infixion in bisyllabic stems that are apparently simple in their origin occurs. Otherwise, suffixing is, on the whole, more extensively used than prefixing; and in some languages only one of these two methods is used, in others both. There are probably no languages in which prefixing alone occurs.

Change of stem is also a device that is used with great frequency. We find particularly that methods of reduplication are used extensively. Modifications of single sounds of the stem occur also, and sometimes in peculiar form. Thus we have cases, as in Tsimshian, where the lengthening of a vowel indicates plurality; or, as in Algonquian, where modality is expressed by vocalic modification; and, as in Chinook, where diminutive and augmentative are expressed by increasing the stress of consonants. Sometimes an exuberance of reduplicated forms is found, the reduplicated stem being reduplicated a second and even a third time. On the other hand, we find numerous languages in which the stem is entirely unchangeable, excepting so far as it may be subject to phonetic contact phenomena.

The following grammatical sketches have been contributed by investigators, each of whom has made a special study of the linguistic stock of which he treats. The attempt has been made to adopt, so far as feasible, a uniform method of treatment, without, however, sacrificing the individual conception of each investigator.

In accordance with the general views expressed in the introductory chapters, the method of treatment has been throughout an analytical one. No attempt has been made to compare the forms of the Indian grammars with the grammars of English, Latin, or even among themselves; but in each case the psychological groupings which are given depend entirely upon the inner form of each language. In other words, the grammar has been treated as though an intelligent Indian was going to develop the forms of his own thoughts by an analysis of his own form of speech.

It will be understood that the results of this analysis can not be claimed to represent the fundamental categories from which the present form of each language has developed. There is not the slightest doubt that, in all Indian languages, processes have occurred analogous to those processes which are historically known and to which the modern forms of Indo-European languages owe their present forms. Grammatical categories have been lost, and new ones have developed. Even a hasty comparison of the dialects of various American linguistic families gives ample proof that similar processes have taken place here. To give an example, we find that, in the Ponca dialect of the Siouan languages, nouns are classified according to form, and that there is a clear formal distinction between the subject and the object of the sentence. These important features have disappeared entirely in the Dakota dialect of the same group of languages. To give another example, we find a pronominal sex gender in all the dialects of the Salishan stock that are spoken west of the Coast range in the states of Washington and in British Columbia, while in the dialects of the interior there is no trace of gender. On the other hand, we find in one of the Salish dialects of the interior the occurrence of an exclusive and inclusive form of the pronoun, which is absent in all the other dialects of the same stock. We have no information on the history of American languages, and the study of dialects has not advanced far enough to permit us to draw far-reaching inferences in regard to this subject. It is therefore impossible, in the few cases here mentioned, to state whether the occurrence and non-occurrence of these categories are due to a loss of old forms in the one dialect or to a later differentiation in the other.

Although, therefore, an analytical grammar can not lay any claim to present a history of the development of grammatical categories, it is valuable as a presentation of the present state of grammatical development in each linguistic group. The results of our investigation must be supplemented at a later time by a thorough analysis and comparison of all the dialects of each linguistic stock.

Owing to the fundamental differences between different linguistic families, it has seemed advisable to develop the terminology of each independently of the others, and to seek for uniformity only in cases where it can be obtained without artificially stretching the definition of terms. It is planned to give a comparative discussion of the languages at the close of these volumes, when reference can be made to the published sketches.

ETHNIC DIVIDING LINE BETWEEN NORTH AMERICA AND SOUTH AMERICA

It has long been conceded that the linguistic element (if it may be termed so) of South America, at the time of the Spanish Conquest, extended into the southern sections of Central America. Brinton says

The mountain chain which separates Nicaragua from Costa Rica, and the headwaters of the Rio Frio from those of the more southern and eastern streams, is the ethnographic boundary of North America. Beyond it [going south] we come upon tribes whose linguistic affinities point towards the southern continent. Such are the Talamancas, Guaymies, Valientes, and others.

So far as the present writer is aware, however, Sapper is the first to lay down definitely this dividing line. Beginning at the extreme northwestern corner of Honduras, where it meets the bay, it runs thence southeast almost in a direct line to the eastern end of Lake Nicaragua; and thence in nearly the same direction to the head of the Gulf of Dulce on the southern coast of Costa Rica. This demarcation, allowing the following modification, is accepted: Carry the line from the east end, or near the east end, of Lake Nicaragua almost directly south to the mouth of the Gulf of Nicoya, the tribes east of this line—the Jicaque, Paya, the Ulvan tribes, Carib, Mosquito, Rama, and all the tribes of Costa Rica (except the Orotina), and those of Panama—being considered as belonging ethnically to the southern continent. Brinton's dividing line was laid down before he had discovered the correct relation of the Rama. He assigned the Jicaque, Paya, and Ulvan group to the northern continent, but, in the judgement of the writer, Sapper's division is the better one. On this point the only question in doubt is, whether or not the Xincan, Lencan, Matagalpan, and Subtiaban tribes, west of the dividing line thus drawn, should not also be added to the South American list.

CHARACTERISTICS OF SOUTH AMERICAN INDIAN LANGUAGES

South American Indian languages have no uniform or even usual characteristics that differentiate them from North American languages. The same may be said of American languages fundamentally, as opposed to Old World languages. Languages were formerly grouped into categories according to morphological pattern; isolating, agglutinating, polysynthetic, and inflective, with an implication of evolution and betterment toward the inflecting ideal—of course, of our own Indo-European languages. However, research has shown that, so far as there has been any evolution, the isolating is the last, not the first stage. American languages were once classed with the polysynthetic,

ship of French, Spanish, and Italian; even if we did not know their descent from Latin, the resemblance is obvious. The relationship of dialects such as Catalan, Provencal, and Gallego is even closer and more evident.

Related languages are grouped in "families" or "stocks," presumed, on present evidence, to be unrelated. These families are then subdivided into divisions, groups, branches, languages, types, dialects, varieties, etc. The terminology is indefinite and there are no established criteria. When families heretofore considered independent are determined to be related, a more inclusive term is required; phylum has been accepted. For instance, if Indo-European, Hamito-Semitic, and Finno-Ugrian are "proved" to be related, as has been posited with considerable ground, they would compose a phylum. Most of the 85-odd "families" of North America, formerly considered independent, are now grouped in relatively few phyla.

Good scientific grammars of South American languages are practically nonexistent, and grammars of any kind, even of the older type based on analogy with Latin grammar, are very few. Comparisons of morphology, one of the important criteria for linguistic connections, are, therefore, in most cases impossible. Most of the classifications are based on lexical grounds, on vocabularies, often short, usually taken by travelers or missionary priests, and generally with the help of interpreters. The recorders were almost always untrained in phonetics and each used the phonetic system of his native language—Spanish, Portugese, French, German, or English; sometimes Dutch or Swedish. Scientific deductions made on the basis of such material have little claim to acceptance. Yet on many languages, extinct or living, nothing else is available. An independent family should not be posited on the basis of one such vocabulary, no matter how apparently different from any other language.

Of many extinct languages, and even of some living ones, nothing is known; of others there are statements that the natives spoke a language of their own, different from that of their neighbors, but without any suggestion as to how different, or that the language was intelligible or unintelligible or related to that of other groups. Of some, only place and personal names remain; of others, recorded lexical data ranging from a few words to large vocabularies and grammatical sketches.

Owing to the magnitude of the field it has been possible for me to make very few independent studies and comparisons of lexical and morphological data with a view to establishing linguistic connections, and even most of the articles published by others in support of such relationships have not been critically studied and appraised. The greater number, and by far the most cogent, of these studies have been written by the dean of South American linguists, Dr. Paul Rivet. Similar studies in *Marco-Ge* languages have been published by Loukotka. In almost all of them the authors were, unfortunately, limited to comparing vocabularies collected by others and pregnant with the faults already herein set forth. Words from lists in one group of languages are compared with words from languages of another group. Rarely are the roots or stems isolated or known, and morphological elements may often be mistaken for parts of stems. Rarely has it been possible to deduce any rules of sound-shift, the best proof of linguistic relationship, or the examples given are too few in proportion to the number of comparisons to carry conviction. Few of these proposed linguistic relationships can be said to be incontrovertibly proved; good cases have been made for many, and many or most of them have been accepted by later authorities, and are accepted herein. Others are doubtful validity, and all require reappraisal and reworking, especially those in which new data may later become, or may already have become, available.

It is a truism of linguistic research that, given large enough vocabularies to compare, and making allowances for all possible changes in the form of a word or stem, as well as in its meaning, a number of apparent similarities, convincing to the uncritical, can be found between any two languages. Especially is this true if the comparison is made between two large groups, each consisting of languages of admitted relationship. To carry conviction, laws of sound-shift must be deduced, obeyed by a large proportion of the cases in question, and a basic similarity in morphological and phonetic pattern must be shown. Few of the comparative works on South American languages attempt such obligations, and almost all suffer from the faults above listed. There is not a really thorough comparative grammar of any South American, or for that matter of any American, native linguistic family, except possibly Algonkian.

One of the pitfalls to be avoided in linguistic comparison is that of borrowing. Languages easily adopt words from neighboring languages; these must be discounted in seeking evidence on genetic relationship. Words for new concepts or new objects are likely to be similar in many languages; generally their categories and very similar forms betray their recent origin. Phonetic pattern and morphological traits are also borrowed, but to a lesser degree. Grammatical pattern is the most stable element in a language, phonology next; vocabulary is most subject to change. There are several areas in America where a number of languages with little or no lexical resemblance have a relatively uniform phonology, and/or similar morphological peculiarities.

Many American languages, North as well as South, show resemblance in the pronominal system, often *n* for the first person, *m* or *p* for second person. Whether this is the result of common origin, chance, or borrowing has never been proved, but the resemblance should not be used as evidence of genetic connection between any two languages. Many of the languages of central and eastern Brazil are characterized by words ending in vowels, with the stress accent on the ultimate syllable.

In some cases, the amount of borrowed words and elements may be so great as practically to constitute a mixed language. Linguistic students are in disagreement as to whether a true mixed language with multiple origins is possible. Loukotka, considers a language mixed if the foreign elements exceed one-fifth of the 45-word standard vocabulary used by him for comparison. Lesser borrowings he terms "intrusions" and "vestiges."

The situation is further complicated by the fact that, in a large number of instances, the same or a very similar name was applied by colonists to several groups of very different linguistic affinities. This may be a descriptive of European derivation, such as *Orejon*, "Big Ears", *Patagon*, "Big Feet"; *Coroada*, "Crowned" or Tonsured"; *Barbados*, "Bearded"; *Lengua*, "Tongue." Or it may be an Indian word applied to several different groups in the same way that the *Mayan Lecandon* of the Chiapas are locally called "*Caribs*," and the rustic natives of Puerto Rico and Cuba "*Gibaros*" and "*Goajiros*," respectively. Thus, "*Tupaya*," the *Tupi* word for "enemy," was applied by them to almost all non-*Tupi* groups, "*Botocudo*" to wearers of large lipplugs, etc. Among other names applied to groups of different languages, sometimes with variations are *Apiaca*, *Arara*, *Caripuna*, *Chavante*, *Guana*, *Guayana*, *Canamari*, *Caraya*, *Catawishi*, *Catukina*, *Cuniba*, *Jivaro*, *Macu*, *Tapiete*, not to mention such easily confused names as *Tuscano*, *Tacana* and *Ticuna*. Many mistakes have been made due to confusion of such names.

One of the main reasons for the great difference in the proposed number of linguistic families in North and South America is that the study of South American linguistics is now about in the same stage as that of North American languages thirty years ago. Since that time many trained students, both in the United States and in Mexico, have studied the native languages intensively, largely under the direction or example of Drs. Franz Boas and Edward Sapir. Except for the indefatigable Dr. Paul Rivet and Curt Nimuendaju, South America has had few linguistic scholars of wide interests and scientific viewpoint, and until recently very few trained younger people. The North American languages have been grouped into six phyla, mainly on grounds of morphological resemblance and intuition, and in this the students have been aided by the fact that the languages are fewer, and fewer of them extinct, so that such morphological studies could be made. South America suffers not only from lack of students, paucity of grammatical studies, multitudes of languages, extinction of many of them, but also from the practical problems of linguistic research: immense distances, poor transportation, difficulties and expense of expeditions, lack of capable interpreters, and similar handicaps.

The history of attempts to classify the languages of South America was reviewed by Chamberlain in 1907. The earlier classifications, such as those of Adelung and Vater, Balbi, Castelnau, Gilij, Hervas, Ludewig, Von Martius and D'Orbigny, were not considered therein, and need not be here. Modern classification began with Brinton in 1891. With his usual far-seeing good sense, not "curiously enough" as Chamberlain remarks, Brinton refused to enumerate or list his "stocks," but apparently recognized nearly sixty. In many later short articles Brinton continued to alter his groupings. Other lists published in the next few years were McGee, 1903; Chamberlain, 1903 ;Ehrenreich, 1905. All these differ more than the slight variation in total would suggest. Chamberlain then gave his own list, totalling 83. Later, in 1913, he published a revision of this, which became the standard classification in English for a decade or more. Though the total of 83 stocks is exactly the same as in his earlier list, the number of alternations, deletions, and additions is great.

Since 1922 a number of classifications have appeared. Krickeberg (1922) stressed only 15 most important families; based on this Jimenez Moreno

(1938) published a large distribution map in color. P. W. Schmidt (1926) also wisely did not attempt to enumerate and list every family, but discussed them under 36 families or groups. The late Curt Nimuendaju never attempted a complete linguistic classification of South America, and his unpublished map and index do not include the far north, west and south, but his first-hand knowledge of the rest of the continent is unexcelled. In this restricted region he recognizes 42 stocks, 34 isolated languages, and hundreds of unclassified languages, the latter generally without any known linguistic data.

Two comprehensive classifications of all South American languages have been made. Paul Rivet (1924), combining some of Chamberlain's families, separating others, reached a total of 77. Pericot y Garcia (1936) follows Rivet very closely, but not in numerical or alphabetical order. The most recent classification and the most radical—or most conservative, according to the point of view—is that of Loukotka (1935). Dividing more of Rivet's families than he combined, he enumerates 94 families with a total of some 558 languages. Later he revised the details somewhat, but only regarding the languages of Brazil. In this latter article he notes the linguistic sources for each language (Loukotka, 1939).

In view of the great uncertainty regarding the relationships and classification of the South American native languages, and the great differences of opinion, the example of Brinton, Schmidt, and Krickeberg is herein followed, in not attempting to enumerate and rigidly to separate the genetic families.

The classification of the languages of South American herein given is, therefore, presented without any pretense of finality or even of accuracy; the data are too insufficient. Future research will indicate many errors and change the picture decidely. It is hoped that the present article incorporates all the accepted revisions since the appearance of other classifications, and improves on the latter. As regards exactitude and finality I can but cite the opinion of a great linguist:

> To attempt to make an exact and complete classification of all languages in rigorously defined families is to prove that one has not understood the principles of the genetic classification of languages. [Mellet and Cohen, 1924, p.10.]

South American linguistic history or philogy does not extend before the beginnings of the 16th century with the first words and observations made by European voyagers. No native alphabets had been developed; there were no hieroglyphs, and even pictographs, petroglyphs, and picture-writing seem to be less than in North America. The Peruvian quipus were arithmetical, astrological, divinatory, and mnemonic. There was a tradition among the *Quechua* at the time of the Conquest that they had once had a system of writing on tree leaves that was later forbidden and forgotten (Montesiños, 1920 chs. 7, 14, 15; Bingham, 1922, ch. 16; 1930, ch. 9.), but this is given little credence by modern scholars, and no trace of it remains. However, it has been suggested that painted symbols were employed by some natives of the North Peruvian Coast (Larco Hoyle, 1944). A system of writing has been claimed for the *Chibcha,* also, based, not on tradition, but on the peculiar, and apparently nonpictorial character of many pictographs in Colombia; this also has received no credence among archeologists. On the other hand, the modern *Cuna* of Panama have developed an interesting existent system of mnemonic picture-writing.

Two of the native languages merit special mention as having become, after the Spanish Conquest, lenguas francas of wider extent and use than formerly. The *Tupi* of the Brazilian coast became the basis of the lingua geral, the medium of communication of priests and traders throughout the Amazon drainage; it is now generally replaced by Portuguese. The Cuzco dialect of *Quechua* became the culture language of the "*Inca*" region and extended its area even before the Conquest, after the latter it continued its spread and was adopted as a second language by the Spanish in Peru. Neither language has today, however, the cultural position of the *Maya* of Yucatan, for instance, though both have added many native terms in the Spanish and Portuguese of their regions, and even throughout the world as tapioca, jaguar, llama, and quinine. It has been estimated that 15 percent of the vocabulary of Brazilian Portuguese of *Tupi* origin. In Paraguay, *Guarani* is considered a culture language, and some newspapers are published in it.

America, and especially South America, is probably the region of greatest linguistic diversity in the world, and of greatest ignorance concerning the native languages. On the very probable presumption that each homogeneous group, tribe, band, or village spoke a recognizable variant dialect or variety, there may have been 5,000 such in South America. The index of Rivet lists some 1,240 such groups (including a few synonyms), and this is far from the total. For instance, in the above index, Rivet lists 13 component members of the small and unimportant Timote family of Venezuela; in his monograph on the Timote he mentions 128 names for local groups, apart from the names of the villages occupied by them.

The multitude of languages in America has often been given as an argument for a comparatively great length of time of human occupation of this hemisphere. This concept presupposes that the first immigrants to America had a common speech. This is unlikely; it is more probable that each migrating group had its specific language, and that number of presumably independent linguistic families may originally have been even greater than at present. Such a reduction has been the linguistic history of the rest of the world. These "families" may either have had a remote common ancestry or multiple unrelated origins; of the origin and early forms of speech we know nothing. All known "primitive" languages are highly complex and evidently have had a long period of development. Of course, the minor dialects and obviously related languages were differentiated in America.

Since the main migration to America is believed to have been via Alaska, we would expect to find in South America languages of older migrations than in North America, the speech of the earliest migrants forced to the peripheries and to cul-de-sacs by later and more aggressive groups, and also small enclaves of moribund independent linguistic families. This applies expecially to southernmost and easternmost South America, and to the speech of natives of paleo-American physical type, such as the *Ge* and the Fuegians.

Regarding extracontinental relationships, many ill-conceived attempts have been made to show connections between South American native languages and Indo-European or Semitic ones; all these are so amateurish that they have been accorded no scientific attention. Dr. Paul Rivet is firmly convinced of the connection between Australian languages and *Chon,* and between Malayo-Polynesian and *Hokan*. Instead of by direct trans-Pacific voyages, he believes that the Australian influence came via the Antarctic during a favorable postglacial period not less than 6,000 years ago. This radical thesis has met with no acceptance among North American anthropologists. The data offered in its support fall short of conviction, but probably have not received sufficient careful consideration.

It is possible that some of the South American languages belong to the great *Hokan* or *Hokan-Siouan* family or phylum of North America. (Cf. *Yurumangui, Quechua.)* Since isolated *Hokan* enclaves are found as far south as Nicaragua, evidence of migrations across Panama would not be entirely unexpected. A number of languages from Colombia to the Gran Chaco have *Hokan*-like morphological patterns. Dr. J.P. Harrington is convinced of the *Hokan* affiliations of *Quechua,* but his published article fails to carry conviction, and no other argument for *Hokan* in South America has been presented. Such *Hokan* migrations, if proved, were probably at a relatively early period.

On the other hand, several of the great South American families have penetrated the southern peripheries of North America. *Chibchan* languages occupied a solid area, with possible a few small enclaves of other families or isolated languages, as far as the Nicaraguan border, and the probably affiliated *"Misumalpan"* *(Miskito-Sumo-Matagalpa)* would extend this area to cover Nicaragua. *Arawak* and *Carib* extended over the Lesser and Greater Antilles, and the former may have had a colony on the Florida coast.

In 1797 the native *Carib* Indians remaining in the Lesser Antilles, mainly on St. Vincent Island, were transported to Roatan Island off the coast of Honduras. Mixing with the Negro population there, they have spread over much of the coast of Honduras and parts of Birtish Honduras. They now number some 15,000, most of them speaking a *Carib* jargon.

The trend in the classification of American languages has been quite opposite in North and in South America. In the former, radical scholars believe that all the many languages formerly considered independent may fall into six great phyla: *Eskimo, Na-Dene, Algonkian-Mosan, Hokan-Siouan, Macro-Penutian,* and *Macro-Otomanguean,* plus the South American phylum *Macro-Chibchan.* In South America, on the contrary, the more recent classifications have increased rather than reduced the number of families or groups given independent status. Most of these new ones, it must be admitted, are one-language families, many of them extinct, and generally based on on or a few short vocabularies that show little or no resemblance to any other language with which they have been compared. These should be considered as unclassified rather than as independent familes. It is certain that the number will be greatly reduced as the languages become more intensively studied, but doubtful if it will ever reach such relative simplicity as in North America. Almost certainly the linguistic picture will be found to be far more complex than in Europe and Asia.

When travelling, fire was sometimes carried by means of a slow burning material such as decayed wood, bark preparations, or fungi. The starting of a fire and the particular method used were at times given religious significance. Some ceremonies involved extinguishing all fires in a community and restarting them from a ritual new fire. After adoption of matches, the native methods of fire making retained their importance for the most part only as religious rites.

LITERACY is the ability to read and write the English language. Today, Indian students are typically older than standard for their grade levels, or else achieve below academic norms; and Indian children often score lower than whites on I.Q. tests. Both of these circumstances are due to cultural differences, often related to differences in the structures of native and English languages, rather than to differences in innate intelligence. For example, many Indian children do not realize that the written word is related to the spoken word — a natural area of confusion for people whose own languages were never reduced to script. Furthermore, there are many structural differences between English and native languages. Indian children, for example, often have difficulty comprehending the meaning of tenses in the English language, since there are no counterparts to them in their native tongues — while English-speaking people refer to the past, present, and future, Indians usually refer to relative time, in terms of duration and sequence.

Recent testing at selected schools indicated that roughly 40 percent of Indian students in elementary schools needed remedial work in reading. An even larger percentage of high school students needed such help.

At schools run by the Bureau of Indian Affairs, curriculum now includes a strong emphasis on oral English — a subject that is unnecessary in schools whose students come from English-speaking homes, but which is essential to the Indians, for whom English is a second, and quite foreign, language.

Until recently, many Indians have been openly hostile to education of the sort they could get in schools run by whites. During the nineteenth century, Indian children were often placed in schools great distances from their homes, where English text books were used, English culture was emphasized, and the use of native languages was prohibited. Under these circumstances, Indian hostility to education was quite predictable and understandable. During their five-year captivity at Fort Sumner, the Navajos resisted government efforts to convert them to Christianity and teach them English. After they were placed on a reservation, they continued to resist the white man's education, keeping their children at home despite a Bureau of Indian Affairs order of compulsory attendance. At Round Rock, violence erupted over the issue. Only since World War II have the Navajo become more willing to have their children learn English. Many older persons also desire to learn English now, and have returned to school to do so. Among the Apache Indians the most modern audio-visual devices are used to teach English to the children, but only as a second language. The same devices are used to teach their young the Apache language. As with the Navajo and other Indian peoples, the Apache are willing to learn the white man's ways — but not at the expense of their own culture. Familiarity with English is simply recognized as a necessity for survival in the modern world.

LONGHOUSE. The characteristic dwelling of the Iroquois was a log and bark community house known as the longhouse (ganonh sees) designed to accommodate five, ten, or twenty families. The longhouse ranged in length from 30 to 200 feet, in width from 15 to 25 feet, and in height, at the center, from 15 to 20 feet. The average longhouse was 60 feet in length, 18 feet wide, and 18 feet high. It was built with a framework of upright posts with forked tops. The lower ends of the posts were set one foot into the ground to form a rectangular space the size of the building to be constructed. Horizontal poles were tied with withes to the vertical poles, along the sides and across the tops. A steep triangular or rounded roof was formed by bending the slender, flexible poles toward the center above the space enclosed by the poles.

The framework of logs was sheathed with bark. The bark was gathered in the spring or early summer up to mid-July. Slabs of bark 4 feet wide by 6 or 8 feet long were removed from the elm, hemlock, basswood, ash, or cedar trees. The elm bark was considered best. The bark was pressed flat under weights, and laid horizontally over the framework of poles, the slabs of bark overlapping one another like shingles. Basswood withes or strips of bast from the inner bark of basswood and hickory trees were used to fasten the pieces of bark together and to secure them to the framework. Holes for use in sewing were made in the bark by means of a bone puncher.

A series of poles, corresponding to the poles of the framework, were set up outside the bark, and close to it, on the four sides and across the roof. They were tied to the first set of poles, binding the bark firmly in place. No metal tools or commercially manufactured materials were used in the erection of the longhouse.

The longhouse had no windows. Light came from the high, wide doors at each end, and from above. A movable piece of bark or tanned hide, which could be easily tied back, was used as a door, at the entrance. In the roof were square openings to admit light and to allow for the escape of smoke. Pieces of bark were provided on the roof to close the holes when wind, rain, or snow made it necessary. They could be controlled from within by pushing with a long pole.

A central hallway from 6 to 10 feet wide ran lengthwise of the longhouse. The hallway served as a place for social visiting where children played while their elders reclined on the mats of reeds and husks provided for the purpose.

Raised 18 inches from the ground along the two sides there ran a series of compartments or booths to accomodate family groups. The booths were from 6 to 12 feet long and from 5 to 6 feet wide. Each compartment belonged to a given family and was not to be violated by members of other families. Private ownership existed, though life was carried on in a communal way. Platforms about 3 1-2 feet wide, running along the sides of the booths, provided bunks for sleeping. Small bunks were sometimes built for the children. Several layers of bark, reed mats, and soft fur robes covered the platform. About 7 feet from the ground a second platform was erected over the bunks, to be used for storage. Cooking utensils, clothes, hunting equipment, and other possessions were stowed away wherever a place could be found for them. Pits were often dug under the beds for the storage of household treasures. On the cross poles or rafters were hung large masses of dried corn (united by braiding the husks of the ears together), strips of dried pumpkin, strings of dried apples and squash, herbs, and other supplies.

At each end of the longhouse, storage booths and platforms were provided for the food kept in barrels and containers.

Down the central passage, between the booths, rough stone fire places were arranged to provide fires for comfort and for cooking, and for light at night. One house might have as many as 12 fires. Each fire place served two families. The fire built by the Indian was always a small one, not like the White camper's roaring bonfire.

During Revolutionary times the bark house of the Iroquois was fitted up with sturdy furniture. Corn husk rugs were used on the floor. Splint baskets, gourd containers, skin bags, and other handicraft products were among the furnishings. Braids of sweet grass were sometimes hung in a house to decorate and perfume it. A strong, straight bough or a thick board that had been deeply notched up one side served as a ladder

cobs served as scrubbing brushes and scratchers. As a fuel corn cob served to smoke meats and hides.

Corn husk mats. The corn husk sleeping or lounging mat is thought to have been used by the Indians prior to the coming of the Europeans. There are many references to the use of mats in the folklore of the agricultural tribes. The corn husk lounging mat was made up of rows of husks of equal length neatly rolled with the ends folded. The husks for the second row were inserted in the ends of the husks of the first row and tied or stitched in place with basswood cord. Thus row after row of husks was added. The finished mat

Maize-leaf ball.

showed a stitching of basswood cord crossing the corn husks at regular intervals several inches apart. The edge of the mat was finished with a tight husk braid.

Another type of mat was made from husks that had been loosely braided, coiled and sewed together with bark thread.

A thick husk door mat was made by braiding strands of the husks in such a way that on one side of the braid the ends were left protruding for an inch or more. The braid was then coiled to form a round or oval mat with the rough side on top. The coils were sewed together with corn husk or other fiber. When the mat was finished the protruding ends of the husks were neatly trimmed to form a short, stiff pile.

Corn husk dolls. Corn husk dolls with hair of corn silk were made both with and without facial features, to be used in certain medicine rites. Some of the dolls were without clothing. Others were dressed in skin or in the textiles used by the Iroquois after White contacts.

Arthur Parker gives the following description of the making of a corn husk doll. "Dolls are made by folding the husk in a pestlelike form for the neck and body. Room is left for the head and neck and the central core is pierced to allow a wisp of husk to be pulled through to be braided into arms. The lower portion is pierced in the same way and the husk for the legs pulled through. Husks are rolled around the upper portion of the neck and the head is formed. Husks now are placed over the back of the neck and carried diagonally across the chest from either side. The same process is repeated from the front and the husks drawn diagonally across the back. This produces the body and shoulders. The legs are then braided or neatly rolled into shape, wound spirally with twine , and tied tightly at the ankles. The foot is then bent forward at right angles to the leg and wound into shape. The arms undergo a similar process, but no attempt is made to simulate hands. The head and body are now ready for covering. For the head the wide husks are held upward against the top of the head and a string passed around

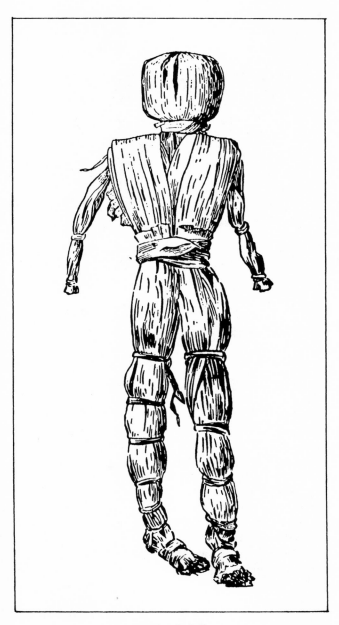

Corn husk doll.

Corn designs on mugs.

them. The husks are then bent downward and the string tightened. This leaves a little circular opening at the top of the head.

MARRIAGE: *See courtship customs.*

MASKS, were powerful tools to most Indian tribes and are still used by some. By wearing a mask, an Indian could call into himself a supernatural spirit: his voice and actions became those of the spirit, and other unmasked Indians could communicate directly with the spirit by talking, singing, or dancing with the maskwearer. Masks have been used by North American Indians since prehistoric times for purposes as various as curing the sick, bringing game to a hunter, and assuring rain for crops. They may not have always succeeded in changing the physical world, but in their heavy dependence on mask ceremonies, the Indians made use of an effective psychological princi-

Zuni mask and Bellacoola mask.

Mehinacu and Bacairi masks. a, b, Mehinacu; c, Bacairi.

Some mask ceremonies are oriented more towards psychological than physical survival. Hopi and Zuni mask dancers, for example, sometimes enact satirical skits that parody their own social customs, the Catholic church, American soldiers, and the neighboring Navajo and Paiute tribespeople. In this way, they can get rid of their frustrations without physical violence.

Masks have been found even in prehistoric times. Southeastern tribes made eerie, white, oval, and seemingly faceless masks from shell with pinhole eyes and mouth. Others had flat, white shell eyes staring out of dark-grained, wooden faces. In the southwest, prehistoric painting of katchina masks and dancers have been found on cave walls. Historically, maskwork became a highly developed art. Materials varied from whalebone or driftwood in the far north, to leather or basketry in the southwest, to wood or cornhusks in the east. Plains Sioux used buffalo and bear heads. Masks from all areas were often painted and decorated with strands or tufts of bark, fiber, hair, or feathers. Intricacy of design included hinged masks that could change expression, eyes and mouths that opened and closed, whole faces that parted in the middle and swung away on hinges to reveal another carved face beneath, and katchina masks that blended into an entire outfit.

In the latter part of the 20th century, mask ceremonies have lost their importance as Indian tribes become more acculturated to white traditions: the pulpit and the couch, cloudseeding and operating tables. It may be impossible for any contemporary Indian to believe fully in the supernatural power of masks, subjected as they are to the urbanized, technological white culture. The Hopi, however, still attend the katchina dances enthusiastically each year, and the Iroquois preserve some mask traditions. If these traditions die out, the North American Indian will have lost a little of his ability to commune with the

Mexican mask.

It is evident that among the primitive civilizations, the dance originated as part of the functions of the shamans. In Mexico, representations exist of masked dancers which date back to 1600 BC and which bear an extraordinary resemblance to the Yaqui dancers of Pascola. Thus many ritual dances have maintained masks as a basic part of their costume, a parallel phenomenon both in those indigenous origin and in those of European influence.

During carnivals or costume parties, masked guests lose their identity and all inhibitions disappear in the magic world in which they find themselves. Of the Mexican carnivals, the most interesting and traditional is that of Huejotzingo, Puebla. It represents the capture and death of the legendary bandit-hero Agustin Lorenzo, who tried to abduct the daughter of a wealthy land-holder. It is a confused mixed-up story with recollections of the defeat of the French and Zouave invaders in 1862.

Mexican masks take on many forms: that of the tiger, from the State of Guerrero, carved in wood and painted, with applied boar tusks and hairs; the owl, from Puebla, made of papier-mache and very popular among the children at carnival time. The two bearded masks are European in type and are frequently seen in such dances as the Santaigueros, Moors and Christians, etc., and others of mestizo origin. The upper left-hand mask is very old and possibly related to the indigenous dances of western Mexico. The devil is a pantomimical character in many dances, e.g., the dance of the Concheros, and its purpose is to scare the children or to make way for the dancers.

METALLURGY. Four metals, copper, gold, silver, and iron (meteoric), were shaped mainly by cold-hammering and grinding, but heat no doubt was employed to facilitate the hammering processes and in annealing. It is believed that copper was sometimes swedged, or in sheet form pressed into molds. But the remarkable repousse figures representing elaborately costumed and winged personages in sheet metal, found in mounds in Georgia and other more highly conventionalized figures from Florida mounds, give evidence of a degree of skill seemingly out of keeping with what is known of the general accomplishments of the northern tribes. Pousse work of like character can be accomplished by simple methods—the employment of pressure with a bone or an antler point, the sheet being placed upon a yielding surface, as of buckskin; but some of this work, especially the Georgia specimens, shows a degree of precision in execution apparently beyond the reach of the methods thus suggested.

Examples of overlaying or plating with thin sheets of copper, in the mounds of Florida and Alabama, and in the mounds of Ohio, are hardly less remarkable; but that these are well within the range of workmen of intelligence employing only stone tools has been amply proved. The thin sheets of copper are readily produced by hammering with stone tools with the aid of annealing processes and the skillful use of rivets. It can hardly be doubted that copper, gold, and silver were sometimes melted by aboriginal metalworkers and that bits of native copper were freed from the matrix of rock by this means. There seems to be no satisfactory record, however, of casting the forms of objects even in the rough, and there is no proof that ores of any kind were reduced by means of heat. It is a remarkable fact that no prehistoric crucible, mold, pattern, or metal-working tool of any kind whatsoever has been identified. No metal-worker's shop or furnace has been located, although caches of implements and of the blank forms of implements more or less worked have been found in various places, suggesting manufacture in numbers by specialists in the art. The use of artificial alloys was unknown, the specimens of gold-silver and gold-copper alloys obtained in Florida being of exotic origin. Stories of the hardening of copper by these or other American tribes, otherwise than by mere hammering, are all without a shadow of foundation. A few of the tribes, notably the Navajo and some of the Pueblos of Arizona and New Mexico, and the Haida. Tlingit, and others in the far Northwest, are skillful metal-workers, although the art as practiced by the Navajo and was adopted from the Spaniards. The Haida, Tlingit, and other tribes of British Columbia and Alaska have probably retained the aboriginal methods in part at least.

"The tools with which the Indian artisan works out the surprisingly well-finished metal ornaments and implements of this region are few in number. For bracelet making the silversmith has a hammer, several cold chisels, and an etching tool which is merely a sharpened steel point or edge. Improvised iron anvils replace the stone implements of this kind doubtlessly used in former days. Copper is beaten into the required shapes. Steel tools now used are very deftly tempered and shaped by the native artisan, who retains the primitive form of his implement or tool, and merely substitutes the steel for the former stone blade or head. The ingenuity which the Indians show in adapting iron and steel to their own uses is but one of the many evidences of their cleverness and intelligence."

SOUTH AMERICA

The use of metal by the pre-Columbian Indians of South America were almost entirely confined to the western edge of the continent, where the Andes provided an abundant supply of gold, silver, and copper, and smaller amounts of platinum and tin. The first objects of metal were probably made on the Peruvian Coast and in Colombia, and each of these two regions developed a distinct type of metallurgy. That of Colombia was based on gold, and the gold-copper alloy called tumbaga. That of Peru was based on gold, silver, copper, and bronze. The processes used in each region were much the same, but the emphasis was entirely different. The variations in local styles within these two metallurgical regions are sufficient to differentiate the metalwork of the various tribes although the technical processes are the same for all.

Sources of Metal. Native gold is found in great quantities in Colombia, Ecuador, Peru, and Bolivia. It is found to a lesser extent in the Antilles, Guiana, other parts of Central America, and in Chile and the Brazilian highlands. It is found almost entirely in the beds of mountain streams. Often, especially in Colombia, it contains as much as 15 to 20 percent of silver. Early Spanish writers state that the richest gold-producing region of all was Caravaya on the eastern slopes of the Andes near Lake Titicaca. Another rich region was the upper Cauca Valley of Colombia.

Native silver and silver ores are abundant only in Peru and Bolivia.

Native copper is found through the Andes in moderate amounts, and easily reduced copper ores are abundant in the Highlands of Peru, Bolivia, Chile, and Northwest Argentina.

Native platinum is found only in southern Colombia and Ecuador. Tin ore is found only in Bolivia and Northwest Argentina.

Various attempts have been made to determine the source of the metal used by the Indians through a comparison of the impurities found in the objects with the impurities found in the native metal and the ores from different mines, but the results have been disappointing. The characteristic impurities are too widely distributed, and there are too few ore analyses available. More work needs to be done on the ores from South America, and more analyses need to be made of objects of known origin.

Mining. Various accounts of the mining operations of the Indians have come down to us. They show that most of the gold was obtained by the washing of gravel from stream beds, and only a little by digging into the earth. Most of the silver seems to have been obtained in the form of native silver from pits and from the smelting of ores. Copper was obtained as native copper, and perhaps from the smelting of ores.

One of the best accounts of mining as carried out by the *Inca* is given by Pedro Sancho.

The [gold] mines [of La Paz] are in the gorge of a river, about half-way up the sides. They are made like caves, by whose mouths they enter to scrape the earth, and they scrape it with the horns of deer, and they carry it outside in certain hides sewn into the form of sacks or of wine-skins of sheep-hide . . . The mines go far into the earth, one ten brazas [60 feet], another twenty, and the greatest mine which is called Guarnacabo goes into the earth some forty brazas [240 feet]. They have no light, nor are they broader than is necessary for one person to enter crouching down, and until the man who is in the mine comes out, no other can go in . . . There are other mines beyond these, and there are still others scattered about through the land which are like wells a man's height in depth, so that the worker can just throw the earth from below on top of the ground. And when they dig them so deep that they cannot throw the earth out on top, they leave them and make new wells.

This is probably an accurate description of an early Peruvian mine. In the American Museum of Natural

History at New York are the bodies of two copper miners with their stone hammers full of blue sand (atacamite), who were caught in the collapse of a mine at Chuquicamata, Chile. The mine is similar to that described by Pedro Sancho. The mines of Colombia and Central America were probably like those of Peru.

Smelting. There is still some doubt whether the Indians of Peru knew how to smelt the ores of silver and copper. Most writers on the *Inca* civilization have assume that they could, but the evidence is not conclusive.

Early Spanish writers describe the production of silver plate and bars by the Indians from the native metal and its ores. In every case the account seems to refer to the smelting of silver at Potosi and Proco in southern Bolivia. Potosi was the richest silver region in all America. It was discovered inn 1545, 12 years after the Conquest. Porco, known to the Indians, was nearby.

Cieza de Leon visited Porco and Potosi in 1549. He wrote:

In Porco, and in other parts of the kingdom where they extract metal, they make great plates of silver, and the metal is purified from the dross by fire, in which operation large bellows are used.

But at Potosi the silver could not be melted with the aid of bellows in the usual way. The Indians—

. . . . therefore, made certain moulds of clay, in the shape of a flower-pot in Spain, with many air holes in all parts. Charcoal was put into these moulds, with the metal on the top, and they were then placed on the part of the hill where the wind blew the strongest, and thus the metal was extracted, which was then purified and refined with a small bellows. In this manner all the metal that has been taken from the hill is extracted. The Indians go to the heights with the ores to extract the silver, and they call the moulds *Guayras*. In the night there are so many of them on all parts of the hill, that it looks like an illumination.

This is the earliest account of the furnaces called huayras.

I believe that the evidence now available leads to the conclusion that the Indians of Peru in their efforts to melt native silver in their furnaces and free it from earthly impurities inadvertenly reduced certain silver ores to metallic silver because of the hot charcoal inside of the furnace. This was a simple form of smelting. It is doubtful if they knew what they had done and it is probable that they regarded it as merely one way of fusing the naturally occurring metal.

It was found that the infusible silver ores when mixed with soroche (galena, or lead sulfide) could be easily fused and reduced to metallic silver. The lead was then removed as dross by repeated fusions of the silver. This fusion of the silver ore with soroche is true smelting, but there is no reason to think the process was known to the Indians.

None of the early writers make any mention of how copper was obtained. Garcilaso de la Vega, quoting Blas Valera, writes:

Copper, which they called anta, served them in place of iron for making warlike arms, knives, carpenter's tools, pins for fastening women's cloaks, looking glasses, spades for digging ground, and hammers for the plate workers. For these reasons they value copper very highly, for it was more useful to them than gold and silver, and the demand was greater than for any other metal.

But there is no hint how it was obtained. In none of the various descriptions of the huayras is there any indication that they were also used for the smelting of copper. Furnaces, crucibles, etc., have been found at various sites, notably in the *Diaguita* region of western Argentina. It is thought these were used for the smelting of ores, but they may have been used for the fusion of the native metal.

At Cobres in *Diaguita* country, a prehistoric copper mine, a maray or place for crushing the ore, foundations of huayras or furnaces, and broken crucibles. The ore from the mine consisted of a copper silicate (chrysocolla), which is easy to reduce with hot charcoal. From one of the huayras, and a bit of metallic copper from a crucible, come the following results:

These results led to the conclusion that the metal and slag were produced by the smelting of the ore from the adjacent mine. The natives of the *Diaguita* region smelted copper carbonate (malachite, azurite) and the oxyuchloride (atacomite).

The weight of evidence is thus in favor of the view that the smelting of copper was known in the Highlands of Peru, Bolivia, and the *Atacameno-Diaguita* region. It has not been proved, however, and more work needs to be done on this problem. There is no evidence as yet that the smelting of silver or copper was practiced in Ecuador, Colombia, or Central America.

The smelting of tin by the Indians is even more uncertain. None of the early writers throw any light on the question. There is no doubt that the *Inca* knew how to make bronze, and how to regulate the tin content in a rough way. They may have smelted tin stone (cassiterite), which is common in Bolivia, and added tin to the copper; or they may have mixed the tin stone with the copper ore and smelted them together.

It has been stated that the Peruvians knew how to refine gold and silver, but there is no evidence that they could do more than free silver from copper and lead by the continued heating of the molten metal. It is unlikely that they could separate gold and silver once they were melted together, or make gold of good quality from a silver-rich gold.

Working of Metals. Before considering the details of the technical processes used in the manufacture of the metal objects that have come down to our day, there is some evidence from the early writers on how metals were worked in Peru.

The metal workers were located in the principal cities of the provinces, and worked under the direction of the chiefs.

In all these capitals the kings had temples of the Sun, and houses with great store of plate, with people whose only duty it was to work at making rich pieces of gold and great bars of silver.

The Indian chiefs when visiting the *Inca* Emperor, in addition to giving him gold and silver, would bring to him—

the men who excelled in any art, such as silversmithing . . . . For the Incas had men skilled in all these arts, and the Curacas presented such men, as worthy to serve their King. The common people did not require the aid of such artizans.

And from Blas Valera,

There were certain arts and employments which had their masters, such as workers in gold, silver, and copper . . . . Their children learned the same trade as their fathers.

Benzoni gives a well-known account of the melting and working of gold as practices by the *Inca* goldsmiths at Quito.

This province of Quito has a temperate climate, wherefore the kings of Cuzco lived ther the greater part of their time, and had in many parts houses of goldsmiths, who, though not using any tools of iron, still manufactured wonderful things. They worked in the following manner:

In the first place, when they wished to melt the metal, they put it into either a long or round grisolo, make of a piece of cloth daubed over with a mixture of earth and powdered charcoal; when dry, it is put into the fire filled with metal; then several men, more or less, each with a reed, blow till the metal is fused. It is now taken out, and the goldsmiths, seated on the ground, provided with some black stones shaped on purpose and helping each other, make, or more correctly speaking, used to make during their prosperity, whatever they were commissioned to do; that is, hollow statues, vases, sheep, ornaments, and, in short, any animals they saw.

Cieza de Leon, in 1553, wrote:

When they work they make a small furnace of clay where they put the charcoal, and they then blow the fire with small canes, instead of bellows. Besides their silver utensils, they make chains, stamped ornaments, and other things of gold. Even boys, who to look at them one would think were hardly old enough to talk, know how to make these things.

Garcilaso de la Vega, although trying to show the Indians of Peru in the best possible light, has a curious chapter in which he considers some of their shortcomings.

. . . . it will be well to show how unskillful their mechanics were in their crafts . . . To begin with the workers in metals: although they were so numerous, and so constantly exercising their calling, they knew not how to make an anvil, either of iron or of anything else, and they could not extract iron, though there were mines of that metal in their land . . . . They used certain very hard stones, of a color between green and yellow, instead of anvils. They flattened and smoothed one against the other, and held them in great estimation because they were very rare. Nor could they make hammers with wooden handles. But they worked with certain instruments made of copper and brass mixed together. These tools were of the shape of dice with the corners rounded off. Some are large, so that the hand can just clap them, others middling size, other small, and others lengthened out to hammer on a concave. They hold these hammers in their hands to strike with as if they were pebbles. They had no files or graving tools, nor had they invented the art of making bellows for blast furnaces. They blasted by means of tubes of copper, the length of half-a-cubit, more or less, according as the furnace was large or small. The tubes were closed at one ends, leaving one small hole through which the air could rush with more force. As many as 8, 10, or 12 of these were put together, according to the requirements of the furnace; and they went round the fire blowing with the tubes. They still use the same method not being willing to change their customs. They had no tongs for drawing the metal out of the fire, but did this with poles of wood or copper, and threw the heated metal on small heaps of damp earth which they had ready to cool it. They drew it from one heap to another, until it was cool enough to hold in their hands. Notwithstanding these inconvenient contrivances, they executed marvellous works, chiefly in hollowing things out . . . . They also found out, in spite of their simplicity, that the smoke of certain metals was injurious to the health, and they consequently made their foundaries in the open air, in their yards and courts, and never under a roof.

The only description of the working of metal from Colombia is given by Raleigh, who obtained his information from an old Indian.

I asked [Topiawari] after the manner how the Epuremei wrought those plates of gold, and howe they coulde melte it out of the stone; he told me that most of the gold which they made into plates and images was not secured from the stone, but that on the lake of Manoa, and in a multitude of other rivers they gathered it in graines of perfect golde and in peeces as bigg as small stones, and that they put to it a part of copper, otherwise they could not worke it, and that they used a great earthen potte with holes round about it, and when they had mingled the gold and copper together, they fastened canes to the holes, and so with the breath of men they increased the fire till the mettell ran, and then they cast it into moulds of clay and stones, and so make those plates and Images.

The quotations from Benzoni, Cieza de Leon, and Garcilaso de la Vega give a good idea of how the metals were melted, hammered into sheets, and worked into cups, etc., by the *Inca* metal workers just before the Conquest. Unfortunately, some of the most interesting processes used by the metalworkers are not mentioned at all—such as casting, soldering, and gilding. Knowledge of these can only be obtained from an examination of the actual cups, ring, knives, figurines, etc., made by the metalworkers of Colombia and Peru.

Hammering, Embossing, and Engraving. The first processes used by primitive peoples in working of metals are hammering and embossing. The earliest metal objects from South America are of gold hammered into very thin sheets. Some of the gold masks from Pracus (ca. A.D. 500) are 0.04 to 0.06 mm. thick. They were embossed and cut to the desired shape. The embossing was probably done with a rock of suitable shape while the gold sheet was lying on a piece of wood.

At a somewhat later date (AD 1000) gold effigy cups were made at Ica by shaping the sheet of gold over a wooden form carved to represent a head. This was also done in the Moche-Lambayeque region, where necklaces of identical small gold pendants are quite common. In the Sinu region of Colombia numerous stone molds have been found which were similarly used for shaping gold sheets into pendants. This was probably common practice wherever gold was used.

Large cups were frequently made in two pieces. The upper portion was allowed to overlap the lower portion several centimeters and the two portions were then hammered together. The joint is often nearly invisible. Occasionally, the upper portion was joined on the side by a staggered joint.

Gold is very soft (Brinell hardness of 30). It is the easiest of metals to work as it remains soft when hammered and thus does not need to be annealed. The whole operation can be carried out without the use of a furnace or blowpipe. Silver is even softer than gold (24) and can be hammered into very thin foil, but it becomes hard and brittle on cold working (90) and should be annealed. For this reason pendants, masks, and cups of silver are usually thicker than those made of gold. Copper is the most difficult of the three metals to work into sheets. It is a little harder than gold (53). When cold worked it becomes very hard (135) and objects may crack unless annealed. On annealing it becomes soft (35). Masks and pendants of sheet copper are fairly common especially in the Chimu region.

Of many copper and bronze axes from Peru, Ecuador, and Mexico, nearly all of them had been hardened by cold hammering. Cold-worked copper is harder than unworked cast bronze of low tin content.

This is probably the basis of the legends concerning the "lost art" of hardening copper supposedly possessed by the *Inca*.

In Colombia similar use was made of the hardening of a gold-copper alloy (tumbaga) under hammering. A gold-copper alloy containing 20 percent of copper becomes much harder than cold-worked copper and somewhat less hard than cold-worked bronze (8 percent of tin) as is shown in table 1.

SOUTH AMERICA

Metallurgy. Furnaces, crucibles, etc., have been found at various sites, notably in the *Diaguita* region of western Argentina. It is though these were used for the smelting or ores, but they may have been used for the fusion of the native metal.

Cobres in *Diaguita* country, a prehistoric copper mine, a maray or place for crushing the ore, foundations of huayras or furnaces, and broken crucibles have been found. The ore from the mine consisted of a copper silicate (chrysocolla), which is easy to reduce with hot charcoal from one of the huayras, and a bit of metallic copper from a crucible, come the following results:

These results led to the conclusion that the metal and slag were produced by the smelting of the ore from the adjacent mine. The natives of the *Diaguita* region smelted copper carbonate (malachite, azurite) and the oxychloride (atacomite).

The weight of evidence is thus in favor the the view that the smelting of copper was known in the Highlands of Peru, Bolivia, and the *Atacmeno-Diaguita* region. It has not been proved, however, and more work needs to be done on this problem. There is no evidence as yet that the smelting of silver or copper was practiced in Ecuador, Colombia, or Central America.

The smelting of tin by the Indians is even more uncertain. None of the early writers throw any light on the question. There is no doubt that the *Inca* knew how to make bronze, and how to regulate the tin content in a rough way. They may have smelted tin stone (cassiterite), which is common in Bolivia, and added tin to the copper; or they may have mixed the tin stone with the copper ore and smelted them together.

It has been stated that the Peruvians knew how to refine gold and silver, but there is no evidence that they could do more than free silver from copper and lead by the continued heating of the molten metal. It is unlikely that they could separate gold and silver once they were melted together, or make gold of good quality from a silver-rich gold.

Engraving. Engraving of metal was occasionally used in Peru, but was much less common then embossing. Some of the early sheet gold cut-outs from the Titicaca region (Early Tiaguanco?) have details added by means of incised lines, but they are poorly done. They are the earliest examples of engraving (about A.D. 700). The laters cups from Cuzco and the Chimu region are carefully engraved in complex designs.

Garcilaso de la Vega states that engraving tools were not known. The lines on some objects are so carefully done, however, that it seems probable that some instrument was used, perhaps a hardened bronze needle.

Sheathing. In the Mochica Period sheet gold was used to cover wooden poles, etc. It was fastened to the wood by tiny gold, silver, or copper tacks. In the

Nazca region metal sheathing has so far been found only in the Late Period, when it was extensively used. It is not known whether the Coast cultures used sheets of metal to cover stone or adobe. In *Inca* times fairly heavy gold sheets were used to cover parts of the walls of the temples and certain of the palaces.

It is not known whether sheathing was used at an early period in Colombia and Central America. It is found frequently in the later periods, not only with wood, but with objects of stone and other materials. The gold and silver foil was probably attached by some adhesive, such as "Pasto varnish" or gum.

Casting. The origin of the casting of metal in South America is not known. It is one of the problems which cannot be solved without more knowledge of the archeology of Colombia and Ecuador and the Peruvian Highlands. Before casting was known, small amounts of gold beads at Esmeraldas on the Ecuadorean coast were probably made in this way. Larger pieces of metal were hammered into shape. Then the furnace was discovered and casting became possible.

The earliest examples of true casting now known are from mochica sites (earlier than A.D. 900). Two copper chisels excavated from the Huaca de la Luna at Moche have elaborate cast handles and seem as complex as anything from a later period. Casting may have been known at the very end of the Early Nazca Period (Navca B) but does not seem to have been known at Chavin or Paracas. However, by the Middle Periods (A.D. 900-1100) knowledge of casting had spread to all parts of the Peruvian Coast and Highlands. Cast objects, some quite simple, are frequently found in Colombia, Ecuador, Bolivia. and the *Diaguita* region of Argentina. Their relation to Peruva in casting is not known.

The first metals to be cast were gold, silver, and copper, then the alloys of gold and copper and copper and copper and silver were used, and finally, bronze. Platinum was used in Ecuador for hammered ornaments but was never cast, as it has such a high melting point. Gold and copper have fairly high melting points, and the Indians must have had difficulty in fusing them without the aid of a blowpipe or a furnace with a forced draught like a huayras. The alloys of the metals have melting points that range from that of the pure metal to that of the eutectic. The eutectic has the lowest melting point of any alloy made from a given two metals. One reason for the use of alloys was their easier fusion and greater liquidity. The alloys also had special properties which made their use advantageous in certain circumstances. In table 2 are given the melting points of the pure metals and their eutectics, and the differences between their melting points and that of gold.

The alloy of gold and silver (electrum) consists of an unbroken series of solid solutions. As silver is added to gold the melting point of the alloy gradually decreases from 1,063° to 960°. The alloy is a little harder than gold. With 40 to 50 percent of silver is of an unattractive gray color. This alloy was sometimes used in Peru but infrequently. Since the alloy is no better than gold or silver in its physical properties, and is inferior to either in appearance, its occurrence is probably due to the careless melting together of gold and silver.

Tumbaga (gold-copper alloy) was extensively used in Colombia and Central America and to a slight extent in Ecuador and Peru. It is impossible to say at present when or where it is discovered. It seems to have originated in Colombia or Venezuela sometime before AD 1000 and spread from there to Central America, and to Ecuador and northern Peru. Its discovery is as important as that of bronze.

Gold and copper form two compounds, Cu-Au with 75 percent of gold and Cu_3Au with 51 percent of gold. These exist only below 420° C. They are hard and brittle. If a Au(82)-Cu(18) alloy (the eutectic) is allowed to cool slowly from 800° C. the compounds have a chance to form, and the Brinell hardness may be as great as 190. If cooled rapidly they do not have a chance to crystallize out and the hardness is 122. With a Au(50)-Cu(50) alloy the compounds do not form at all, and the hardness of rapidly cooled and slowly cooled alloy are 80 and 40. This means that gold alloys containing 20 percent of copper become hard when annealed below 420°C., while alloys with 50 percent or more of copper remain fairly soft.

If copper-gold alloys are annealed for a long time the copper on the surface oxidizes and the Cu_2O or "fire" that is formed diffuses along the crystal edges and makes the metal brittle. If the "fire" is removed from the surface by an acid pickle the color changes from red to yellow (the process of gliding by mise en couleur).

If the gold in a gold-copper alloy is replaced by silver the hardness is increased until with Au(52)-Ag(22)-Cu(26) the hardness of the rapidly cooled metal is 150. On cold working this is increased to 200. This is as hard as an annealed low-tin bronze. The melting point of this ternary alloy is 890°C.

The Colombians thus had at their disposal an alloy which had a lower melting point than bronze, which could be made almost as hard, and which unlike bronze could be gilded.

The silver-copper alloy was sometimes used in Peru, notably on the South Coast at chincha. Silver and copper dissolve in each other only to a slight degree and the molten mixture contains two phases, *a* and *B*. At 779°C. (the eutectic temperature), the silver-rich (*a*) phase contains 9 percent of copper, the copper-rich (*B*) phase contains 8 percent of silver. At room temperature they are practically insoluble in each other. The *a* and *B* phases are soft; the eutectic is hard. Hence rapid cooling results in a soft metal; slow cooling or annealing below 779°C. results is a harder metal. If the alloy contains from 6 to 72 percent Ag it consists of copper-rich crystals surrounded by eutectic. If it contains 72 to 95 percent Ag it consists of silver-rich crystals surrounded by eutectic. The presence of a silvery and a coppery phase gives the metal a characteristic mottled or streaked appearance.

A silver-rich alloy containing 7.5 percent of copper (sterling silver) has a Brinell hardness of about 60. On cold working this increases to 183, almost as hard as bronze.

If a silver-copper alloy is annealed too long or heated to a high temperature the copper oxidizes to Cu_2O and this oxide, diffusing along the grain boundaries, makes the metal brittle. If such an oxide-coating alloy is placed in an acid pickle, the oxide dissolves leaving a coating of pure silver. This method of silvering, the equivalent of the mise en couleur method of gilding was apparently not known.

Bronze (an alloy of copper and tin) was, next to tumbaga, the most important alloy used for casting. It was probably discovered in Bolivia about AD 1000 and spread from there to the Peruvian Coast and to Argentina. Later it was introduced by the *Inca* into Ecuador. Copper and tin form a very complex system with many phases. Alpha, or low-tin, bronze contains less than 16 percent tin and is soft and malleable. Its melting point varies from 1,083.°C. to about 950°C. On cooling below 525°C. it changes in part to delta bronze (32 percent Sn), which is brittle and very hard. A mixture of alpha and delta bronze is also obtained on cooling bronzes with 16 to 32 percent of tin (m. pts. 950-750°C.)

All South American bronzes are of the alpha type, and contain less than 12 percent of tin. When such bronzes are rapidly chilled, or annealed above 525°C. they remain malleable; when slowly cooled, or annealed below 525°C. they are partly converted to the delta form and become brittle. The malleable bronze can be worked both cold and hot. The brittle bronze can be worked only if frequently annealed at a low red heat. The hardness of low-tin bronze increases with the tin content. Well-annealed copper has a Brinell hardness of 40, bronze containing 5 percent tin has a hardness of about 55, hammering increases the hardness of a bronze containing 5 percent of tin to about 200, of a 10-percent bronze to about 275. Low-tin bronzes expand on solidification. The maximum expansion (0.12 percent) takes place with 10 percent tin. Such a bronze melts at 1,005°C. or 80° lower than pure copper. Bronze is more liquid than copper at a given temperature and thus easier to cast.

Some have considered in detail the question of bronze in South America, and the relation between the tin content and the type of object. It is found that in Peru, Bolivia, and Argentina the greatest amount of tin found in ornaments and other fairly complex castings. Objects that should be hard are generally either of copper or contain only a small percentage of tin, and the hardening was brought about by cold hammering. In Ecuador, on the contrary, the greatest percentage of tin is found in objects like axes, knives, needles, and fish hooks that should be hard. They were further hardened by cold hammering.

Native copper containing a high percentage of arsenic is sometimes found in Peru. It is much harder than ordinary copper and in many ways resembles bronze. Objects of this arsenical copper are found in the Chimu region.

Little has come down to us about the method of casting metal, there exists a fairly clear description of casting by the cire-perdue, or lost-wax, method. This method was without doubt the one used both in Columbia and in Peru. In no other way can intricate castings be easily made. A model of the object was built of wax. This was covered with layer on layer of clay until all the interstices were filled, then clay was packed around the outside. A roll of wax extended from the object to the bottom of a clay cup. After the clay was thoroughly dry the object was inverted and warmed until the wax melted and ran out, leaving a hollow of the same shape as the object, connected to the cup by a small channel. The mold was then placed with the cup upward and heated to a high temperature in a furnace. Molten metal was poured into the cup. It ran down the channel and filled the mold. The mold and metal were then allow to cool. The clay was broken away from the metal, the plug was cut off, and the object was polished or gilded. Hollow objects were made by encasing a clay core in the wax.

Many hollow figurines and bells have been found with a core of burned clay, though no fragments of clay molds have yet been found. In the *Diaguita* region of Argentina simple stone molds have been found for the casting of axheads, etc., and in the *Chibcha* region of Colombia stone molds for the casting of figurines are also known. In both cases the cast objects involved simple forms and had no filagree or wirework details.

The results of casting by the cire-perdue process are sometimes very complicated and have led some observers to assume that details must have been added by soldering or welding. This is particularly true of some of the *Chibcha* figurines, which often appear to consist of a flat plate to which wires have been fastened. Sections through such figurines have been made and in every case the crystal structure of the metal has extended right across the juncture, proving that they were cast in one piece and involved no soldering or welding. This has also been found to be true of some of the jewels from Esmeraldas made from minute gold beads, and of a cast-copper necklace of Mexican origin.

Annealing. When a metal object is heated for some time to 200 to 400° C., well below its melting point, a change frequently takes place in its crystal structure which alters its properties. This is known as annealing or tempering. This process was probably discovered at a very early period, perhaps even before casting, and not long after metals were first hammered into thin sheets. Knowledge of annealing was widely distributed. For example, bronze *Inca* axheads, knives, pins, etc., from Machu Picchu were found to have been annealed, some several times. Annealing was most common where the object was to be hammered, for example, the flat head of a pin or the blade of a knife. Apparently, the part to be annealed was placed in a hot fire until dull red, then removed, and hammered. It does not seem to have been too carefully carried out. Likewise tumbaga figurines from Veraguas (Panama) were found to have been frequently hammered and then annealed.

Annealing was usually resorted to when hammering was found to have made a metal hard and brittle, as with copper and silver. Annealing for half an hour at 400° softens copper and silver and makes them ductile again. It has the opposite effect on tumbaga and bronze. Annealing hardens them. This softening in one case and hardening in another must have baffled the Indian metallurgists if they observed it.

Welding. Welding is the junction of two pieces of hot metal by hammering along, no molten metal being present. To make a good weld the surfaces must be clean and in close contact and heated to a high temperature. Fusion welding is the melting together of the edges of two pieces of metal or their joining by the heating of the adjacent edges and the running of some molten metal of the same kind into the intermediate space. Welding is frequently said to have been practiced in Peru and Colombia, but no certain example of welding has so far been discovered. It must have been hard to do with the primitive equipment used by the Indian metallurgists and it must have been rarely done, if at all.

Soldering. Soldered objects have been found from Guatemala to Bolivia. None are known from Mexico or Argentina. The earliest known examples of soldering are from Mochica and Early Nazca sites. One object from Moche is a gold ear spool with small beads soldered around the rim. The beads are evenly spaced and the junction shows only a trace of solder. It is as fine an example of soldering as anything found in later periods. By the Middle Periods knowledge of soldering has spread up and down the Coast and perhaps to the Highlands. Soldering was also practiced in Ecuador,

Colombia, and Central America but it is not known at what period it began to be used. As with other technical processes, much more information must be obtained about the archeology of Colombia and Ecuador before the relation between soldering in these regions and in Peru can be worked out.

It is easier to say what method of soldering was not used in Peru than to tell how it was done. It was not done with a blowpipe and a low melting solder. Analysis of a fragment of solder from a beaded Chimu ear spool shows its composition to be nearly the same as that of the beads. It was not done by use of mercury or an amalgam. There is not the slightest evidence that anywhere in North or South America mercury was used for either soldering or gilding.

MOCCASIN. The Indians wore soft-soled buckskin moccasins of two types. The moccasin of the Cayuga and the Seneca was made of one piece of skin with a seam at the heel and over the top of the foot, but the bottom was seamless. At the back a quarter of an inch was lapped over from each side giving added strength to the seam. The seam up the front of the moccasin was gathered with notches cut out between the gathers so that the two sides could be brought closely together. After the seam had been made the gathers were beaten or pounded so that they would lie flat. The gathered seam was often covered with a narrow strip of quill or bead work. In some cases fine bead work was done directly on the moccasin at the sides of the seam. The thread used in sewing was of sinew. The needle was made of a small bone taken from near the ankle joint of the dener and was known as the "moccasin needle."

The Mohawk in the eastern part of New York made a moccasin of different type, similar to the moccasin of the Algonquin, in which the toe of the moccasin was gathered into a U-shaped vamp that was sometimes decorated. In some cases a separate piece of the same shape as the vamp was elaborately embroidered with quills or beads and tacked over it. These decorative

Zuni clay moccasins.

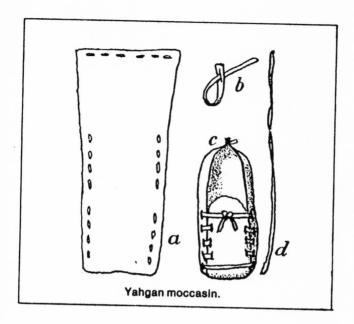

Yahgan moccasin.

Velvet and broadcloth cuffs were popular on the later moccasins. Both black and brown velvet and red and black flannel were used for cuffs. The edges of the velvet cuffs were bound with cotton cloth or cotton braid or with a silk ribbon. An old pair of Tuscarora moccasins shows black velvet cuffs bound in red woolen braid.

The moose hair embroidery on moccasins was worked out in delicate scroll and floral patterns. Bead embroidery patterns ranged from very fine triangles, scrolls and double curve designs on the Seneca and Cayuga moccasins to heavy floral designs on the Tuscarora and Mohawk moccasins. Opaque, translucent, and transparent beads in many different sizes were used in moccasin decoration at different periods.

At one time the Iroquois made moccasins of braided or twined corn husks or basswood fiber.

MUSIC. What was the music like among the aboriginal peoples of the American Continents, the

music have evolved if not interrupted by the European invasion and what is the state of this music today?

The answers to these and many implied questions have puzzled scholars and musicians for several centuries, or at least since the moment that the first serious listener among the explorers and ravagers of Colonial America became aware that what he was hearing from the native people was to him recognizable as music. This moment of recognition was in itself a milestone in the history of libertarian thought for a 16th century European, especially since his colonistpioneer-conquistador-explorer-settler counterparts were supremely non-cultured and non-musically oriented soldiers of fortune having concepts of music related primarily to the Byzantine and Early Renaissance varieties heard in the far-away courts and monasteries of "high civilization", in the Old World. From all historical accounts of Conquest days the prevalent thinking seemed to be: "How can savages and barbarians be cultured to the point of having music when they are infidels and are bloodthirsty animals incapable of civilization" . . . which finally culminated in the famous quote of General Phil Sheridan, who said, "The only good Indian is a dead Indian!" With such attitudes of genocide and cultural superiority, it is a great wonder indeed that any Indian music survived, not to mention the Indians themselves!

However, it is almost impossible to kill an idea being made of intangibles which arise from the indomitable human spirit itself . . . and such is the case with aboriginal music, the voice of the soul of autochthonous man arising from the earth's clay and from every minuscule grain and fibre of existence in a land for 1,000,000 years (a debatable time span for the Indian occupation of our Western Hemisphere since most archaeologists now say 100,000 years, but this is extended further back with each new study). Music being the most intagible of ideas, therefore, has survived and has been the key to survival for many Indians. This mother of all the arts is also a clue to better understanding of the Indian which the white man (also no-such-being, but rather a state of mind) has yet to utilize with skill and perception, for Indian music has remained mysterious, unintelligible, exotic and alien to

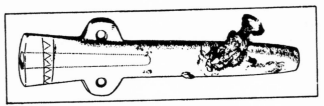

Silbato, or whistle of pottery.

the non-Indian and has remained wonderfully un-
influenced, in many cases, from outside forces.

Indian music has been the most dissected, analyzed
and annotated of aboriginal musics, yet it has
remained the least understood and the most vilified of
musics. Perhaps because it is so close to life itself and
like life it is so immediate and evanescent in terms of
total comprehension. The only really cogent method of
knowing Indian music is to know Indian life by
association as well as by observation. For the general
reader, this may be a remote possibility. Therefore, this
treatise will predicate answers to the aforementioned
questions upon the strength of scholarly research plus
logical positivism resulting from the author's own
associations and tribal affiliations as a singer of tribal
songs, composer and music ethnoeducator-
musicologist.

Much has been written based upon conjecture as the
basis for inferences concerning Indian music while
much knowledge has been gained via archaeological
research and the use of radio-carbon dating techniques
to substantiate claims of pre-Cortesian musical relics,
but very little is known of actual music textures and
tessituras in very eary Indian music, not to mention the
same situation in any pre-literate society in other parts
of the world. Musicologists still argue widely over the
exact nature of early Hellenic music and other European pre-notational forms of musical expression.
Exact answers to certain questions may never be
known, music being the dynamic art form that it is and
having adaptability plus constant state of flux in every
culture which it serves. Also, in terms of 20th century
scientific implacability it is a truism that the powers of
oral transmission, used by all pre-literate cultures, are

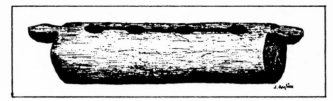

Jivaro drum.

greatly underestimated and vilified in learned circles as a means of knowledge diffusion. Yet, in the field of humanities and the arts, oral transmission as a means of empirical knowledge has been responsible for centuries of retention and evolution. In short, we cannot rely solely upon written accounts where none exist but must rely upon this most ancient and reliable of techniques for the furtherance of our understandings.

It is not enough to acknowledge that American Indian music is different from other music and the Indian, somehow, 'marches to a different drum', as a way of paying obeisance to the unique cultures of our Native American peoples. What is needed in America, as it has always been needed, is an awakening and reorienting of our total spiritual and cultural persepective to embrace, understand and learn from the aboriginal American what it is that motivated his musical and artistic impulses. To do so may very well be the one significant step toward our survival as rational and stable beings who need to be in tune with a rational and stable environment where dynamic art forms can flourish and where mankind can truly hope to be uplifted in spirit and in everyday existence. The arts of any people in the history of mankind have often been the only element to survive . . . and it is a curious fact that the surviving art forms are mainly those with a richly heterogeneous influence wherein intrinsic differences are allowed freedom of expression. America has an historically artistic imperative to glorify and foster American Indian music and art in any viable traditional and/or contemporary terms . . . for upon this basis we will ultimately be judged by posterity.

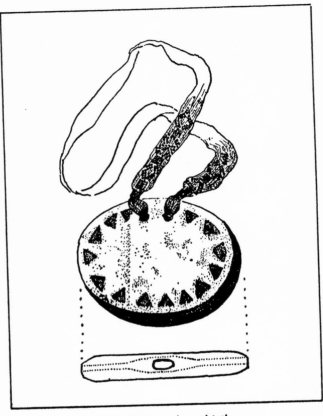

Pilaga flat wooden whistle.

PRE-COLUMBIAN
TRADITIONAL AMERICAN INDIAN MUSIC

A. In North America
B. In Meso America
C. In South America

A. Pre-Columbian life and culture, consequently the musical forms of all aboriginal Americans, the Native Americans, was invariably tempered by the respective environmental phenomena which the people encountered whether in relatively sedentary states as one-place villages dwellers or in migratory states as nomads. In each climate zone represented in continental North America from the near-tropical zone of the Florida Everglades to the arid desert lands of the Great Basin to the frigid reaches of the Artic Circle, there were native singers, dancers and music makers as well as avid listeners.

Scholars have categorized the people by various means: 1. Division into geographical areas (Eastern Woodland, Southeast Woodland, Great Plains, North and South, Southwest, Great Basin and Plateau, Pacific Coast of California, Pacific Northwest, Alaskan Tundra and Artcic); 2. Division into linguistic "stock", "family", "phylum" of "macro-group" (Algonquian, Iroquoian, Siouan, Caddoan, Shoshonean, Piman, Yuman, Salishan, Eskimauan, to mention only the major groups while there are smaller groups having no relation to these); and 3. Division into body structure types and appearances (short frame or tall, facial features, personal adornment, hair styles). Such divisions are at best arbitrary in the face of such variety, and in terms of nomenclature it can be safely stated that there was not one type of Indian, therefore it follows that there was not one form or type of Indian music ... but, there were many musics!

These musics of pre-Columbian American natives were primarily vocal and monodic. Songs or chants were an outgrowth of languages, and that distinctive feature of all Indian songs, the vocable (non-meaningful vocalization) came into being as a form of rhythmic embellishment before languages and verbal utterances reached the highpoint of palatalization. To place these developments in an exact time period would be sheer folly since no one can establish actual initiatory dates of aboriginal inhabitation and oral expression. Vocables are quite significant and seemingly indispensable in most Indian songs as a method of propelling the rhythmic thrust of chant having percussion accompaniment which in itself was another important achievement, the date of which is lost in the dawn of pre-history. Actual throat and oral cavity formation in the production of most vocables found in Indian songs today are not palatally produced and can best be described as functioning like the European Melisma with added breath pulsations originating in

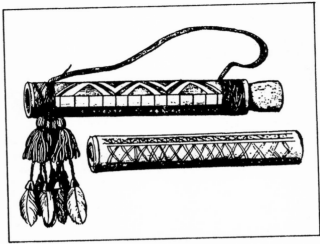

Canella end-blown trumpet.

organic fashion from various sources of the breathing apparatus, diaphragm to palate. Also, like the Old World counterpart the vocable probably developed slowly from simple grunts in animal-hunting gesture-chant intended to imitate animal sounds and thereby insure success in the hunt, to the extended vocable used in more vocally impassioned war dance songs.

Intrinsic meaning, sense and value in every song was also of paramount importance in the development of aboriginal musics. This brings us to another very vital characteristic of all pre-Columbian Indian musics, the functionalism of all musical expression whereby the song served a specific purpose, whether appeasing the alien and/or friendly spirits to aid in survival: good harvest, good hunting, good fishing, or purposes that related to work, play, courtship, healing, lullabies, etc. But even on the very earliest level, Indian melodies were never anarchic or arbitrary but followed certain, almost unbreakable rules of composition. If a particular song seemed to work magic in its purpose and function, then that song was not likely to be forgotten ... hence, the developing powers of oral transmission.

Where are we in terms of chronology? Suffice it to

to Meso America. However, it goes without saying that decidedly unique and distinctive musical expression emanated in organic fashion here just as it did elsewhere and in like manner it will probably never be known to what extent the forces of diffusion have accounted for certain isolated characteristics from one region to the other.

For reference to music beginnings we must again turn to native mythology. The *POPUL VUH* or Sacred Book of the ancient Quiche Maya is probably the most distinguished example of native American literature which has survived, through translation by colonial priests, the passing centuries on this hemisphere. The Quiche Indians were a branch of the Maya and were the most powerful nation of the Guatemala highlands in pre-Conquest times. The original manuscript has never been lost, but from a 16th century version in the third book we find a reference to the origin of music. After the world was created and was peopled with many races, the Maker or Great Creator was going to make the sun, and when the sun came up . . . *"When the sun arose, when it dawned on the face of the earth and the whole world was lighted, here the people began their song, which they called 'camucu' which means 'we see' or 'our dove', mucuy in Maya. They (the first people) sang it, but only the pain their hearts and their innermost selves they expressed in their song."* A striking parallel to the Pima-Papago version of North America!

In the northwestern sector of Mexico, along the Baranque del Cobre, the Tarahumara Indians have remained generally isolated from outside influences and, believably, even more so in colonial times. Hence, many researchers and scholars have viewed Tarahumara music as a basis for inferences on the state of pre-Conquest expression. The Tarahumara world for singing and dancing, "novaloa", meaning literally "to work," gives us the hint that music was taken in a very serious and ceremonious context rather than a form of amusement, thus dance and music was functional in appealing to the deities for rain and for other favors. Furthermore, the Tarahumara assert that they learned their dance and music from the animals who also appealed for rain in their dry, arid environment. ·

In the words of a Tarahumara Indian, "We pray by dancing and the gourd (rattle)."

Properly speaking, any mention of the Lumholtz expedition of A.D. 1902 belongs chronologically in a discussion of post Conquest times, but since early colonial chroniclers, mainly clergymen, largely neglected the highland Indians and their music, I concur with other scholars that a perusal and summary of highlights witnessed by this late study is significant in pre-Conquest terms. Also, it only adds to our earlier premise that native arts and music were held in such low esteem by the conquerors and their immediate successors that no in-depth interest and research was completed from the time of early contact until the 20th century, nearly 400 years . . . yet, a scant time span for the full measure of orally transmitted music.

Two ceremonies considered to be the oldest music and dance forms among the Tarahumara Indians are the Rutubari and the Yumari Dances, observed by Lumholtz, and these oft-quoted examples of melodic notation are considered by many scholars to have pre-Columbian origins as evidence by lack of Spanish influences. The Tarahumara believe that their ancestors learned the Rutubari from the turkey and the Yumari from the deer. In each ceremony, the ever-present shamans with their gourd rattles were the foremost singers of many song stanzas of entreaty and supplication. The dance formation of the Yumari as described by Lumholtz was not unlike that of the Walk Dance of the Mississippi Choctaws, by way of observation, having men and women seperated in single file stance. Both dances, the Rutubari and the Yumari, are for the sun and the moon, the former being the more serious of the two. Feasting and drinking generally follow after the dances with a prayer that the shaman may have the power to cure. During the dry season, the Tarahumara danced these two dances nearly every night. Also, it was not unusal for the men to perform the Yumari alone in front of their houses for two hours before going on a hunting expedition to insure success on the hunt. Therefore, it was not necessary for an entire group of people or a special occasion at which these ceremonies were performed.

Lumholtz also observed, near Aboreachic, a dance

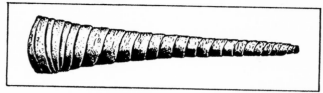

Ipurina bark trumpet.

called "Valixiwami" and another called "Cuvali" further south, both being danced for the same reason as Rutubari. The Tepehuane Indians danced mainly the Cuvali and also another dance for snow as a supplication dance called "Yohi"; for clouds to make rain a dance called "Ayena" was performed. On several occasions during very serious droughts it was not unusual for the following dances to be performed in the following order: Rutubari, Yumari, Valixiwami and Cuvali. The Tarahumara Indians, reports Lumholtz, believed that Rutubari and Yumari were once young men of mythology who taught them how to dance and sing. These two men lived with the Father Sun, and Valiximwai and Cuvali were also mythological male companions to Rutubari.

Medicinal and ritual uses of peyotl, or peyote, and other cacti plants having hallucinogenic effects when taken internally, probably originated in Meso America. Among the originators of the hikuli (peyote) cult, hence many songs pertaining thereunto, the Nahuatl-speaking Huichol Indians were located also in northwestern Mexico about 200 miles south of the Tarahumara. Nahuatl was the language of the Aztecs who also used peyote. Both the Huichol and the Tarahumara believed that the hikuli plant possessed music and also that the plant sang many songs and was a very powerful personage, being addressed on ceremonial occasions as a person. The hikulu or peyote was not as important as Father Sun (according to mythology) but sat next to him and so was addressed as Uncle. "One man had a bag of hikuli and wanted to use his bag as a pillow but could not sleep, he said, because the plants made so much noise and music." It is generally believed that ritual uses of peyote did not occur in North American tribes until much later in the

18th century, but the peripheral tribes in southwestern Arizona and New Mexico were probably users having shaman practioners of the healing arts. The following transcription of a Hikuli song was made by Lumholtz from field recordings.

None of the Indians visited by Lumholtz were descendants of the ancient Aztecs and no tunes of absolutely proven antiquity from the Aztec melodic system have survived due to a complete void of musical quotations in the 16th century chronicles of pre-Conquest life. The following general principles were deduced from numerous examples of Tarahumara and Huichol melodies: 1. Melodies mainly pentatonic; 2. Nonexpressive in Western sense; 3. Generally adhere to "toniclike" endings in Western terms; 4. Range of octave or tenth; 5. Non-climax goal oriented; 6. Strong, rhythmic, propulsive force driving all songs; 7. Nearly all are cult or ritual songs; and, 8. Dance and song closely used. Aztec melodies often covered a wide vocal range into falsetto, Stevenson further reports, quoting from the early writer Sahagun (16th century).

So, we actually know very little about the exact sound of vocal music in the ancient and magnificent temples and city states from the flourishing days of the Pyramid of Cuicuilco (meaning in the Nahuatl language, "place of singing and dancing") and the metropolis of Teotihuacan, city of the gods, both dating back to Archaic culture periods (A.D. 1500). Without doubt, music was a focal and moving force throughout the entire religious practices of each suceeding culture: Teotihuacan's golden age, 200 B.C.-A.D. 900; Toltecs of Tollan, A.D. 900-1168; Aztec culture, A.D. 1324-1521; and the Gold Coast cultures of La Venta, 800-400 B.C. and Tajin, A.D. 0-1200 (Olmecs, Totonacs), and in the heartland of Meso American peoples with the Maya and their predecessors, the Zapotec and Mixtec cultures, 400 B.C. to A.D. 1546. Music was functional in every aspect and always related to religious observance. Professional musicians existed in the form of a caste who were responsible for the production of music for the religious ceremonies. The musical training was extremely disciplined for a career in the priesthood of music since only the most highly trained singers and

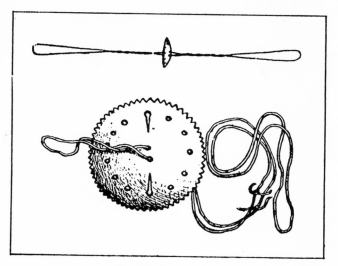

Canella buzzer disk.

players could properly accompany the religious
ceremonies. Since music was performed to appease the
gods it was therefore necessary that musical performances were perfectly executed and often a musician
suffered a death penalty for a faulty performance. The
prestige of the musicians, singers and players, was very
high in the social scale and the musicians were accorded much prestige. Music was a form of communal
expression rather than an expression of individual
technique or individual emotion. Singing always accompanied instrumental performance. Some musicial
instruments were treated as idols as well as musical instruments because they were thought to be of god-like
origin, such as the teponaztle and huehuetl (drums).
These instruments were said to have a life of their own
and mysterious powers of another world. Apparently
the early Spanish conquistadors could grasp the
emotional religious feelings of the Aztec music,
whereas the Indian tribes further inland made music
that meant little or nothing to the European ear. All
music performed was composed, not extemporized,
and was meant for a certain place a certain time,
therefore the musician had to have a vast memory to

Top; dance rattle, Bottom; Mlwatani society rattle.

call forth the appropriate song at the proper time. No form of notation has been discovered other than mnemonic aids. Composers of songs were especially highly regarded and creative ability was an important part of the musical caste system, as the musicians not only carried on by oral tradition the old songs but created new songs for the special occasions. A sense of musical pitch was apparently very acute and the musicians tuned their instruments with great care even though they lacked a string system.

One of the more important 16th century chroniclers was Fray Torobio do Motolina (1490-1569), a Franciscan priest who wrote two works deemed authentic in describing the music of this time. In the *Memoriales*, Two, Motolinia gives a description of pre-Conquest music and tells how music functioned in Aztec life, what instruments they used, how the Aztecs rehearsed songs and dance music and other aspects presumed to established pre-Conquest musical information, but actual quotations are sadly lacking. Both Aztec and Mayan music associated with ceremonialism held to the credo (recorded by another scribe, Sahagun) of Aztec qualifications for an ideal singer which was, "The worthy singer has a clear mind and strong memory. He composes songs himself and learns those of others, and is always ready to impart what he knows to the fellows of his craft. He sings with a well trained voice, and is careful to practice in private before he appears in public. The unworthy singer, on the other hand, is ignorant and indolent. What he learns he will not communicate to others. His voice is hoarse and un-

trained, and he is at once envious and boastful."
(SAHAGUN, *Historia General de las Cosas.*)

C. Any reference to pre-Columbian cultural
achievements in South America invariably centers
around the accomplishments of the Inca Empire
located in the Central Andean Mountain Range and
Peru including the peripheral areas of Bolivia, Ecuador
and Chile. What we term the *Inca Civilization* was
created by the Quechua people who spoke a language
known in ancient times as Runa Simi, now called simply *Quechua*, which has become the most widely spoken
language in South America. The center or the "navel"
of this empire was a place called *Tahuantinsuyu*, now
known as *Cuzco*, Peru. The actual period of empire as
it dominated the whole course of ancient history in the
Andean world was relatively short, between the dates
of A.D. 1200 and 1438, having been preceded by many
older civilizations who can be credited with actual
beginnings in many cultural manifestations not
excluding musical developments, function and style.
Ancient artifacts attest, again, to the uses of musical
expression far back in the dawn of pre-history,
however, several distinct musical achievements stand
out and the Incas are generally given the credit for
developing these to a high point of importance:

1. Development and use of the quipu (knotted rope)
as a form of musical memory.

2. Establishment of formal music instruction (Inca
Roca).

3. Development and use of a micro-tonal music
system.

The "archives" of ancient Inca history were locked
up in numerous contrivances of colored threads and
knots known as the *quip*, or *quipu*. Through the use of
these contrivances by the official knot-string-record interpreter (called *quipu-camayoc*) and the singing bard
(called *haravec*), entire blocks of history relating to the
Inca Empire could be recorded and recalled . . . or
deliberately forgotten as in the case of newly crowned
leaders whose authority and choice it was to record important events of the realm. Nevertheless, the *quipus*
were used by the singers who must have possessed fantastic memories to go along with their musical abilities.

Guapore musical instrument.

The different colors of the wool threads apparently were given special meaning; the method of twisting or intertwining the knot in the thread or the distance of the knots from each other or the thickness of the knot each gave special nuance to the interpreter who, in turn, sang the story whether in poetic form or in narrative style. Furthermore, it is asserted that the singers by using the *quipu* could even express abstract ideas and subtle meanings going far beyond mere numbers and narrative accounts. As a supplement for the memory of historical events, the use of the Inca *quipu* was without equal in the history of mankind.

Written accounts from colonial times, particulary those of Pedro de Cieza de Leon in 1549, relate almost incredulous observations regarding the fantastic memory of the *quipucamayoc* in demonstrating the value of the quipu. Historical events, trading activities, counting systems and other numerous facts were recalled to the astonishment of the observer. So elaborate and efficient was this method of recording information, in fact, that the Incas seemingly never felt the need for any form of writing and, consequently, never developed in this direction any syllabary.

The *quipu* was the logical end-result in the process of oral transmission and thereby was considered no substitute for writing, but to the Inca mentality it was "the" form of writing. Also, in this sense, it served as a form of music notation to the singers and court musicians. "Why develop anything else?" was apparently the conclusion of the ancient Inca scholars and scribes who must have felt that their world and their culture was to last forever, thereby living under a delusion not unlike that of other races in other empires the world over. Is this one of the inevitable and

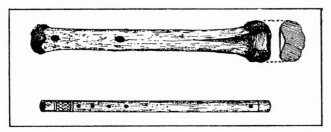

Huari bone flutes.

paradoxical dilemmas to accompany the uses of great
power and the resulting state of euphoric security that
results when a people or a nation become quite
satisfied that their way of life and their cultural mores
have reached a zenith of development? For it seems to
occur when a civilization (whether Incan, Roman or
Egyptian) reaches a state of effete and arrested
development as evidenced in a jaded existence and attitude when the leaders ignore the possibility of change
by being simply unprepared for any sudden and
cataclysmic deviation. The ancient Greek musicians, in
like manner to the Incas, did not rely upon any form of
musical notation, much to our dismay.

The natural drawback of the Inca *quipu-camayoc*
system was the fact that absolutely no pitch determination or other salient musical features of interval, meter
and rhythm could be recorded in the knots which were
meant to be interpreted by none other that the special
singing bards ... who, of course, would not live
forever. Twin disasters in Andean history, and in
musical history, struck in the form of 17th century
crusading padres of the Roman Catholic Church
(resulting from a zeal to stamp out idolatry, in this case
the quipus which were naively considered to be "works
of the devil") who proceeded to destroy all known
quipus and to persecute the "rememberers", or the interpreters of the *quipus* whose skills were no longer
practiced and who gradually died off leaving no
successors ... in short, the "archives" were
destroyed, being composed of two elements: the *quipu*
and the *quipu-camayoc*. This could have been

prevented if the invading European scholars had the foresight to do so, but it will forever stand as mute testimony to the practitioners of cultural genocide that by A.D. 1569 when Pedro Sarmiento de Gamboa attempted to write an offical history of the Incas he discovered that it was practically too late, the interpreters as well as the quipus had all but disappeared from the face of the earth. De Gamboa himself was probably as responsible for this as anyone since he was the principal executioner who exterminated the remaining survivors of the Inca nobility. Thus, in one monumental stroke of concerted destruction, an entire history, not to mention a vast body of musical literature, was completely obliterated. It is true that archaeological sites and graves yielded much useful and authentic information about the ancient Inca culture, namely the existence and use of the *quipus*, but the few surviving *quipus* are virtually meaningless to us today.

The practice of formal schemes of musical training known to exist in the Inca Roca schools (*ca.* 1350) gave to the Incas the added and equally admirable distinction of being the first Americans to establish formal instruction in music. These schools were mainly in the royal city of Cuzco where the *amautas* (masters) instructed in poetry and music plus those sciences which the royal family and the nobles of the empire needed to know. Oral transmission of countless songs throughout the four-year course of study in the yachahuasi (school) culminated in oral examinations to test the memory of wars, sacrifices, conquests, travels and other myriad details of Inca life all recited and celebrated through music. The songs were taught by rote and by actual participation based upon the memories of the amautas who were accorded great honor and status in the society for upon them was vested the responsibilities of actually preserving rites, precepts and ceremonies of the Inca religion. Thus music and musicians occupied a place of high esteem and the singing bards (*haravecs*) were not unlike the Medieval Troubadours and Jongleurs in Europe who added the element of imaginative spontaneity to the developing arts of music.

During the reign of Pachacuti (1438-1471), the

ninth Inca emperor and builder of the Cuzco Temple of the Sun, it was ordered that standard collections of songs be assembled and rehearsed to be never forgotten throughout the Empire. A form of dance-song called an *arabice* was the occasion for recounting the old happenings through responsorial chant and group singing which lasted many hours. Thus, ceremonial music flourished and reached its highpoint in the preConquest era of the Inca Empire which began with the legendary Manco Capac (*ca*. A.D. 1200) and ended with the massacre of Inca Atahualpa by Francisco Pizarro in A.D. 1532.

Recent discoveries of musical artifacts dating back to A.D. 500, when the Tiahuanaco culture flourished near the southern tip of Lake Titicaca, and back to A.D. 850 during the Chavin Period, aptly support the use of various areophones, idiophones and membranophones of musical signigicance among the pre-Inca cultures. Double-row panpipes, rasps, clay and bone flutes, ocarinas and other instruments attest to the fact that the Indians of pre-Conquest South America need not be considered musical inferiors to the Aztecs, Mayas or other Indians throughout the Western Hemisphere. Moreover, some of the *antaras* (panpipes) and bone flutes attest to a definite melodic and musical syntax, the exact code and nature of which is yet to be accurately deciphered. Therefore, the genesis and growth of the art of music in South America obviously antedates the Incas by many centuries with roots firmly planted in the dawn of pre-history as in the other Americas.

The area of pitch discrimination and fixed systems of scale structure and tuning give rise to ethnomusicological controversy, but it seems fairly certain that some musical artifacts reveal that microtonal pitch discrimination and non-overtone based tunings were the deliberate intent of the musical craftsmen. It follows that the vocal melos was similarly concerned. In my own experience with nearly all aerophones of the flute variety found in native North and Mesoamerica, the melodic characteristics adhere to and possess vocal adumbrations.

The Incas apparently did not borrow musical ideas from the Aztecs or Mayas, having no direct contact with either of these groups but, in fact, being virtually unaware of their existence. For further study in this area, the reader is advised to look at the research works by Raoul and Marguerite d'Harcourt, *La musique des Incas et ses survivances* (1935), the work of Jimenez Borja (1951), Izikowitz (1935), and most certainly the work of Robert Stevenson, *Music in Aztec and Inca Territory* (1968).

As to other vast reaches of the South American plains and forests, especially throughout the Amazonian jungles to the Matto Grosso and Gran Chaco regions, the other major groups of Arawk, Carib, Aymara, Atacemeno, Araucanian, Alacaluf, Chono and Yahgan, Tupian, Panoan, Ge, Guaycuruan, Puelche and Tehuelche . . . all probably possessed the basic membranophones, a scattering of flutes and pan-pipes and most certainly those mesolithic uses of ceremonialism with music. The term pre-Conquest has no meaning whatsoever when one considers the fact that the Spanish invaders and all following invaders have yet to successfully penetrate the deepest rain forests with any ease and security much less to conquer all of the native peoples. Without the incentive of gold and the attendant riches of empire builders, only the most intrepid of explorers dared venture far into the dense hinterlands. In conclusion, the early inhabitants whose life style remained largely at the hunting-gathering stages were less likely to have any complex and highly developed music as compared with the inhabitants whose life style centered around the chief-dom and state-like social structures.

POST-COLUMBIAN AND CONTEMPORARY AMERICAN INDIAN MUSIC

A. North American

From colonial times in continental North America, beginning with the 16th century until late in the 19th century, very little useful information and study has survived regarding the sum and substance of aboriginal tribal music. Among the original 13 colonies along the Atlantic seaboard, those tribes who first encountered the Europeans certainly possessed a musical culture along with their ceremonialism and it

part into Indian music and ceremonialism. Recently, in the 1960s, a Catholic priest in the mission church at San Felipe, New Mexico, was promptly expelled from the Indian village when he attempted to discourage Indian music and ceremony.

This writer feels that the general area of the Southwest (Arizona, New Mexico), more than the other cultural areas where the Indian Wars waged on before and during the 1900s, today contains the purest body of American Indian music and ceremonialism. Perhaps it was due to the Spanish Indian policy of containment and co-existence, or to the large population of Indian people, but, whatever the reason, there is certainly a great variety and abundance of age-old ceremonialism, religion, art and music among the Pueblo, Hopi, Navajo and Apache peoples in the Southwest region. Even the post-Conquest, panIndian movements of the Ghost Dance and the peyote cult can trace their beginnings to this part of the country. Also, some of these Indian groups have taken the precautions to strictly forbid photographs, recordings and even the presence of outside visitors during their religious observances. Furthermore, the added devotion to detail and restriction of costume material and musical purism that avoids outside influences has been rewarded by a virtually unadulterated and continuing tribal musical tradition which promises to last for many years.

Regional differences, language variations and vocal mannerisms among the more than 200 tribes in the continental United States, account for an immense and diverse body of vocal music repertoire today. This vast and largely untapped reservoir of oral literature has come to light only in recent years with the work of ethnomusicologists who have attempted to classify, record and transcribe Indian musics. Today there are numerous ethnological studies published by the Bureau of Ethnology which contain song transcriptions dating from the 1890s to the present. Also, record companies have numerous field and studio recordings of tribal music, namely, Canyon Records, Indian House Records, Folkways, Library of Congress, Indian Soundchiefs, to name a few.

Edward Lee Natay, recording on Canyon Records

in 1951, did much to promote the popularity of Indian recordings and the Library of Congress field recordings from the 1930s including a cross-section of tribal musics from every cultural area, both made Indian music accessible and desirable, especially to the Indian communities. Today, the pan-Indian use of "other tribes" songs in vogue and tribal singers borrow/exchange songs with much zeal and enthusiasm.

The Pow-Wow as an inter-tribal meeting place has done much to foster musical growth and the proliferation of songs. Originating mainly in Oklahoma among the Plains tribes of Kiowa, Comanche, Cheyenne,

Timbira type flute made of gourd from the Apinaye.

Arapahoe, Ponca and Otoe, these events are today matched in activity and intensity by the Sioux, Blackfeet, Arikaree and other tribes of the Northern Plains. Also, in large cities like Chicago, Los Angeles and San Francisco, the relocated pow-wow fervor shows no signs of diminishing.

Inasmuch as Indian songs are all composed by an individual, the creation of modern day chants by tribal singers, usually termed "head singers," continues apace with other social dances, round dances, two-steps and other pow-wow features. The 49-songs of Oklahoma are just such a modern creation with roots in the old war-journey songs of the Kiowa. In other regions, the sway songs and squaw dance songs of the Navajo at "sings" in New Mexico and Arizona; bone and stick game songs in the Pacific Northwest; stomp dances among the Shawnee, Creek, Cherokee, Yuchi and Seminole are important events outside of the pow-wow circuit in Oklahoma.

MUSICAL INSTRUMENTS were nearly always played with singing and dancing as part of a sacred ceremony. Occasionally instruments were played for enjoyment or to accompany social dancing, but music was important primarily for its metaphysical power as opposed to its aesthetic or entertaining aspects.

Percussion instruments, those where the sound is made by objects striking or rubbing against each other, were nearly universally used and appeared in many variations. Drums were made of hide simply folded or stretched over a hoop or pot. Canoes, logs, boxes, baskets, boards, and even buildings served as drums, and were beaten with hands, feet, sticks, and wands. Rattles were either containers with small objects loose inside, such a gourd rattles, or junglers with similar objects dangling together such as animal hooves or shells. Decorations on drums and rattles included carving, paint, and feathers. Examples are the carved cedar raven rattles of the Northwest Coast and the painted hide drums of the Plains. Copper bells were made in Central America and Mexico from A.D. 900, and traded and imitated widely. Musical rasps consisted of a long, regularly notched stick rubbed with a shorter wooden or bone piece. Clappers were split sticks or two pieces of wood that might be shaken, beaten together, or clacked like castinets. Thin sticks or reeds slit severals times made a soft, rustling sound when shaken.

Of wind instruments, the simplest was the whistle. Producing one note, whistles were not only ceremonial, but also used in hunting and war. When two or more whistles were joined together side by side, they became a panpipe; when holes were added along the sides, or a slide over the vent hole, to produce more than one note, it became a flute or flageolet. These variations of whistles were the most common melodic instruments used by North American Indians. Panpipes were used in California and Central America. Also in California and in the Northwest, two whistles were bound together, said to have "two

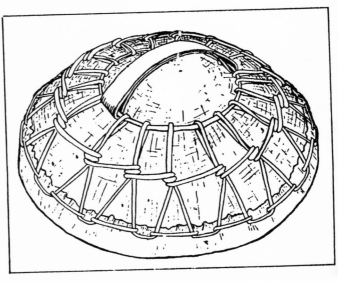

Smithsonian Institution, National Anthropological Archives.
Machi drum.

voices." Flutes seem to have been used everywhere for courting — for young men signalling to their lovers and for casting love charms. But in some areas the flute was present in ceremonies and dances. The Yaqui tribe of southwestern U.S. and northern Mexico had a clown dance where one person played a drum with the right hand and flute with the left. A similar combination was played in the *volador*, flying dance, of eastern Mexico. California and northwest coast tribes had tubes with reeds resembling oboes and clarinets. Conch-shell trumpets were used by Aztecs and by Indians of the southeast and Carribean for war bugles. Aztec priests also used them in religious rites, and such trumpets survived in 20th century Mexican festivals. Trumpets and reeds were also blown by hunters to attract animals — the trumpet for moose and caribou, and a reed to bring deer.

A musical bow is the only stringed instrument believed to be indigenous to North America. In the

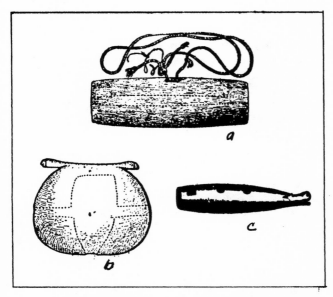

A,b; wooden whistle, c; wooden flute.

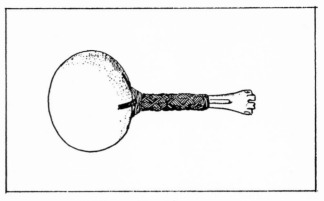

Rattle used in girls ceremony.

rulers' enjoyment and, primarily, for rituals. The Aztec religious cycle had 260 days, and each day had its own musical composition. The music reflected the cosmos and any mistake would bring disorder, hence musical errors were severely punished. The best composers, performers, and vocalists were highly honored. Instruments included trumpets, flutes, musical rasps, slit drums (capable of playing up to five notes), and hide drums.

In the Southeast where religious music was an important part of the knowledge of priests who served hereditary kings, and on the northwest coast where musical education existed and mistakes were sometimes punished, there were also complex styles and as armadillo-shell lutes, are believed to be derived from Spanish instruments. Also derivative is the Apache "fiddle," made from a hollow yucca stalk and played with a horse-hair bow. The Eskimo "guitar," a hollow stringed instrument played with a pick, probably developed from continuing contact with Asia. North American Indian instruments generally were similar to Asian instruments because of the Indians' Asian origin.

The Aztec had professional, full-time musicians, many instruments, and orchestras that played for the

great basin — the inland northwest — a hunting bow was held in the mouth and played by striking a stick against the string. The shape of the mouth determined sound and tone. In the Sierra Madre mountains of Mexico, a gourd was placed over a small hole in the earth and a bow called a *tarahumare* was held vertically upon it. The bow was struck with a stick and the gourd and hole acted as resonator. The Maidu people of Mexico connected much magic with the musical bow, and it occupied an important place in their rites.

MUTILATIONS AND DEFORMATIONS.

the first of these, the flat-head form, the forehead is flattened by means of a board or a variety of cushion, while the parietes of the head undergo compensatory expansion. In the second form, known as macrocephalous, conical, Aymara, Toulousian, etc., the pressure of bandages, or of a series of small cushions, applied about the head, passing over the frontal region and under the occiput, produces a more or less conical, truncated, bag-like, or irregular deformity, characterized by low forehead, narrow parietes, often with a depression just behind the frontal bone, and a protruding occiput. All of these forms present numerous individual variations, some of which are sometimes improperly described as separate types of deformation.

Among the Indians north of Mexico there are numerous tribes in which no head deformation exists and apparently has never existed. Among these are included many of the Athapascan and Californian peoples, all of the Algonquian, Shoshonean (except the Hopi), and Eskimo tribes, and most of the Indians of the Great Plains. Unintentional occipital compression is observable among nearly all the southwestern tribes, and it once extended over most of the United States (excepting Florida) south of the range of the tribes above mentioned. It also exists in ancient skulls found in some parts of the northwest coast.

Both forms of intentional deformation are found in North America. Their geographical distribution is well defined and limited, suggesting a comparatively late introduction from more southerly peoples. The flat-head variety existed in two widely separated foci, one among the Natchez and in a few other localities along the northeast coast of the Gulf of Mexico, and the other on the northwest coast from southern Oregon as far north as southern Vancouver Is., but chiefly west of the Cascades, along Columbia River. The Aymara variety existed, and still exists, only on and near the northwest extremity of Vancouver Island.

The motives of intentional deformation among the Indians are the same as those that lead to similar practices elsewhere; the custom has become fixed through long practice, hence is considered one of propriety and duty, and the result is regarded as a mark of distinction and superiority.

The effects of the various deformations on brain function and growth, as well as on the health of the individual, are apparently insignificant. The tribes that practise it show no indication of greater mortality at any age than those among which it does not exist, nor do they show a larger percentage of imbeciles, or of insane or neuropathic individuals. The deformation, once acquired, persists throughout life, the skull and brain compensating for the compression by augmented extension in directions of least resistance. No hereditary effect is perceptible.

South American Indians

Three kinds of artificial changes have been observed frequently in the skeletons of South American Indians. These are cranial deformity, trephining, and dental mutilation. Bones showing amputations have been found in Peru but are far from being as common as Mochica pottery represents.

Deformity. Intentional shaping of the head in infancy was being practiced by a number of Indian tribes when they were first seen by Europeans, but the practice was probably on the wane and in most places soon was banned. In prehistoric times there were three general centers of cranial deformity on the continent: (1) The Caribbean coast, with an extension through the Antilles; (2) the Pacific Coast in the region of Ecuador, Peru, and North Chile and extending back into the Highlands; and (3) the Coast of Argentina in the region of Rio Negro and other Patagonian valleys. It is convenient to consider these centers separately, although they are not altogether discontinuous.

(1) The Caribbean center is limited to Colombia, Venezuela, probably British Guiana, and all of the inhabitable islands of the Antilles. There is no evidence that the custom extended much farther inland. Neither is there evidence that this custom spread from the Antilles into the Southeastern United States. Also, it is absent from Panama and thus there is no direct connection with the Maya center.

The deformity here is predominantly of one type and should be classified as parallelo-fronto-occipital (or tabular oblicua of Imbelloni); that is, the frontal and occipital parts of the skull have been altered by pressure exerted in directly opposite directions. However, the occiput usually is not flat but is symmetrically rounded, whereas usually the frontal is markedly flattened and even concave. From this form it is judged that a small board was placed on the frontal and held in place either by a band passing around the occiput or by attachment to the ends of a board shaped to the occiput. Some of the early writers speak of the use of two boards, and yet it is difficult to visualize such an arrangement in the cases where the frontal is more extremely distorted than the occiput.

The only evidence of the antiquity of this custom here comes from Cuba. Harrington found undeformed "*Ciboney*" skulls that appeared to antedate the *Arawak* and *Carib* who practiced deformity.

(2) The Pacific Coast center begins in Ecuador and includes most of Peru, Bolivia, Northwest Argentina, and North Chile. There is no evidence as yet of the

presence of this custom in southwestern Colombia connecting the Pacific and Caribbean centers. For instance, deformed skulls have not yet been found in association with the San Agustin culture. However, at the southern end of this area there is probably a thin connection with the Patagonian center.

In this great area all the principal types of deformity were present at different times or in different places. Little is known about the distribution and types in Ecuador, but at Paltacalo, near the coast, the parallelo-fronto-occipital type occurs. In North Peru, or at least in the Mochica area, the type becomes fronto-vertico-occipital (or tabular erecta of Imbelloni); in South Coastal Peru it is chiefly parallelo-fronto-occipital; in the Highlands of Peru and Bolivia it is chiefly circular; in Norhtwest Argentina it is again fronto-vertico-occipital; and in North Chile it is parallelo-fronto-occipital.

The different types were produced by various kinds of apparatuses, some of which, owing to the aridity of parts of this area, have been found with mummies. The circular type was produced, of course, by a band of cloth. A pseudocircular type resulted from the use of a band in combination with a doughnut-shaped pad on the occiput. When the child was placed in a cradle and the head held in place by pressure on the forehead, the fronto-vertico-occipital type of flattening was produced.

These variations in type are closely associated with culture and thus have chronological as well as geographical distributions. The oldest skulls yet found — Cupisnique, Paracas — are deformed. Thus the custom may have considerable antiquity here. Late crania are not so extremely deformed, as a rule.

(3) The Patagonian center comprises mainly Rio Negro, Chubut, and Santa Cruz Territories of Argentina. A single type of deformity — fronto-vertico-occipital, with variations simulating the circular type — is found here. Some of the material showing this deformity is recent, but a considerable age is claimed for the so-called fossil Man of Monasterio, which shows marked frontal flattening.

A large portion of the literature on the subject of cranial deformity is devoted to classifications of types. Thus the terms *"Aymara"* and *"circular"* have become synonymous when applied to cranial deformity, although there is little justification for this.

Imbelloni has done more than anyone else to bring order out of this confusion. His classification is simple; it distinguishes primarily between the forms produced by small boards or other flattened surfaces (tabulares) pressed against the head and the circular form produced by a constricting band. Both of these forms are subdivided into vertical or erect and oblique forms, depending upon variations in the direction of the applied pressure.

Trephining. Surgical removal of parts of the cranial vault during life has been practiced during historic times in Bolivia and Peru. The geographical and chronological distributions of the custom, as well as variations in technique, on the other hand, are known chiefly from skeletal remains. Judging from these remains, the custom rarely occurred outside the above-mentioned countries. A few specimens have been reported from Northwest Argentina, and it would not be surprising if others were found in North Chile.

Thus far, a few localities have furnished the majority of the reported specimens. Except for the Paracas Peninsula, where numerous specimens have been found, Coastal Peru has furnished only scattered examples. On the other hand, large numbers have been found in the Peruvian Highlands, particularly around Huarochiri and Cuzco. The Bolivian remains have come mostly from around La Paz. The frequency of the trephined skulls in collections from these several places are as follows: Huarochiri, 2-4 percent; Cuzco (Urubamba River region, except Macchu Picchu), 17-21 percent; Bolivia, 5 percent; Paracas, 40 percent.

The Paracas skulls furnish the earliest record of this custom. Elsewhere, the skulls are usually attributed to the Late cultural period. Of the numerous sites about Cuzco yielding *Inca* remains, it is note-worthy that the burials at Macchu Picchu did not include trephined skulls, perhaps because the majority were females.

Three techniques for removing the trepan are generally recognized: (1) cutting or sawing, (2) scraping, and (3) drilling. Cutting was done in both straight and curved lines. Straight-line cutting, perhaps better designated sawing, produced angular openings, usually square or rectangular, with the cuts extending into the bone beyond the opening. Curved cuts were perhaps slower, but left a neater, rounded opening. Scraping usually damaged an area larger than the final opening and probably was slow. Drilling seems to have been used seldom, and then for small openings. The instruments employed were chiefly obsidian and quartz flakes.

Straight-line cutting or sawing seems to have been most common in the central Highlands about Huarochiri. Elsewhere, a combination of circular cutting and scraping was used. At Paracas some of the skulls present immense areas in which the bone has been removed by cutting and scraping down to the thin inner table. There is some question in these cases whether they may have been done post mortem, since there are no signs of healing.

The rate of survival from this primitive surgery was surprisingly high.

The reason for the operation is not always apparent. This absence of apparent cause in a series of 19 skulls led to the suggestion of thaumaturgy as an explanation. Subsequent writers have stressed the therapeutic nature of the procedure. Fractures are the principal indication for the operation. The Paracas skulls are an exception in this regard, and this is further reason for believing that many of them may have been trephined after death.

The defect in the skull is said to have been covered in some instances by a disk of shell, metal, or other material. These disks, if discovered in situ, rarely have been described. A thin gold plate over a small trephine opening was found in one Paracas mummies.

Dental mutilation. Chipping and filing of the teeth was practiced more commonly in historic than in prehistoric times, owing to the introduction of the African version of this custom by Negro slaves. Inlaying of the teeth, on the other hand, was practiced only in Ecuador and in prehistoric times.

The prehistoric skulls with filed teeth thus far found come from Ecuador, Bolivia, Chile, and Argentina. Mutilation of the teeth by chipping was not practiced in prehistoric times, having been introduced by the Negroes. In Ecuador the filing was dome primarily to make a bed for the inlay. However, in one case an upper canine and lateral incisor appear to have a shallow U-shaped groove on the occlusal border of each.

From the other countries of South America only about seven specimens from prehistoric times have been reported. In some of these specimens the upper anterior teeth alone are involved, whereas in others it is the lower anterior teeth. In none is the full pattern of mutilation determinable, because of post-mortem loss of various elements. In most cases there is a single V- or W-shaped notch in the occlusal border of the tooth. A unique case from Santa Cruz, Argentina, presents a longitudinal V-shaped groove along the labial surface of the lower right first premolar. The practice in general was not common and probably was not old.

The examples of inlay are limited to three specimens, all of which come from Esmeraldas in Ecuador. Gold is the material inlaid. The number of teeth involved is variable; in the three specimens on record it is two, six, and eight — all upper anterior teeth. In most cases the inlays are circular but in one it is in the form of a band. Except in the use of gold, the Ecuadoran examples of dental mutilation resemble those commonly found in the *Maya* area.

In addition to these forms of mutilation, in which the teeth bear witness of their maltreatment, there is some evidence that a negative form known as ablation or the knocking out of a tooth — inferred from its absence in the skull — was also practiced in prehistoric times. Since teeth are lost in life through in prehistoric times. Since teeth are lost in life through various causes, including accident and disease, a subjective element necessarily enters into the interpretation of the post-mortem dental remains. Hrdlicka, who alone has summarized the evidence from crania on ablation, has examined considerable material from North America and Siberia, but of South American material only that from Peru. Here he found evidence of the practice in about four percent.

In historic times this practice has been separately introduced by black slaves.

N

NECKLACE is a body decoration worn around the neck. Of symbolic and ceremonial use as well as decorative, necklaces were made and worn in all areas of North America from prehistoric times, and were created from as many and diverse materials as were available. Beads were made from stone, bone, teeth, shell, seeds, pottery, wood, and metal. Pendants and "danglers" might be attached to leather thongs or combined with beads to make a necklace. Shell beads were often cut in small, flat discs, and are the most common at archaeological sites, followed by stone and bone. Other prehistoric materials, including the fiber or leather used to string the beads, have often decayed.

Among the gifts given, in the early 16th century to the Spaniard, Cortez, by the Aztec ruler, Montezu-

Ancient pendants and ornaments.

food employ many water symbols in their art, such as lightning, clouds, and water animals.

Northwest coast tribes had excellent woodcarvers. Houses, utensils, pipes, rattles, masks, and totem poles were carved and painted in stylized forms of animals, birds, people, and spirits. The architectural pieces were of monumental size, and all were monumentally awesome religious art.

In the first half of the 16th century, the record of De Soto's Spanish expedition through the southern part of the U.S. describes a temple on the Savannah River whose ceiling inside and roof outside were decorated with strands of shells and pearls.

Leather shirts, tipis, drums, and other hide objects were often painted with symbols and designs. Leather was often embroidered. All the way across the continent in the Subarctic latitudes, moose hair was used as embroidery thread, dyed in different colors. In Mexico, dog and rabbit hair was embroidered on cotton clothing. Copper, used for much jewelry and many ornamental objects, was sometimes made into wire or thread for embroidery.

Porcupine quills were used throughout the hunting region. They were dyed and sewn to leather or bark clothing and objects. Sometimes they were flattened and softened by chewing, then wrapped around leather thongs to be applied to clothing or utensils. The Micmac tribe in Nova Scotia decorated things made of birch bark, such as boxes with geometric designs of dyed porcupine quills. As European glass beads became available they replaced porcupine quills to a great extent.

Buttons were used as decoration in many areas. Small designs cut out of thin sheets of copper were found in Hopewell mounds (Ohio, C. 900-1300 A.D.) that were probably sewn to clothing for decoration. Silver buttons were used similarly by mid-19th century Navajo. In 1910, a Kwakiutl (Northwest Coast) chief who was also a priest wore a factory-made blanket

tion of Hopi katchina dolls is traditional; often the use of colors is symbolic. The painted designs include geometric shapes, plants, animals, and parts of the heavens: stars, moon, sun, lightning, clouds. The bodies are painted with flat geometrical shapes, making Hopi katchina dolls extremely colorful and theatrical. Zuni and Rio Grande katchina dolls are not as elaborately painted.

Rock paintings in the Great Lakes area, especially around the northern United States and southern Canada are quite figurative. There are infrequent abstract elements, but on the whole, these paintings in red pigment on cliffs and in caves show fairly realistic representations of people, animals, and boats.

Among the art of the Indians of the Eastern Woodlands, painting was used in a decorative symbolic manner similar to that of the Northwest Coast Indians. Significant buildings were ornamented with carved posts resembling reptiles and fish. The walls of the buildings were covered with paintings depicting animals, humans, and some figures which combined both animal and human elements. In addition, body coloration in the form of tattooing, using indigo dyes, was significant. A variety of intricate design elements (celestial bodies, geometric scrolls, animals, human figures, battle and chase scenes) covered the bodies of Indians living in this area.

Modern painting by 20th century Indian artists has achieved widespread recognition and critical approval. The establishment of the School of Indian Art in Santa Fe (New Mexico) in the 1920's led to an effort on the part of Native Americans to become a part of the contemporary art scene. The Institute of American Indian Arts in Santa Fe, which emerged from the auspices of the Indian Arts and Crafts Board, as well as the Taos (N.M.) Colony and the ever-expanding interests of non-Indians in Indian artists has led to the training of Indian artists in non-craft painting. There are many contemporary Indian painters whose works reflect the traditional influences of subject matter and design, but their works are unique blends of those traditions with the more painterly traditions of non-Indian western arts, and are of great aesthetic and commercial value today.

PETROGLYPHS. A distinction has been made between a petroglyph, or rock-writing, and all other descriptions of picture-writing. The criterion for the former is that the picture, whether carved or pecked, or otherwise incised, and whether figured only by coloration or by coloration and incision together, is upon a rock either in situ or sufficiently large for inference that the picture was imposed upon it where it was found. This criterion allows geographic classification. In presenting the geographic distribution, prominence is necessarily (because of the laws authorizing this work) given to the territory occupied by the United States of America, but examples are added from various parts of the globe, not only for comparison of the several designs, but to exhibit the prevalence of the pictographic practice in an ancient form, though probably not the earliest form. The rocks have preserved archaic figures, while designs which probably were made still earlier on less enduring substances are lost.

Throughout the world in places where rocks of a suitable character appear, and notably in South America, markings on them have been found similar to those in North America, though until lately they have seldom been reported with distinct description or with illustration. They are not understood by the inhabitants of their vicinity, who generally hold them in superstitious regard, and many of them appear to have been executed from religious motives. They are now most commonly found remaining where the population has continued to be sparse, or where civilization has not been of recent introduction, with exceptions such as appear in high development on the Nile.

The superstitions concerning petroglyphs are in accord with all other instances where peoples in all ages

Mountain sheep pictographs.

and climes, when observing some phenomenon which they did not understand, accounted for it by supernatural action. The following examples are selected as of interest in the present connection.

It must be premised with reference to the whole character of the mythology and folk-lore of the Indians that, even when professed converts to Christianity, they seem to have taken little interest in the stories of the Christian church, whether the biblical narratives or the lives and adventures of the saints, which are so constantly dwelt upon throughout the

Petroglyphs on the Puye cliffs, Pajarito Park.

Christia.. world that they have become folk-lore. The general character of the Christian legends does not seem to have suited the taste of Indians and has not at all impaired their affection for or their belief in the aboriginal traditions.

Among the gods or demigods of the Abnaki are those who particularly preside over the making of petroglyphs. Their name in the plural, for there are several personnages, is Oonagamessok. They lived in the caves by the shore and were never seen, but manifested their existence by inscriptions on the rocks. The fact that these inscribed rocks are now very seldom found is accounted for by the statement that the Oonagamessok have become angry at the want of attention paid to them since the arrival of the white people and have caused the pictures to disappear. There is no evidence to determine whether this tradition should be explained by the fact that the ingenious shamans of the last century would sometimes produce a miracle, carving the rocks themselves and interpreting the marks in their own way, or by the fact that the rock inscriptions were so old that their origin was not remembered and an explanation was, as usual, made by ascription to a special divinity, perhaps a chieftain famous in the old stage of mythology, or perhaps one invented for the occasion by the class of priests who from immemorial antiquity have explained whatever was inexplicable.

At a rock near the mouth of the Magiguadavic river, at the time immediately before the Passamaquoddy Indians chose their first governor after the manner of the whites, the old Indians say there suddenly appeared a white man's flag carved on the rocks. The old Indians interpreted this as a prophecy that the people would soon be abandoned to the white man's methods, and this came to pass shortly after. Formerly they had a "Mayouett" or chief. Many other rock carvings are said to have foretold what has since come to pass. Strange noises have also been heard near them.

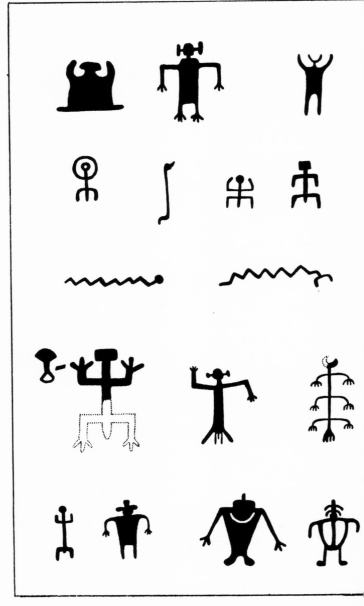

Human and other pictographs.

the age of the great waters, at the time when their fathers were able to reach the heights in their canoes.''

If these legends and these petroglyphs are proof of an extinct civilization, it is astonishing that their authors should have left no other traces of their culture. To come to the point, it is admissible that they were replaced by savage tribes without leaving a trace of what they had been, and can we understand this retrograde march of civilization when progress everywhere follows an ascending course? These destructions of American tribes in place are very convenient to prop up theories, but they are contrary to ethnologic laws.

The remarkable height of some petroglyphs has misled authors of good repute as well as Indians. Petroglyphs frequently appear on the face of rocks at heights and under conditions which seemed to render their production impossible without the applicances of advanced civilization, a large outlay, and the exercise of unusual skill. An instance among many of the same general character in the petroglyphs at Lake Chelan, Washington, where they are about 30 feet above the present water level, on a perpendicular cliff, the base of which is in the lake. On simple examination the execution of the pictographic work would seem to involve details of wharfing, staging, and ladders if operated from the base, and no less elaborate machinery if approached from the summit. Elevated drawings were made by the ingenious use of stone wedges driven into the rock, thus affording support for ascent or descent, and reports that he actually saw such stone wedges in position on the Yenesei river. A very rough geological theory has been presented by others to account for the phenomena by the rise of the rocks to a height far above the adjacent surface at a time later than their carving.

But in many cases observed in America it is not necessary to propose either the hypothesis involving such elaborate work as is suggested or one postulating enormous geological changes. The escarpment of cliffs is from time to time broken down by the action of the elements and the fragments fall to the base, frequently forming a talus of considerable height, on which it is easy to mount and incise or paint on the remaining prependicular face of the cliff. When the latter adjoins a lake or large stream, the disintegrated debris is almost immediately carried off, leaving the drawings or paintings at an apparently inaccessible altitude. When the cliff is on dry land, the rain, which is driven against the face of the cliff and thereby increased in volume and force at the point in question, also sweeps away the talus, though more slowly. The talus is ephemeral in all cases, and the face of the cliff may change in a week or a century, as it may happen so its aspect gives but a slight evidence of age. The presence, therefore, of the pictures on the heights described proves neither extraordinary skill in their maker nor the great antiquity which would be indicated by the emergence of the pictured rocks through volcanic or other dynamic agency. The age of the paintings and sculptures must be inferred from other considerations.

Pictures are sometimes found on the parts of rocks which at present are always, or nearly always, covered with water. On the sea shore at Machias Bay, Maine, the peckings have been continued below the line of the lowest tides as known during the present generation. In such cases subsidence of the rocky formation may be indicated. At Kejimkoojik Lake, Nova Scotia, incisions of the same character as those on the bare surface of the slate rocks can now be seen only by the aid of a water glass, and then only when the lake is at its lowest. This may be caused by subsidence of the rocks or by rise of the water through the substantial damming of the outlet. Some rocks on the shores of rivers, e.g., those of the Kauahwa, in West Virginia, show the same general result of the covering and concealment of petroglyphs by water, except in an unusual drought, which may more reasonably be attributed to the gradual elevation of the river through the rise of the surface near its mouth than to the subsidence of the earth's crust at the locality of the pictured rocks.

It must be admitted that no hermeneutic key has been discovered applicable to American pictographs, whether ancient on stone or modern on bark, skins,

nomenclature. The following general remarks of Schoolcraft are of some value, though they apply with any accuracy only to the Ojibwa and are tinctured with a fondness for the mysterious:

For their pictographic devices the North American Indians have two terms, namely, *Kekeewin,* or such things as are generally understood by the tribe, and *Kekeenowin,* or teachings of the *medas* or priests and *jossakeeds* or prophets. The knowledge of the latter is chiefly confined to persons who are versed in their system of magic medicine, or their religion, and may be deemed hieratic. The former consists of the common figurative signs, such as are employed at places of sepulture or by hunting or traveling parties. It is also employed in the *muzzinabiks,* or rock-writings. Many of the figures are common to both and are seen in the drawings generally; but it is to be understood that this results from the figure alphabet being precisely the same in both, while the devices of the nugamoons or medicine, wabino, hunting, and war songs are known solely to the initiates who have learned them, and who always pay high to the native professors for this knowledge.

In the Oglala Roster, infra, one of the heads of families is called Inyanowapi, translated as Painted (or inscribed) rock. A blue object in the shape of a bowlder is connected with the man's head by the usual line, and characters too minute for useful reproduction appear on the bowlder. The name is interesting as .giving the current Dakota term for rock-inscriptions. The designation may have been given to this Indian because he was an authority on the subject and skilled either in the making or interpretation of petroglyphs.

The name "Wikhegan" was and still is used by the Abnaki to signify portable communications made in daily life, as distinct from the rock carvings mentioned above, which are regarded by them as mystic.'

One of the curious facts in connection with petroglyphs is the meager notice taken of them by explorers and even by residents other than the Indians, who are generally reticent concerning them.. The resident nearest to the many inscribed rocks as Kejimkoojik Lake, Nova Scotia, was a middle-aged farmer of respectable intelligence who had lived all his life about 3 miles from those rocks, but had only a vague notion of their character, and with difficulty found them. A learned and industrious priest, who had been working for many years on the shores of Lake Superior preparing not only a dictionary and grammar of the Ojibwa language, but an account of Ojibwa religion and customs, denied the present existence of any objects in the nature of petroglyphs in that region. Yet he had lived for a year within a mile of a very important and conspicuous pictured rock, and, on being convinced of his error by sketches shown him, called in his Ojibwa assistant and for the first time learned the common use of a large group of words which bore upon the system of picture-writing, and which he thereupon inserted in his dictionary, thus gaining from the visitor, who had come from afar to study at the feet of this supposed Gamaliel, much more than the visitor gained from him.

SOUTH AMERICA

Petroglyphs. Rude linear designs engraved or painted on rocks are widely distributed in South America, where they are variously knows as petroglyphs, pictographs, "letreiros," "pedras lavradas," "piedras escritas," "piedras garabteadas," "pintados," and "riscos." In scientific usage, there has been a tendency to restrict the use of the term "petroglyph" to the engravings and to call the paintings "pictographs," but this is not always done. In the present article, the two varieties will be termed engraved and painted petroglyphs.

Whether engraved or painted, the petroglyphs are ordinarily found upon large boulders or outcrops of rock. Some lie close to the sites of Indian villages; others do not. The engraved forms are most common in and along streams, frequently in the vicinity of rapids and falls, but they also occur in open fields, on cliffs, in caves, and in rock shelters. The painted petroglyphs appear more often in caves and rock shelters than in the open, probably because protection is needed for the preservation of the painted markings. Rarely, engraved or painted petroglyphs are found on

occurring singly as in the other areas, are common, but many of the designs portray scenes and a few are presented in perspective. Pictures of birds, animals, and human beings are characteristic, the llama being the most common, Geometric designs are in the minority; some of them tend to resemble the designs on pottery and other artifacts.

The Ando-Peruvian petroglyphs vary considerably from place to place. Pictures of the llama are most common in the central part of the area. As one moves north into Peru, feline figures become more important; to the south, the typical design is an entanglement of irregular curved lines. Most of the drawings of scenes are in Northwest Argentina, while North Chile is characterized by enormous petroglyphs, which are often traced in the desert sands rather than on rocks, or by planting stones in the ground.

The earliest petroglyphs of North Chile were composed entirely of rectilinear geometric motives, with the exception of the circle. He postulates a later period of Chincha influences, marked by the introduction of meandering lines, hooks, spirals, concentric circles, rhomboids, stepped figures, and pictures of men and animals, all of which, according to him, are motifs found on *Chincha-Atacameno* gourds and pottery. A subsequent group of petroglyphs are said to show *Inca* influences and still others are believed to be post-Spanish. The extension into Spanish times, however, has been verified by the discovery of pictures of riders on horseback in Northwest Argentina.

Petroglyphs of the Columbian-Venezuelan group are largely restricted to the Andean sections of those countries. Rough paintings and engravings are present in the open and in caves and rock shelters. The figures of human beings and animals are common, but they never show the details of clothing and ornament characteristic of the Ando-Peruvian area, nor are they used to portray scenes. A typical practice is to draw a geometric outline and fill it in with other lines; these are commonly rectilinear.

In Colombia, to the south, in the department of Narino, only engravings are mentioned; these comprise mainly human and animal figures located on rocks and in caves. In the San Agustin region, engraved petroglyphs are located on the slabs lining megalithic temples and tombs, as well as on natural rocks. Geometric figures are more common than pictures of animals and human beings; the spiral is notable for its absence. Modern Spanish petroglyphs have also been reported from this area. Both rock paintings and engravings occur in the valley of Cauca and the Tierradentro region. They have been found on boulders and on the steep slopes of rock and comprise mainly human and animal forms. Rock paintings and engravings are also known from boulders and rock shelters in the northern part of the department of Huila, where geometric figures and pictures of human beings are said to have a certain resemblance to *Chibcha* goldwork. The plateau of Boyaca and Cundinamarca farther north contains engraved boulder markings of geometric and human figures, some of them with recognizable sex organs. In the Sierra Nevada de Santa Marta, engraved petroglyphs occur on boulders and on figure stones. They consist of animal as well as human figures. The eastern slopes of the Andes, finally, have yielded engravings like those of the Amazon Basin, in which human faces and possibly supernatural beings are emphasized. No attempt has yet been made to work out the chronological implications of these regional styles.

The petroglyphs of Brazil and the surrounding lowlands are too poorly known for adequate characterization, and it may eventually be possible to group them with the Colombian-Venezuelan forms. There seem to be centers of concentration near the headwaters of the various tributaries of the Amazon, in the region around Pernambuco and Natal in Brazil, in the Guianas, and in the West Indies; these may be correlated with the availability of rocks. The petroglyphs occur both in the open, in rock shelters,

Europe—even persecuted on account of its nightshade affinity, and maliciously slandered for its alleged poisonous properties—the potato remained for a long time the sustenance of the poor only. Yet during the last century and a half it has conquered all classes of society in both Europe and North America. It is now a fundamental of white man's civilization; like bread, it is a prime necessity and mainstay of his daily life, an indispensable article in his home.

In one respect it was lucky: its American ancestry has never been called into question. As yet no one has tried to prove its African or Chinese origin. In Africa it is of no importance to the natives; in China as well as in Japan it holds an inferior position. The same holds good for the Near East, the Malay Archipelago, Melanesia, and Polynesia with the sole exception of New Zealand, where it has been able to transform the economic life of the Maori. Spain and Portugal remained sadly inactive in propagating the plant. Spain merely served as a stepping-stone an a way of transit from Peru to Italy. The Spaniards, although the first discoverers of the useful tuber, were slow in recognizing its nutritive value and woke up to the knowledge of its importance at a later time than any other European nation; all they did was confined to the transplantion of the tuber to the Philippines. The Portuguese may have brought it to India, but whatever importance it may have gained there is due to British initiative and energy. It followed the British as well as the Hollanders into their colonies. Clusius and Parmentier are the two brilliant names standing out in the history of science as students and propagators of the plant in Europe.

An illustration of Peruvian potato varieties inserted in the March number of the *Journal of Heredity* of 1925 is accompanied by this legend: "The potato is the most valuable of the gifts that the ancient Peruvians made to the agriculture of the world. One year's potato crop amounts to from four to six billion bushels, which represents in money value probably far more than the treasure taken from Peru at the time of the conquest. In spite of this, the potato is not an unmixed blessing, for by making possible a greatly increased population in northern Europe it is to be regarded as one of the contributing causes of World War." Poor potato! It was not enough to brand it with the stigma of lacking Biblical authority, causing leprosy, spreading poison and disease, and ruining soil; now it must also bear responsibility for a war. True it is that the potato is somewhat revolutionary in character, inasmuch as it has engineered an economic revolution in human and animal nutrition and to a remarkable degree has lessened the dangers ensuing from famines. In this manner it has largely contributed to the saving and preservation of human lives, perhaps even to the increase of population; yet the role of a life-saver is by no means ignominious. The factors which tend to increase the population of a country cannot be laid at the door of this or that plant, but are complex and organically interrelated: improved conditions of housing and sanitation, the progress of medicine and hygiene; superior standards of living, amelioration of wages and labor conditions, rapidity of progress in commerce, industries, and agriculture, number of marriages, etc. are all contributing or concomitant factors. If it is true that overpopulation has a tendency to cause wars, it is certainly not fair to blame a war on just one of the numerous causes which go to make for overpopulation.

A French naturalist, l'Abbe Armand David has observed that maize and potatoes, both novel to China, have allowed the Chinese to live in the gorges of the high mountains; he is disposed to think that what takes place in China may occur in many other mountainous regions of the temperate and subtropical zones, and he concludes that, consequently, in ancient times our earth was never populated so densely as it has been since the acquisition of these two alimentary resources.

The variability of the potato is stupendous. The varieties have increased by leaps and bounds. Culture, so to speak, created new varieties almost daily. While about a thousand are known at present, sixty were know in France in 1815, 493 in 1855, and 528 in 1862. The degree of variability has doubtless increased with the intensity of culture, which simultaneously improved quality. The general aversion to the potato in the time of its initial cultivation in Europe may have been due partially to inferior or underdeveloped specimens, partially to lack of understanding of its cultivation and preparation. The superior quality of our present potatoes is the outcome of long-continued selection and improved methods of cultivation. There can be no doubt that several varieties existed in the Inca empire as the result of the achievements of Peruvian agriculture. This is still demonstrated by the many varieties grown by the natives of Feru. The tubers show a wide range of variety as to shape, size, color, and texture; some varieties are deep purple under the skin, and others purple throughout. The natives of the tableland districts plant many varieties together, but know the names and qualities of the different kinds. In general, the color varies from pale gray to yellow, red, violet, and even black; the size, from that of a nut to that of a small melon.

No less admirable is the adaptability of the plant to climate, altitudes, and soils. It lives at an elevation of 12,000 and even 14,000 feet, yet also flourished in coastal areas. It thrives in sandy soil and at elevations where cereals do not grow. The tubers can be preserved easily and for a long time.

EARLY HISTORY OF
THE POTATO IN SOUTH AMERICA

At the time of the Spanish conquest of America the cultivation of *Solanum tuberosum* was strictly limited to the Andean region of South America. It was not cultivated and not found anywhere at that time in the Antilles, in Mexico or Central America, in North

America, or in the central and eastern portions of South America. All statements to the contrary are erroneous, being prompted by misunderstandings and confusions with other species like the batata or sweet potato, *Apios tuberosa*, and wild-growing species of *Solanum*. The subsequent propagation of *S. tuberosum* from its original home on the west coast of South America to other parts of the continent is not due to Indian agency, but to the activity of the white man. It is notable also that while other cultivated plants of South America spread rapidly northward after the conquest, the potato moved at a comparatively slow pace.

The first documentary evidence for the existence of *Solanum tuberosum* is presented by the account of Pedro Cieza de Leon, who in 1538 encountered it in the upper Cauca Valley between Popayan and Pasto, in what is now Colombia. Subsequently he found it at Quito, the present capital of Ecuador. In his journal, entitled *Chronica del Peru*, he describes what the aborigines call *papas* as "a kind of earth-nut, which, after it has been boiled, is as tended as a cooked chesnut, but it has no more skin than a truffle, and it grows under the earth in the same way." In this writing of the elevated Collao region in Peru, he speaks of it thus: This country of the Collao was once very populous, and was covered with large villages round which the Indians had their fields, where they raised crops for food. "Their principal sustenance is *papas*, which as I have already stated in this history as like *turmas de tierra*. These they dry in the sun and keep from one harvest to the other. And they call this *papa* after it is dried, *chuno (chunu)*; and among them it is esteemed and held precious: for they have no ditches like many others in this kingdom to irrigate their fields; and if there is a dearth of natural water to make their crops grow they suffer from lack of food and work, unless they are provided with this sustenance of dried *papas*. And many Spaniards have become rich and returned to Spain prosperous only from carrying *chuno* to sell to the mines of Potosi.''

Markham annotates that ''frozen potatoes are still the ordinary food of the natives of the Collao. They damn up square shallow pools by the sides of streams, and fill they with potatoes during the cold season of June and July. The frost soon converts them into *chunus*, which are insipid and tasteless.'' Cieza's account refers to the Chibcha, the ancient inhabitants of Colombia, of whom also Oviedo says that they subsisted principally on maize and potatoes, called in their language *yoma*.

Jose de Acosta, who was in South America from 1571 to 1576, describes *papas* in the old English translation thus: ''These rootes are like to ground nuttes, they are small rootes, which cast out many leaves. They gather this *Papas*, and dry it well in the Sunne, then beating it they make that which they call *Chunu*, which keeps many daies, and serves for bread. In this realme there is great trafficke of *Chunu*, the which they carry to the mines of Potosi; they likewise eat of these *Papas* boyled or roasted.'' W. E. Safford gives a fuller version, translated from the Spanish text: ''In the elevated region of the Sierra of Peru and the provinces which they call the Collao, composing the greater part of that kingdom, where the climate is so cold and dry that it will not permit to cultivation of wheat or maize, the Indians use another kind of roots which they call *pappas*, a kind of *turmas de tierra* that send up scant foliage (*echan arriba una poquilla hoja*). These *pappas* they collect and leave in the sun to dry well, and breaking them they make what they call *chunyo* which will keep for food in that form many days and serves them for bread; and of this *chunyo* there is great commerce in that kingdom with the mines of Potosi. *Pappas* are also eaten fresh either boiled or roasted; and from one of the mildest varieties which also grows in warm situations they make a certain ragout or *cazuela* which they call *locro*. Indeed, these roots are the only wealth of that land, and when the season is favorable for the crop they [the Indians] are glad; for many years the roots are spoiled and frozen in the ground, so great is the cold and bad climate of that region.'

"In preparing *chunyo*, potatoes were subjected to freezing as well as drying. The process is described in detail by Padre Bernabe Cobo who writes as follows: "The tubers are gathered at the beginning of the cold season, in May or June, spread on the ground and exposed, for a period of twelve or fifteen days, to the sun during the day and frost at night. At the end of this time they are somewhat shriveled, but still watery. In order to get rid of the water they are then trampled upon and then left for fifteen or twenty days longer to the action of the sun and frost, at length becoming as dry and light as a cork, very dense and hard, and so reduced in bulk that from four or five fanegas of fresh tubers there results only one fanega of *chunyo*.' Cobo adds that *chunyo*, thus prepared, will remain unspoiled for many years and that the Indians of the Collao provinces eat no other kind of bread. A choicer and more highly prized quality is prepared by soaking the tubers in water for about two months, after their preliminary drying. They are then taken out and dried in the sun once more. This quality of *chunyo*, which is chalky white within, is called *moray*. From it a kind of flour, finer than wheat·flour, is prepared by the Spanish women, who use it for starch, biscuit, and sweetmeats of all kinds, like those confections usually made with sugar and almonds." The natives of Peru have a sort of root like truffles, but possessing very little flavor.

Size, shape, and color of potatoes depend much on the composition and fertility of the soil, and upon weather, climate, care, etc. This was well known to the Inca. According to the Jesuit P. Morua, the Inca Urko, a member of the royal family, a famed engineer and architect, to whom the construction of the fortress of Cuzco is also ascribed, had the best potato soil carried from Quito to Cuzco and made into the hill Al'pa suntu ("Earth-Hill") east of the fortress, and there the

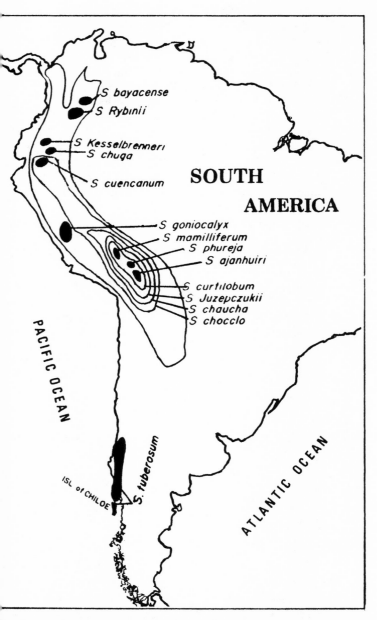

Distribution of potato varieties cultivated by South American Indians.

potatoes were grown for the ruling Inca.

In the worship of the ancient Peruvians the *papa* played a certain, though inferior, role. At times the female fortune-tellers placed heaps of potatoes before them and took the tubers up by pairs; if none was left, they predicted a favorable year; if one was left, however, the year was unlucky. The Kol'a styled this mode of divination *piu irute* ("potato-counting").

In a Peruvian prayer addressed to the Creator, it is said: "Thou who givest life to all things, and hast made men that they may live, and eat, and multiply. Multiply also the fruits of the earth, the *papas* and maize (*papa-sara*) that thou hast made, that men may not suffer from hunger and misery. Preserve the fruits of the earth from frost, and keep us in peace and safety."

There were two ways of preserving potatoes: (1) They were peeled and then exposed to the cold for several nights and dried in the sun during the day. This process was repeated as many times as necessary; thus prepared, the tubers were stored in a dry place and kept for years. (2) Another method was to freeze the potatoes for several nights and to dry them in the sun during the day. Then they were pressed with the feet and again exposed to the sun and frost; when dry and without moisture, they were preserved. In this state they were shriveled and small, of gray black color, and, when boiled, made a slimy pap of bad taste.

In the higher elevations of Peru, where maize does not thrive, living was rendered possible only by the potato. In Cuzco, potato-farming is carried on throughout the country from 12,000 feet above sea level upwards to nearly 15,000 feet

The accounts of the Spanish authors did not fail to attract attention among the scholars of Europe. Girolamo Cardano summed up the subject as follows: "In Colla or the country of Peru, the *papa* is a genus of tuber, utilized like a kind of bread and generated in the soil; thus nature everywhere cares wisely for all necessaries. The *papas* are dried and then called *ciuno*.

Some people found means to profit from transporting only this article into the province Potosi. They say that this root bears an herb similar to that of the Argemone. They are shaped like chesnuts, but have a more agreeable taste: they are eaten cooked or made into meal. They are likewise found among other peoples of this Chersonesos, as well as among the inhabitants of the province of Quito.'' Cardano is the first Italian author and the first in Europe who speaks of the potato on the basis of Spanish accounts, without knowing the plant, which has not yet been introduced into Italy at the time he wrote.

Fortunately there is also archaeological evidence testifying to the great antiquity of the potato in Peru. This evidence comes to us in twofold form—plant remains and reproductions of the tuber in ancient pottery. Dried potatoes were discovered by Safford in 1887 in graves at Africa, on the coast of northern Chile, together with arrow points and llama-drivers' slings from the elevated plateau about Lake Titicaca.

Potatoes were also cultivated by the aborigines of southern Chile at an early date. There they were encountered as a food staple of the Indians in 1578 by Sir Francis Drake who observes that their occurrence at sea level in this part of South America is not singular; for, as all students of plant distribution know, many species characteristic of Andean vegetation thrive at altitudes lower and lower as they extend southward, reaching sea level in the region of the Chonos Archipelago and the Straits of Magellan. Within less than a decade after Drake's visit, potato tubers had become a regular food on Spanish ships. On March 16, 1587, Thomas Cavendish, stopping at St. Mary Island near Concepcion in southern Chile, found ''Cades full of Potato Rootes, which were very good to eate, ready made up in the Store-houses for the Spaniards, against they should come for their tribute.'' The center of potato cultivation is to be sought in ancient Peru, and from there the potato spread northward into the territory of Ecuador and Colombia as well as southward into Chile.

The statement has frequently been advanced that the potato occurs spontaneously in Chile, and that there also its cultivation was initiated. From there the cultivated form is supposed to have spread to Peru and Bolivia into the empire of the Inca, who largely contributed to its extension. The Indians of Chile were skillful agriculturists long before the conquest of the Inca and that by no means do they owe to this invasion the first steps to civilization, as almost all Chilean writers believe. This does not mean that the Peruvians did not independently discover the utility of the *papa* which grows wild everywhere along the Pacific coast. There is no doubt that in no other territory than Chile was the cultivation of the *papa* in pre-Columbian times more extensive and intensive, and it is more than probable that from Chile this tuber has conquered the world. What the ancient Chileans cultivated was really *Solanum tuberosum*. The fundamental question is one of species. The term *papa* was extended by the Spaniards to all tuber-bearing species of *Solanum*, and is therefore an unreliable, nay, misleading criterion in an investigation of this character.

Potato culture was practiced in Venezuela in prehistoric times. The potato was doubtless introduced into that country by the Spaniards from Peru or Colombia and thrives well only in higher altitudes, best of all in the *tierra templada* and *fria*.

POTLATCH, throughout the aboriginal cultures of the Pacific Northwest, the potlatch was the principal means whereby class distinctions, family honour and privilege, and social prestige were maintained. This system of gift distribution was universal in this area and regulated the social life not only of village communities, but also of whole linguistic groups.

In order to maintain his social status, a member of the ruling class was obliged to give away large amounts of property on nearly every public occasion. The assuming of a new title on the decease of a former chief required several potlatches in order to honour the dead suitably and to establish, in the eyes of the community, the new chief's right to the position. The building of a new house also required a potlatch, as did the naming of a new-born, or the granting of new names to sons or daughters entering puberty or adulthood. The lavish distribution of gifts was the sole accepted method of establishing one's right to new ranks and privileges and of maintaining those already held.

Among the northern coastal Indians the potlatch was a form of investment. The rules of the system, hallowed by the traditions of generations, insisted that repayment, often to the extent of 100 per cent interest, was the only acceptable answer to the potlatch gift. Thus family groups would labour for months or even years in order to accumulate the required amount of potlatch material necessary to establish their head man in the position desired. After the distribution had been made, the family members might be completely destitute, but so strong were the rules of the game that they were regarded by other members of the community and surrounding villages as being both wealthy and influential. Their social position rested on the tacit recognition of debts owed to them by others.

The potlatch has been described as a "humiliation device" and a form of "economic warfare," but such broad terms are inadequate to describe individual differences in temperament, ambition, and social aspirations. It is true that one method of humiliating an enemy was to utterly degrade him by making large gifts to him and to members of his family—gifts which they could not possible repay. Under the existing customs, refusal of the gifts was tantamount to acknowledging defeat and social disgrace, and suicide was not unknown as a means of escaping from this fate. This form of warfare often involved not only the giving-away of property, but also the destruction of valuable pieces of equipment. After distributing the bulk of his possessions to those above whom he wished to rise, a chief might make a final vainglorious gesture by destroying his most valued article—perhaps by throwing into the sea a famous "copper" (a plate of beaten copper inscribed with heraldic designs) or by smashing beyond repair his best canoe. Such actions would long be remembered among the villagers, until some other chief made even greater sacrifices and by so doing rose to even greater eminence.

On the other hand, although admittedly stimulating aggressive competition, the potlatch was normally conducted with less vicious intent. Among the Haida it was distinctly a method of raising the social status of one's children. To these Queen Charlotte Island people, it was the parents' providence which counted. No man, no matter to what extend he potlatched, could offset his parents' failure in this respect. His status remained that which they bequeathed to him.

Again, among some groups, one major potlatch could raise a man from the position of commoner to that of petty chief, and a member of the ruling class. But among other groups where the caste system was more firmly entrenched, although it was possible to become wealthy and respected within the commoner class, no magnitude of potlatch could effect acceptance into the upper ranks of society.

The more aggressive attitude of the northern Indians was modified somewhat in the southern area. There the interest-bearing aspect was less evident, and in consequence less rivalry was created. The potlatch distribution included gifts to the poorer members of the community, from whom no possible repayment could be forthcoming, and in general the motive appears to have been a simple striving for social prestige through a moderate display of generosity.

POW WOW is a form of council meeting common among North American Indians, usually convened to consider some immediate problem. Speakers presented different views on the matter at hand, after which there followed a general discussion. Praying, dancing, and singing often accompanied these procedures. Sometimes pipes were smoked, the Indians intending for the spiritual beings who protected their tribe to join in the deliberations. The term *pow wow* was originally used by only a few Indian peoples in New England. Other tribes across the continent called such gatherings "sings" or "dances." But the term *pow wow* rapidly gained currency in the English language and has become, for English-speaking peoples at least, the name applied to all council meetings of this type.

PRAYER STICKS are lengths of wood with feathers attached that serve as messages to the spirits. There is infinite variety in the length and shape of stick, the kinds of feathers, and the method of attachment. They are not sent out to the shrines of the spirits until they have been treated, often with drops of honey but always with tobacco smoke. The blowing of smoke from the lungs of the giver is symbolic of a signature on the message.

Among the Pueblo, prayer sticks were planted for the dead at certain times of the year, as they were for various gods and spirits since the dead do not forget. The Pueblos and Navajos in the West placed their prayer sticks near spirit haunts before a ceremony and they served as invitations rather than offerings. Each stick carried the feather symbols of the spirit for whom it was intended, as a substitute for calling the name. At the end of the Soyal ceremony the Pueblo distribute a tremendous number of prayer sticks to the sun, to the God of the Underworld, and to every house in the village. In the days of preparation clan men of all societies made prayer sticks and the simpler prayer feathers.

The Zuni koyemshi or mudheads, a group of sacred funmakers, planted prayer sticks before every performance while fasting. While priests often made the sticks, every citizen also made one for the sun at the beginning of each moon and planted it in his cornfield. After this planting, he had to practice the usual abstinence for four days or the offering would have no power. He made one also for his wife to the moon, but she did not fashion the offering or fast. Prayer sticks were amongs the sacred objects collected by the Navajo chanter. These were two-inch lengths of hollow reed, stuffed with pollen and bird down and fragments of the Navajo jewels. Some have called these sticks cigarettes, for they are symbolically lighted with a crystal.

PROPERTY. Broadly speaking, Indian property was personal. Clothing was owned by the wearer, whether man, woman, or child. Weapons and ceremonial paraphernalia belonged to the man; the implements used in cultivating the soil, in preparing food, dressing skins, and making garments and tent covers, and among the Eskimo the lamp, belonged to the women. In many tribes all raw materials, as meat, corn, and, before the advent of traders, pelts were also her property. Among the tribes of the Plains the lodge or tipi was the woman's but on the N.W. Coast the wooden structures belonged to the men of the family. Communal dwellings were the property of the kinship group, but individual houses were built and owned by the woman. While the land claimed by a tribe, often covering a wide area, was common to all its members and the entire territory was defended against intruders, yet individual occupancy of garden patches was respected. In some instances, as among the Navajo, a section of territory was parceled out and held as clan land, and, as descent in the tribe was traced through the mother, this land was spoken by members of the clan as "my mother's land." Upon such tract the women worked, raising maize, etc., and the product was recognized as their property. The right of a family to gather spontaneous growth from a certain locality was recognized, and the harvest became the personal property of the gatherers. For instance, among the Menominee a family would mark off a section by twisting in a peculiar knot the stalks of wild rice growing along the edge of the section chosen; this knotted mark would be respected by all members of the tribe, and the family could take its own time for gathering the crop. On the Pacific slope, as among the Hupa, varying lengths of river shore were held as private fishing rights by heads of families, and these rights passed from father to son, and were always respected. Clan rights to springs and tracts of land obtained among the Pueblos. The nests of eagles were also the property of the clan within whose domain they were found. The eagle never permanently left the vicinity of the nest where it was born, so, although the bird remained in freedom, it was regarded as the property of the clan claiming the land on which its nest was situated. This claim upon the eagles held good after the clan had left the region and built a new village.

Names were sometimes the property of clans. Those bestowed on the individual members, and, as on the N.W. Coast, those given to canoes and to houses, were owned by "families." Property marks were placed upon weapons and implements by the Eskimo and by the Indian tribes. A hunter established his claim to an animal by his personal mark upon the arrow which inflicted the fatal wound. Among both the Indians and the Eskimo it was customary to bury with the dead those articles which were the personal property of the deceased, either man or woman. In some of the tribes the distribution of all the property of the dead, including the dwelling, formed part of the funeral ceremonies. There was another class of property, composed of arts, trades, cults, rituals, and ritual songs, in which ownership was as well defined as in the more material things. For instance, the right to practice tattooing belonged to certain men in the tribe; the right to say or sing rituals and ritual songs had to be purchased from the owner or keeper. Occasionally a spectator with quick memory might catch a ritual or a song, but he would not dare to repeat what he remembered until he had properly paid for it. The shrine and sacred articles of the clan were usually in charge of hereditary keepers, and were the property of the clan. The peculiar articles of a society were in the custody of an appointed officer; they were property, but could not be sold or transferred. Songs and rites pertaining to the use of healing herbs were property, and their owner could teach them to another on receiving the prescribed payment. the accumulation of property in robes, garments, regalia, vessels, utensils, ponies, and the like, was important to one who aimed at leadership. To acquire property a man must be a skillful hunter and an industrious worker, and must have an able following of relatives, men and women, to make the required articles. All ceremonies, tribal festivities, public functions, and entertainment of visitors necessitated large contributions of food and gifts, and the men who could meet these demands became the recipients of tribal honors. *(See Potlatch.)*

Property right in harvest fields obtained among the tribes subsisting mainly on maize or on wild rice. Among the Chippewa the right in wild-rice lands was not based on tribal allotment, but on occupancy.

PROPERTY AMONG THE TROPICAL FOREST AND MARGINAL TRIBES

The property concepts of Indian peoples often differ radically from whites. There is often collective ownership of utilitarian goods, and even when individual rights are acknowledged in theory they may be overshadowed by moral obligations of sharing with kindred or neighbors. On the other hand, objects that seem trivial figure precisely as those which for the Indian are important enough to establish the basis for differences in wealth. In short, we must at every step envisage the law of property in the perspective of the total culture.

REAL ESTATE

Land is generally conceived by the Indians as something inalienable; any report of their selling and buying it under aboriginal conditions is suspect. Further, major tracts are at least most commonly held by a social group, the individual merely acquiring possessory rights over the section he uses. Among the *Cubeo,* where the clan coincides with the political unit, headsman and council divide the communal territory among adult clansfolk, who acquire property rights for their families in particular plots only after expending labor on making clearings and planting there.

However, the group owning land or values connected with it on a larger scale is not always the same in character. It may be a dialectic division, a patrilineal band, a tribe, a moiety, or a men's society. Among the *Yahgan* it is each of the five dialetic groups taht claims a definite district, but since much of these people's time is spent on the water their interest in landownership is less intense than with the neighboring *Ona,* whose 39 patrilineal bands jealousy guard their respective domains, held by mythological sanctions. Each range was marked off by natural topographical boundaries. Both Fuegian tribes allow encroachment in cases of real necessity and also when a whale is beached by some lucky fluke. The latter windfall creates a superfluity in which all fellow *Yahgan* or *Ona,* respectively, are free to share, and with in comes the rare opportunity of having large assemblies of people in one spot over a space of weeks, hence the chance to celebrate a major festival. Among the *Tehuelche* the several bands claimed each a district and regarded trespass as a fighting matter. Correspondingly, the *Botocudo* hordes guarded their respective bailiwicks by means of sentries stationed at the border procedure similar to that of the *Northern Maidu* in California. Farther north, the *Yaruro* bands are credited with specific hunting grounds. In the Jurua-Purus region each family is said to mark off the grounds it claims by setting bunches of animal hair in the cleft of a stick along the paths. The *Sherente,* whose sense of solidarity was wider than that of most Brazilian Indians, did not allow any property to the single village, but recognized a certain tribal domain. On the upper Xingu the tribe figures as the major landowner, territories being marked off by watercourses; the *Nahukwa,* e.g., occupy one bank of the Kulisehu River; the *Mehinacu,* the other. Of course, a tribe is sometimes limited to a single settlement, as in the case of the *Canella* of Ponto village. In other cases the settlement, such as the *Tucano* maloca, asserted rights over a definite tract. Even when, as among the *Taulipang,* communal rights were not so rigourosly delimited, the people would hesitate to stray more than a few days' journey from their village, being restrained by distrust of their fellow *Taulipang* in other localities and by the fear of being penalized by sorcerers.

It is possible for distinct social units to exercise each a distinctive form of sovereignty. The sparse pieces of ground that permit the growing of quinoa are regarded by the *Chipaya* as tribal property, the total area of 1 km. by 300 m. being divided into strips about 300 by 10 m. each for annual redistribution among the several families. But the pastures nowadays required for sheep and pigs are alloted on a different principle, for they belong to the moieties, whose respective shares are separated by boundaries. If the beasts of one moiety encroach on the other's territory, they are instantly slaughtered and consumed by the aggrieved party.

To sum up, the total domain for economic exploitation is collectively owned, most commonly by a local group (band, localized clan, tribe), but sometimes by other units. In non-Andean South America the chief cannot as a rule be said to exercise sovereign territorial rights. He may act as a supervisor (*Yugua*) with power to grant outsiders temporary fishing privileges (*Cubeo*), but he no more than any other individual freely disposes of the soil. Thee *Chiriguano* chiefs are far from mere figureheads, but though declared to

own the land in certain districts the statement is at
once qualified with the sifnificant addition "not for
their own interest, but on behalf of the tribe."

Within the limits of the generally recognized range
of jurisdiction individuals or families are permitted to
hunt, gather, fish, plant, and build at will. A Barama
Carib may thus be said to own his house and his fields.
The extent and manner of such individual claims,
however, are often modified by coexisting institutions
and idealogies. Among the *Sherente,* e.g., the men's
associations are, apart from other functions, economic
corporations. An individual may choose a spot to be
cleared, but his society performs the task of deforesta-
tion, later aids in weeding and foresting, and has at
least a moral claim to the aftermath of the maize crop.
Again, any joint hunting party, even if numerically insignificant, will distribute their kill among fellow
members. Perhaps still more significantly, the two
most important wild plant species of the region, the
buriti and the babassu, both palms, are not free for
general use, but belong to the four associations, none
of which ventures to trespass on another's stand of
trees without danger of a fight.

Whereas the *Sherente* men own the fields and
houses, the matrilineal *Canella* and *Apinaye* recognize an indisputable feminine proprietorship in both.
As regards the dwellings, however, this can hardly be
conceived as individual: it is rather a corporation of
kinswomen—say, a grandmother with her daughters
and daughters' daughters—that is in control. Further,
the males associated with this group continue to frequent their maternal homes, where their position is far
more secure than that of their brothers-in-law. Like
their *Hopi* brethren in Arizona under corresponding
circumstances, they seem to have a moral claim to
being sheltered by their matrilineal kinswomen even
though no amount of labor expended on a house can
ever give a *Timbira* male a claim to legal
proprietorship.

A curious limitation of individual feminine rights

over cultivated fields is imposed by the *Apinaye*. A couple of men, one from each moiety, assume magico-religious charge of the plantations from the first sowing until they publicly announce the maturity of the crops. In the meantime they pray for a good harvest, plenty of rain, and freedom from insect pests, also supposedly promoting the growth of the plants by songs and magical acts. Any woman who dares remove a single sample from her plot before the official signal is at once punished by the two officials, who break utensils in her dwelling and flog or gash her if she has not taken to her heels.

Ownership of houses and plots must be viewed not according to abstract principles of law, but according to associated ideologies. In some instances there is a clear-cut connection between a proprietor and his property: when a *Cubeo* headman dies, the communal dwelling of which he is reckoned the owner is deserted and his garden is no longer used. In a great many tribes death nullifies property rights in a different sense. Among the Barama *Carib,* anyone's death in the house leads to its abandonment along with that of the clearing in which it is situated. It is tempting to conjecture that as dwellings increase in complexity the natives will recoil from the inconvenience resulting from such change of domicile, but this hypothesis is only partially true. The *Cayapa,* e.g., reoccupy a house if only an infant has passed away, but the demise of any important child, is followed by removal. This is no small matter, for the cutting and adzing of the long, heavy hardwood posts is a major task. Moreover, when the family home is suddenly deserted, the inmates have to put up a temporary shelter while the new structure is in process of erection or must crowd into some relative's house. If the new site is at some distance, this further implies the making of new clearings. In short practical utility is here overriden by idealogical motives.

There are, of course, contrary instances, for tribes naturally differ in the precise balancing of contradictory urges, and their responses may even differ in different periods. The *Yagua* do not now abandon a maloca even after a chief's death, but only when the men's council decides that too many persons have been interred under the floor of the maloca. The *Yecuana,* like contemporary *Yagua,* are not deterred from remaining in their abode by a single death, but if there are several successive deaths the settlement is shifted, possibly at the distance of an hour and a half's journey.

However this may be, fear of the spirit or a vaguer sense of uncanniness or merely the desire to get away from scenes that recall the mourned person frequently leads to evacuation of both huts and plantations. The neighbors of a bereaved *Caingang* family at once give up their settlement to pitch hastily erected lodges in the neighboring woods; and the immediate mourners cut and burn up all the dead person's maize plot, since to partake of the crop would cause a tribesman's death. Desertion of the hut is reported from such diverse peoples as the *Botocudo, Puri, Guarani, Paressi,* and *Cubeo.* The *Yamiaca* destroyed many of the cultivated plants in the deceased man's fields. *Yuracare* practice differs in that it is held proper to harvest the crop of a deserted plantation even though a death is followed by firing of the hut, departure to a considerable distance, and the establishment of new clearings.

What the data cited illustrate is the impermanence of ownership as the result of native superstitions connected with death. Possession of a dwelling evidently has a distinctive meaning when any death precipitates a general migration of the inmates. Supernaturalism produces similar consequences apart from death. The *Aparai* of Kopoko deserted their village and took up residence three days' journey away because a visionary had seen a giant ounce that threated to devour all the people if they stayed in their settlement. Classical illustrations from another area are furnished by the *Apapocuva-Guarani,* who, under the obsession of an impending world catastrophe, were constantly migrating during the 19th century at the behest of messianic shamanchiefs, who promised to guide them to a place of refuge in the form of an earthly paradise revealed to the leaders in visions.

Instability, however, is likewise the inevitable consequence of practical considerations. The technical stage of aboriginal agriculture does not safeguard against a rapid exhaustion of the soil. Lack of fertilizers thus forces the *Aparai* to shift their plantations every 4 to 10 years and corresponding difficulties arise elsewhere. Again the *Canella,* a steppe people, are unable to farm anywhere with their crude implements except in the galeria forests within their territory. As the timber in their vicinity disappears, the journeys to their plots grow longer and longer, finally obliging them to resettle near new clearings. After possibly another decade or so they are able to return to their then reafforested old haunts. The *Chiriguano* are, indeed, said to maintain their rights to abandoned plantations, so that fallow land is claimed and inherited years after effective use; such cases, however, are highly exceptional.

Where the primary economic activity is not farming, but fishing, a different emphasis on immovable property rights is natural. Each *Cubeo* clan jealously guards its fishing rights along the river frontages, and where several clans are involved the weirs are opened and shut according to a definite schedule.

It should be understood that in the economic use of land, as well as with regard to other property, deep-rooted ethical postulates often tend to limit assertion of absolute property rights. Thus, as noted, the plea of necessity is accepted by one *Yahgan* group in admitting aliens of another to their territory; on the upper Xingu anyone is free to shoot fish with bow and arrow, tribal barriers to the contrary notwithstanding; and the *Tucano* do not interfere with travelers who hunt and catch fish while traversing their area.

CHATTELS

Movable property is generally owned by individuals

on the principle that one has a right to whatever one has produced. This fact is attested by various collectors who found it impossible to buy coveted ehtnographica, no matter how commonplace, in the rightful owner's absence.

Several observers emphasize the exclusive rights of women to dispose of their belongings. The tribes in question represent widely divergent status and institutions, including the *Alacaluf*. *Aparai* women, for example, claim whatever they manufacture and use—carrying-baskets, fans, basketry bowls, and pottery. A husband may temporarily help himself to such belongings but never ventures to sell them without his wife's express consent. Several cases are especially noteworthy. A Barama *Carib* wife controls not only her pottery, dress, and personal decoration, but even the baskets made by men; her *Caraja* sister owns houses and boats, and among the uxorious *Palicur* a wife will even interfere with her husband's sale of his personal possessions.

With striking investigators have also been struck by the fact that even young children are solely qualified to dispose of their trinkets and toys. A *Choroti* or *Ashluslay* would never give away his child's belongings without asking his consent. Corresponding observations hold for the *Caraja,* and other central Brazilians. The same attitude has beeen encountered in Patagonia and both of the main Fuegian tribes.

As in the case of real estate, however, the claims of the individual may yield to those of official authority but generally a certain reciprocity is assumed as a foregone conclusion. Though the political heads of many tribes, e.g., in the Chaco, perform exactly the same labors as the rank and file, notable exceptions occur even among relatively simple peoples. The *Caraja* chief neither hunts nor works in the fields beyond directing operations, and he attempts to catch only certain species of fish. But such exemption from ordinary tasks is balanced by duties toward the subjects:

the chief must support the poor, including widows and orphans, as well as entertain visitors. Where chiefs work exactly like common folk, they are, nevertheless, often entitled to gifts of food and drink, which among the *Canella* are likewise due to the councilors. A successful *Macushi* hunter will send part of his kill to the headman. The explorers the upper Xingu distributed beads among the Indians, who promptly passed them on to the chief, but then it was recognized duty to treat his people to food and drink on pain of losing their respect.

The moral obligations which hold between chief and commoner are not restricted to this relationship. "In spite of individualism in ownership there is in fact a certain communism in practice". This principle, formulated for the Barama *Carib,* has much wider application and certain natural consequences. A Barama *Carib,* being permitted to borrow from his coresidents, is inevitably better off de facto if he is the inmate of a large household, though his legal rights over property are not increased thereby. It also follows that, notwithstanding the absence of theoretical communism, differences of wealth in our sense of the term are insignificant. Riches may, indeed, simmer down to the possession of pure luxury articles and the holding of prestige-conferring incorporeal property, matters of great importance to the aborigines, but immaterial from a rational economic point of view. The *Caraja* phrasing of the situation is instructive: "A wealthy man has everything—axes, knives, pots; the poor man has nothing. He goes to the rich man and says, 'Give me a pot or an ax.' The wealthy man is obliged to give it to him." The chiefs as wealthy par excellence are expected to distribute their surplus among the poor. A *Choroti* who has made an extra fine catch of fish or received useful presents at once shares his good luck with his fellows: "Every object has its owner, but since he is charitable and regards all his tribesmen as brothers, he generously shares with them". As already suggested, altruism asserts itself with special force in respect to the basic conditions of human existence. A *Yahgan* who has shot a seal will divide it into seven parts, retaining two for his household and distributing the rest equally among the five fellow tribesmen present; his wife similarly distributes the mussels she has collected. This obligatory unselfishness does not altogether efface prior rights: When a whale is beached, those who first sighted it hold the privilege of keeping choice slices, of distributing the spoils themselves, or of delegating the task to their appointees. Nevertheless, to all intents and purposes the theoretical claimant derives very little more advantage from his legal status because of the tremendous traditional urge to let others partake of his bounty. In view of the widespread South American attitude it is distinctly surprising to learn that the *Yagua* never lend hunting weapons and cooking pots.

Altruism is not necessarily restricted to fellow tribesmen or even to Indians. *Taulipang* hospitality proved veritably embarrassing to a White guest when his hosts pressed bowl after bowl of native dishes upon him and poured out an infinitude of kashiri for his benefit. Similarly, the Indians brought their visitors large bowls, prettily woven food baskets, and 16 manioc flat-cakes from as many households; balls of twine were also favorite forms of presents to visitors. Characteristically, the natives expect presents in return. The *Yahgan* have systematized the practice of gift-offerings. A visitor generally brings fresh meat or a fine hide for his hosts and on parting is likely to receive weapons, raw materials and, if a woman, ornaments and little baskets. Anyone who should fail to offer presents for an indefinite period would become the butt of gossip; and similarly anyone who does not return an equivalent after a reasonable lapse of time is branded as a miser throughout the district. Since it would be a grievous affront to decline a proffered gift, the beneficiary of an extra fine donation is sometimes sorely embarrassed for want of any article of approximately equal value. This institution seems to be quite lacking among the neighboring *Ona*.

It is clear that such mutual property exchange between alien groups can go far toward cementing intertribal relations. A curious variant of the custom binds together several of the *Timbira* tribelets. During a visit the hosts will specially decorate one of their guests, formally present him to the council, and thereby create him their courtesy chief, a great honor that invests him with quasi-consular functions. On a return visit the former hosts go to this champion of their interests, who is expected to find quarters for them in a house owned by his kinswomen and to board them. In 1931 the entire body of these honorary chiefs numbered 34 among the *Canella;* they are called King Vultures and share certain ceremonial rights of active tribal chiefs. Generosity towards their electors is a primary duty of the King Vultures; they must give presents to the group that chose them and are expected to conform to the highest *Timbira* standards in their general behavior. On the other hand, they share with other officers of honorific order of "hamren" claims on the first part of the kill when hunters bring in a large game bag. Notwithstanding their enhanced standing and the prerogatives attached thereto, many King Vultures find the associated obligations so burdensome that they abdicate according to a fixed procedure.

Intermediate between individually and communally controlled possessions are those belonging to a family in the narrower sense of the term. Thus, a *Yahgan* canoe is made by the man, but propelled and tended by the woman, so that neither is entitled to exclusive ownership, which may be said to be vested in the group composed of the father, mother, and children so far as they are still with their parents. Here, as in many other cases, the individual family forms at the same time the economic unit. Different arragements may result in complications of property law. Thus, the *Macushi* families have each its own plantation and crop, but the processing of vegetable food—the preparation of flour, cassava bread, and festive beverages—requires implements used by all members of the common residence. It is *Cubeo* practice to have cooperative labor on objects like canoes or weir screens, which are difficult to manufaccture, and to have the whole clan share in their use. Manioc ovens are likewise used by anyone in the house.

Property marks occur in the Chaco. Sheep are shorn in distinctive fashion and indicate the owner, and for the same purpose the *Ashluslay* mark their cloaks with designs. It is, however, possible that the idea has been copied from white men's horse brands.

As already suggested, the aboriginal point of view often stresses the value of nonutilitarian objects, so that sheer luxury articles according to our standards assume an inordinate importance. Ceremonial regalia and other decorative property correspond to our pearls and diamonds. Thus, a complete *Cubeo* dance costume is reckoned the equivalent of the bride-price. *Bororo* women specially prize certain neck ornaments, which are passed down from a grandmother to her daughters and granddaugthers. The prestige derived from the possession of these heirlooms thwarts an ehtnographer's efforts to buy them for even incredibly high prices. In some instances labor expended on the production of a decorative outfit indicates the importance attached to them. One *Chacobo* youth was seen wearing a neck and chest ornament composed of 1,506 front teeth of a particular monkey species, implying that he had killed 189 monkeys in order to attain his wish, not counting the work of trimming the edges with red toucan feathers.

As in North America, persons ostensibly owning ceremonial emblems may turn out to be mere custodians, the actual proprietorship being vested in the community or its representatives. Though the dance regalia of the *Kejara Bororo* are scattered over the settlement, only the chief has the right to settle on their sale, and he rarely decides to do so without the support of his confidant and heads of the clans. For corresponding reasons it is extremely difficult to buy *Tucano* dance regalia: they were considered communal property, the individual holding them being merely a keeper who was not qualified to dispose of them without general consent. Ordinarily, the ethnographer is able to obtain only isolated pieces that happen to be heirlooms in individual households or to get the complete outfit from a chief whose settlement has broken up.

The stock in trade of a medicine man can be classed under the head of chattels when viewed as tangible objects or as incorporeal property insofar as a vision or other supernatural sanction copyrights their use. Widespread shamanistic possessions of a material nature include gourd rattles, carved wooden stools, plant emetics, and crystal rocks, which latter are constantly worn or carried about for use in curing practices. All of them are typical of Guana. The *Apinaye* recognize a vast number of medicinal plants as antidotes against illness springing from the shadowsouls of plants and animals which have pathogenically intruded into the patient's body. Such remedies are not restricted to the shamans. As a matter of fact, a newborn infant's grandmother at once stores his navel cord in a little basket together with other medicines; if the child suffers from some eye trouble, a little of the navel cord is scraped off, the scrapings being then mixed with water and used as a lotion. Other contents of these receptacles include porcupine quills as a cure of snake bites, neck pendants with snail shells against the jaundice, the root of a forest shrub to provide an infusion against catarrhs and stomach ache, and a host of others.

Slaves form a special class of chattels whose social significance is discussed in the article on slavery. They generally originate in warfare, though by no means all tribes made a practice of keeping captives. The motivation for the custom varies. Whereas in some case prisoners taken in warfare are impressed into economic service so as to consitute a vertiable lower caste (Panama), the *Tupinamba* waged war mainly to capture enemies for ceremonial slaughter and consumption. The *Caraja,* on the other hand, generally engage in fighting in order to steal the wives and children of their enemies, the adult males being killed. The prisoners are subjected to slave labor, the women being further conscripted as sex-mates for *Caraja* bachelors.

INCORPOREAL PROPERTY

Though rarely so labeled, incorporeal property exists in many forms, even among the simpler south American peoples. This should be obvious from the fact that this category logically includes any exclusive privilege, whether held by single persons or a group. Thus we have to reckon with the prerogatives of chiefs and shamans, but also with those of organizations, favored hereditary classes, and men as opposed to women. The right to eat human flesh, open to both sexes among the *Tupinamba,* was reserved for *Witoto* males, hence is part of their incorporeal property. Similarly, the knowledge of secret ceremonials, wearing of masquerade costumes, use of a clubhouse, or playing of sacred flutes falls under this head if the female sex is barred on principle from taking part in relevant activities. It is inessential whether or not the privilege in question finds embodiment in a tangible way, for what counts is not owning the object, such as a mask, but the privilege of making and using it.

Every *Bororo* treasures feathers for use in dances, but the method of using them and the very techniques of manufacturing ornaments from them are linked with particular clans, and the chief alone holds the monopoly for making the crowns worn by leaders in the ceremonials. That one clan should arrogate to itself an ornamental style appropriate to another is hardly conceivable for these Indians. The Caterpillar people, e.g., glue red feathers on their ceremonial bowstaves, whereas the Porcupine clansfolk have a specific fashion of alternating bands of different color and length on their articles. Even the pennantlike wings projecting from the penis-sheaths worn on special occasions, though all painted in black and red colors and trimmed with white down, differ according to clans in the arrangement of these elements and in superadded features. Thus, the Tapir clan pennant bears in the center a red puma figure (one of the linked "totems" of the group) and that of the "Chief" clan is cut out at one extremity into the semblance of an alligator. Similary, an ornamental pendant of armadillo claws bears the symbol of the clan, which is indicated by the color of the central cotton fringe as well as by the number and shape of the mother-of-pearl framgents inlaid in a rosinous matrix. Not only the clans, but the dual divisions hold dinstinctive prerogatives, only the chief's moiety being entitled to make the bull-roarers which play so important a part in *Bororo* festivities.

Incorporeal property is also amply developed among the *Ge*. The four *Caingang* sections—subdivisions of their moieties—are distinguished by their painted facial patterns, say, a small circle in the middle of the forehead; the five subdivisions of the *Aweicoma* correspondingly differ in their body paint. Among the *Apinnaye* red and black paint normally characterize the Kolti and the Kolre moiety, respectively; and village chiefs are always Kolti. Most of the social units into which the *Canella* are split have particular stations which they take up on festive occasions and exercise peculiar rights and functions; the two Rainy Season moieties, e.g., are contrasted by the application of red and black pigment, respectively, and the logs they carry in races are colored accordingly.

Sherente individuals, clans, moieties, age classes, associations may all be credited with incorporeal property. Precisely as in North America, a visionary may acquire from his supernatural patron chants, styles of decoration, and material objects, such as a box enabling him to stave off a world catastrophe and to shorten a solar eclipse. Articles thus obtained should be handled only by the original beneficiary, though in exceptional instances he may convey them to a brother or son; since, however, there is a belief that transfer hastens the visionary's death, he is likely to make the transfer only when his end is approaching. True visions are restricted to the male sex. The clans of this tribe are largely connected with the preparation of ceremonial adornment, most of which is manufactured for either moiety by one of its three original clans. Members of one clan have the most extensive tonsure used in the tribe and wear a red cotton cord on the forehead, and deer or tapir hoofs hanging down the back. Again, although any one may play with balls made of maize husks, only the Prase clan is entitled to throw balls of rubber enclosing a core of dry grass. The moieties, though sharing black body paint, differ in their designs—series of horizontal lines as against series of circles. In worship, the moiety residing on the south side of the village is linked with the sun, the northern complement with the moon; and an individual communicates with the god and the spirits subordinate to him that belong with his moiety. As to the age classes, each of the bachelors' grades owns a form of hair sheath and of body paint peculiar to it. The associations, apart from the material possessions noted in a previous section, hold special sites within the village circle, and also names (to be discussed presently), and one of them had the privilege of forming the vanguard on the march or in battle. To these manifold prerogatives might be added the right to diverse emblems or to special treatment accorded to various dignitaries and their wives.

Incorporeal property is further exemplified by sacred spells, songs, and other possessions of magico-religious nature.

A Barama *Carib* shaman carefully "guards the proprietary interest" in his incantations, which are regarded as peculiar to him, being either revealed in a trance or invented by himself, the chant taught by a spirit during the medicine man's novitiate serves to summon it on subsequent occassions. Certain appurtenances of the office, notably the rattle enclosing pebbles that represent the shaman's familiars, are, of course, material objects, but the right to use them seems distinctive of the trained medicine man.

Similarly, the full-fledged *Yahgan* yekamush is distinguished by a special type of feather decoration, and because only men are allowed to wear it, no woman, even though practicing sorcery, is reckoned as in the fullest sense a shaman. The definite call to office consists in receiving the gift of a chant from one's supernatural patron, and when a tyro spontaneously intones such a song he is recognized as a potential practitioner who will be qualified by several months' training under an experienced professional. Subsequently when a party of *Yahgan* plan a hunting trip on the water, it is the shaman's prerogative to lure the spirits of the game animals by intoning a certain tune. Other privileges relate to the treatment of the shaman's corpse, which unlike that of common folk, is painted red all over and adorned with this distinctive feather diadem.

The siginficance of songs appears clearly among the *Apapocuva Guarani.* Usually acquired in a dream of some dead kinsman, they are all regarded as sacred, and their possession and nature determines social standing. Young people lack songs, hence are regarded as uninspired; adults of either sex have songs for private purposes; medicine men or women, possessing more of them, are qualified to lead in the dances; but the highest grade is reserved for the owners of the most sacred chants, who direct the principal ceremony and act at once as chiefs and shamans. A Mataco acquires exclusive rights to sing a song by dreaming about some singing bird and remembering its tune. *Caraja* songs and dances are at least in part invented by individuals, who transmit them in their family lines; "others know them, but do not execute them".

Under this head may be further mentioned the

magical formulae reported from the *Taulipang* and also in less pretentious form from the *Aparai* and *Jivaro*. Their purpose is to drive away disease by reciting spells of the appropriate character. That is, the declaimer refers to animals assumed to stand in a special relationship to the ailment to be removed. Such formulae are rarely uttered except in the bosom of one's family and are not readily communicated to Europeans. Some of them are prophylactic. There are likewise evil charms which cause illness. All recitations are supposed to be preceded by the telling of a brief myth.

Names constitute a particularly important category of property. South American Indians share the common primitive reticence concerning. The *Taulipang* suppose a name to be intimately linked with the bearer and hardly ever employ it. The owner certainly will not pronounce it, but is somewhat less reluctant about nick-names and does not mind at all uttering appellations bestowed on him by whites. Corresponding attitudes occur among the *Yecuana*. However, the personal names are not necessarily inalienable; they may be exchanged as a mark of mutual affection and, in some tribes are altered in order to excape the wrath of spirits (*Tupinamba*) or after the killing of a brave enemy whose name is then assumed (*Island Carib*). To whites the *Guarani,* too, do not divulge native names, which are considered a kind of souls and are changed in case of illness in order to separate the disease from the patient. In the upper Xingu area, as among the *Palicur* there is very little disinclination to uttering masculine names. The *Yahgan* call a child after the place of his birth, altering the name at his initiation according to the site of the festival, and dropping it after the death of a namesake. Persons born in a canoe receive a special appellation indicative of the fact and are distinguished from one another by nicknames.

Names are not always the property of individuals, but may belong to social units as well. Even if the connection is not formally crystallized, it is indicated by the bestowal of some ancestor's name, as among the *Pilaga.* The five *Aweicoma* subdivisions have each a set of personal names. *Sherente* moieties own distinctive sets of masculine names, which are passed on from grandfather or great-uncle to grandson and great-nephew. On the other hand, feminine names, oddly enough, belonged to the men's associations, which conferred them according to an obscure principle somehow connected with the society of the girl's father. The *Apinaye,* who lack comparable men's organizations, vest ownership of all personal names in their moieties. Ideally the transfer is from maternal uncle to sister's son and from maternal aunt to sister's daughter, but sometimes the mother's maternal uncle, the maternal grandmother or her sister, or the mother's adoptive sister are the name-conveyors. With the *Canella* only boys obtain their names from matrilineal kinsmen, girls getting theirs from patrilineal female relatives. Theoretically, a man bestows his names on his sister's son and she in return gives hers to her brother's daughter; but in the absence of appropriate recipients of the proper sex, substitutions are allowable, but always on the principle of reciprocity so that the male name-transferrer must have a daughter to whom a patrilineal kinsman of hers can give her set.

The importance attached to names appears from the frequency of *Ge* ceremonies connected with the bestowal of names. It is further demonstrated by the social consequences of bearing a given name. Thus the *Apinaye* distinguish between "little" and "great" names, the latter imposing specific ceremonial rights or obligations on the bearer or his kin. For example, men called Vanme and Kt'tam, each representing one of the moieties, have the privilege of first shouldering their team's log in a log race; the girls Amdyi' and Koko' serve as female auxiliaries in the youths' initiation; and Panti's father is obliged to start a special plantation in order to provide a feast for the people.

Among the *Canella,* names determine membership in one or the other of the agamic Rainy Season moieties, in the masculine plaza groups, and in certain festive societies. Finally, a *Bororo* personal name determines into which clan or subclan the bearer is to marry.

INHERITANCE

Many tribes have no rules of inheritance because virtually or even literally no legacy remains. This extreme is illustrated by the *Yahgan.* who make a point of destroying the deceased person's possessions, including his dwelling. Eager to obliterate all possible mementos that might recall the dead and renew the sense of their bereavement, the mourners cast a man's spear into the sea or burn up a woman's paddle. If there were other facilities available for transport, a widower has even been known to annihilate his wife's canoe. Sometimes, however, these Indians compromised by exchanging valuable implements for equivalents owned by an outsider. The mourner thus evaded the necessity of constantly seeing the actual objects employed by the deceased and yet retained the use of valuable, if not indispensable, tools or weapons.

Although the Fuegians exemplify a limiting case, annihiliation of economic values at a relative's death commonly reduces the heritage, as already explained with regard to habitations. Although the deceased *Mataco's* animals are not killed, all his personal belongings are cremated. His house, too, is pulled down, but its materials are allowed to go into the construction of a new one only 10 yards away. The domiciliary situation of *Cayapa* mourners has already been described. They exhibit some individual variability concerning treatment of chattels, ordinarily keeping one or two articles, yet often the "legacy" is deposited with the burial or destroyed, for a prevalent attitude coincides with Fuegian mentality in trying to get rid of anything that might recall the mourned person to mind.

The sacrificing of material goods is thus not by any means restricted to the simplest peoples and turns up in an exceedingly large number of tribes, though the extent of the self-denial practiced varies. A representative series of illustrations may be cited in support of this statement.

Common *Aparai* fold are interred, and shamans or chiefs are cremated on a funeral pyre, but in both cases the material possessions of the deceased accompany them. The *Tiatinagua (Tacanan)* bury belongings with the corpse, the *Yamiaca (Southwest Panoan)* go beyond this, also destroying many of the cultivated plants in the deceased person's fields.

Whereas in the foregoing cases little remains for distribution among the survivors, other tribes manage to salvage some property for the accepted heirs. A *Siusi* son will put an ax and sundry trifles into his father's coffin, but cling to his most important tools, weapons, and ornaments. The Barama *Carib* desert the dwelling and put food, clothing, and articles of decoration with the corpse, but bows, arrows, and pottery go to the kindred, with sons getting the lion's share. The *Yagua* demolish a dead person's pottery and weapons, but household pottery and minor artifacts remain; dogs are inherited by the son if he is old enough or otherwise by a brother, and pet animals are appropriated by the children.

It naturally makes a considerable difference whether or not the house and plantations are retained. *Apinaye* survivors dispose of chattels by depositing them in the grave or use them to compensate the corpse-decorators and gravediggers. Some minor object might remain for the dead person's children. Here, however, the preservation of stable dwellings and of farms modifies the picture; and inasmuch as these forms of property are invariably owned by women, the daughters and other kinswomen of the deceased fall heir to them.

In some cases the coming of Caucasian innovation has altered ancient usage. In the first third of the last century, the *Sherente-Shavante* are known to have buried tools and weapons with the corpse and cremated all residual possessions. In recent times, however, the value set on guns, iron implements, and trade clothes has led the people to give up the traditional practice of destruction, yet no fixed rules of distribution have evolved, so that disputes often arise now. Siblings, spouses, parents, and children are all potential heirs, but, interestingly enough, no one inherits from an uncle despite the fact that both the father's and still more the mother's brother play a significant part in the social life. Of great suggestiveness in this context are the data concerning the *Goajiro*, whom 16th- and 17th-century accounts describe as nomadic gatherers, but whose latter-day economy revolves largely about cattle. This comparatively new type of property, along with personal possessions, theoretically passes from maternal uncle to sister's son in accordance with the matrilineal system of the people. However, it is only the man's eldest sister's senior son who ranks as legatee. What is more, a man will deliberately strive to thwart the principle by transferring livestock to his own sons during his lifetime, so that actually few, if any, head of cattle remain for the nephew after his uncle's demise.

The disposal of widows constitutes a special phenomenon fully considered in the article on Social Organization. Suffice it to say that the principal types known from other continents are represented, viz, the levirate, filial and, more rarely, nepotic inheritance. The latter, characteristically, is reported from the matrilineal *Goajiro*. In general, however, it cannot be said that the rules of inheritance are very conspicuously related to those of descent. This is doubtless due to the factors set forth above, viz, the material reduction, if not elimination of movable goods; the frequent abandonment of houses and fields; and the impermanence of agricultural holdings.

PUNISHMENT by recognized authorities of a social unit is directed against persons who have in some manner offended the laws or mores of the groups. Among North American Indians, methods of punishment varied greatly, depending on local custom and the nature of the offense committed. Among the Yuroks, there was no punishment whatsoever. Disputes of all kinds were settled by negotiations between the two parties. No social body or individual had authority to punish wrongdoers, and punishment—even in the form of retaliation—was considered the equivalent of a new crime, even when revenge was seen as morally justified.

Among Eskimos in Alaska and Greenland, disputants settled their differences by facing each other in a song duel, called a Nith Song. Each party sang insulting verses at the other. Facility in the art of singing and wit were highly valued. The issue was settled by other villagers, who gathered to watch the song duel, and who indicated their preference for one contestant or the other with applause. Right and wrong played no part in the decision—the ritual duel was aimed at ventilating hostilities, not at reaching a "just" settlement in terms we would understand today.

Public crimes among the Eskimos were handled differently. A person who violated traditional hunting mores was thought to have offended the souls of the animals on whom the group depended for sustenance. Such an offender was required to abstain from eating certain foods, or to avoid sexual activities, for a certain time as a penance. Murderers could be dealt with still more directly. If someone was considered a murderer, a person from his village went about obtaining the approval of everyone in the community, including the murderer's relatives, to seek revenge in the name of the whole group. If everyone agreed, he could then execute the murderer without fear of retaliation.

Among the Navajo, law was based on shared customs and values, and there was no institutionalized means of enforcing these laws. People who deviated from them were dealt with through public ridicule and ostracism. Parties to a dispute often settled the issue by compromise and arbitration. Aliens and witches were dealt with by force; witches could even be killed.

Among the Cheyenne, murder was punished by banishing the offender for a period of from five to ten years. Someone who broke the rules of the tribal buffalo hunt was severely beaten; sometimes his bones would be broken, and personal property such as horses, weapons, or a tipi, could be destroyed.

In Oregon, members of a tribe could become debt-slaves to others through the infringement of tribal laws, such as those prohibiting striking someone or destroying another person's property. Debt-slaves could regain their freedom by paying off their debt, or they might be ransomed by relatives.

PYRITE was rather widely used in both North and South America. It in not unusual for Maya pyrite mirrors and the firestones in Eskimo graves and those of the Maine Red Paint People to be altered to limonite, a possible scale of the rapidity of pyrite alteration.

In Labrador, northern Canada, and Alaska, the Eskimo used pyrite to strike fire as did the Indians of northwest and northern Canada and Newfoundland. It may be mentioned that the Aleutians to obtain fire strike together two flints rubbed in sulfur, the spark falling on lint powdered with sulfur which is obtained from the nearby volcanoes. At Point Barrow, the Eskimo miners believe the pyrite, which occurs massive and as spherical concretions, to have fallen from the sky and hence it is called "firestone." Among the Cumberland Bay Eskimo snapping a whip with a piece of pyrite at the tip drives away evil spirits. These people believe that some seals break a breathing hole through the ice with a stone held under the flipper. A hunter, if he kills such a seal, should, without looking at the stone, throw it over his shoulder, which changes it into pyrite and thereafter insures good luck in sealing. Iglulik Eskimo protect themselves from thunderstorms by laying out an amulet consisting of pyrite, a piece of white skin, and a small kamik sole. The Haneragmiut Eskimo procure pyrite for fire-making to the northwest of Coronation Bay and trade this to the Copper Eskimo.

It is common in the Mound Builder mounds of Ohio, that of the Muskingum Valley presumably coming from the adjoining hills where pyrite abounds. In 1826 an English traveler, Ash, found in a mound what from its luster he believed a large lump of gold. His laborers carefully covered up their work and secretly in a private room gave it the fire test. Their "gold" turned "black, filled the place with a sulfurous odor and then burst into 10,000 fragments."

Pyrite was used extensively by Aztecs as inlays in their mosaics, as eyes for their statues, and, well polished, as mirrors. Pyrite mirrors were used in the sun-cult, to concentrate the rays of the sun and so light the sacred fire at noon on the days of the vernal equinox and summer solstice. Crushed marcasite was used as a face powder by certain Aztec priests.

The natives of Tierra del Fuego who, like the Eskimo, used iron pyrite for fire-making, obtained it from at least two mines known to us; one on the northern part of Tierra del Fuego Island and another near Mercury Sound, Clarence Island. As its use to produce fire is noted as early as A.D. 1580, it was doubtless a pre-European custom. The Fuegians prize it highly. Their neighbors, the Patagonians, not only used it for making fire but weighted the globular hide bags at the end of their bolas with it. Presumably they obtained it from the Fuegian country.

QUARTZ. Rock crystal and quartz, jasper and chalcedony were used by practically all tribes. Agate was known to the Indians of British Columbia, eastern Canada, the North Atlantic states, Virginia, the Mississippi Valley, the northern plains, the western mountains, the American Pacific coast, and the Pueblos. It was also used by the Aztecs, the Mayas, and the Peruvians and the Indians of Costa Rica, Panama, Colombia, Bolivia, British Guiana, Chile, Argentina, and Brazil. Carnelian artifacts have been found in Georgia, Illinois, the western mountain states, California, Oregon, and Washington, and among the Pueblo ruins. It was used by the Aztecs and the Mayas and the Indians of Costa Rica, Panama, Montserrat Island, Lesser Antilles, Colombia, Venezuela, Ecuador, British Guiana, and Brazil. In certain Colombian graves, as many as 8,000 beads, largely carnelian, have been found together with pebbles of carnelian, suggesting a stream origin. Such beads are readily sold to the present-day Indians living to the east, and a brightly colored one may be worth a mule. The local source is not sufficient for today's demand and beads are actually imported from Germany to satisfy it.

In North America amethyst was used by the Eskimo and by the Indians of eastern Canada, the southeastern states, the upper Mississippi Valley, and California, and by the Pueblos and Aztecs. It was also used by the aborigines of Costa Rica, Panama, Montserrat Island, the Lesser Antilles, and Peru. Smoky quartz was used by the Eskimo, the Indians of Newfoundland, Rhode Island, the southeastern states, upper Mississippi Valley, Colorado, Washington,

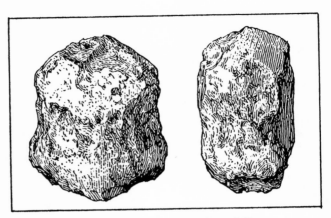

Roughly grooved hammer of quartzite.

Oregon, and California, and the Pueblos and Peruvians. Other species of quartz were used as follows: Moss, agate (Saskatchewan, New York, southeastern States, Wyoming, Colorado, Texas, Utah, California Oregon, and the Pueblos); rose quartz (New Jersey, Maryland, Virginia, Georgia, South Dakota, Aztecs, and Brazil); gold quartz (Georgia, California, and Arizona); citrine (Georgia, upper Mississippi Valley, and Dakota); prase (Pueblos and Aztecs); bloodstone (Oregon, Aztecs, Panama, and Peru); chrysoprase (Peru, Colombia, and perhaps California); iris (Mound Builders); Aventurine quartz (Aztecs and Mayas); plasma (Aztecs and Panama); and onyx (southeastern States and Washington).

AMETHYST
The Aztecs had some amethyst of fine color.

ROCK CRYSTAL
Quartz was doubtless obtained largely in river, marine, and glacial gravels but pits were sunk on quartz veins in New England, New York, and in the Appalachian Mountains of Virginia and North Carolina and it must have been a byproduct of mica

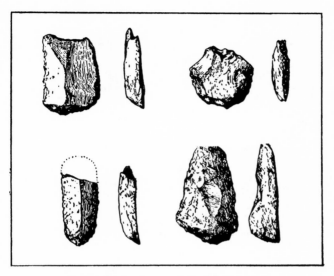

Quartzite scrapers of duck-bill type.

mining. Quartz was, indeed, quarried at many places
in the Piedmont region of the southeastern states, but
since here, as elsewhere, it occurs so frequently as pebbles, gravels were the main source. Twelve miles above the
falls on the James River was a Christall Rocke
wherewith the Indians doe head many of their arrows.
When Albert de la Pierria founded Beaufort, Fla.,
about 1563, the Indians brought the Frenchmen
presents of "pearls, crystals, silver, etc." In 1587, the
Frenchmen of Charles-fort were given by the chief,
Ovade, pearls, fine crystal, and silver ore said to come
from 10 days' journey inland (Georgia probably)
where the "inhabitants of the countrey did dig the
same at the foote of certaine high mountaines where
they found of it in very good quantitie. Being joyfull
to understand such good newes and to have come to
the knowledge of that which they most desired" the
Frenchmen returned to their fort. When John Verar-
zanus, a Florentine writing in 1524, states that the
Florida natives were the possessors not only of crystal

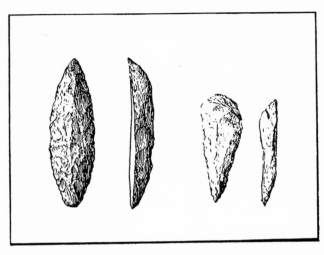

Blades of quartzite.

but also of turquoise, we become skeptical of his mineralogic attainments.

The Hot Springs, Ark., rock crystal locality was as well known to the Indians as to present-day mineralogists. Rock crystal and arrowheads made of it are common in Arkansas Indian graves. In Cavelier's account of La Salle's voyage, he says "about 50 leagues from the spot where we were [mouth of Rio Bravo, Tex.] were two or three mountains on the banks of a river from which were taken red stones as clear as crystal," possibly a distorted reference to Hot Springs.

Father Gravier (1900) in his voyage on the Mississippi in 1700 "found in a small basket," in a temple in the village of the Taensas, a subtribe of the Natches Indians, "a small piece of rock Crystal."

The Navajos are stated to light their ceremonial fire from the sun by means of crystal. The Pueblo Indians of the upper Rio Grande during their rain ceremonies beat the drum to imitate thunder, and rubbed together pebbles of white quartz to produce an incandescent glow simulating lightning. At Pecos, New Mex., a

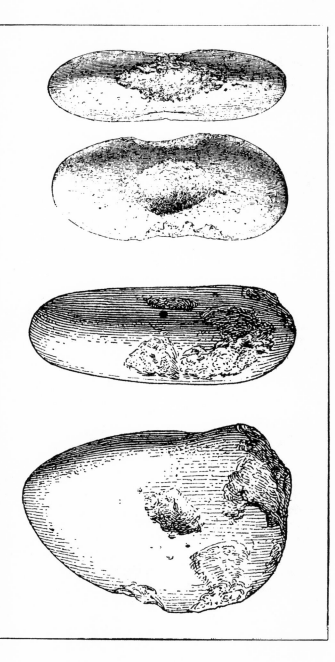

Hammer of quartzite with pitted faces and battered end and sides.

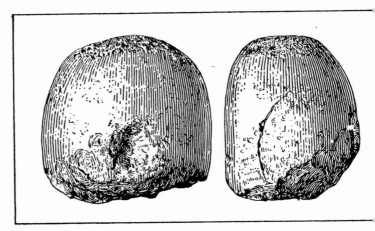

Hammer-anvil of quartzite.

cylinder, set in a rectangle with a shallow groove into which the cylinder exactly fitted, both of white vein quartz. The cylinder is about 3 inches long and 1½ inches in diameter. Knowing that "lightning sets" still were used in religious ceremonies at San Ildefonsa, that night he rubbed the cylinder in the groove and finally the stones "became visible a strange pale glow which flickered and died for all the world like distant lightning." Here we have a perfected machine perhaps 700 years old; the first Indian to observe the luminescence of quartz must have done so centuries earlier.

The Hopi used rock crystal in religious ceremonies, as well as in divinition. It was also used in the religious ceremonies of the Zuni, being, for example, placed on certain fraternal shrines, and by other Pueblos it was used to reflect sun into kivas and into medicine bowls. Rock crystal was used in diagnosing disease both by the Pueblos and the Pima. Rock crystal is a common charm among the Yuma Indians. The Australian medicine man parelleled his American confrere in many uses of rock crystal in the curative art.

According to a Shasta legend, a long time ago there was in the East a white and glistening firestone like the purest quartz. The coyote brought this to the Indians, and thus fire originated. Quartz was supposed by the Chippewas to protect its owner against thunderstorms as the thunderbird would no more hurt it than a hen "the egg she has laid." The most prized possession of the Cherokee medicine man was a rock-crystal-like mineral once embedded in the head of the Horned Serpent so prominent in Iroquois mythology. It was invaluable in treating the sick and foretold which of the braves should shun certain raids as their deaths were shown by it to be probable. Among the Ojibways white flint was called *mik kwum me wow beek,* or ice stone and as the name was also doubtless applied to rock crystal, it parallels the Greek from which our word crystal was derived. Similarly certain Alaskan Eskimo believe rock crystals are the centers of ice masses so solidly frozen that they become stone: they are, therefore, prized amulets. A Mandan medicine man, among other wonderful performances vouched for by white witnesses, could roll a snowball in his hand "so that it at length becomes hard, and is converted into a white stone, which when struck emits fire." Near the village of Lansingburgh, N.Y., is Diamond Rock, a mass of Quebec sandstone containing innumerable quartz crystals which glitter in the sunlight. According to Mohawk tradition, these are the joyful tears of a devoted mother upon her reunion with a wandering son.

The Aztecs had crystal mines and these come from the mountains on the Gulf coast between Veracruz and Coatzacualco River; that is, those of Chinantla and the Province of Mixtecas.

The present-day medicine men among the Yucatan Indians pretend that they can see hidden things with the aid of rock crystal, and it is successfully used in the diagnosis of the ills of their patients. When Hans Stade was about to be eaten by his eastern Brazilian captors, an old woman of the tribe shaved off his eyebrows

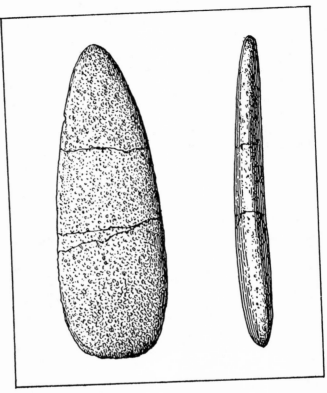

Quartzite muller-pestle.

with a rock-crystal razor. The Venezuelan Indian lover must shape for his beloved, as a betrothal gift, a cylindrical bead of rock crystal to be worn around her neck.

QUILL WORK. Indian quill weaving and embroidery were at one time among the most prevalent arts practiced. The early skin robes, moccasins, and quivers were elaborately decorated with porcupine quills in woven or embroidered patterns by the Northern Algonquian tribes (Ojibwa, Cree, and Ottawa). Quill work in birch bark was not developed to so great an extent by the Iroquois as among the other Woodland

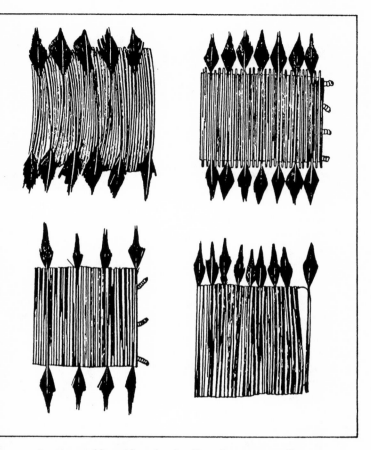

Sections of head bands of yellow-hammer quills.

tribes and is not carried on today. Only a few examples of the woven quill work remain.

Fine geometric designs in well blended colors were developed in the weaving. Elaborate techniques that are no longer used were practiced.

In the embroidery work some delicate floral patterns were worked out with very fine, young quills, but most of the embroidery designs were geometric because of the stiffness of the quills.

The craft workers sorted the quills as to diameter and length, dyed them various colors as desired, and kept them in cases made from bladders of the elk or some other larger animal. The undyed white quills, with their brown tips, were used effectively in working out the early designs.

In the quill embroidery, sinew was used as thread and a sharp thorn served as a primitive needle. A steel awl later replace the thorn. When the quills were to be applied they were soaked for an hour or more in water, flattened between the teeth, then fastened to the skin with the sinew thread. Holes through which the sinew thread could be drawn were made in the buckskin with a fine awl. Patterns seem not to have been necessary to the early workers, but old tribal designs were used repeatedly.

QUIPU. As far as is now known, no form of writing was ever used in the Andean area before the Spanish Conquest, and it seems most unlikely that pre-Columbian writing will ever be discovered. Suggestions have been advanced that certain motives found on pottery, cloth, and stone represent hieroglyphic symbols, but these are all too few and too symmetrically placed to be conceivable as linguistic symbols. Some are probably heraldic motives and others may represent divination or games, but most are purely ornamental. The fact is that the Andean peoples possessed substitutes for writing which were so satisfactory that they probably never felt the need for anything more elaborate.

In *Inca* used an ingenious apparatus, the quipu (KHIP, "knot"), which consisted of a main cord from which hung smaller strings with groups of simple knots on them at intervals. Frequently, subsidiary strings are attached to the main pendant strings, and often the strings are distinguished by color or method of twisting. A large number of quipus found in graves on the Central and South Coast (Chancay to Ica) have

Wooden rattle, Tlingit.

east, gourd rattles were used in the diagnosis and cure of disease, and the Iroquois False Face Society used turtle-shell rattles in healing rites. Southwest tribes used gourd rattles to imitate the sound of hoped-for rain. Tlingit chiefs of the northwest coast used wooden rattles carved in the shape of a raven as a chairperson's gavel. When hunting, Eskimos shook rattles to attract seals into the water.

Sometimes the two types of rattles were combined, as when deer hooves were attached to a tortoise-shell rattle then tied behind the knee to sound in time with a dancer's motion. This rattle was used widely, as by Hopi men in Snake and Kachina Dances and by women dancers in the Southeast. Today sleighbells may replace it.

Among some groups, including Eskimo and Pueblo,

rattles were children's toys. But in general they were reserved for sacred rites. In the Plains Indians' sign language, the sign for "rattle" was the basis for every word meaning "sacred." In a large ancient archaeological site in Kentucky (c. 3000 B.C.) rattles were found only in graves. Rattles were often made or decorated in symbolic ways, The turtle and raven, for example, were figures from tribal creation myths.

RESIDENCE CUSTOMS, patterns of residence, are usually dependent on kinship or other social ties and often influenced by environmental considerations. Among the Eskimo, for example, the difficulty of finding enough food to sustain large groups was reflected in the predominance of the nuclear family as the most common residential unit. Even these units, however, were often broken up by high mortality rates. In central and eastern arctic regions, snow, earth, stone, and whalebone houses were used by individual families. These structures became useless with the arrival of summer, at which time their occupants abandoned them. The next season, the remains of these houses could be claimed by anyone who happened to find them. Winter settlements occasionally reached a population of one hundred, although sometimes less than fifty persons was a more common size. Also, winter settlements were composed of different families each year, since the same families did not always return to the same place.

Similar residence customs arose in a quite different, although equally harsh environment—the desert regions around the Great Basin and in Nevada. Here, single families were the basic residential units among such Indians as the Shoshoni and the Paiute. Related groups of families sometimes lived together for brief periods, usually during the winter months. Occupying villages for no more than two or three weeks at a time, such groups frequently banded together for a rabbit or antelope drive, which could be pursued more effectively with larger numbers of hunters. None of these settlements, however, reached the proportions of a permanent village.

On the Northwest Coast, where subsistence activities revolved around fishing, permanent villages of up to a thousand people were common. These were usually located at or near the mouths of streams. After the establishment of European trading posts in the area, villages often grew up near them instead of near the more traditional fishing spots. These villages were usually composed of members of a single kinship group, such as a clan, although the population of some of them included a number of separate kinship groups. The Haida Indians lived on the Queen Charlotte Islands. Among them, the nuclear family was the basic residential units, although it shared a large plank house with the extended avunculocal family of which it was a part. Groups of such houses were organized into villages. The entire village population usually made up a clan, which was composed of each of the avunculocal extended families.

Many Indian peoples of the Plains area of North America were seasonally nomadic hunters who travelled in small groups or larger bands. The Cheyenne and Arapaho bands returned to favorite campsites each winter. Among these tribes, men lived with their wive's families. Among the Blackfoot and Assiniboine Indians, families sometimes travelled by themselves, although here too the band was the more common unit. Among the Chippewa of Minnesota and Wisconsin, permanent villages were the major centers of settlement. Bands of hunters and warriors were drawn from the village population, and, in fact, often broke from their parent village to form entirely new settlement.

ROCK ART of the Indians of the Americas comprises incised and painted pictures on stone. The most prevalent form of rock art appears in petroglyphs

Rock engraving from Camoodi Rock Essequibo.

which are drawings usually made by pecking but also made by carving, engraving, scratching, and abrasion using a stone harder than the one being incised. There are also many pictographs which were made by painting on stone usually with brushes of twigs or yucca but sometimes by crude finger painting. The colors of most pictographs were red, black, or white. Polychrome pictographs generally combine these colors but there are some more elaborate polychromes in which blue, green, and yellow were added. Both incised and painted pictures are usually found in the same area with one form predominating. Thousands of petroglyphs and pictographs have been found in caves and on cliffs, especially in the West where smooth surfaces of sandstone, basalt, and granite lent themselves to making such pictures. There are only a few hundred known rock art sites east of the Mississippi River.

American Indian rock art was made for several thousand years continuing into the 20th century with paintings of the Kwakiutl Indians of British Columbia. Prehistoric Indians produced pictures in a variety of

Rock-engraved ship.

styles both naturalistic and abstract. Important design motifs which appear in almost all rock art areas are the hand, bear track, thunderbird, and mountain sheep.

Rock art was generally made in conjunction with ceremonies seeking supernatural help for success in hunting and fishing, for rain, fertility, and good health. It was also produced in connection with initiation and puberty rites and to record legends and events. Many were made by shamans or under their supervision.

There are four main areas of rock art in the West; California, where the Chumash Indians produced some of the finest painting, the Columbia Plateau, where many pictures were flooded by the Grand Coulee Dam, the Great Basin region, where perhaps the earliest rock art was produced, and the Southwest with its great variety. There are petroglyphs of life sized figures pecked in Utah, pueblo motifs such as kachinas, feathered rattlesnakes, and flute players in New Mexico, and naturalistic Navajo paintings of the 18th and 19th centuries in Canyon de Chelly. Also in the Southwest in another type of rock art consisting of enormous human and animal figures made by outlining with piles of gravel on the ground or by taking away stones thereby creating figures in the sand underneath.

Other noteworthy rock art is that of Northwest Coast Indians incorporating stylized animal motifs similar to their wood carvings and of the Northern Plains whose most prominent motif is a shield figure. In the Eastern Woodlands there is one concentration of petroglyphs on horizontal limestone in Missouri.

ROPE MAKING. The Iroquois made thread, twine, and woven burden straps from the fibers of the inner bark of the basswood (Tilia americana L.), the moose wood or leather wood (Dirca Palustris L.), and the slippery elm (Ulmus fulva Michx). Indian hemp or Dogbane (Apocynum—Cannabinum and androsaemifolium L), nettle fibers (La porte canadensis L.) and milkweed fibers (Asclepias syriaca L.) were also used in Iroquos weaving. Basswood fiber was especially valuable for rope and for the heavier burden belts.

Bark that was to be used for thread was usually gathered in the spring when the sap was running. The outer surface of the bark was removed, then the inner bark was peeled off in narrow strips six or eight feet in length, loosely braided, and tied in bunches until needed for use. It was then boiled and pounded to

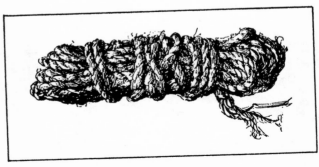

Iroquois rope.

render it pliable. It was sometimes necessary to repeat this process three times. Then it was washed thoroughly and dried in the sun. After it was dried the strips of bark were separated into the natural fibers running with the grain. Many of the fibers ran the entire length of the strips of bark and were often several feet in length. When separated the fibers were usually neatly braided into skeins and laid aside until needed for use as thread or twine.

In addition to many other uses twine was made into nets for use in fishing. When netting was to be done, all the strands were caught at one end so that they ran lengthwise. Then each strand in turn was twisted or knotted with the neighboring strands on either side to form meshes of uniform size producing an open, elastic fiber. The work was done with a wooden needle and was often carried on by the old men of the tribe. Wild hemp was the favorite thread for fish nets but the inner bark of the mulberry, elm and basswood were also used.

The Burden Strap or Tump Line. Before the coming of the White settlers, the Iroquois were using Indian hemp and bark fibers from the elm, basswood, and cedar to weave or braid the long straps that were used for carrying burdens. The straps were variously known as burden straps, tump lines, pack straps, and carrying straps. Slippery elm fibers made burden straps of the best quality, being finer, stronger, and more pliable than basswood fibers. Basswood fiber were good for very heavy straps. The fiber were prepared by boiling, stripping, rubbing and twisting into cords.

The burden strap consisted of a woven belt about two feet long and two and one-half inches wide with narrower tying strips at each end, usually woven all in one piece. In making the belt a twined weave was used, two weft-strands of fine fiber being twined over one another between two coarser warp strands. The weaving was started in the middle of the belt which narrowed in width near the ends. The remaining length of

Coil of rope.

the warp strands were then braided to form the tie-strings for the packs. On some straps the tying strips were reinforced by braiding strips of tanned deer hide with the fiber. The tie-strings usually extended about seven feet from each end of the belt. The finished strap was fifteen feet or more in length and three of four inches wide.

Few burden straps have been made since 1820. An old craft worker on the Seneca Reservation who knew how to make them taught the technique to others during the recent revival of the native arts.

Though made for use, the belt of the burden strap was often elaborated by the development of geometric designs in the weaving. A ribbed appearance was obtained by using a finer cross thread. Hairs of the moose, buffalo, deer, and elk were commonly used.

RUBBER—When early British golfers were playing with a ball made of feathers packed into a leather cover, Indians were playing a game with a ball made of rubber. For untold centuries before the time of Columbus, Indians had known and used rubber, and they were the only people anywhere of which this can be said. Very elaborate stone ball-courts were erected in Middle America to provide a suitable place for their ball games, which were religious in character, and ball-courts probably of similar significance were used as far north as northern Arizona.

When the Spaniards first saw rubber balls, they were amazed at the remarkable way they would bounce. Not only balls, but many other articles, including waterproof bags and the original "gum boots," were manufactured from rubber by the Indians, for they had mastered the required processes just as they had devised ways for obtaining the sap and treating it.

Several kinds of rubber trees were utilized, principally in Middle America and in the valley of the Amazon. Nowadays most of the planting of rubber trees is in distant countries, but it is well to remember that all of it is rubber of the American Indians.

Long after the time of Columbus the name rubber was applied by the English, who first used the product to rub out pencil marks.

To people who ride on rubber and to all nations who wish to win wars, it would be difficult to exaggerate the importance of rubber as a crop, as we learned during the recent war.

History. The discovery of rubber is undoubtedly one of the greatest Indian contributions to modern civilization. It was used in South America long before the Conquest. One of the first to mention this substance was Oviedo y Valdes, who gives us an involved and quite inaccurate description of the fabrication of rubber balls by the *Taino* Indians of Haiti.

Throughout tropical South America the principal use for rubber was to make balls for the famous games in which the ball was butted with the head or shoulders. Consequently, the list of tribes said to use the rubber ball, may well serve as a basis for mapping the distribution of the use of rubber. In his list are included the *Taino*, the *Otomac*, the *Huari* of the Guapore River, the *Paressi*, the *Chiquito*, the *Chane*, the *Chiriguano,* and the *Aueto* Indians of the Xingu River. To these should be added the *Apinaye, the Mojo,* and the *Guarani-Itatin* of northern Paraguay.

The *Mojo* made their balls by coating a round clay core with liquid rubber. When it had hardened, the clay was dissolved by dipping the sphere in water and was removed through a hole. After this the ball was inflated with air, wrapped with a strip of rubber, and smeared with several coatings of liquid rubber. The finished ball weighed about 25 pounds.

A similar procedure exists among the *Apinaye,* where the making of rubber balls was a ceremonial operation that took place at the end of the boys' initiation rites. Latex of the mangabiera tree *(Hancornia speciosa),* which was tapped with a stone knife, was smeared on the novices' body and limbs in strips about three fingers' wide. As soon as the liquid had dried, a second and third coating followed. A core, 4 cm. in diameter, shaped out of hard clay from termite nests, was wrapped with the rubber bands by rolling the strips off the boys' bodies. As soon as the ball had attained a certain thickness, the core was knocked into pieces and was removed through a small slit cut into the rubber rind. The hollow sphere was further strengthened by additional rubber strips, which covered the slit and finally yielded a very elastic ball.

Several tribes of the upper Amazon Basin *(Omagua, Maina, Caripuna,* and *Cacharary)* made rubber syringes, which were provided with a bone mouthpiece to blow parica *(Piptadenia* sp.) into the nostrils, but which were used most often to administer powerful clysters prepared with the same intoxicant. These syringes were made on clay molds. The Indians may have got the idea of making syringes when they observed that they could spout the water with which they dissolved the clay core of their balls.

Otherwise little use was made of rubber. The Indians of the Caiari-Uaupes and Orinoco Rivers smeared rubber on the ends of the heavy wooden mallets with which they beat their huge slit drums.

nets, harpoons, or gaffs. As soon as the fish were taken they were thrown to the women, who split them open, spread them with pointed sticks, and hung them in the sun to dry. Later they were stored in special elevated caches.

SHAMAN AND SHAMINISM. The Shaman, witch doctor, or medicine-man, whose function has been described as that of an "unorganized priesthood," was only such in the sense that he supposedly held the ability to control the souls of men, and was so considerably above average in the potency of his "mystery powers" that he could exorcise evil influences and mischievous spirits. However, shamans did not conduct prayers or ceremonies, although they played a leading part in the latter, particularly those designed to bring good fortune in hunting and warfare.

Shamans appear to have exerted more direct authority among loosely integrated migratory groups. Settled village communities, with their more complex social structure, gave greater authority to chiefs and the wealthy upper class, relegating the medicine-man to the position of a combination of community doctor and spiritual adviser or intermediary.

During the period of guardian-spirit seeking, certain visions or significant signs were accepted by the seeker as evidence that he was endowed with shamanistic ability. Among some Indian groups, bleeding at the mouth was of great portent in this respect. If visited by this sign, the novice from then onward must spend much of his time in improving and extending his powers by subjecting his body and mind to increasingly difficult trials of fortitude and endurance. Long periods of fasting, the intense observation of natural and animal phenomena, and the development of magic skills were all part of this training. Apprenticeship to older shamans was a common practice, and societies or brotherhoods of shamans were maintained among certain coastal groups. Shamanishm was in many instances regarded as a hereditary function, with novices being obtained from among the nephews of old established shamans.

It must be recognized that much as we tend to disparage the "cunning" and "trickery" of the shaman, in most cases, at least, he held a firm and sincere conviction in the efficacy and righteousness of his powers. The tricks he applied in effecting cures, such as that of concealing some foreign substance in his mouth and later pretending to withdraw it from the body of a sick person, were devices of a strictly pragmatic nature, the value of which, as suggestion cures, had been known to the fraternity for many generations.

Among some groups, shamans were specialists in afflictions of certain parts of the body. Because of this, a patient might require the services of more than one shaman. Young shamans were often preferred because of the freshness of their spiritual experiences and also because of their alleged greater purity. However, this did not entirely offset the respect shown to the older shamans, whose experience in practical magic often gave them the advantage and a reputation for "powerful medicine."

Normally young shamans did not charge for their first experiments in curing the sick. This was something in the nature of a test, upon the success of which their future reputations were likely to depend. Nor did any shaman charge for treatment if that treatment was unsuccessful. Shamans also had considerable knowledge of herbs and other natural remedies, but since many of these were common knowledge, they did not depend on such things to display their powers. However, it is indicative of their ability to use such remedies, in conjunction with suggestion cures and "spells," that few shamans were poor men. In this respect it might be noted that the patient's belief in the reputed effects of the "medicine" were in most instances much more important than the actual medicinal value.

It was believed that a good shaman, by sending

forth his own spirit, or that of one of his guardians, could follow the trail of a soul which had wandered away from its body, and could effect its return. Some shamans actually claimed to have reached the land of the dead, but others were less presumptuous.

The various spells, incantations, dances, and procedures used by shamans in the practice of their art differed in detail from group to group and from one practitioner to another, but fire and water usually played a large part in all magic. Considerable competition existed between shamans. Nor was their field restricted to cures alone. Upon payment of sufficient fee, a shaman would attempt to place an evil spell on one's enemies. Among certain groups such "evil working" was considered illegal, or at least unethical, and, if used against a member of the local community, was punishable by death or banishment.

Shamanism was not restricted to men, but women shamans were generally less powerful and confined their activities to women's ailments and childbirth.

The following is a description by the early wandering artist, Paul Kane, of a shaman he observed while among the Klallums of the Coast Salish group:

Cross-legged and naked, in the middle of the room, sat the medicine man, with a wooden dish of water before him. Twelve or fifteen other men were sitting around the lodge. The object in view was to cure the girl of a disease affecting her side . . . The officiating medicine man appeared in a state of profuse perspiration from the exertions he had used and soon took his seat among the rest as if quite exhausted. A younger medicine man then took his place in front of the bowl and close beside the patient. Throwing off his blanket he commenced singing and gesticulating in the most violent manner whilst the others kept time by beating with little sticks on hollow wooden bowls and drums, singing continually. After exercising himself in this manner for about half an hour until the perspiration ran down his body, he darted suddenly upon the young women, catching hold of her side with his teeth and shaking her for a few minutes . . . . He then relinquished his hold and cried out that he had got it, at the same time holding his hands to his mouth; after which he plunged them in the water and pretended to hold down with great difficulty the disease which he had extracted lest it spring out and return to its victim.

At length, having obtained mastery over it, he turned around to me and held something up between the finger and thumb of each hand, which had the appearance of a piece of cartilage; whereupon one of the Indians sharpened his knife and divided into two leaving one end in each hand. One of the pieces he threw in the water and the other into the fire, accompanying the action with a diabolical noise which none but a medicine man can make.

Indians may approach the gods individually, but in the majority of cases they appeal to religious specialists to intervene in their behalf. One of these intermediaries is the Catholic priest; however, he seldom visits the highland villages. Over the centuries, the Indians have evolved religious practices that do not require the services of a priest. When he does come, his time is primarily occupied with baptisms, a few marriages, and with the annual Mass of the patron saint, all of which occur within the church. The priest is not expected to intervene in other areas, and one who attempts to change the traditional beliefs is labeled a Protestant.

Because of the scarcity of priests Indians have never placed great emphasis on the sacraments other than baptism, which has pre-Columbian roots, but do value the elaborate processionals, ceremonies, and *fiestas* sponsored and conducted by the religious brotherhoods. Composed of local men, these groups are responsible for the care of the Church and particular saints, for the sponsoring of *fiestas,* and the celebration of various Catholic holy days. These duties are performed in the name of the whole village so that the saints, in turn, will bless all its inhabitants with good fortune. The offices in ther brotherhood are rotated annually, and all men assume the responsibility and honor of serving both the saints and the village (see Ethnic Groups and Languages, ch. 4).

In the more isolated areas, which almost never see a priest, older men who have passed through all the offices of the brotherhood become unofficial native priests. They maintain the adherence to folk-Catholic ceremonies, conducting many of these, since they have amassed a vast knowledge of religious and magical ritual; however, they seldom administer the sacraments other than baptism. These native priests are found primarily in the north in Verapaz and Chiquimula Departments.

One of the most important religious specilaists is the *chiman,* or shaman. His duties and powers vary from one township to another, and in some areas he maintains strong ties with the official Roman Catholic structure, working closely with the brotherhoods and conducting a large part of the cermonies. In the areas the shaman has wide knowledge of Maya lore and is similar to the native priests, but usually has not passed through the offices of the brotherhoods. This type of shaman is found mainly in the eastern part of the country.

In most townships, however, the shaman is associated with supernatural beliefs and rituals, which exist outside of the formal religious organization, and is more involved with personal and family problems rather than village ceremonies. Although he consults and pays homage to Catholic saints, he usually propitiates and appeals to the nature gods or supernatural spirits of legends and folklore. He is the prime user of the ancient Maya calendar, or at least portions of it, employing it for selecting sacrifical days in the cultivation cycle and for divination.

Two of the shaman's greatest abilities are divination and curing. Most possess a bundle of red beans, called *miches,* which were supposedly given to them by God. With these they can predict the future, discover the cause of an illness and, in conjunction with the calendar, pick a good day on which to conduct rituals. Some shamans, however, do not use the beans exclusively, but rely on the twitching of their leg muscles, which can be read either as a positive or negative answer to a question asked of the gods.

The curing rituals vary, but often involve an appeal to certain deities and a tour of ancient shrines and chapels where prayers are said and candles and incense burned. In many cases the subject must submit to a complete confession with members of his family present. Generally, the shaman will accompany these rituals with divination, in an attempt to locate the cause and source of the illness. Often the curer pretends to extract worms or frogs from the patient's mouth, supposedly placed there by witchcraft. The curers have various rituals for different illnesses, but, as a rule, they mix propitiations of the supernatural with herb remedies.

In solving personal problems, the shaman uses both his power of divination and his supposedly direct contact with the spirit world. Indians claim that he can find lost articles, discover if a wife or husband has been unfaithful, predict the sex of an unborn baby, and other similar matters. He can also intercede with the gods on behalf of someone who has offended them. If a man's crop is not doing well he can go to a shaman, who will offer sacrifices to the proper gods in the man's name.

Most of the divination and curing process is based on set rituals, which are performed the same way each time. Many of the shamans contend that their knowledge of these rituals comes directly from God, who speaks to them in dreams. Others admit that they acquire the knowledge informally by early and constant attendance at ceremonies and rituals conducted by older shamans. There appear to be no instances of formal training, although this may occur covertly.

It is sometimes hard to separate the witch or sorcerer from the shaman, for in certain areas one man performs both roles. Generally, however, the shaman seeks only to help the individual, whereas the sorcerer deals primarily in black magic. This sort of witchcraft has been officially outlawed; nevertheless, it still does exist and is considered quite powerful. Although definitions vary in most places the sorcerer is considered a practitioner who sells his knowledge of witchraft to clients wishing to cause bodily harm to, or to place a supernatural curse on, an enemy.

The sorcerer is an ordinary man who supposedly has learned magic formulas and rituals from another sorcerer. It is doubtful that this type of training is done formally, but many *ladinos* insist that schools of witches and diviners exist in the highlands. The knowledge of black magic is fairly common though in legends and folk beliefs, and anyone who wants to practices these rituals can obtain the information with little trouble.

The sorcerers usually make their victim ill by allegedly casting animals into his body. As a rule they needs some possession of the victim, and often the client must participate in the ritual. No complete black masses are performed, but sorcerers supposedly conduct religious rituals backwards and burn candles upside down.

It is also believed that many sorcerers do not sell their knowledge; rather they practice witchcraft against their own enemies and against anyone they envy. For this reason Indians do not wish to flaunt their good fortune, as this would be inviting witchcraft against themselves. When a man's luck goes bad, he immediately suspects witchcraft from an enemy and will seek out a shaman or a sorcerer to counteract the curse.

SHELLWORK was a highly developed art and prized commodity among Indians of North America. Shell was a favorite material for making both useful ornaments such as beads and pendants. Tribes who lived far from a supply of shell on a shoreline obtained shell by trade. In prehistoric times shell was cut, drilled, ground, and polished using techniques and tools similar to those used today.

In the Eastern Woodlands wampum, which was clam shell made into cylindrical beads strung on thongs, was used in ceremonies and for barter in Colonial times. The white and purple shell beads were woven into belts, necklaces, and bracelets.

Top; shell gorget, Missouri. Bottom; shell gorget, Lick Creek Mound, Tenn.

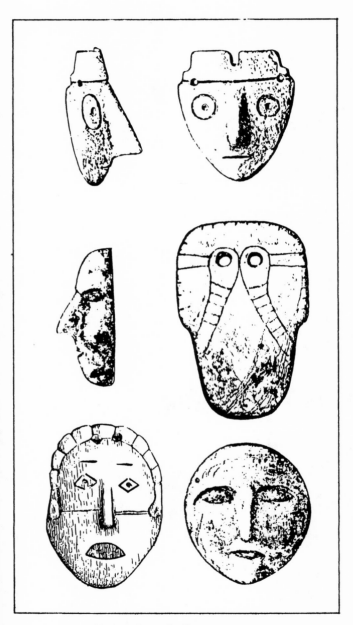

Human face shell ornaments.

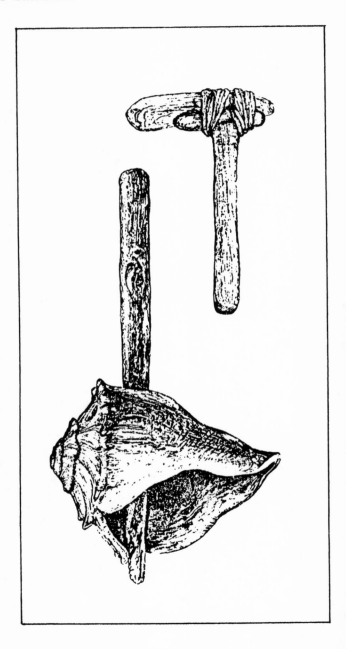

Atsidi Sani who was taught by a Mexican called Naki Tsusi, probably between 1853 and 1868. Around 1873 another early Navajo silversmith, Atsidi Chon, taught the first Zuni, named Lanyade, silversmithing. In 1898 a Zuni, probably Lanyade, taught silversmithing to a Hopi named Sikyatala, who taught others. The craft spread to most other pueblos.

Coins were the Indians only source of silver until 1890 when the U.S. government enforced the law which made it illegal to deface American coins. Mexican coins were used until 1930 when Mexico prohibited their export. After that Indians bought sterling silver slugs and sheets from white traders who bought it from silver refineries.

Although tools and techniques have improved since the Navajo began silversmithing, early silver jewelry was hammered, filed, and decorated with simple stamped or incised designs much as it is today. The first designs were copied from Mexican leatherwork. In 1875 Navajos began sandcasting. Turquoise was set in silver for the first time in 1880.

The first silver objects made by Navajos were those made for Navajos and other Indians who used bridles and tobacco canteens and wore bow guards, bracelets, beads, buttons, rings, and concho belts. Indians began producing silver for white men in the 1890's when the railroad coming West created a new market. There is commercial silver jewelry which is not authentic handmade Indian jewelry. However, some of the finest Indian jewelry is made today in both traditional and contemporary designs.

The Navajo, Zuni, and Hopi are the leading producers of silver, each using distinctive designs. Navajo style is generally massive, simple, and uses torquoise to enhance the silver. Zuni silversmiths set turquoise, coral, shell, and jet in silver using inlay and channel techniques. Since 1938, encouraged by the Museum of Northern Arizona, the Hopi have developed a style in silver based on their pottery, basket, and textile designs executed in an overlay technique.

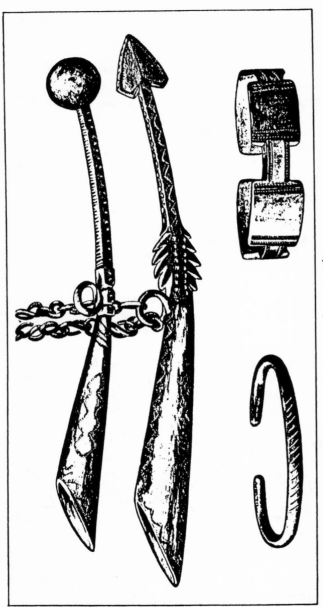

Navojo objects in silver.

The art of silversmithing was unknown in Mexico until the time of the Toltecs (10th Century). It was introduced from the south, perhaps from Colombia, Costa Rica and Panama, even Peru. Due to the traditional manual dexterity of the Indians, marvellous silversmiths soon appeared, particularly among the Mixtecs who produced an infinite assortment of objects which ended up in the Spaniards' coffers and which, fortunately, are still preserved in museums.

During the Spanish colonial era in Mexico, the working of silver had reached a high degree of perfection and the silversmiths united into guilds or confraternities. The authorities set up ordinances to determine the competence of the artisans, watched over the quality of the products, applied the "fifth" to gold and silver, that is to say, they required that the tribute to the Crown or "royal fifth" be paid, and, among other rulings, established discriminatory laws for the Indians by which they were allowed to work as laborers but not in any official capacity.

Colonial silversmithing produced real masterpieces which later inspired modern craftsmen such as Alfredo Ortega, who has designed many exquisite pieces like the illustrated silver pitcher.

During the second half of the 19th Century, due to the political situation to the closing of many mines, to the mining industry's interest in exploiting other metals, to the Mexican public's loss of taste for silver objects and, in consequence, a reduction in the number of silversmiths, this craft suffered a heavy decline and was only sustained by the efforts of a few men. Around 1928, Fred Davies, the great lover and promoter of Mexican handicrafts, for the first time combined silver with obsidian, thus creating a revival in the buying public's interest.

But it was not unti 1931 when the young American architect and artist, William Spratling, who had settled in Taxco where a few mines still functioned, got the idea of establishing a small silver workshop in that town. He called Artemio Navarrete, a silversmith from

Iguala, and with him founded the shop called "Las Delicias", with the idea that "Taxco had been producing silver during four hundred years without ever benefitting its own inhabitants".

With the flourishing of Taxco, an enormous demand for silver objects has sprung up. In Mexico City, as in other places, the importance of this handicraft has greatly increased and shops such as Codan, S.A. have created magnificent silver pieces like the illustrated coffee pot, inspired in the Danish silver designs. The other objects in the attached illustration are: Of William Spratling, a salad set, in silver and ebony, and a centerpiece of blended metals, in silver, bronze and copper; and the brooch with little hanging fishes, made by the native silversmiths of Patzcuaro, Michoacan.

SLAVERY was the involuntary servitude of one person or group enforced by another. Among so-called primitive peoples, slavery is a rare occurrence. The Eskimos, for example, have left no traces whatsoever of the possible existence of this institution in their society.

Although slavery in one form or another was common among other native American groups, its character was markedly different from slave systems found in European and other advanced cultures. The Indians in the southern part of North American learned slavery from the whites and, in fact, traded in black slaves. Black slaves were often highly valued by their Indian masters, for the possessed skills, learned from the whites, that the Indians did not possess. In any event, the social mobility of these slaves was very great in Indian society. They were frequently adopted as full members of the tribe to which they were bound. Seminole Indians frequently married black runaways, and the position of black slaves in their society appears to have been identical to other Seminoles. And the Seminole tribe included several settlements of runaway

Sweden also cut their pots directly from the rock outcrop.

At Johnston, R. I., the largest pits are 10 feet long, 6 feet wide, and are now 5 feet deep although originally doubtless 15 feet deep. The Narragansett Indians were famous steatite artisans and traders, and their pipes made of local steatite were in demand not only among the Mohawk but also by "our English Tobacconists for their rarity, strength, handsomeness and coolnesse".

The Cumberland Sound Eskimo when breaking steatite from a quarry, "deposit a trifling present at the place, because otherwise the stone would become hard". The Eskimo on the west coast of Hudson Bay and the Copper Eskimo believe that steatite should not be worked while the people are living on the ice. The former sometimes use steatite as bullets when lead is scarce. It is mined by Eskimo at the mouth of Tree River, which flows into Coronation Gulf, 75 miles east of the Coppermine mouth. The Coppermine Eskimo are dealers in soapstone lamps and pots, and at many of the soapstone localities the main occupation of certain Eskimo is pot making. Families from as far away as Cape Bexley visit the Tree River for the stone, being en route 1, 2, or more years and such trips are the subject of local songs. It is also distributed by tribal barter. It is believed by Stefansson that this and localities east of it once supplied soapstone cooking utensils as far west as Siberia. A pot takes all an Eskimo's spare time for a year and that certain of the more skillful members of the tribe specialize in making such utensils.

SQUASH is classified by botanists as belonging to the gourd family, of which there are representatives in the Old World as well as in the New World.

The English colonists, on seeing a yellow vegetable growing in the cornfields of the Indian farmers, gave it the name pumpkin, a word from the Greek *pepon,* meaning mellow, ripe. However, the word *squash* is thoroughly Indian, being an abbreviation of one of those long Massachusetts Indian words, *askutasquash,* meaning "eaten while green".

American pumpkins and squash occasionally were referred to by European travelers as melons, and this gave rise to the belief that melons were native to the Western Hemisphere, which is incorrect.

There is much confusion as to which are pumpkins and which are squash. Common names do not help much. The so-called summer squash, such as crookneck squash and scallop squash, are pumpkins; and among the winter squashes the mammoth Chile squash takes first prize at county fairs as the biggest pumpkin. In England all large squashes are called pumpkins. Vegetable marrow, so popular there, is a variety of the American pumpkin.

American squash and pumpkins were developed probably in Middle America and South America, and their prehistoric distribution extended well over both western continents.

STORYTELLING. There is almost unanimous agreement among writers on primitive education concerning the importance of storytelling as a pedagogical device. This section presents supplementary evidence from North American Indian cultures concerning the applications of storytelling to the educational process and the possible stimulus provided by these applications to the development of oral literature, its themes, and its style.

Statements have been made that myths and legends were not told to children, or that certain of these stories were usually told only to adults. For the most part, however, children and young people appear to have been important in the storyteller's audience, and in many instances be directed a considerable share of his effort to them. Ray is one of the few authors to mention that myths and legends were not told directly to children. He says, for the Sanpoil and Nespelem of Washington: "They learned at such times, too, the lore of their fathers. The myths and legends were not customarily told to the children, but were recited in their presence." Another comment of this type is made by Barbeau for the Huron and Wyandot. After stating that great care was taken to teach myths and legends to the children, he says: "It appears that on such occasions children were not always welcome, and that they were sent to bed with the remark that 'for little folks like them, it was not good to listen to these stories.'" This remark is clarified, however, by a footnote: "Repeating this statement on two occasions, Henry Stand was apparently repressing laughter, as if he did not care to say what the stories were about." We may gather that these stories fell into the category of "erotica". Mead reports, for an area outside North America, that among Manus of the Admiralty Islands legends were not considered to be for children at all, but were for old people. She implies that the Manus children did not like imaginative stories and cites this fact as casting doubt on a story appetite as an inherent attribute of children. Later, however, without attempting to harmonize the two statements she implies that children did know folklore, by stating that they regarded the animals in myths and legends as men, because men were frequently named after animals.

To counterbalance this evidence of, at least, a selective process in the stories told to children, there are scores of reports, representing all cultural areas, to show that much energy was expended by the elders in general, or by specifically designated elders, to inculcate in the young a knowledge and appreciation of the traditional oral literature of the tribe. Malinowski points out that it is a function of myths to substantiate belief, enhance moral precepts, give validity to faith, and give weight to all that has to be believed, obeyed, or accepted, by referring authority to a Golden Age.

A Shasta informant states emphatically that stories

were told primarily for the children, and not to entertain adults, because the myths and legends gave the elders a ready means of indicating to a child why he must behave in one way and not in another. The stories were told only in winter, but allusions to them were made at any time in encouraging or discouraging the activities of children. John Hunter, who lived for years among the Plains Indians, says: "The rest of the Indian's education, apart from what is acquired by experience, is obtained from the discourses of the aged warriors. The elderly women, also, frequently perform these offices, more particularly as they relate to narratives and traditions, of which they are by the consent of custom the unerring and sacred depositaries."

Among the Menomini a whole winter would sometimes be given over to one series of legends and myths, told in sections, one a night, to the assembled people. It is implied that the youth of the village were present by the added statement:

Some myths, of course, were too sacred for public narration except on ceremonial occasions, and these were bought in private from the older men by the youths, segment by segment. Thus a young man would appear some evening at the lodge of one of the elders, heap up a pile of goods on the floor and then, with a preliminary offering of tobacco, would request the elder to tell him such a myth. Asked in this ceremonial manner, the older man might not refuse for fear of angering the gods. On the other hand, without the customary present, it was equally offensive to mention the great powers.

Elsewhere, it said of Menomini folklore:

The part that folklore has played in influencing Menomini social life and vice versa, can scarcely be overestimated. Even today folklore forms an important factor in determining many usages. In disputes over etiquette, for example, these tales are resorted to for reference. . . . A significant point. . . . is that of the transmission of apparently trivial stories, presumably for no other reason than that they contain practical information. . . . A few "true stories" are told for the purpose of inculcating the principles of honor, virtue and bravery among the children. Many of these have a moral, either stated or implied, contrary to the popular idea of North American folklore.

Curtis says of the Wichita: "Each culture legend conveys a teaching. . . . In fact, in a measure, the moral lessons taught overshadow consciousness of the Infinite." Dorsey points out for the Caddo that there was an extended series of stories for children which presented in dramatic fashion just what would happen to those who misbehaved in specific ways, and also what would happen to those who did right. A boy who whips his dog will have to through Dog Land when he dies and will probably turn into a dog himself. A boy who is lazy and talks too much will be turned into a tree when he dies. If a boy does not listen to advice and remember it, he will be smashed between two huge rocks on the path to the Land of Spirits. If a boy is disobedient and a laggard, he will not be able to cross a river on the road to the Spirit Land. If a boy is greedy he will not be able to resist eating persimmons on the way to the Spirit Land and he will lose his way and his memory. If a boy does not finish tasks given to him he will spend many hours drying bones, dying, being born again, working himself to skin and bones, and so on.

According to Benedict there is no clear classification of esoteric folklore among the Zuni. All stories are told at the family fireside by any layman. The stories are never the same, though they deal with similar episodes. But all expressions of politeness, of etiquette, and proper behavior, are repeated over and over again whenever the story gives opportunity. "In most mythologies the picture of cultural life that can be abstracted from the tales, as in the studies of the Tsimshian, Kwakiutl, and Crow, is a comparatively adequate description of most phases of social life, but in Zuni there is in addition a loving reiteration of detail that is over and above this faithful rendition." A Zuni narrator is almost always free to incorporate his special knowledge into any tale he is telling. Elsewhere, it is reported that stories exercise a profound influence on children of the Pueblo. The reasons for all rules are given in dramatic story form.

A Walapai father told traditional stories to his son when he grew old enough to hunt. "On such a trip a boy would learn more than hunting, for it was about the campfire at night that he heard from his father the old myths and tales, knowledge about the stars, and the like." The Apache girl is taught by stories. "She is overwhelmed with tales of what has happened to those who disobeyed this injunction in the past."

By footnotes to various folk tales he collected on the Northwest Coast, Swanton indicates the use of myths and legends in training children. For example: "When older people were giving their children advice they would bring up this part of the story and tell them not to be greedy and selfish, but honest. They would say they did not want him to be like Raven, who ate up all his playmate's fat." Nichols was so struck by Swanton's examples that he used Tlingit myths as one of his major sources in discussing moral education among the North American Indians.

Among the Thompson, myths and legends were interspersed with lectures admonishing the audiences, especially the young, on tribal virtues, namely: purity, cleanliness, honesty, truthfulness, bravery, friendliness, hospitality, energy, boldness, virtue, liberality, kindness, diligence, independence, modesty, affability, sociableness, charity, a proper respect for the supernatural, gratitude, initiative on the warpath, honor, pride in seeking revenge from enemies, industry, and so forth. The Carriers used folk tales as one of the principal means of conveying religious and social knowledge. Elsewhere, the same author says of the Carrier:

> On quiet winter evenings, when the people had gathered inside their big, plank houses, dimly lighted by one or two small fires, an old man seated in a corner would narrate some tradition or folk-tale of the distant past, and point the moral of the story with reference to the conduct of the children during the preceding hours. The education of children in other parts of Canada followed among the same general lines, but was not always organized into so definite a system.

On the other side of Canada, among the Naskapi, it is reported:

> During the long winter nights or during the periods of cold or inclement weather in which Indians may not venture out, they sit

around the fire and relate stories intended for the instruction as well as entertainment of the younger people. The older men have a great stock of these stories, and many of the women are noted for their ability in entertaining the children, who sit, with staring eyes and open mouths, in the arms of their parents or elders.

Farther north, among the Eskimo, Rasmussen states that the legends are known to all, it being the responsibility of the grandmothers to see that they are taught to the children. Many horror stories are also told to illustrate what happens to those who transgress the traditional rules.

These quotations, chosen from accounts of Indians in the various culture areas, are numerous enough to indicate that folklore enters into the educational program to a great extent, and that it does so in two principal ways. The folklore is literature, and is transmitted for its own value, and at the same time, is utilized as an authority for cultural beliefs and practices which are taught in other ways. One of the purposes of this study is to indicate how the various methods of transmitting a culture to successive generations have influenced the content of the culture. This is especially true in the transmissions of folklore. Several of the notes already cited indicate this directly or by implication. It is probable that mythology and legendary love reflect the needs of the youthful auditor quite as much as those of adults since children form a large part of the storyteller's audience, and curiosity about nature and the cosmos is a trait of the young more than of adults. Moreover, the development of the child was a matter of universal concern. So far as could be discovered, however, this probability has not been specifically covered in discussions of the origin and development of oral literature among primitives.

Unquestionably many factors are involved in the development of an oral literature as extensive and complex as that found in the cultures of many American Indian tribes. But recalling Mead's statement that Manus children do not confirm a love for stories as an innate human trait, it would seem that the educational value of these stories has been a strong factor in promoting their use for children and youths and in developing adult appreciation of them. It has been aptly said that an appreciation for music is acquired by most people in the same way as is a suntan—through constant exposure. The same undoubtedly holds true with most people for other forms of art. The pleasure of the adult American Indian in storytelling is recognized in all areas. The taste was acquired, apparently, through listening to stories as a child or adolescent.

Almost all bodies of oral literature in North America are characterized by a greater or lesser explanatory content. That is, episodes in myths and legends are explicitly or by inference used to explain why things exist in their known form. These etiologic elements range all the way from an explanation of the cosmos, in creation myths, to an explanation of the length of animals' tails and of the performance of ceremonial acts. Boas believes that the explanatory elements are not a result of philosophic cogitation primarily, but are merely finishing touches added to previously existing stories. A similar conclusion is reached by Waterman: "From the places they [the explanatory elements] occupy in a given tale, and the manner of their appearance, they seem to be chance features, put in for good measure, or for other reasons, perhaps, which are not concerned directly with the plot."

Waterman also holds that for adults, the satisfaction derived from stories is more emotional than intellectual, the explanatory element being of minor importance. This naturally leads us to ask why the storyteller bothers to use his artistic skill in adding explanatory elements? One reason here proposed is that a good part of the audience is normally drafted from the juvenile population, and the storyteller, being aware of this audience, puts in a tag now and then, referring to things that the children are normally curious about, to hold their attention, keep them awake, and impress them with the practical importance of the tribal myths and legends. We may also hazard a guess that the adult audience got a vicarious enjoyment out of the explanatory elements through realizing that they might be effective in holding the interest of the children and in stimulating them to absorb the traditional lore. In using the term "realizing" a point is being stretched, however, for the process was probably more subconscious than conscious.

Quite probably there are other factors involved in the widespread use of explanatory elements. The individual storyteller may use them, and probably often did, merely because it was standard practice and style to do so; it gave the story a pleasing cadence, or an additional aesthetic value. But even then the underlying problem of training youth probably had its influence; for it is difficult to understand the adoption of etiologic elements a type of literary "ornament" over such wide areas when the adult audience confessedly was not particularly interested in their etiologic character.

In his study of Tsimshian mythology, Boas expressed the opinion that in all likelihood many of the tales have changed as the culture of the people using them has broken down, and that some explanatory elements which would not have been felt necessary in older times are now added in the version told to the young of recent generations, as well as to white people. This confirms my idea that the youths in the audience are often responsible for the direction given to the artistic striving of the storyteller, particularly with respect to the intellectual content of the tales. It is not plausible that the curiosity of adults should still be sufficiently alive about the various aspects of nature around them to demand explanations. Like adults everywhere, they have attitudes set for them before having advanced far into maturity. Yet we know that explanatory elements of widely different kinds are added to old episodes from area to area, and it seem justifiable to ascribe the incentive for this to the young people in the audience.

That the audience does influence the tale, as Boas intimates, is confirmed by Bartlett in his study of the psychology of primitive culture. He says:

Not only does the relation of the story-teller to his group affect the form of the folk-tale; not only does it frequently determine directly particular details of the material dealt with; not only does it influence the general type of social relationship that will be most often depicted among a given people; but it may, together with the group difference tendencies, and the individual instincts, settle the dominant themes of the tales, and how these themes are developed.

I conclude that in the explanatory element of the folk tale and myth is found a possible influence of primitive education problems on the form of the oral literature. That this influence may be considerable is attested by Waterman, who counted 1,053 explanatory elements dealing with earthly matters, and 138 dealing with celestial or cosmic matters in twenty-six collections of folklore from American Indian tribes. He points out that in addition there are many explanatory. features which are not explicitly stated in the versions collected by ethnologists, but which are known to the natives.

There is other evidence, however, which seems to imply that the educational problem and the need of meeting the demands of young audiences have influenced the oral literature even more fundamentally. This evidence is derived from merely a casual analysis of any body of American Indian folklore. Psychologically, the interest of an individual in a given story is to a considerable extent measured by the degree to which he can project himself into the situation depicted. That is, stories written for the entertainment of adults do not generally deal with the doings of children. Conversely, stories written for children tend to deal with children. Keeping this fact in mind, it is significant to note that a considerable proportion of the legends and myths in North America, even the most important of them, have as their leading characters young children or youths still in the process of winning their spurs.

Lowie says: "The Grandchild Myth looms large in both Arapaho and Crow consciousness, as is attested by the number of recorded variants." He adds that it is also found in various forms among the Hidatsa, Mandan, Arikara, Gros Ventre, Kiowa, Skidi, Dakota, Assiniboine, and Blackfoot. This grandchild is sometimes the offspring of a beautiful Indian girl and the Sun god. In a collection of Gros Ventre myths and tales made by Kroeber, the longest tales are invariably those dealing with children who accomplished miraculous feats, or who showed outstanding character in meeting difficult situations.

Among the Blackfoot, Old Man, the dominant elderly character in the myths, is not an exemplary model, because he is constantly getting into trouble through stupidity, but he does illustrate what happens to people who do not do right, and the laughter of the audience is a reflection of social ridicule. On the other hand, in the cosmical myths, called Star Myths, where miraculous things happen and difficulties are overcome, the characters are all children. Among the Coeur D'Alene, where Reichard says the moralizing character of the tales is most noticeable, a popular opening for a mythical legend is, "A boy lived with his grandmother," and the characters of tales tend to assume a family organization, though a few deal with fear-monsters. In fact the folklore of the Assiniboine, as collected by Lowie, eleven miscellaneous tales deal with the accomplishments of poor orphan boys who did not have a chance. The rest of the tales in this classification, with few exceptions, have boys or girls as leading characters or in the supporting cast. Among the Ojibwa, legendary vision quests by youths of other days are common. Among the Shoshone, there are a number mythological gigantic ogres and monsters in the tales, and usually they are overcome by the efforts of twin boys or youths. Many Shoshone bands have a mythical character of miraculous powers called Nu numbi, usually described as an Old Man, but among the Wind River group he is a little boy of remarkable strength.

In the Southwest, the mythology of the Pueblo of Santo Domingo presents adventurous young people as myth characters in a number of instances. At Zuni, Benedict finds that the deserted child is a strong theme in the folklore. "The plots are all concerned with the supernatural assistance and human success of the poor child, and often the whole plot is directed toward the triumph of the abandoned child over the mother or the parents." The point does not seem to be a warning to parents against deserting children—they never do—but is rather a glorification of what boys and girls can do if they have the approval of the supernaturals. Examination of the myths of Zuni indicates also that children are popular characters in other than desertion stories. Frequent characters are a poor boy living with his grandmother, or the youngest daughter or son of a priest, or two brothers. Bunzel adds that the origin story of the Koko gods is a story of children, and that the myth explaining why Katcinas always wear feathers in an adventure story of a boy who was lost. At Isleta a large number of myths and legends deal with children, and in the telling of them the favorite closing is: "Thus far we are going to see who remembers tomorrow night." The same large percentage of children's adventures appears in the myths of Sia. An excellent example of Apache legends indicating the way in which dramatic stories are used to promote valorous behavior is offered by Opler in the minor epic "Dirty Boy."

Wherever large collections of myths and legends have been made this same tendency to cast children in important roles relating to the origin and development of the tribe, or with the creation of cosmological phenomena, is apparent. Boas says of the Eskimo on the northern edge of the continent: "Tales of poor maltreated children who later on become very powerful are a frequent and apparently a favorite subject of story-tellers." Elsewhere it is said that the "orphan boy" is the hero par excellence of the Eskimo myth. Other citations might be given, but as this point is verifiable in many if not all adequate collections of mythology, it is not necessary to give further space to it.

The frequent occurrence of child heroes or juvenile leads in myths and legends of American Indian tribes strongly indicates that the problem of holding the interest of children and of inculcating traditional beliefs in the minds of the immature, has powerfully influenced the development of myth characterization, just as it has the factual content and style.

In the sections on personal names and the vision quest, reference has been made to the custom of relating stories concerning family ancestors as a means of stimulating the self-development of the boy or girl. The frequent incidence of field reports from many areas in which statements to this effect appear, seems to indicate that extant collections of myths and folk tales of the Indians are not in any true sense representative of the entire body of oral literature of any of the cultures involved. Such evidence as is available seems to affirm that for every tribal or group folk tale and myth that might be told during the year there were a great number of lesser stories, sacred to particular families, or merely anecdotal, concerned with individual biography. Tribal myths and legends were almost universally told only in the winter months. The only group noted in this survey where myths and legends were deliberately told in the summer was the Southeastern Yavapai. It was believed by these people that to tell stories in winter would cause a storm. Consequently, to speak of the oral literature of the Indians solely in terms of myths and legends is akin to speaking of English literature in terms of the King James version of the Bible, Chancer, and Shakespeare. During many months of the year the sacred myths and legends could be no more than alluded to as references. And even in the winter months there were, apparently, many stories told which were too individualistic or ephemeral to be included in folklore collections.

Rasmussen alludes to the great number of personal anecdotes of great hunters and adventurers which he listened to around Eskimo oil lamps. Bilby implies that the old legends and myths were told after younger hunters and adventurers of the Arctic wastes had done their best to amaze the audience. In the Great Bear Lake area, Osgood found that "the commonest type of story is scarcely describable as a myth, but rather as a more or less exaggerated narrative of events, many of which have a historical basis." He had an opportunity to follow the history of one such story apparently made up on the spur of the moment, but so fantastic that it caught on and was soon circulating throughout the whole area. In speaking of the Tanaino, the same author says:

> Myths of the actions and adventures of people and animals living long ago are popular . . . Autobiographical accounts of childhood experiences of old men they like very much as they serve to explain the way of meeting difficulties in the woods and on the sea. Stories of animals, and their habits, never fail to create interest. Also storytellers beguile their time with historical accounts and narratives with a moral . . . Some men are said to be able to tell a different story every night for six months.

On the Northwest coast, the Nootka, it is said, told a multitude of stories about young men of past generations who had gone forth on vision quests and on winter evenings there was an interminable list of adventure stories, legends, and myths. Among the Lummi:

> At every available opportunity, the old people of the village relate the accomplishments of the heroes of the past in the presence of the children with the intention of educating them in tribal traditions and customs . . . bystanders participate by interjecting enthusiastic comments to make the exploits of the ancestors appear more vivid and to impress the children with the honor and the esteem with which great men are regarded.

Among the Ojibwa, aside from such myths and legends as might be told, a father regaled the boys with long tales of the adventures of famous men, and the ambition of boys was aroused by the applause with which the women and girls greeted each accomplishment. Of the Assiniboine it is said:

The traditions related to the young in their lodges are usually extravagant fables and exploits of former warriors, exaggerated, of course, to make them interesting . . . The grandmothers are also well versed in this and night after night the children learn a great deal . . . The lives and actions of former warriors and other events of real life form a portion of the instruction thus conveyed.

The Menomini had a large number of summer stories, spoken of as "true stories," which related the personal adventures of men on the warpath, in vision quests, and in dreams. Dreams were particularly regarded as true stories. The true stories of the Menomini form the great mass of the oral literature, ranging from simple narratives of daily life to supernatural experiences, told to arouse laughter, to excite or to convey facts or explanations of phenomena. Among the Iroquois, of course, much true or slightly legendary history was told, particularly on the occasion of the raising of a sachem. Special officers recited the history, using strings of wampum as mnemonic devices.

In some areas, the Southeast particularly, the teaching of the important legends and myths was restricted to specific children selected because of the interest that they showed, and their retentive memories. In the Southwest and elsewhere, there were special tales for children particularly. At Zuni the myth and legend episodes are used merely as the springboard from which the narrator leaps into the story he wants to tell in order to convey some bit of knowledge. Collections of myths from this area are merely collections of episodes used in stories rather than the stories themselves.

On the Plains, Dorsey states that Siouan legends varied from family to family and were apparently told as a family affair. It is also stated of the Sioux that the ambitions of boys are aroused by listening "to the tales of the old men, as they recall the stirring senses of their youth, or sing their death-songs, which form only a boasting recapitulation of their daring and bravery." Lowie states that the tales told by the old men of vision quests and the success achieved as a result of them, were probably responsible for encouraging boys to seek a guardian spirit with so little urging. The Comanche are reputed to have had few or no culture tales, but many stories of hunting and war, according to Curtis. Grinnell supplements his remarks on the myths and legends of the Cheyenne with the following:

> Old men discussed the happenings of past years, their war journeys, their meetings with other tribes, visits they had received from white people, or mysterious events that had taken place within their knowledge. Sometimes, near groups of these old men might be seen two or three growing boys, seated at a little distance behind them, eagerly drinking in the talk that flowed from the lips of these wise elders.

This type of biographical, autobiographical, historical, or anecdotal story, dealing with individuals or families rather than with clans or tribes or natural or supernatural matters of general concern, is well known to the field worker. Many such stories are recorded in case histories or biographies. But since little is said in the ordinary collection of myths and folk tales concerning the oral literature of a genre of an ephemeral nature from which the more formalized and dignified stories are sifted, it is necessary to draw attention to them specifically. We cannot speak of the part played by folklore in primitive education unless the term "folklore" is used to mean the entire range of "oral literature." Important as were the myths and folk tales, as a body of literature, and as a source of quotations and allusions in everyday training and discipline, the practical stimulus to individual achievement probably was provided in equal measure by autobiographies, biographies, and dramatized historical episodes.

The stories that a boy heard concerning the name that he bore, and new ones that he might win; the stories of how other specific individuals had achieved success in vision quests; of how men had built their reputations in the chase or on the warpath; of how girls won and held husbands or built respected reputations—few of these are sufficiently generalized to be dignified as folk tales or myths—yet they provide much of the background for the lives of primitive children.

SUICIDE, the taking of one's own life, is today the second leading cause of death among North American Indians and occurs in that group at a rate exceeding the national average by three times. Historically, as might be expected, suicides by Indians were precipitated by a wide variety of events.

Among the Iroquois, public criticism by a mature man might cause a younger man to kill himself. The same criticism voiced during the War Dance, however, would be taken lightly, since traditionally all spectators were permitted to voice their opinions freely. Iroquois parents frequently treated their children permissively, being fearful of a child's suicide. Child suicide did in fact occur among the Iroquois, usually when a child felt too restricted by his or her parents.

Among the Kwakiutl, a man might commit suicide if his child died, even though the child's death was in no way his fault. If a son failed to qualify for membership in a secret society, his father might kill himself; but in this situation the cause of the suicide was usually financial—the high cost of the ceremonies frequently absorbed all of a man's financial resources. Among the Tlingit Indians, someone might commit suicide if, wronged by someone else, he found himself unable to attain satisfaction. In this situation, the offender was considered to be the murderer of the suicide, and the deceased's relatives continued to seek compensation for the wrong that had been committed.

SUN AND MOON. For many Indian tribes, Sun and Moon are not only mythological characters, but true deities, the Sun usually claiming precedence. Both sometimes appear directly to *Apinaye* votaries, and are addressed for rain and good crops by the *Canella,* who expect no theophany. To the *Sherente,* Sun and Moon do not appear either, but they send their distinctive astral deputies according to the solar or lunar affiliation of the visionary's moiety. The *Tapuya* worshiped the "Northern constellation," celebrating it with chants and "leaping," and at a special festival with athletic contests and dancing. According to their mythology, life had been easy for the Indians until Fox caused them to fall into this deity's bad graces, whence their subsequent need to worry about food.

The *Cariri* are supposed to have had a trio of gods, the "Father" being also represented as having two sons who quarreled. According to another source, God (Touppart) sent a friend to the Indians who was called their Grandfather; after a while Grandfather retired to the sky and sent them Badze (Tobacco) to be worshiped through offerings.

Ceremonial.—The preponderantly profane nature of much of eastern Brazilian ceremonial has been pointed out; on the other hand, certain phases of religious ritual have been necessarily discussed under other headings. The elementary rites of prayer, offerings, dramatization, and self-mortification are probably general. Certain cryptic forms figure in early sources, such as "confession in the woods" by the *Cariri.* There is likewise the clubbing of a kneeling person by the *Cayapo* chief till the blood flows from his forehead and is wiped off by attending women—a rite that reappears in the obsequies on behalf of a distinguished man, whose corpse is smeared with the blood. The *Tapuya* "king" owned a sacred flask or case, containing several holy rocks and fruits. This could not be touched without his consent, but was consulted before serious undertakings after tobacco smoke was blown upon it. Among these people priestly consecration was also deemed necessary to prosper the fields. The *Timbira* favored a retreat with ceremonial taboos in periods of crisis, such as birth or mourning. Arrows are shot at the sky during an eclipse by several tribes *Cayapo, Bororo)*.

Major festivals are usually highly composite. Mortuary rituals are elaborate among the *Bororo* and *Caingang,* whereas the boys' initation is stressed by the *Apinaye, Canella, Aweikoma,* and in the special form connected with an animistic cult and a tribal society by the *Mashacali.* Name giving is a common occasion for solemnities, but often without manifest religious connotation. Performances are sometimes definitely linked with social units *(Timbira, Caingang).*

MYTHOLOGY

A Sun and Moon cycle, with Moon as the less intelligent member of the pair who is teased by his companion, spoils things by foolish chatter, gets killed as a result of his stupidity, and has to be revived by Sun, is important in *Timbira, Sherente,* and *Camacan* mythology and at least adumbrated among the *Mashacali.* Both are generally male, but frequently comrades rather than brothers. The *Bororo,* however, though also telling tales about the Sun and Moon, have for their principal mythical heroes genuine twin brothers unconnected with the heavens, but appearing as hosts of the dead, as inventors, transformers, and slayers of monsters.

Significantly distributed in eastern Brazil are a number of motifs of which the following may be mentioned: A deluge; a world-fire; marriage to a star-woman *(Cayapo, Timbira, Sherente)*; the deserted boy acquiring fire for Indians from a friendly jaguar (same tribes); the destruction of a man-eating falcon by two brothers (*Timbira, Cayapo*); and Sharpened-Leg (*Timbira, Cayapo).* The primeval hoarding of all water by Hummingbird and its liberation for general use is shared by all the *Caingang* and *Botocudo.* The were-jaguar motif, popular among the *Camacan,*

Mashacali, and *Cayapo,* is lacking among the Botocudo, Timbira, and *Sherente.*

SUN DANCE, also called the New Life Lodge and the Sacred or Mystery Dance, was a rite that was practiced to renew communion with the earth, the sun, the spirits, and the winds in order to bring health and fertility to the tribe and make the buffalo flourish. The dance was a prolonged exercise that was done by men who fasted and gazed steadily at a sacred object such as the sun. There was often self-torture in this elaborate pageant that was replete with symbolic honors of all the forces of nature. Few words were spoken during the Sun Dance, but every movement of hand and foot and the lines drawn on the ground held sacred significance and were understood by all. Official equipment included a "bundle" of an ancient pipe, sinew, and dried herbs. The organization was informal. A Pledger, or holy man, acted as chief priest during the ceremony. On the night of the altar dedication he was required to have intercourse with the wife of the Pledger who handed down the ceremony. In this way the ceremony was kept alive and was passed down through living bodies.

The Sun Dance took place with no organzied priesthood or permanent temple. Tribesmen brought their decorated tipis and buckskin clothing. Most tribes performed the ceremony in summer and it was an occasion of excitement. In the Sun Dance of the Dakota and Mandan the men were tortured in a group as they awaited coming visions. Among the Oglala Sioux men were not considered brave, generous, or filled with integrity unless they could exhibit scars on their bodies that had been acquired as part of the Sun Dance ceremony. It was a way too for a man to raise his status. Self-torture was not a necessary part of the Sun Dance and when it occurred it was done in a way so as not to cause permanent injury. Nevertheless, the United States government banned the ceremony on the basis of its destructiveness. The torture was meant to convince the Powers of the Indians' earnestness in seeking the help of the supernatural.

The ceremony continued for two to four days while outside the main ceremony there was fasting, singing, and minor ceremonies. At the time of the Sun Dance children were given names and some had their ears pierced, marriages were arranged, acquaintances between young men and maidens were made during dancing and parading. In warrior societies there was feasting and talk of exploits, along with future vows. Women performed endless cooking and other tasks.

The Sun Dance is considered one of the most famous and spectacular of all Indian ceremonies. As a tribal rite it dates around 1800, established as a midsummer pause after the great buffalo hunt when food was plentiful. The last tribe to adopt the ritual was the Utes in about 1890. It grew from the ancient Algonkian quest of the vision quest by ordeal to become an elaborate Plains production in less than a hundred years.

SWEET POTATO (*Ipomaea batatas*) was cultivated in Middle America, the West Indies, and northern South America in prehistoric times. The exact place of origin is as yet unknown, but some evidence suggests northern South America. There is fairly general agreement that the sweet potato had also reached some of the islands of the Pacific in pre-Columbian times. Although it seems probable that its introduction there was by the agency of man, a natural means of dispersal cannot yet be entirely ruled out.

TABOO. The familiar, worldwide concept of taboo implies that the focus of power or mana is dangerous to a person who is not in a sacred state. The focus of power is untouchable because it is part of the supernatural world with which contact is dangerous. In most tribes, anyone who has been in contact with a supernatural power, whether voluntarily or against his will, must negate the danger by withdrawing from human society and all bodily activity. This might mean seclusion, fasting, abstaining from speech, sleep, glancing at the sun or fire, touching the most important part of the body, the head, or touching water to the lips. Among the Creeks, hunters, warriors, women in menstruation or in labor, and young men who were in training to become medicine men secluded themselves, fasted, and observed numerous taboos that would protect them from harm in their pursuits.

Gradually the concept of taboo changed from the status of one who is powerful or sacred to one who is unclean. There was a wide diffusion of taboos among tribes that involved restrictions for women during her reproductive life. There were incest taboos, pregnancy taboos, and taboos against intercourse at specific times, such as after the birth of a child. Among the Navajo, taboo transgression brought the universe into a lack of harmony. Spirits favored hunters and others who observed taboos. The breaking of a taboo might cause disease, or famine, or even death. In the Arctic, Sub-Arctic, Great Basin, and Northeast Mexico there were certain taboos that centered around funerals. Among Osage warriors, if victory did not result in a battle it was attributed to the breaking of a taboo; if animals did not come during the hunt it was the breaking of a taboo; if a man became diseased or died it might be that an angry spirit had taken away his soul because of a transgressed taboo.

Dietary taboos were common among the native North Americans. Eskimo children were forbidden to eat young seal meat, entrails, heart, lungs, liver, narwhal, small game, and eggs before they had fully demonstrated themselves to be accomplished hunters. Pregnant women generally were not allowed to eat meat. Among certain California and Great Basin tribes a husband observed food taboos along with his pregnant wife. Anyone who was ill or associated with illness had to refrain from eating meat for fear of diminishing the luck of the hunters. In the Natchez tribe it was taboo to eat the first ripe corn of the season until the firstfruits ceremony had been held. A family whose corn was ripe would rather starve then break the taboo on corn.

Hundreds of taboos surrounded hunting among most of the tribes of North America. Sometimes a hunter could not hunt when his wife was menstruating. She could not touch his hunting gear or any game that had been slain previously. In northwestern California meat was brought into the house through a removed wallboard instead of through the regular entrance for fear a menstruating woman had dropped blood in the doorway. A hunter often did not have sexual intercourse for at least one night before his hunt. A taboo broken in the manner of hunting or disposing of the animal's body parts could bring down the wrath of an animal spirit. Animals showed themselves in a hunt only if all taboos had been observed and the spirits pleased. Among the Elk clan of the Osage on the Prairies the killing of elk cannot be done by the same persons who make the elkskin coverings for sacred objects.

Taboos across North America were intimately involved with religious phenomena and were often known by hundreds of different names.

TATTOOING. The Mohave Indians of the lower Colorado River, like most primitive peoples, are fond of personal adornment. Two favorite methods of self-embellishment are tattooing and painting. Men and women have marks tattooed on the chin and usually on the forehead as well. Both sexes, in addition, paint striking designs on the face, hair and body. The use of tattooing relates the Mohave to the California tribes, most of whom practise this art. Facial painting, except

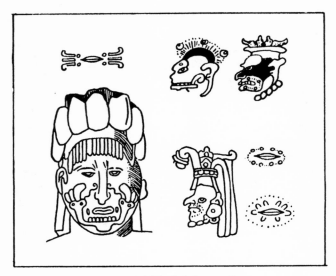

Tatooing and facial decoration.

for ceremonial occasions, is not highly developed in California. The Mohave, who paint regularly, show more of an affinity in this trait to the Southwest where painting is elaborate and frequent. On the contrary, a few Southwest tribes tattoo. It is noteworthy that tattooing and non-ceremonial painting occur together among the Mohave, as these traits are often regarded as mutually exclusive.

TATTOOING

Chin tattooing *(bakuich thompol,* 'mark chin') usually is applied to a person between twenty and thirty years of age. As there is no special class or guild of tattooers, anyone may do the tattooing. Some individuals, however, are regarded as more proficient and frequently are asked to perform the tasks. The client, lying flat on the ground with his head resting in the operator's lap, holds his chin up so that the tattooer may have an unobstructed view. First a design is drawn on the skin with charcoal; then a series of pricklings are made close together along the lines of the pattern. In recent years a steel needle has been used to puncture the skin, replacing the aboriginal sliver stone. When the blood flows, finely ground mesquite or willow charcoal is rubbed into the wounds. The operation is extremely painful and takes about two or three hours to complete. One Mohave reported typically: "My chin hurt awful when it started, but after a while it was so numb that it hardly hurt at all. It took a whole morning to finish." Not a few individuals refuse to continue after the first pricklings, because of the pain.

The wounds, which usually swell after the operation, are bathed from time to time with warm water, and fresh charcoal is rubbed in with the palm of the hand. While the sores are healing, care must be taken not to break them open; consequently only soft foods are eaten for four days. Said one, "After I got tattooed I could only eat young roasted pumpkin, so I wouldn't chew hard and break open the sores." Furthermore, a freshly-tattooed person must retire early and sleep lying flat on the back with body extended. If he should sleep on his side, "the chin would crack and the tattoo would be crooked." Normally the tattoo would heal in three or four days. The marks are dark-blue if the operation is well done, otherwise they are light-blue, and some may not even be visible. Occasionally the design may have to be tattooed on the skin a second or even a third time.

The chin design is selected by the tattooer, who chooses one which, in his opinion, will best suit the facial features of his client. A design for a narrow-faced person usually consists of narrow lines or rows of dots to accentuate the length of the face (fig. *l, a, b),* because a long face is much admired among the Mohave. Patterns for broad faces tend to have wider lines and cover more of the chin (fig. *l, c, e),* and seemingly make the face look even broader. Some

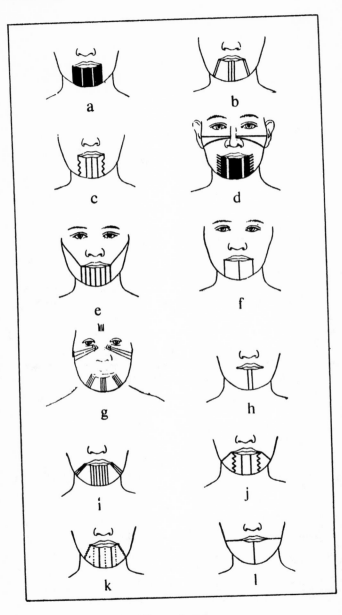

Women's tatoo.

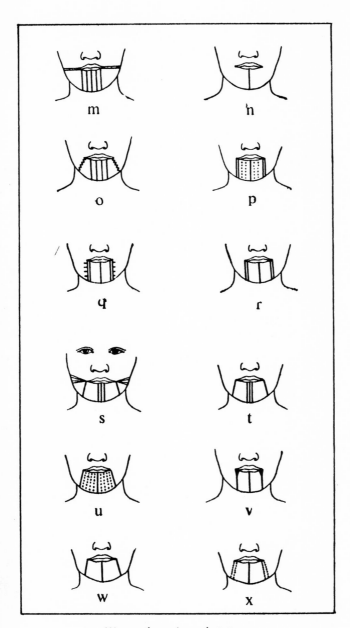

Women's and men's tatoo.

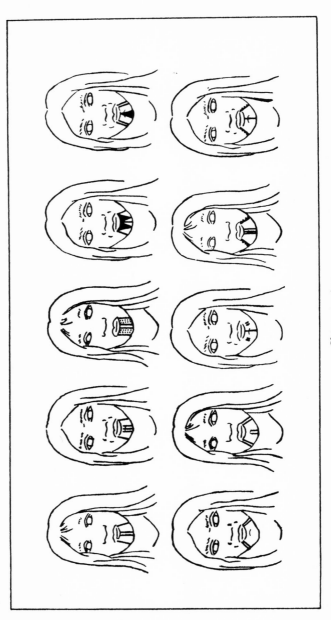

Chin tatooing.

motives are limited to males (fig. *l, d, f, j*). others to females (fig. *k, c, g, i*), and a few may be used by either sex (fig. *l, a, b, e, h*). Women occasionally may have the entire lower lip colored; men only the corners. The upper lip is never ornamented. The designs are only decorative and have no symbolic meaning; their names are descriptive, i.e., "dots", "put on lines", "lines with peaks", "points", etc.

Small marks (hakiuch hia, 'marked forehead') are tattooed in the middle of the forhead just above the eyebrows, and this is usually done some years after the chin tattoo. Simple lines, dots, and circles are used. A person may choose his own forehead design, but again some sex differences prevail. A few women may have a single or a double band ·tattooed on the front of the upper arm, and occasionally also just above the wrist. Men never have these. However, some men may have parallel, transverse, or intersecting lines tattooed on either one or both middle fingers, and they may also have lines, bands, or human figures ("boys") tattooed on their thigh.

A warrior may have a large circle (or two smaller ones) tattooed on the chest with one or two lines radiating toward the shoulders. An important man, such as a scalp-keeper (*gi hot*), frequently has a T-shape design tattooed on both sides of the face just below the cheek-bone.

Almost everyone tattooed, because a man or woman without marks on the face would be refused entrance to the "land of the dead" and had "to go down a rat-hole" instead.

It was related, "A kind of judge looks over each one who comes to Sil'aid (Land of the Dead) and if a man don't have marks on his face, he sends him down to where the desert rats are." Black paint is rubbed on the tattoo marks of dead person that they will be more visible on Judgment Day.

A few individuals, either because of the pain or for other reasons, refuse to be tattooed. Their relatives try to prevail upon them to have it done. Said one. "I couldn't stand getting tattooed when I was young, so I didn't. When I got older my daughter kept getting after me to let her do it. So I finally did," Some wait until they are very old and death is not far off before undergoing the operation.

TIPI. Of all types of primitive dwellings, the *tipi,* of the Plains Indians, with its conical form, tapering poles, and ingeniously devised flaps or wings at the top to regulate the draft of air for the fire, is the most picturesque and beautiful. Like the *iglu* of the far-distant Eskimo, it displays much skill in the adaptation of available materials to the necessities of environment. Evolved in the distant past to meet the requirements of a more or less nomadic people, the design and interior arrangements of the tipi were so complete that they never changed. For comfort, convenience, and good ventilation, it was unexcelled. By reason of its adaptability to prairie life, the Indian tipi was adopted by Gen. H. H. Sibley as a model for the army tent which now bears his name.

The Crows and the Blackfoot were said to make the finest tipis of all the Indian tribes. Their poles were long and tapering, the buffalo-skins which they used for covers skillfully tanned and whitened, the sewing materials of the best, and their tipis large and tall and well proportioned.

The manufacture, erection, and decoration of tipis differed more or less among the Plains tribes. The information about Blackfoot tipis was gained at first hand by my owning several of them. I used them while living in Blackfoot camps on the prairies, and learned their superiority to a modern tent for comfort in all kinds of weather when traveling with packhorses in the Rocky Mountains.

The establishing of a tipi by a Blackfoot family

welcome—other women, even a grandmother or some relative, were generally the helpers.

Women selected and cut the poles which were secured on the mountain slopes. The heavy forest at the head of Cutbank River was a favorite place, because of its growth of lodgepole-pine. There the trees grew tall and straight, and were free from branches.

The women used the tall and slender trees of lodgepole-pine, peeling off the bark and drying the poles slowly in the sun in order that they would be light and straight and easy to handle, cutting off the twigs and branches, and trimming smoothly and carefully, as a rough lodge-pole might wear holes in the cover and cause the lodge to leak.

Tipi-covers were generally made, in the spring or early summer, from the skins of buffalo cows sewed together. Old-time lodges were made of an even number of skins—fourteen, sixteen, twenty, sometimes even thirty or more. There were some magnificent family lodges having a base diameter of forty feet, with poles forty or more feet in length. But very large lodges were unusual, for they required two or more fires to heat, while the heavy cover and the long poles were hard to transport. Heavy covers were carried on the backs of horses, the poles fastened to the horses' sides, with the thicker ends dragging behind on the ground. In their life as nomads and hunters, the Blackfoot changed camp so frequently and traveled so far that the poles were soon too short for further use, hence a new set was required every year. Long ago, before the days of horses, when they had only dogs to draw their travoix, and carried things on their backs, smaller tipis were necessarily used.

A good-sized lodge had twenty poles, averaging twenty-five feet in length; for a very large one, thirty poles were used. The more poles employed in the construction, the better the cover could be stretched, consequently the lodge-cover would be taut and free from wrinkles; besides, it would not be so liable to leak, and it would last longer. Those who used the most poles usually had the best-looking lodges. My Blackfoot friends said that they could tell the lodges of the Crows from a distance by the shortness of their tipis poles, which had a cut-off appearance. It was customary for the Blackfoot to have their poles extend from four to six feet above the tops of the lodges.

A tipi-cover in constant use usually did not last more than a year, but with care it would endure for several years. Holes were worn in the cover by packing on horses; badly trimmed poles might wear other holes. Frequent wetting and drying of the sinew stitching in the hot sun caused seams to open; and even if patched, the cover would be likely to leak when heavy rains came.

Then the woman began to think of making a new lodge, and told her husband that skins were needed for the covering. She procured the sinew, which was split for thread: coarse strands for heavy work, medium fine or very fine for decorative work. These strands were folded into little bundles which the woman placed in her sewing kit. She prepared the bone needles and awls; and when the skins were brought in she tanned them herself, stretching them on the ground, hair-side down, to dry in the sun, and held by wooden stakes. She raked the hide with a large tool of bone sharpened at one end, and hacked it free from flesh and fragments. She left the hide to cure and bleach in the sun for several days, then scraped it to an even thickness with an adze-like tool.

After the flesh-side was finished, the woman turned the hide over and scraped off the hair. The skin was further dried and softened by drawing back and forth through a loop of twisted sinew fastened to a lodge-pole; then it was whitened by rubbing a piece of fungus—and the skin was ready for use.

Meantime the woman made it known through the camp that she was making a new tipi. She prepared a supply of food—dried meat, service-berries, kettles of soup, and tobacco. Then she invited certain women to eat with her, and by accepting they thus signified their desire to help. Tipi-covers were so large and heavy that it was necessary for the women to cooperate and to make their manufacture a social affair. Smoking, feasting, and gossiping, they enjoyed the work. The women whose tipi was being made superintended the work, seeing that the half-circle of the cover was true and of the right length, and that the wings and front pieces werre properly put on. The work of sewing was usually finished in one day.

Next the tipis was set up and rested—the sides pinned down close to the ground, the door-flap put on, and the smoke-hole closed. A fire was built inside and sagebrush used to make a thick smudge, that the lodge-skins be thoroughly smoked so that they would not harden when wet.

A marked feature of Blackfoot culture was the superiority of women in the household arts, in which they were trained from childhood. Women were the industrialists, the men were providers and defenders. And the women were not dissatisfied nor felt oppressed; they were proud of their work and were known throughout the camp for the quality of their product.

A mother trained her daughter in the tanning of skins and in making them into clothes and shelter and she instructed her also in the use of herbs and plants and wild vegetables used both for food and in healing. Women considered it their vocation and allowed no interference from the men, who knew nothing about such things. Not only the manufacture but the care of the tipi, was the work of the women; and they were so expert at pitching and striking a tipi that it took them only a few minutes.

In later years, after the extinction of the great buffalo herds canvas and cotton duck were used for tipi-covers. In the days when skins were used, the Blackfoot cut up the tops of old lodges for wet-weather mocassins, because they were well smoked and would not harden or shrink.

Although the use of paints as a preservative was unknown, the decorative painting of tipis and the symbolic marking of sacred objects were in such general use among the Blackfoot as to make the procuring and preparation of paints an occupation in itself. Onesta and Nitana, my friends who took me to visit the camp of Brings Down The Sun among the Northern Piegan in Canada, were known as "paint-gatherers." They traded in paints with their own people and also with other tribes.

Onesta said he obtained some paints from the ground—a white earth, a red earth, also a red from burned yellow earth. Most of the yellow came from a place on the Yellowstone River near some warm springs, but there was also a yellow from buffalo gall-stones. Yellow and black were both found along the Marias River; but there was also a black from charred wood, blue from a dark-blue mud, and a green was once procured from the scum of a lake northeast of the Katoyisix (Sweet Pine Hills).

Nitana, wife of Onesta, told of her experience in digging paint on Birch Creek. While at work she had been praying for the recovery of old chief Many White Horses, only to find the paint she gathered had turned into worthless dirt. A few days later, Many White Horses died.

Onesta explained to me that it was customary for women, while digging paint, to pray to the Sun in behalf of some prominent medicine-man. He warned his wife, saying, "If you had prayed for Heavy Breast who was then giving the Sun Dance ceremony, as you should have done, your paint would not have changed to dirt."

SOUTH AMERICA

Tipis are relatively rare in South America. In southern Tierra del Fuego, where wood is available, the *Ona* make a conical dwelling with a frame of a number of stout saplings arranged in tipi fashion, and a cover of branches, bark, or other material. The floor may be scooped out and covered with branches. Larger tipis are covered with sod, and used for ceremonial centers. The *Yahgan,* in the southern archipelago, make similar shelters. In eastern Brazil the *Timbira* used conical tipis for ceremonial centers and for temporary dwellings. The *Caingang* in northeast Brazil once made a tipi with a central forked pole against which four saplings were leaned, and the whole covered with palms. The interior was quartered by partitions, and each compartment was occupied by one family. Small doorways connected the compartments. The *Guaranoca* of the Chaco used a similar dwelling.

TOBACCO is exclusively an Indian product; but after Europeans discovered its use it was distributed so widely throughout the world and adopted by so many peoples in distant lands that now it is difficult to picture it as having once been confined to the Western Hemisphere.

The tobacco plant first was brought into Europe in 1558 by Francisco Fernandez, a physician who had been sent by Philip II of Spain to Mexico to investigate its agriculture. For some years tobacco in Europe was regarded as a medicinal plant only.

It was Sir Walter Raleigh, who, in honor of the Virgin Queen gave the name Virginia to the region covered by the patent Elizabeth granted him for colonization. The claim to Virginia then extended from Newfoundland to Florida and westward to the Pacific. Although he never visited Virginia, Sir Walter financed out of his private fortune the first two unsuccessful attempts at settlement there, which were in what is now North Carolina near Cape Hatteras. Sir Francis Drake searched for the earlier Roanoke colony, where the discouraged governor, Ralph Lane, and his settlers asked Sir Francis to take them back to England, which he did. This was in 1586 when, so far

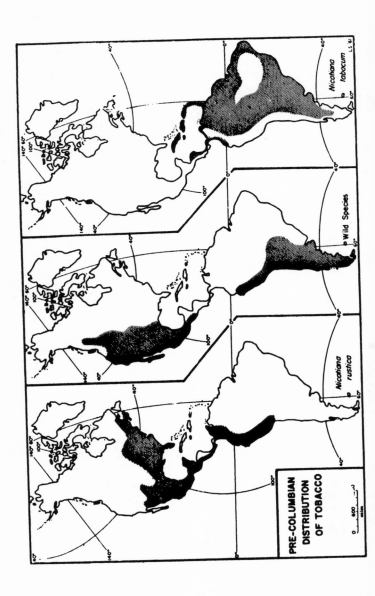

PRE-COLUMBIAN
DISTRIBUTION
OF TOBACCO

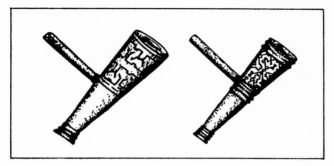

Tobacco pipes of wood.

as know, Ralph Lane was the first person to smoke tobacco in Europe.

Ralph Lane had brought with him from Virginia a quantity of Indian tobacco and tobacco pipes with which he supplied his patron, Sir Walter Raleigh, and taught him to smoke. Sir Walter being a gentleman of fashion, the Elizabethan courtiers followed his lead, and soon the custom of smoking commenced to spread.

Life went badly with Sir Walter Raleigh, however, and in 1618 he was beheaded. About the last thing he did before he walked to the block was to smoke a pipe of tobacco.

The pipe-makers of London became an incorporated body in 1619. Throughout the XVII century the custom of smoking spread far and wide in spite of opposition by priests and statesmen, severe laws, flogging, excommunication, and even captial punishment.

Tobacco was introduced into France by a French consul to Lisbon, Portugal,—Jean Nicot, from whose name is derived the term *nicotine.* Later, French aristocrats set the fashion of taking snuff from exquisite snuffboxes. In time this fashion was copied in England by the upper classes, among whom snuff-taking largely supplanted smoking for many years. Meanwhile the habit of chewing tobacco grew rapidly, especially among sailors and Americans.

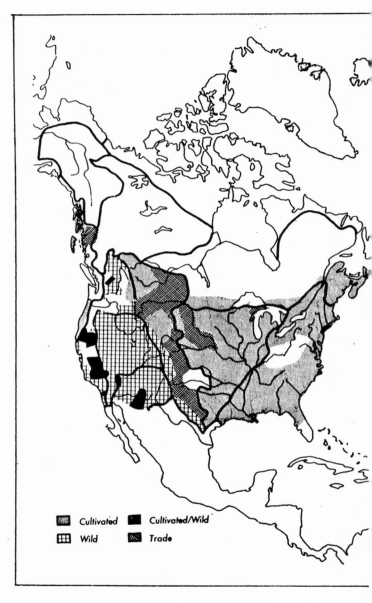

Native source of tobacco.

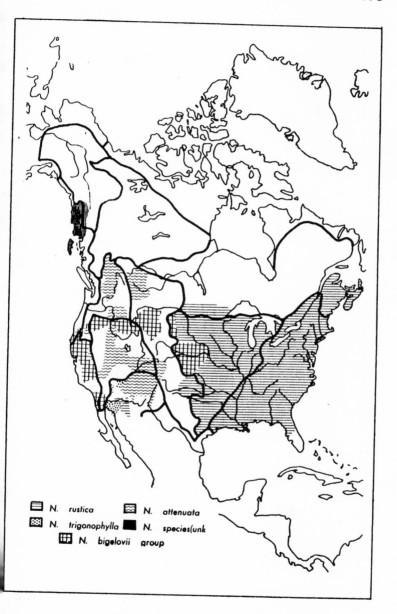

Dominant tobacco species.

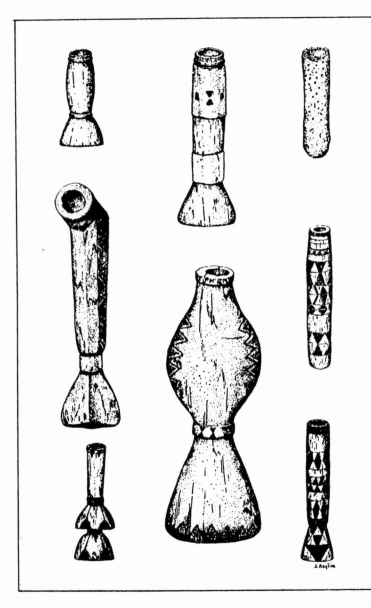

Chaco tobacco pipes.

The word *tobacco* is Indian, probably from the Taino word *tabaco,* meaning the pipe in which it was smoked, though it may mean tobacco leaves rolled for smoking.

There are many different species of tobacco, several of which were grown by the Indians. Two species were evidently cultivated by Indians in South America; and in pre-Columbian times one or both of these had been distributed over most of South America and as far north in North America as the climate permitted cultivation by Indian farmers, which was in Canada. Both of these species are still grown, one much more than the other, and in all countries in the temperate and tropic zones of the world.

TOMAHAWK. The story of the tomahawk, a "distinctive American production," deserves to be told in its proper historical setting. Symbolic of both war and peace, in its later form as a combination war axe and pipe, its history goes back into the distant past.

Centuries before the coming of the white man the aborigines who inhabited the upper Great Lakes region stumbled onto outcroppings of native copper metal. Pieces of this metal were broken off from larger masses and beaten into tools and implements of war. Among these were artifacts called celts, may of them shaped much like a modern axe head. These were mounted on hafts of wood or bone and used as a cutting tools, and no doubt frequently as a weapon.

Such implements inevitably found their way along trade routes all over the northern and eastern United States and Canada. But after the supply of copper was no longer available these metal weapons became scarce and the Indian was obliged to go back to his old stone axes.

When later Indians finally learned what the white man's axe was for (at first they hung them around their necks as decorations), they were happy to adopt them as tools. In keeping with long-established tradition the heavy axes were turned over to the squaws (and hence came to be called "squaw" axes), while the smaller hatchets were used to cut kindling wood or, if the situtation warranted, to cleave the skulls of their enemies.

The physical make-up of the typical pipe-tomahawk as is still seen today is a fairly simple affair. The metal head is made of iron or steel, brass, bronze, copper or pewter. The blade is of light weight and varying shape, with the sharp edge of the bit from three to four inches in width. It may be decorated by simple mechanical or patterned designs, cut-outs or insets of some decorative metal. Adjacent to the socket the blade usually becomes thicker, thus making it more sturdy. The socket hold the upper end of the handle, or helve, and is marked by way of vertical thickenings which serve as reinforcements as well as decorations. The bowl, which holds a couple of thimblefuls of tobacco or some allied smokeable substance may be shaped and marked by thickened rings at its orifice or base. It may also be inlaid by a decorative metal.

The handle was usually made of wood, although early battle-axes probably had metal handles, judging from their thickness. They were fairly uniform in diameter and rounded, oval or ovoid on cross section. They were usually made of hard or semihard wood, native to the region in which they were produced. But soft woods *(e.g.* pine*)* were sometimes used, especially when carving was to be done. Some handles were painted or covered with designs made with brass-headed nails or tacks.

Trinkets of "medicine," or of totemic significance were often attached to the lower third of the handle in the form of feathers, bits of fur, tufts of hair, strands of ribbons, or thongs of buckskin with strings of glass bread, bangles of metal, or animal or bird claws.

Perhaps one reason why the Indian took such a strong fancy to the hatchet was the fact that he had long been used to war clubs of various types, called *casse-tetes* ("skull crushers") by the French. But to distinguish the wood clubs, whose terminal knob was sometimes equipped with a sharp stone, a deer antler or metal spike, from the hatchet the latter came to be called a *tomahog* or *tomahack*, identified in the native tongue as a "cutting weapon." When the white traders learned that these tools were also in demand as weapons they introduced actual antique battle-axes from Europe for this purpose, or made axes to conform to this style. It is said, therefore, that the tomahawk has a double ancestry—the frontiersman's hatchet on one hand, and the European or Asian soldiers' battle-axe on the other. Until the turn of the 17th century (some say just before the Revolutionary War), it was these broad expanding-bladed battle-axes that were used primarily as war weapons.

It is not known who conceived the brilliant idea of attaching a pipe bowl to the axe, thus combining in one implement the Indian's two hobbies of smoking and skull cracking. By drilling a hole through the length of the handle and plugging its upper end, the bowl mounted on the butt end of the blade could be smoked as a pipe. Many of the old pipe-tomahawks still reek with the odor (or taste) of scorched tobacco. But once the idea was out, there was little demand for the old-fashioned battle-axe. The genuine pipe-tomahawk now brings a fancy price while the much rarer non-pipe war axe brings little more than would a modern hunting axe.

With the increasing opportunities to trade the relatively cheap tomahawks for fine furs, the British came out with the. model pipe-tomahawk, a well-balanced blade and "well-turned bowl" which came to represent the craftsman's art. On the other hand, the French incorporated their traditional *fleur-de-lis* into a spear-shaped blade with a pair of tangs sprouting sideways just in front of the socket. While this lily pattern had many modifications, it readily distinguished the French weapon, made specifically for British crania. Thus the two countries encouraged their Indian allies to carry on the fight along the borderlands.

Because of a natural reticence in having one's own head split open by a savage Indian so armed, there was some reluctance on the part of the English to arm their Indian allies with tomahawks. For Indian warfare along the frontiers usually resulted in the killing of women and children as well as the men. To quiet such fears an English proponent of Indian allies, Colonel Guy Johnson, made light of the viciousness of this weapon in a letter to Lord George German when he wrote: "The tomahawk which is so much talked of, is seldom used but to smoak thro, or to cut wood with."

On the other side of the question, Morgan (1901) writes of the use of this weapon by the Iroquois in these words: "The tomahawk succeeded the war club, as the rifle did the bow. With the invention of this terrible implement of warfare, the red man had nothing to do except in having it fashioned as to be adapted to his taste and usage. The tomahawk is known as widely as the Indian, and the two names have become apparently inseparable . . . They used it in close combat with terrible effect, and also threw it with unerring certainty at distant objects, making it revolve in the air in its flight. With the Indian, the tomahawk is an emblem of war itself. To bury it, is peace; to raise it, is to declare the most deadly warfare."

And thus was fought an almost constant warfare along the frontier. Urged on by his desire to destroy the invaders who were taking over his homeland, sometimes allied to English, sometimes to the French, the Indians raided isolated Colonial farms or surprised small villages in their version of "total war." Even if captives were taken, many were subsequently murdered in cold blood if they were too slow or collapsed of their wounds on the trail. And frequently, after the prisoners had arrived at their captors' village, some Indian squaw, mourning for a husband or son

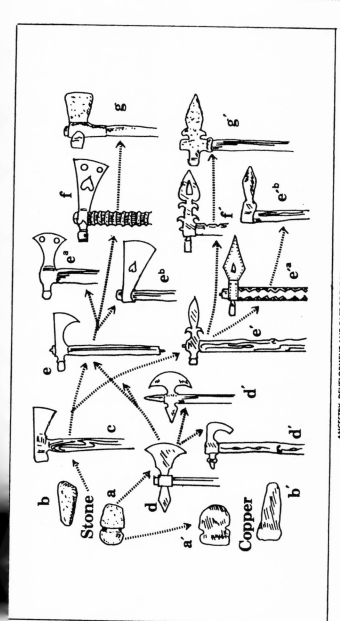

ANCESTRY, DEVELOPMENT AND FATE OF THE TRADE TOMAHAWK

a. Stone axe. b. Stone celt. a1. Copper axe. b1. Copper celt. c. Colonial iron handaxe or hatchet. d. Battle-axe type of tomahawk. d1 Battle-axe. Indo-Persian type. d11. Battle-axe. Viking type. e. English type pipe-tomahawk. e1a. Minnewauken type tomahawk. e1b. Diamond-bladed tomahawk. f. Ceremonial blunt-edged tomahawk. English-type blade. f1 Ceremonial *fleur-de-lis* tomahawk. French type. g. Catlinite tomahawk. English style 'blade. g1. Catlinite tomahawk. French style blade.

dead at the hands of a frontiersman, would seize a hatchet and split open the skulls of captives while their heads were held by the braves who had captured them. The tomahawk also became a means of capital punishment for Indians who had transgressed the mores of the tribe.

The skull wound made by a blow from a bladed (English style) tomahawk is quite characteristic (Courville 1948). The central part of the wound is incised by the sharp cutting blade. On either end of this wound there is an irregular crack, or "split," in the bones due to the wedging effect of the blade. The wound of the underlying brain also occurs in the form of a cut associated wtih bleeding.

Individual tomahawks were traded to the Indian for his beaver pelts, or were given wholesale to tribes whose favor the white man hoped to gain. Highly ornate and decorated pieces made by British or French artisans were also presented to noted warriors among their allies, or bestowed with flowery references to a future "unending chain of friendship" when making peace with a previously hostile tribe. The pipe was often smoked in friendship between individuals as well as groups.

All this made good business and many English and French companies which manufactured pots and kettles, as well as knives and hatchets, supplied the frontier with such material. But even wars must sometimes cease, and after the American Revolution and the War of 1812 the red man finally had to make up his mind which side to line up with in accepting the white man's ways. Beaver hats were also going out of style. The French traders had first been displaced by the English and English by the Americans after the Revolutionary War, so there was then a shift in the fur trade. By 1825 the market for tomahawks was greatly limited, and for cutting fire wood an ordinary hatchet would do.

Meanwhile, the opening of the West had created a new contact with the numerous tribes of Plains

Indians. At first these Indians were friendly to the white explorers and traders and fought mostly with one another—until they realized that the growing horde of palefaces really meant to take over their country. They fought desperately with their own weapons and the invaders' when they could get them. But the tradition of the tomahawk as a weapon of authority died hard. The portraits of many chiefs and notable warriors painted by a Catlin, Kurz, or an Eastman show weapons slung over one arm, and these weapons are usually war clubs or tomahawks.

While it is presumed that some American hardware manufacturers supplied tomahawks to the midwestern tribes, many of these weapons were made to order by the village blacksmiths. Throughout Colonial days the local smith had his price to turn out a simple axe or hatchet, or even the more complicated pipe-tomahawk (which would cost two or three dollars, depending upon the amount of workmanship in it). However, the tomahawks carried by the middle plains Indians, both shown by the artists or found in current collections, were usually hand made. The larger exception was the brass-headed weapon, which by its very nature had to be cast. The artistic talents of the ironmonger were thus put to the test, with the result that some remarkable productions were forthcoming.

The destiny of the tomahawk was ultimately settled by the repeating rifle and six-shooter in the years after the Civil War. There was no use in carrying around a *striking* weapon when it was no longer possible to get close enough to make a pass at your enemy. Even though the handle of the tomahawk was lengthened to make it more effective on horseback, and beautifully decorated to make its "medicine" more powerful, it was a thing of the past. This fact was significantly remarked by Colonel Richard Dodge (1890): "While there are yet many elaborately ornamented toma-hawks, they are regarded as an insignia or rank, to be carried on ceremonial occasions but scarcely thought of as weapons; even as pipes they are beginning to be noted a bore by the average Indian." Some of these ceremonial weapons have blades of magnificent size, with the handles often tastefully embellished by large-headed brass tacks. Occasionally a sample of bead work on a banner of buckskin is attached as "medicine". All this has served only to make them an attractive antique or memento of the days of the Old West.

The tomahawk was to have its *exitus* in effigy. In the land of the Sioux there is a pipestone mine which contains a peculiar claylike material appropriately named Catlinite. Fresh from the ground, this substance can be carved in detail to make smoking pipes of all sizes and styles. When dry it becomes hard, like fired clay. The Sioux in particular have made many simulated tomahawks of Catlinite which are actually smokeable pipes. Even the French type of weapon with its tradiitonal *fleur-de-lis* pattern has been imitated. Of special interest is a group of pipes which are made of Catlinite and a soft lead alloy. One of these, now in the Southwest Museum, has the blade of the simulated tomahawk made of this metal.

TOMATO—Whether or not the tomato was poisonous was a question that aroused controversy in times past; but nowadays the tomato is known to be wholesome, a great source of vitamins, and a valuable addition to the modern table. The United States leads all countries in appeciation of its merits. The word is Indian, derived from the Nahuatl *tomatl*. It is believed that the plant was developed in South America; and its pre-Columbian distribution was in South America and Middle America. By the time Europeans arrived there were several distinct species of tomato, and a great many varieties. In the United States we ordinarily see only one of these species.

TORTURE is inflicting pain of an unusually severe nature upon a person. Among the North American Indians, torture was usually associated with prisoners of war, although it could also have religious overtones. The Huron Indians, for example, tortured prisoners throughout the night. They were careful, however, to insure that they survived until morning, since both the god of war and the Sun god were thought to witness the ordeal. After many hours of burning, stabbing, mutilating, and even dismembering a prisoner, they finally decapitated him. At times the remains of the victim were cannibalized.

The emphasis on torture of prisoners that is found in the East seems to be unusual compared to practices in other regions of North America. Instances of torture in the Plains and Prairies, for example, seem to have been derived from Eastern practices during the historic period. Some California tribes practiced torture, included the Maidu and the Gabrielino. In this region, however, torture seems to have been merely a prelude to execution.

Self-torture was common among the North American Indians. Hidatsa warriors, for example, endured the ordeals of self-torture as a preparation for the trials of war. Leaders of unsuccessful war parties often punished themselves with self-tortures. The most usual self-torture involved inserting sharpened thongs into the flesh and attaching various objects to them, which would then be dragged about without the use of hands. The Teton's used a similar method of self-torture, tieing a cord to the thong and attaching the other end of the cord to a tree. The victim was required to free himself by pulling until the thong was ripped from his flesh. The goal of this ordeal was to faint from pain and fatigue, since in that condition a man was thought to be in touch with the gods. This self-torture could be undertaken at any time, although the annual Sun Dance provided the most usual occasion for such displays.

Other relatively minor tortures were employed in a variety of situations. Puberty rites, for example, were often accompanied by some mild torture, as among the Pueblo Indians whose children were ceremonially flogged. The Alibamu Indians flogged their children until they bled. The Tlingit Indians tied suspected witches to a pole for ten days in order to extract confessions. If no confession was obtained, and if the victim survived the ordeal, the suspect was presumed innocent. Most suspects, however, confessed to the charges, since the only punishment was the requirement that the witch remove his spell. On the Northwest Coast, rude guests were forced to eat a trayful of repulsive foods, or to drink urine.

TOTEM POLES. The totem poles of the north Pacific Coast of America, in British Columbia and Alaska, are known all over the world. The excellence of their decorative style at its best is nowhere surpassed by any other form of aboriginal art, and as an expression of native personality and craftsmanship they are impressive and unique. Many of them, along with vast collections of carvings and paintings, are treasured by the museums of Europe and America. Other monumental carvings of the same coast stand in the public parks of western cities. Seattle, Victoria, Vancouver, Prince Rupert, Ketchikan, Juneau, and Sitka. But it is in their true home that these picturesque creations can be seen to best advantage. At the edge of the ocean, amid tall cedars and hemlocks, and in the shadow of lofty mountain peaks, they create impressions as unexpected as they are exotic. Deep-set in moist, dark green, semi-tropical surroundings in an atmosphere often laden with bluish tints, their bold profiles are strangely reminiscent of Asiatic divinities and monsters.

The art of carving poles belongs to the past. Racial customs and stamina are on the wane everywhere, even in their former strongholds. With the exception of a few poles recently carved and erected in the upper Skeena River, and in southern Alaska under the auspices of the WPA, totem poles as such are no longer made. Most of those erected from forty to seventy years ago have fallen from old age, and since disappeared in decay. Some were sold, cut down, and acquired by museums or public institutions. A few were removed, without the consent or knowledge of the owners, in maritime raids upon deserted Indian villages. A number were destroyed by the owners themselves during religious revivals under the banner of Christianity; for instance, those of a southern Tlingit village in Alaska, and of two Tsimsyan tribes (Gitlarhdamks and Port Simpson) in the winters of 1917 and 1918.

Not even a remnant remains of the famous clusters of former days at Massett, Yan, and Skidegate, among the Haidas of the Queen Charlotte Islands. The Kaigani-Haida totems of Prince of Wales Island have vanished or have been removed to other locations in public parks. Scarcely any are left among the Bella Coolas, the Kwakiutls, and the Nootkas, and in a few years even these will have disappeared. Of the fifty or sixty Haida poles still standing along the sea-coast in several deserted villages visited by the author in 1947, only about a dozen could be removed for preservation elsewhere. The rest are in an advanced state of decay.

The best collection of poles, still fairly complete in 1930, was that of the upper Skeena River in British Columbia, a short distance southeast of the Alaskan border. It comprised more than a hundred poles or carvings in scattered groups of from four to over thirty poles, each in eight tribal villages of the Gitksan nation. (The Gitksans are one of the three nations of the Tsimsyans.) But grave deterioration has since set in, sometimes in the form of "restoration". Another of the three Tsimsyan nations, on Nass River to the north, still possessed, in 1927, more than twenty of their poles; these were scattered from Gitiks, near the mouth of the Nass, to Gitlarhdamks, midway up the river. Although the poles of Nass River tribes were among the finest and most elaborate in existence, ranging up to 80 feet in height, those of the Skeena· were, on the whole, of inferior size and quality. Nearly all the Nass River poles by now have been purchased and removed by the author for various institutions in Canada, the United States, Great Britain and France.

A number of the Skeena poles are crude, archaic, and older than any of the poles on the coast, where constant moisture hastens decay. Only a part of the long shaft in many of them is decorated. They occur upriver, far inland—from 150 to 250 miles—at the edge of the area where this art once was the fashion. Nowhere else but on the Nass were poles to be found so far inland. The Canadian Government and the Canadian National Railways, in 1928 and 1929, inaugurated the policy of preserving the Skeena River poles in their original location, and a decade later the Forestry Branch of the United States Government adopted a similar policy in Alaska.

The fame of this striking form of native art might lead one to suppose that our ethnographic literature concerning it is rich in proportion. But it is not. In the articles, usually illustrated, of such observers as James Deans, Dr. Franz Boas, Dr. J. R. Swanton, Liet. George T. Emmons, Dr. C. F. Newcombe, W. A. Newcombe, and others, we find only brief or casual descriptions of poles or of models. Their notes usually lack the necessary historical context, and it is too late now to recover it. The only substantial contributions to the knowledge of this subject are the author's monograph Totem Poles of the Gitksan, published in 1929, and a smaller, valuable book mostly on the totems of Alaska, by Edward L. Keithahn, entitled Monuments in Cedar.

The figures on totem poles consisted of symbols and illustrations, many of them comparable to our heraldry, and others commemorating historical events. They were not pagan gods or demons as is commonly supposed; they were never worshiped. Usually they illustrated myths or tribal traditions. Their meaning and associations inspired veneration rather than actual religious devotion.

The poles of the Tsimsyans and the Tlingits in particular—though this also largely true of those of the Haidas—were monuments erected by various families in the tribe to commemorate their chiefs after their death. They corresponded to our tombstones. After the people had given up erecting totem poles, they often had some of the same crests carved from stone or marble at Port Simpson or Vancouver, and placed as tombstones in their modern graveyards. The owners' object in showing their coats of arms on poles or posts was to enhance their prestige and to publish at large their claims to vested rights and privileges. These emblems or totems varied with each family; they were their exclusive property, jealously guarded. They embodied legends, phenomena, and the animals of the country. The Eagle, the Raven, the Frog, the Killer-Whale, the Grizzly Bear, and the Wolf are among the most familiar themes. The Thunderbird, the Woodworm (a local form of the Dragon), the Strong Man (the Samson story), and several others were borrowed from mythology. Some animals are less frequently seen, and so seem to be quite recent as crests: the Owl, the Salmon, the Woodpecker, the Beaver, the Starfish, the Shark, the Halibut, the Bullhead, Split-Person, the Mountain-Goat. The Puma, Moon and Stars, Mirage and Rainbow are fairly restricted in use. All these symbols were property marks, proudly displayed on houses, garments, and household possessions.

The legendary origin of most of these emblems is explained in traditional narratives that used to be recited at the winter festivals or potlaches, after totem poles had been erected. In spite of the decay of tribal customs, they are remembered by members of the older generation, who can still tell how their ancestors long ago met with tribulations, and adventures; how they were harassed and rescued by spirits and monsters; how benevolent spirits appeared in visions and invested their 'proteges' with charms; how ancient warriors conquered their enemies in warfare. The carved illustrations of these stories served a definite purpose besides commemoration and ownership; they made familiar to all members of the tribe the legends and traditions of the past.

Soon after the death of a chief, the prospective heirs appointed his leading nephew to the post. The induction of the successor took place in the presence of a large number of invited guests, and during elaborate festivals where liberality was an outstanding feature. The name of the 'uncle' passed on to the 'nephew', and the erection of the totem pole crowned the event. Groups of related families mustered all the resources available to make the feast memorable, for their standing and influence depended on display. Power and wealth were ruling factors in the social life of the Northwest Coast people.

Cutting a large red cedar tree, transporting it overland or by sea for considerable distances, carving and finally erecting it, often required years. Delays were numerous and unavoidable. The owners needed time to gather their resources, and expenditures were necessarily made in installments. First a tree was selected and felled. The 'allies' or opposites (that is, the family of the father) took charge of the work and no relative could accept a stipend. The workers and the guests were fed and paid publicly, before the ceremonies were concluded. Then a carver was hired, also from the 'father's' clan, who, should he lack the necessary skill, was privileged to appoint a substitute over whom he 'stood' ceremonially, assuming the credit for the work. The carving was accomplished as secretly as possible. Figures were selected by the owners from their list of available crests, as these might exceed half a dozen in number. The most costly item was the actual planting of the pole in the ground. When enough food and wealth had been amassed, invitations were sent forth to all the leading families of the neighbouring tribes. Eventually the pole was erected in the presence and with the help of the hundreds—sometimes the one or two thousand—gathered for these festivities which were so important a feature of this tribal life until sixty years ago.

As there was a lack of modern equipment, the raising of a large tree trunk required the greatest ingenuity as well as the closest cooperation of several tribes. The butt of the pole was introduced into a six-foot hole, out of which a trench was dug, and the small end was raised gradually by means of wooden props. A rope of cedar bark, sinew, or trade materials was then attached to the upper end of the shaft and passed over a stout supporting frame. Numerous hands then pulled the rope until the mast was finally hoisted into position.

Though the totem pole villages of the Haidas have been the most widely known, they have now virtually ceased to exist. Those of the upper Skeena are the only ones that still retain some of their earlier features. Kispayaks, Gitsegyukla, and Kitwanga claimed, as late as 1930, about twenty poles each. Their own alien and bizarre appearance was enhanced by the striking background of darkly wooded and mist-shrouded, ice-capped peaks. Gitwinlkul is the most remarkable of these tribal villages. It stands on the Grease Trail from the Skeena to the Nass, claiming the largest number of poles now standing anywhere in a single cluster. Even in 1925 it was still most impressive. Its poles were among the tallest and best, as well as the oldest. Each year, however, brings some veterans down.

These carved memorials usually faced the main highways of river or ocean. They stood apart from each other, in front of the owner's house, and dotted the whole length of the village in an irregular line. Changing times forced the removal of most villages to new quarters in the last sixty years, and the poles were forsaken in the abodes of the past. Here and there trees have grown round them, and sometimes it was not easy to find them in the forest. This was particularly true along the Nass and on the Queen Charlotte Islands. As it is, they lean precariously, tottering in every wind, and destined to crash down, one by one.

Little printed information is available on the actual

carvers among most nations. The author has retrieved enough material from near oblivion for a detailed history of plastic art and the making of totems on the north Pacific Coast. The carving of totem poles once was a very popular art. Although some artists were at times preferred to others for their skill, their choice for specific tasks was governed by customs rather unconcerned with craftsmanship. (This did not apply to the Haidas as it did to the Tsimsyans and the Tlingits). Each family of standing had every inducement to employ its own carvers for important functions in ceremonial life. For instance, the hundred totem poles of the upper Skeena were produced by more than thirty local carvers and thirteen outsiders. Six of the outsiders were from the Nass, and had been engaged in the earliest period when the Skeena carvers were not yet proficient in the new calling; three others were from the lower Skeena, and four from the Bulkley River, a tributary of the Skeena. The Skeena carvers belonged to independent and widely scattered social groups or families: 23 were of the Raven-Frog phratry, 9 of the Wolf, 5 of the Eagle, and 3 of the Fireweed Seventy-eight out of the hundred poles are ascribed to Gitksan artists, and the balance is credited to outsiders.

THE GROWTH OF TOTEM POLE CARVING

It is an error to suppose that totem poles are hundreds of years old. The nature of the materials from which they are made and the climate to which they are exposed render this an impossibility. A green cedar pole cannot stand upright much beyond fifty or sixty years on the upper Skeena, where precipitation is moderate and the soil usually consists of gravel and sand. Along the coast, it cannot endure beyond half a century because of the muskeg foundation and the intense moisture that prevails most of the year. For instance, the totem poles of Port Simpson, which are exposed to warm rainy winds, all decayed on the south side first, and most of them tumbled to the ground in less than fifty years. The well-known poles, now in our parks and museums, were carved after 1860, and many of those seen in Indian villages, such as Alert Bay, were erected after 1890.

The art of carving and erecting memorial columns is not really so ancient on the north Pacific Coast as is generally believed. Popular misconceptions in this respect used to be fantastic. Nobody seemed to question the statement on labels that some poles were one or two hundred years old, when the actual age, still verifiable, was much nearer sixty or seventy. Even such poles as these were among the oldest obtained in the Haida country.

Native technique reached its fullest development in the last century, and after 1860. It hinged upon European tools, the steel axe, the adze, and the curved knife, which were made in imitation by the natives or were traded off in large numbers to them from the days of the early circum-navigators, that is, after 1778. The lack of suitable tools, wealth, and leisure in the prehistoric period precluded elaborate structures and displays. The benefits accruing from the fur trade at once stimulated local ambitions; they stirred up jealousies and rivalries, and incited sustained efforts for higher prestige and leadership. The overmastering desire everywhere was to outdo the others in ingenuity and wealth, power and display. The totem pole came into fashion through the rise of these ambitions, fostered mostly by the fur trade. It became the best way of announcing one's own identity in the commemoration of the dead, the decoration of houses, and in the perpetuation of traditional imagery. The size of the pole and the beauty of its figures proclaimed the fame of those it represented.

Feuds over the size of totem poles often broke out among the leaders. The bitter quarrel between Hladerh and Sispegoot is still remembered on the Nass River. Hladerh, head-chief of the Wolves *(Larhkibu)*, would not allow the erection of any pole that exceeded his own in height. Sispergoot, head-chief of the Killer Whales, disregarded his rival's jealousy. When his new pole was carved, over seventy years ago, the news went out that if would be the tallest in the village. In spite of Hladerh's warnings, Sispegoot issued invitations for its erection. He was, however, shot and wounded by Hladerh as he passed in front of his house in a canoe. The festival had to be postponed for a year. Meanwhile Hladerh managed, through a clever plot, to have Sispegoot murdered by one of his own kinsmen. He later compelled another chief of his own phratry to shorten his pole twice after it was erected; and he was checked only when he tried to spread his rule to an upper Nass village.

Before totem poles had reached imposing proportions among the three leading northern nations, the carvings that preceded them were mostly graveyard carvings. The crests as a rule were painted with ochres on the house fronts or carved on head-dresses and small ceremonial objects. The impressive crop of totem poles that became known from 1880 to 1900 was the first of its kind to stand anywhere. The oldest poles of Gitsegyukla (at Skeena Crossing on the Skeena River) have stood only since the fire destroyed the earlier villages in 1872; those of Hazelton were carved after the establishment of the Indian reserve about 1892. But several of the poles in the other villages —including Kitwanga—were many years older and are, therefore, particularly interesting as an illustration of the growth of totem pole carving within two or three generations in the nineteenth century. The Haida and Tlingit poles were all, with rare exceptions, erected after 1860. The earliest lot, much smaller, is unknown to us.

The poles of the upper Skeena were, on the average, erected in the past fifty or sixty years. The five or six oldest slightly exceed eighty years of age. Many are less than forty years old. It is safe to say that this feature of native life among the Gitksans became fashionable only after 1870 and 1880. Six out of nearly thirty poles at Gitwinlkul—the earliest of these villages to adopt the art—exceed sixty years of age, and only a few poles at that time stood in the neighbouring villages.

Native accounts and the evidence of what the earliest carved memorials were, among the three northern nations of the coast, led to the inevitable conclusion that carved house-front poles and house corner posts were introduced many years before the first detached columns appeared. Several houses and posts of this kind were still remembered by the elders and have been described to us; a few were even to be observed, though most were in an advanced state of decay. The archaic style of house decoration was abandoned as soon as the natives gave up building large communal lodges in the purely native vein, and memorial colums that could no longer serve as ceremonial doorways—or traps—became the new fashion. Actually, some of the upper Skeena villages never adopted the fashion wholesale, and at least four of them boasted of no more than a few poles, some of which were put up only after 1890.

Internal evidence tells the same tale. The carving technique on several of the oldest poles—those erected over seventy years ago—is self-revealing, particularly as it discloses anterior stages in the art. It is essentially that of making masks or carving small detached objects; or again, of representing masked and costumed performers as they appeared in festivals rather than the real animals or objects as they existed. The carvers had not yet acquired the skill of their successors, who had advanced to the point of thinking of a large pole as a unit, which called for breadth of decorative treatment. Haesem-hliyawn and his comtemporaries of Gitwinlkul, among the Gitksans, have been responsible for the advance of the art beyond its first stage; and yet they belong, from the point of view of location and affiliation, to the Nass as much as to the Skeena. The totem poles of Cape Fox and Tongas (southern

Alaska) are said to have been the work of Nass River carvers, and the house posts of Klukwan in the Tlingit country to the north were from the hands of Wrangell craftsmen.

The fashion of erecting large wooden memorials in most parts, except the Haida and Nass River districts, was plainly derivative. During the stages of its evolution it spread from the Nass southeastwards to the upper Skeena, as some of the leading carvers of the coast were invited to transplant their activities to parts still unprovided with native craftsmen. But the demand for foreigners here was shortlived. Local talent soon developed. Stimulus for it was constant, the demand pressing. The imitativeness and inexperience of the new recruits to the art was at first only too evident, and their efforts were often crude. Progress to a point was rapid, but they remained on the whole inferior to their contemporaries of the Nass and the Queen Charlotte Islands to the west.

Haesem-hliyawn and Hlamee, of Gitwinlkul, both represent distinct periods of the craft among the Gitksans. To Haesem-hliyawn, the greater of the two artists, goes the credit of carving some of the best poles in existence. He belonged to the little group of Nass River and Gitksan carvers who excelled their compatriots, among whom we note Nees-laranows and Hlamee. Their carvings were on a par with the best ever produced on the Nass and the Queen Charlotte Islands. In other words, they are nowhere surpassed in excellence.

Haesem-hliyawn and Nees-laranows lived as late as 1868. Hlamee, their junior and follower, died after 1900. No fewer than twenty poles from their hands still stand in the three lower villages of the Skeena, seven of them ascribed to Haesem-hliyawn, three to Nees-laranows, and ten to Hlamee.

The style of Haesem-hliyawn was of the finest, in the purely native vein. He combined a keen sense of realism with a fondness for decorative treatment. With him, as with Oyai of the Nass, Tsimsyan are reached one of its highest pinnacles. It sought inspiration in nature, while keeping within ancient stylistic technique. Haesem-hliyawn belonged to the generation (1840-1880) in which the art of the totem pole saw at once its formative stages and its apogee. His handling of human figures ranks among the best achievements of West Coast art—indeed, of aboriginal art in any part of the world. The faces he carved, with their strong expression and amusing contortions, are characteristic of the race. Many of them are masterpieces. From a purely traditional source his art passed into effective realism. His treatment of birds and spirit-monsters is not inferior to that of the human figure. On several of his best carvings, especially as seen at Gitwinlkul, he reached into the sphere of higher art where the artist yields to his instinct and expresses himself in general terms.

The carved poles of Nass River maintain a higher standard of art than those of the Skeena and adjacent areas. They were less numerous too, as the Nass people gave up their ancient customs earlier than the Gitksans. That was fifty or sixty years ago, and most of the Gitksan poles were erected since. The technique of pole carving in both areas represents well the passage from the earlier and better art of the Haesem-hliyawn type to that of Hlamee. Carving was at first the almost exclusive means of achieving effect, but commercial paint later gained ground at the expense of plastic form.

Nass River tribes made totem poles at an earlier date than the upper Skeena people. Many families on both sides were related, and several of the Gitwinlkul villagers had their hunting grounds on the upper Nass. The Gitksans villagers had their hunting grounds on the upper Nass. The Gitksans used to travel every spring to the lower Nass for oolaken fishing or to trade pelts and dried fruit cakes with the coast tribes. There they came into close touch with the Tlingits of southern Alaska and with the Haidas of the Queen

Charlotte Islands. A strong cultural influence from the more progressive tribes of the coast was unavoidable and it is a trait of all these aborigines that they were keen and gifted imitators, and fond of novelty.

The Tsimsyans of the lower Skeena, or Tsimsyans proper, never wholly adopted the art of carving totem poles. When they were moved long ago to commemorate a historical event of the first magnitude, they erected a tall slab of stone, not a totem pole as they would have done more recently. Such a slab still stands at the Gitsalas canyon, at the former village of Gitsedzawrh, on the north side of the river.

The pole erected at the Tsimsyan village of Port Simpson, established by the Hudson's Bay Company in 1833, have mostly all decayed or been destroyed. Yet they were all erected after 1857, as an early painting, "Fort Simpson in 1857", reproduced in Arctander's Apostle of Alaska contains no trace of a totem pole.

If the Tsimsyans proper were not swayed by the modern fashion of erecting carved memorials to their dead, they retained the older custom of painting their symbols on their house fronts in native pigments. Although not a single totem pole seems ever to have stood in the village of Gitsees near the mouth of the Skeena, five house-front paintings were still remembered and described to the author a few years ago. Many houses of the neighboring tribes were also painted; a feature that at one time may have been fairly general all along the coast.

This remarkable West coast custom of carving and erecting house poles and tall mortuary columns, and of painting coats of arms on house fronts, is sufficiently uniform in type to suggest that it originated at a single centre and spread north and south. Its frontiers coincide with those of the West Coast art, embracing the carving or painting of wood, leather, stone, bone, and ivory.

This art itself seems more ancient in its smaller forms. Its origin may be remote, going back to Asia like the people themselves during late prehistory. It was partly in existence, quite conventionalized, at the time of the early Spanish, English, and French explorers (1775-1880). Most of the early circumnavigators—Cook, Dixon, Meares, Vancouver, Marchand, and La Perouse—give evidence that masks, chests, and ceremonial objects were, at the end of the eighteenth century, decorated in elaborate or grotesque style. They also mention, without details, that house fronts and house posts were decorated with carved and painted designs. There is a striking lack of evidence as to the existence of totem poles proper or detached memorial columns, either south or north. Yet the early mariners often visited the villages of the Tlingits, the Haidas, the Tsimsyans, the Kwakiutls, and the Nootkas. The descriptions or sketches in some of their relations fail to give us any hint of the presence of tall carvings, still less of their actual appearance. For instance, Dixon examined several of the Haida villages on the Queen Charlotte Islands, but fails to mention totem or even house poles; yet he minutely described small carved trays and spoons, and left some illustrations.

There were already—from 1780 to 1800—some carved house posts in existence. Captain Cook (A Voyage . . . Volume 11, page 317) observed a few decorated posts inside the house of the chiefs at Nootka Sound, where he wintered; and Webber, his artist, reproduced the features of two of them in his sketches. Meares, in 1788 and 1789; observed similar Nootka carvings in the same neighbourhood, which he describes (Voyages . . . page 138): "Three enormous trees rudely carved and painted, formed the rafters, which were supported at the ends and in the middle by gigantic images, carved out of huge blocks of timber." And he calls them elsewhere "misshapen figures". The earliest drawing of a carved pole is that of a house-front or entrance pole (not a real totem pole) of the Haidas, in Bartlett's Journal, 1790.

The custom of carving and erecting tall mortuary columns in front of the houses in the villages to honour the dead is comparatively modern, and was probably unknown before the beginning of the nineteenth century. But it is not easy to trace it back to its exact birth-place on the coast. These monuments hastily borrowed their style and features from smaller prototypes, ceremonial objects such as masks, charms, canes, and staffs. The earliest Gitksan poles, the oldest preserved, show this derivative trend, and a few poles among the Haidas and the Kwakiutls are reproductions of ceremonial staffs or carved canes. The figures were carved out of a log as if they were detached parts affixed to its surface with wooden pegs. Even the simple poles of the Nootkas as described by Cook may not represent the art of prehistory free of foreign influences. Iron and copper tools at that date were already available on the coast and were used everywhere with the proficiency of lifelong habit. The West Coast at that date was no longer untouched. The Russians had discovered its northern parts many decades before, and the Spaniards had left traces of their passage to the south. The influence of the French and the British had filtered in through contacts between intermediate tribes, and through the arrival of half-breeds and coureurs-de-bois west of the mountain passes. The north Pacific Coast people, mostly because of the fur trade, had been under foreign influence at least indirectly for more than two hundred years. All the natives were eager imitators. Nowhere more than on the western sea-coast did they show greater avidity and skill in assimilating whatever suited their needs from the sundry goods and crafts of the white man. They quickly adopted the tools introduced by European traders, and improved their native technique to the full measure of their new facilities.

To emphasize the novelty of totem pole carving and single out the causes which, after 1830, promoted its growth, I shall select a few illustrations showing their connection with the fur trade, more particularly with the North West Company and the Hudson's Bay Company.

One of the two upper Gitksan tribes, that of Kisguasas or Sea-Gull near the outlet of Babine River on the Skeena 225 miles from the sea-coast, was not far removed from Fort. St. James, the earliest fur trading-post established in 1808 in the northern Rockies. It seems that the company soon after built a subsidiary post at Bear Lake, under the direction of a Mr. Ross. A Tsetsaut party at that time raided the village of Kisgagas while most of the hunters were away, killed two men with the flint-lock musket in their possession—the first gun seen in the country—and returned home with a female captive, a niece of the head-chief whom they had killed. The young woman was rescued by the white people at Bear Lake and later sent back home. A retaliation party, under her guidance, proceeded to the Tsetsaut country, but decided to visit the white man's fort on the way. Here they had their first opportunity to see the white man and to marvel at his possessions and strange ways; to them all this was nothing less than a supernatural experience. What impressed then most was the white man's dog, the palisade or fortification of the house, and the broad wagon road—so different from their faint forest trails. All three of these they decided to adopt as their own crests or emblems after they had reached home. Waiget, the head of one family, took upon himself White-Man's Dog or Mr. Ross' Dog (called masselaws); Malulek, another chief, assumed Palisade as his own; and other participants shared other similar crests. They gave two big feasts in the course of the next two years, to which they invited representatives of other Gitksan tribes as guests. They exhibited with pride their new acquisitions, which they later carved on their totem poles. The palisade took the form of a small fence built around the totem pole.

Another family lower down on the upper Skeena, that of Harhu of Kispayaks, likewise acquired the

Shingle crest *(ran' arhgyeek),* obviously from the white man's device of that name, after an ancestor once had proceeded either to the trading-post of Bear Lake or Fort St. James. This Shingle emblem on a Kispayaks totem pole is still seen in the form of parallel lines sloping down on both sides of a central ridge cut deep in the cedar.

Many instances of similar origins are noticeable on the totem poles and house frontals of the coast; for instance, the white sailor at the helm of a ship at Bella Coola (a short distance north of Vancouver Island) now preserved at the National Museum of Canada; another white man at the top of a tall pole at Cape Fox, southern Alaska; a sailing ship with a woman on its deck on a pole recently transplanted to Ketchikan, Alaska, and erroneously stated to represent Captain Cook; and the splendid Haida pole now standing in the same park at Ketchikan showing three Russians, two of them in church vestments, one above the other, two cherubs with wings outspread, and two eagles. This pole from Kasaan, a a Haida-Kaigani village on Prince of Wales Island, was carved about seventy years ago and erected during a potlatch, which some old people still remember, for a native family that showed its interest at the time in the Greek Catholic Church of the Russians. Another Kasaan pole with scroll fret-work was said by an old Indian woman to have been carved by her uncle, who wanted to represent on it a Greek Catholic Church certificate in his own possession.

These emblems were at first foreign to the Indians and have remained, since their assumption, the exclusive property of a few families. The bulk of totem-pole figures elsewhere is of a different kind; it symbolizes familiar animals, legends, and natural phenomena.

Definite examples of totem poles erected as a result of relations between officers of the Hudson's Bay Company and the natives are too extensive for full quotation here. Yet these include some of the best and

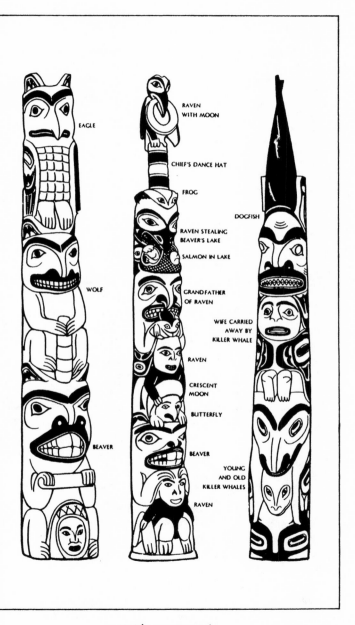

Haida totem post.

tallest samples of the art, in particular on lower Nass River.

A head-chief there named Sakau'wan—Sharp-Teeth —whose pride was deeply wounded by his wife's desertion. The young woman, who was attractive, and either ambitious or fickle, had forsaken native rank for the favours of Captain McNeil, a Hudson's Bay Company's fur trader, and had gone down the coast to live with him at Victoria.

To efface his shame in a way recognized by his people Sharp-Teeth made use of the first opportunity in a tribal feast and, holding up his hand ten beautiful marten skins, he began to sing on an old tune a new challenge which he had composed to cast ridicule on the deserter.

This song of challenge was "Wait and see what chief can do! Wait, sweetheart, that you may learn how I have raised my head again! Wait, O flighty one, before you send me word of how you pine once more for my love! Time is now ripe, woman of the bleached Victoria tribe, for you to send me a bottle of Old Tom (whisky). That is why I now dispatch to you this handful of beaver skins."

Actually the skins we even more valuable than beaver, they meant dollars to the natives, and were picked marten such as an indignant and resourceful chief could sacrifice to heap ridicule upon a woman unworthy of him and surely unable—after her escapade—to reciprocate in kind. The only way now for her to save her face was to return a gift of still greater value. This, unexpectedly, she did.

The gift which, in her absence and through her brother Neeskinwaetk, she used to rebuke her former husband (with the help of her new husband, Captain McNeil) was a large Haida canoe carved out of a huge cedar tree. Thus she had made the Old Tom demanded by Sharp-Teeth into a trade canoe, decorated inside with the Bear, her own heraldic emblem, and beautifully carved at the prow. As the canoe was given in a feast to the challenger, "she went over big"—so we were told—"and had the best of him." He had wanted to discredit her forever in the eyes of the people, becuase she had shamed him and he was proud. Now once more she had brought new humiliation upon him. At the time the tribe was not sure that he would retaliate.

He did. After he had gathered all his wealth in pelts, copper shields, blankets, and trade goods, he gave a big feast, invited all the neighbouring tribes and made it known that he was about to cast off his wife in a way that would brand her as worthless. As he lavished presents upon his guests, particularly those who had derided him, he sang a song which he had composed for the occasion—a taunting song.

Captain McNeil's native mistress, in her turn, smarted under the insult, even though she lived far away from the scene of her disgrace. She decided to fight it out to the end with her former overlord. As her brother Neeskinwaetk, with whom she shared the leadership of a high Wolf clan, had recently died, she decided to erect in his memory a totem pole and herself assume single-handed the leadership of the clan. Bent on using this opportunity to raise a fine totem and enhance the prestige of her clan—one of the oldest on the Nass—she would wipe out the shame which her dismissal by her husband had brought upon her. And she had the means to do it.

The best carver of the Nass at the time—about eighty years ago—was Oyai, of the Canyon tribe on mid-river, who was spending his busy life under the command and the pay of the chiefs of various tribes, carving memorial columns for them. So she made sure of his services for about a year, during which he fashioned a pole for her.

When the carving was ready she came in person to the Nass, bringing much property with her, and had the totem erected to the memory of her brother in the midst of a great celⁿbration. Henceforth, in the esteem of the people, she would assume the rank of a high chief, on a par with her estranged husband, who had lost his power over her. She was a leader among the Wolves, as he was among the Eagles—their respective clans being the Wolf and Eagle.

Her totem pole was a fine memorial, standing at the head of a spendid row of totems at the Old Nass village of Angyadae. After the lapse of about seventy years, I discovered it still standing on the former village site, surrounded by a growth of wild crabapple trees. Its heraldic figures carved out of red cedar were weather-beaten, yet most expressive and original.

It was evident at first sight that Oyai, its carver, deserved his reputation as the best totem carver of his generation on the Nass or anywhere.

The author has since purchased this pole from its owner and removed it for conservation to the Trocadero Museum, now Le Musee de l'Homme, in Paris.

The plastic and pictorial arts of the coast and river villages progressed in new directions throughout the nineteenth century until, after 1880, they came down with a crash among the Haidas and the Tsimsyans, largtly through the conversion of the natives to Christianity and the influence of the Gold Rush into Alaska. They thrived until about 1900 among the Gitksans, owing to their isolation inland, and until 1910 among the Kwakiutls. Argillite carvings, canoe and box-making of the Haidas, and the carving of totem poles, beautiful rattles, and head-dresses among the Nass River people, all belong to this period. These were meant for inter-tribal or foreign trade after prehistoric frontiers had been invaded.

THE ORIGIN OF THE TOTEM OR MEMORIAL POLES ON THE COAST

When and where the totem poles or mortuary columns first appeared is an interesting though elusive point. There are two possibilities. These heraldic monuments first became the fashion either on Nass

be a typically Tlingit practice. Most, if not all the Haida and the Niskae or Nass River tribes, on the other hand, were totem pole carvers and owned many poles in each village. The fashion is more typically theirs that it is Tlingit.

The Haidas might next be dismissed from consideration as likely originators of the totem poles proper. The large Haida carvings, as we know them, are partly house poles, grave memorials, and partly totem poles, and the house poles are far more numerous in proportion among them than among the Tsimsyans. Practically none of the Niskae carvings, as they have come down to us, were house poles. The two large posts observed among the Haidas by Bartlett and Marchand in 1788-1792 were house portals. Though the Haida villages were often visited at the end of the eighteenth century and in the first part of the nineteenth, we find no other reference to large poles, still less to the famous rows of poles at Massett and Skidegate as they were photographed about 1880. The Haida poles, as we know them in our museums, are all of the same advanced type, of the same period (1840-1900), and presumably from the hands of carvers who were contemporaries. Their stylization was largely the result of miniaure argillite carvings made by their craftsmen for the curio traffic with white buyers. The totem poles were from ten to thirty years old when the islanders accepted Christianity, memorials or abandoned them in the bush. It is commonly said that the fine row of poles at Skidegate rose from the proceeds of an inglorious type of barter in Victoria. There is no evidence of totem poles among the Haidas antedating 1840 or 1850, though a few earlier and transitional ones may have served to introduce the fashion.

In all probability detached totem poles actually originated among the Niskaes or northern Tsimsyans of Nass River. From traditional recollections, it is obvious that the custom among them of commemorating the dead with a carved memorial is not an ancient one;

yet it antedated that of the Gitksans or the Tsimyans proper. It is more likely that the Haidas imitated them, as did the Tlingits, than the reverse. The estuary of the Nass was the most important thoroughfare of Indian life in all the northern parts. Oolaken fishing in the neighbourhood of what was called Fishery Bay, near Gitrhadeen—the largest Niskae centre—was a predominant feature in native life. The grease from the oolaken or candle-fish was an indispensable staple along the coast. For their yearly supply the Haidas, the Tlingits, the Tsimsyans, and the Gitksans journeyed by sea or overland every spring and camped side by side for weeks at a time in temporary villages of their own from Red Bluffs eastwards on the lower Nass. Exchanges of all kinds, barter social amnenities, and feuds were quite normal at Fishery Bay and Red Bluffs. Cultural features of the local hosts—whether they were willing hosts or not is open to question—were constantly under the observation of the strangers and often were a cause for envy or aggression. The Tsimsyans, on the other hand, never crossed to Queen Charlotte Islands unless on war raids or isolated visits to relatives.

Nass River carvers were on a par with the best in Haidaland. Their art reached the highest point of development every attained on the north Pacific Coast; many of their totem poles were the best and tallest seen anywhere. The Haida poles in comparison were more stylized and offered less variety. The Tlingit poles closely resembled those of Nass River.

TRAPS AND TRAPPING. Our information on South American traps is satisfactory for only a few tribes and regions. We have very meager data on traps used by the Southern Hunters south of the Chaco and by the peoples of the Andean Highlands and West Coast from Panama the Chiloe. "The Southern Hunters, it seems fairly clear, have few and very simple traps. Whether our paucity of information on the trapping complex of the Andean and West Coast peoples is due to poverty of the complex or to lacunae in our recorded observations is not clear; the first alternative seems the more probable. At any rate most of our information on South American traps is from the Silval region, the forests and savannas of the Guianas and of the Orinoco, Amazon, and Parana-Paraguay watersheds. Even for this great are our records are spotty, and, with rare exceptions, lacking in detail.

For comparison of South American traps with those from other parts of the world, see especially: Lips (1927, world), Lindblom (1925-26, Africa), Keller (1936, Africa), Cooper (1938, northern North America), Sirelius (1934, Finland).

BIRD AND MAMMAL TRAPS

Snares.—The pole snare, consisting of a noose at the end of a pole, for catching birds occurs very widespread from Panama and the West Indies to Cape Horn—as it does in North American and the Old World. Perch and clog snares are not reported, but various types of single and multiple tether snares for birds and mammals are recorded from many parts of the continent, especially in the Marginal and Silval regions.

Of lifting-pole snares, the tossing-pole type, in which the pole works by gravity, as a lever, is not reported, but several kinds of the spring-pole type, in which the pole works from the "spring" of the pole itself, are recorded from the Silval region (map 7). The type illustrated in figure 68, a type of wide distribution in western North America (e.g. *Yuma*, Thompson River, *Kwakiutl)* and the Old World (e.g., *Pahouin* of French Congo, *Kyaks* and *Malays* of Sarwak, *Thadou Kuki* of Assam), is recorded for the *Carib* of Dominica, *Arawak* and othe tribes of Guiana, *Choroti* of the Chaco, *Caingua,* and *Lamisto* and *Amahuaka* of northestern Peru; with tread-bar or leaf-covered release instead of tread-gill, for the *Chane* and *Cavina of Bolivia and the Toba* of the Chaco, the whole Caiari-Uaupes area, the *Pioche, Ocaina, Coto,* and *Quijo* of the upper Putumayo and Nap, and the *Arhuaco-Cagaba*. Five other types of spring-pole snares are found among: (2) The *Pauserna* of Bolivia; (2) the *Cavina*; variants:

Both overhung types, in which the fall log is hung or suspended by a loop from above, and underpropped ones, in which the fall log is propped by a post or other support from underneath, are found, the former being the more common. The trigger, i. e., the whole mechanism—apart from fall log, bed log, weight logs, guide stakes, and pen—which holds set and releases the fall log, is more commonly identical with or a variant of that illustrated supra for the most widespread type of spring-pole snare; but several other trigger types are also found. The trip-spring release is not reported for South American deadfalls.

One type of overhung deadfall, that of the *yagua*, is illustrated. Four other types of overhung deadfalls are recorded and figured in our sources: (1) *Cayapa, Tumapasa,* and *Caingua*, with trigger as in the *Carib* of Dominica spring-pole snare (fig. 68); (2)*Iquito-Kuhuarano;* (3) *Schayawita, Lamisto, Chebero;* (4) *Ica* and Demarara River Indians—the latter believed by Roth to be borrowed from the Negroes.

A *Pioche* underpropped lever-and-stake deadfall is illustrated in figure 70. Four other types of underpropped deadfalls are found among the: (1) *Guarayu;* (2) *Ocaina, Awishira,* with trigger as in the *Pioche* type; (3) *Mosetene;* (4) *Ica*. The samson-post deadfall of northern North America and northern Asia is not reported for South America.

De Brettes gives a cut of an *Arhuaco-Cagaba* deadfall for armadillos, which consists of a heavy flat stone support by trigger—the only instance known to the present writer of Indian use of the trigger in South America (European influence?).

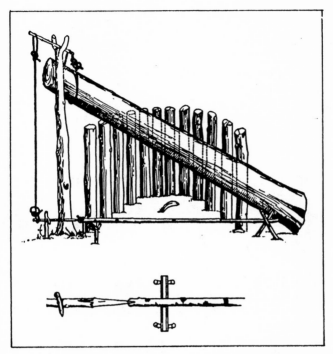

Overhung deadfall. Yagua of northeastern Peru.

The *Mosetene* two-lever deadfall occurs also, with a heavy fall log instead of a stone-weighted fall platform, among the *Guarayu, Ssimaku* (cf. *Omurana*), and upper Barima River Indians.

Deadfalls are also recorded, without however sufficient details for reconstruction and identification, among the *Tupinamba, Guarani,* and many tribes of the northeastern Peru region.

The *Ocaina* (also *Witoto* and *Muinane*) monkey trap set on the branch of a tree, differs from the ordinary deadfall in that the fall or crushing stick, on release, is pulled down on the trapped animal by a heavy weight hanging from the stick.

Fall traps—The basketlike fall trap of the *Carib* of

Dominica, with rabbet-joint supporting post, is identical with a northeaster Peru *(Chama)* and a Guiana trap. Roth considered the last to be perhaps of foreign introduction, but its occurrence on Dominica and in northeastern Peru as well suggests its aboriginality, and the present writer has found a very similar trap, with the identical rabbet-joint supporting post, among the *Yuma* and *Papago* of Arizona. The *Caingua* and *Palicur* fall traps, described but not figured by Wavrin and Nimuendaju respectively, are of similar or perhaps identical construction. The *Caraja* fall trap figured by Krause has a similar fall basket but a quite different trigger. In Farabee's *Wapisiana* trap with basketball fall and in his *Macushi* "beehive trap" the support is released by a boy on watch who pulls the string when the birds come under the basket to eat the seed bait.

The *Yagua* have a quite complicated fall cage-trap. The false floor, as part of the release mechanism, is also reported by Vogt for his *Caingua* underpropped deadfall, with fall platform instead of fall cage. The *Yameo* and *Chebero* "Kastenfallen," with a falling door, reported by Tessmann but not figured by him, may be of the type of Fejo's *Yagua* "door trap." This *yagua* door trap is a conical construction of stakes, with a ground-level opening or "door," thus imprisoning the bird or smaller mammal. A box trap for crabs, used by the Indians of the Pomeroon, is, in ally probability, of foreign introduction—of African origin, Roth holds. (Vf. *Guaymi* box traps)

"Guillotine" traps.—These are reported only for northeastern Peru, southeastern Colombia, and eastern Ecuador, among the *Yagua* (fig. 73), *Coto, Ocaina,* and *Jivaro.* The *Yagua* and *Ocaina* types are essentially identical; the release mechanism of the *Jivaro* type is a "kicker" one, quite like the vertical "kicker" trigger reported elsewhere in the world only, so far as the present writer can discover, from northern North America.

Automatic spear and bow-and-arrow traps.—The *Ssimaku* (and *Omurana*) automatic spear trap is not, to the writer's knowledge, reported from elsewhere in South America. Roth's *Arawak* automatic bow-and arrow trap has essentially the same release mechanism as in the *Ssimaku* spear trap, except that the propelling force comes from the bent bow instead of from the bent sapling; it is also essentially identical with a well-known African trap. In all the forgoing automatic traps, the trigger mechanism is released by the animal striking against a string stretched across the trail. The string release in South America is reported only in such automatic spear and bow-and-arrow traps. Automatic bow-and-arrow traps are also reported among the *Apinaye* of the upper Tocantins and the *Guaymi* of Panama. Automatic gun traps have been recorded among the *Cavina,* Guiana *Arawak,* and *Guaymi.*

Pitfalls.—Pitfalls for large and small mammals are of very wide, but not universal, distribution among the Indians of the Silval region of South America. they are not reported for the Marginal peoples living South of the Chaco, nor for the *Araucanians,* nor, so far as the present writer can discover, for the Andean Highlands and West Coast from Central Chile north. In many cases, pointed stakes are stuck in the bottom of the pit, these being poisoned among some of the northwest Amazon and northeastern Peru peoples. A *Lengua* jaguar pitfall is provided with a tethered looped lasso which tightens around the trapped animal's body.

Hunting nets.—Fixed nets for birds and land mammals are or were of widespread, but far from universal, use in both the Silval and Andean Highland and Coastal regions, but are not reported for the *Araucanians* or the hunting tribes of the open country south of the Chaco. The *Chiriguano* use a clap net spread on the ground for pigeons, and operated by the fowler, who pulls a string when the birds go after the maize bait put between two halves of the net.

Miscellaneous devices.—The use of a resinous or

other viscous substance as bird lime is recorded for the *Carib* of Dominica and the *Yagua, Ocaina,* and *Muinane* of northeastern Peru and southeastern Colombia. Among the *Kahgan* a gorge hook, consisting of three pieces of sharp wood, the ends of which are covered with fish flesh, is used to taking cormorants. A funnel-shaped contrivance, placed at the opening of the hole or hollow log where a peccary has taken refuge, from which contrivance the issuing animal cannot extricate himself, is common among the *Carib* and *Arawak* tribes of the Guiana region.

FISH TRAPS

Spring-hook and spring-basket traps.—Spring-hook traps for fish are reported only from the *Arawak, Carib,* and *Warrau* of the Guianas, mostly Coastal groups, and from the *Tupi*-speaking *Oyampi* of Guina. One type is here reproduced; W.E. Roth describes and figures three other types with variant release mechanisms. Stedman described and figured a very similar type as in use among the Dutch Guiana Negroes of his time.

The *Acawai, Boviander,* and other tribes of the upper Demarara River of British Guiana use the spring-basket fish trap, as did the Dutch Guiana Negroes of Stedman's time. When the release mechanism is sprung, the basket lid closes, but the basket itself remains under water. A somewhat similar spring-basket fish trap also occurs, in which the basket, on release, is jerked up above the surface of the water, with the fish caught head down in the basket; this type is reported by Roth for the *Piricuta* and *Waiwai* of British Guiana, by Farabee for the *Arawak* and *Carib* of the Guiana region, by Ehrenreich and Steere for the *Ipurina* and *Yamamadi* of the Perus River, and, to judge from the descriptions, by Nimuendaju for the *Uaca* of Uaca River, northeastern Brazilian Guiana, and by Martius for the *Tupi* of the Amazon.

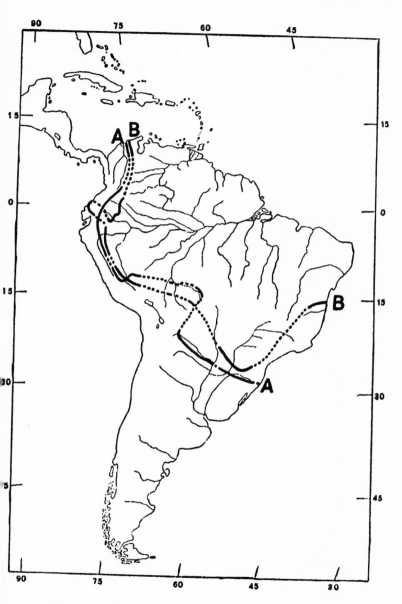

Distribution of traps. A-A western and southern limit
of spring pole snares; B-B dotted sections of lines
represent lacunae.

The fact that these spring-basket traps are first reported by Stedman as in use by the Surinam Negroes and that they are found today in widely separated areas of west and east Africa suggests that they may have been introduced into South America by the Negro.

Cylinder fall trap.-The cylinder fall trap is reported for the Indians of Guiana. When the trap is set, the open bottom of the cylinder is under water, a little distance above the underwater ground level. The fish enters the cylinder from below and nibbles the bait hung inside, thus releasing the trigger, whereupon the cylinder drops and imprisons the fish. A somewhat similar trap is described by Tessmann for the *Ocaina* of southeastern Colombia.

Conico-cylindrical traps.—Fish traps of reed, bamboo, lianas or wicker, pointed and closed at one end, and open at the other, are of widespread occurrence in the Silval area and regions adjacent thereto. In one type, of simple elongated funnel construction with one end fully open, the fish enters freely, gets stuck, and cannot back out. In another type, in principle like our familiar eel-pots, the open end is provided with an elastic funnel of reeds pointing inward, which allows easy entrance but which bars exit. Such traps are often placed in the openings of weirs. The *Araucanians* take fish in ponchos and baskets baited and set under water.

Gill-nets and night-lines.—Set nets are sporadically reported, as among the *Caraja, Cayapa,* and Jivaro. Koch-Grunberg observed a night-line in use by the Indians of the upper Rio Negro. The night-line and the *Caraja* set-net are suspected of having been borrowed from adjacent Whites.

In hook-and-line fishing among the *Patamona* of the upper Potaro River, British Guiana, the line is passed over the leaves of a fibrous plant tied onto a stick fastened upright in the ground; when a fish bites, the loud swishing sound caused by the friction of the lïne over the serrated edges of the leaves warns the fisherman that he has a bite. A similar warning device is used by the *Guaymi* with baited fish traps.

TURQUOISE. Green and blue stones were especially valued by the Pueblos. They highly prized turquoise as an ornament, as a votive offering, and as a fetish; they decorated, in some instances, the lintels of their doors with it and used it as a measure of wealth and a means of investment. It may be added that the Navajo, to assist him in gambling, must needs have a fine piece of turquoise since Noholipi, the Gambling God in the Navajo legend, owed his remarkable winnings to a turquoise lucky piece. Fray Geronimo de Zarate Salmeron says "to them it [turquoise] is as diamonds and precious stones". In more recent times a string of turquoise fragments sufficient for an earring might well be worth the price of a pony. While Prof. J. S. Newberry states that it was "so highly prized that a fragment of fine quality no larger than the nail of one's little finger and one-eighth of an inch in thickness was regarded as worth a mule or a good horse." He states that the Indians "discriminated accurately between the different shades of color" and were "not to be deceived by any base imitation." The value of turquoise beads was judged by the delicacy and purity of their blue colors.

The Pueblo Indians worked turquoise mines in our own Southwest at a number of places long before the Spanish arrived. Turquoise does not occur in ruins previous to those of the late Basket Makers and hence we can date the beginning of turquoise mining in the Southwest to about the fifth century. These people also apparently inaugurated the fascinating mosaic work of the Pueblo Indians. That the industry was an important one long before the discovery of America is shown by the many thousands of turquoise beads and pendants (30,000 in one room and 5,889 beads in a single burial) found at Pueblo Bonito, Chaco Canyon,

N. Mex., dating from about A. D. 900 to 1100. It has furnished more turquoise ornaments than any other American ruin. George H. Pepper describes a turquoise pendant from Pueblo Bonito 3.4 centimeters (1 17/50 inches) long and 2 centimeters (78/100 inch) broad at top and 2.5 centimeters (1 inch) at the bottom. A single mosaic cylinder 6 inches long and 3 inches in diameter was set with 1,214 pieces of turquoise. One can well agree (Pepper, 1920, p. 377) that the nearby Los Cerrillos mines must have been diligently worked by these people 1,000 years ago. John F. Blandy reported that in one grave near Prescott, Ariz., half a peck of turquoises worth $2,000 was recovered. Artifacts, indeed, suggest that over a thousand years ago the Pueblo peoples had greater wealth in turquoise than now and this opinion is strengthened by some of the Indian legends. Along the Salinas River, Ariz., ancient ruins are searched for turquoise after rains by modern Indians. Turquoise is also prominent in the myths of the people of the Southwest (i. e., the Zuni, Pima, and Hopi), including the Navajo creation myth, suggesting the length of time it has been known to them. The extent of the commerce in turquoise in the sixteenth century is further proof that the mines were relatively old.

The most famous of these old turquoise mines, that at Los Cerrillos, N. Mex., the Tewa Indian place-name for which is the equivalent of "the place where turquoise is dug" was reworked by the Spaniards until 1686, when the workings caved. From the size of the Cerrilos open-cut and of its dumps, and the large trees, thereon, some of the latter being considered to be 600 years old, a considerable age for these pits is indicated. George H. Pepper, judging from country rock attached to some of the Pueblo Bonito turquoise pendants, is satisfied that Los Cerrillos was the mine from which they were obtained. In 1540 the Indians at the head of the Gulf of California told Captain Fernando Alarchon that the Pueblos dug the turquoises "out of a rock of stone". Los Cerrillos workings have been described by many geologists. Rather extensive ancient workings occur all over Mt. Chalchihuitl and on Turquoise Hill, 4 miles distant. Modern mining on Mount Chalchihuitl, according to Silliman, broke into open stopes in which were many stone hammers, some to be held in the hand and others grooved for handles. One of 20-pounds weight had the scrub-oak handle still attached by a withe. He adds that fire was used in breaking the rock. Sterrett says the "main pit on the northwest side of the hill" is "about 130 feet deep on the upper side and about 35 feet deep on the lower side, the rim is about 200 feet across and the bottom nearly 100 feet across. The large dumps of waste rock removed from this are about 150 yards long by 75 yards wide and from 1 to 30 feet deep. These dimensions do not correspond closely with those given by the earlier writers since this would give the dump an area of less than 2 1/2 acres as compared with some 20 reported by Silliman." It does, however, suggest the removal of some 100,000 tons of rock. Silliman mentions aboriginal open chambers in solid rock, 40 feet long, and he states that at places modern mining has encountered aboriginal workings in depths of at least 100 feet. W. P. Blake says that 75 years ago it was visited by Indians from a distance and the Indians continue to this day to get turquoise at this mine. Although this mine is undoubtedly old, the Zuni tale of the migration of the Turquoise Man and the Salt Woman suggests that, before the discovery of Los Cerrillos, turquoise was obtained from some mine farther north possibly from the locality of La Jara, Colo.

There are also ancient Indian turquoise mines presumably of pre-Columbian age in the Burro Mountains at several localities, on Hachita Montains, and Jarilla Mountains, Sierra County, near Paschal, N. Mex.; Sugar Loaf Peak, Lincoln County and Crescent, Clark County, Nev.; Turquoise Mountain, Cochise County, and Mineral Park, Mohave County,

Ariz.; Manvel, and Silver Lake, San Bernardino County, Calif., and near La Jara, Conejos County, Colo. Several of the Burro Mountain localities known to white miners were discovered by evidence of aboriginal workings. The presence of charcoal indicates the use of fire in breaking the rock, followed by hammer work. The larger rock fragments were broken into small pieces in the search of turquoise. The stone hammers are "of rounded form, 4 to 8 inches or more in diameter and were evidently used without a handle". Pits were sunk to a depth of 20 feet at least. Fire was also used at Turquoise Mountain, Cochise County, Ariz. Prehistoric turquoise mines occur over a large area in northwestern San Bernardino County, Calif., Manvel being one of the chief centers. Stone hammers and crude pottery occur in the old pits while pictographs are common in the vicinity. The pits, which occur in an area 30 or 40 miles in diameter, are from 15 to 30 feet across and up to 18 feet deep. In the Silver Lake district, San Bernardino County, Calif., the pits occur in an east and west line 8 miles long and that short drifts were driven from the main pits.

The aboriginal trade in the turquoise of the Southwest (pl. 4) was widespread, extending from the West Indies and Yucatan on the south to Ontario on the north and from California on the west to Mississippi and Arkansas on the east. About 1527, Alvar Nunez Cabeza de Vaca obtained turquoise from his Indian patients on the Rio Grande, Tex. The men of Hernando de Soto (A. D. 1542), when they arrived in the province of Guasco (eastern Arkansas), found in the possession of the Indains "Turkie stones—which the Indians signified by signes that they had from the West". In a grave in Coahomo County, Miss., 100 turquoise beads and a small turquoise pendant were found. As glass beads were also found in the grave, this commerce with the Pueblos of the Southwest continued after the white man reached America. Vicente de Saldivar Mendoza in 1599 met, near the Canadian River in the vicinity of the present Texas-New Mexican

line, a band of Apaches who had been trading for turquoise ("some small green stones which they use")
with the Picuries and Taos pueblos of New Mexico
years 1630 and 1680 says the Apaches visited the
Pueblo of Pecos to trade for *Chalchuites*. Among the
Apaches, precious stones had a directional symbolism:
white shell, north; jet, east; turquoise, south; and
catlinite, west.

When Sieur Perrot arrived among the Fox and Sauk
in 1683, he was informed that the latter had visited
lands to the Southwest where they met Indians coming
from that direction whence they had brought "stones,
blue and green, resembling the turquoise which they
wore fastened in their noses and ears." They had also
seen mounted men resembling the French, that is, the
Spaniards of New Mexico. Twenty-one years earlier
Radisson claimed that the Crees of the Lake Superior
region had beads of "a stone of Turquoise" as nose
ornaments which they obtained by barter from the
"nation of the buff and beefe". A piece of turquoise
was reported from a Wisconsin Indian site.

The French got turquoises from the Florida Indians
in 1562 but his minerology may have been faulty or the
material may have been derived from Spanish wrecks.

That turquoise, *Xiuitl*, was known to the Aztecs in
early time is proved by the name of their God of Fire
and Water, Xiuhcoatl ("The Turquoise Snakes").
Turquoise was rather commonly used by them, and
also at the time of the Spanish occupation by the
Indians of Sinaloa, Sonora, and Chichuahua. The latter certainly got theirs from our own Southwest,
largely by barter with the Pueblos, although perhaps in
part in mining excursions which they, themselves, may
have made. A Franciscan friar (probably Fray Juan de
la Asuncion) in 1538 found turquoise among the
Indians of Northern Mexico which they got as day
laborers' pay from the Pueblos to the north and the
next year Friar Marcos de Niza repeats the statement.
In consequence, at that time New Mexican turquoise in

quantity was in the possession of at least the northern Mexican Indians and as, in the ruins of Pueblos Bonito sherds of Toltec pottery have been found, trade between our Southwest and Mexico is indicated even 1,200 years ago. While the gem does occur in Mexico at several localities, none of the deposits are important and no aboriginal workings are known, although the Aztec Book of Tribute and the statement of Sahagun that it was found in the "mines" indicated without much doubt that the Aztecs had Mexican sources of turquoise. Turquoise is said by Lorenzana to have been worked at Tollan, the capital of the Toltecs, about 1325. In short, the Aztecs and their predecessors, the Toltecs, probably got their turquoise largely from New Mexico and Arizona but in part from local sources now undiscovered or exhausted. It appears to have been available in smaller pieces to the Aztecs than to the Pueblos and particularly was used as thin plates in mosaic work. Its treatment suggests its high value and possibly its foreign source.

That the Mayas had at their command considerable quantities of turquoise is shown by the 3,000 pieces set in the mosaic plaque found by Earl H. Morris at Chichen Itza in 1928. The turquoise, doubtless was largely of new Mexican origin.

Turquoise was a popular and relatively common gem among the Peruvian Indians. It was also used by the natives of Montserrat, West Indies; Bolivia; Colombia; Ecuador; Argentine; and Chile. Indeed A. Hrdlicka, in 1910, found a turquoise bead at Miramir, Argentina, on the Atlantic Ocean, 270 miles south of Buenos Aires. The natives of Ecuador had some fair-sized pieces of turquoise, a partially worked bead found on the Island of La Plata being 2 1/2 inches long and 1 1/2 inches in diameter. No aboriginal South American mines are as yet certainly known but the gem occurs at certain places in the Andean regions of Peru, Argentina, and Chile. A suggestion as to a source is obtained from the name, Copiapo, which owes its origin, according to the Indian tradition to the great quantity of turquoise found in its mountains. Further turquoise has recently been identified in the Chuqicamata copper deposit in Chile and as this mine was extensively worked by the Indians and as turquoise artifacts are found in the immediate vicinity, this was doubtless a source.

D. Jenness found a turquoise bead some years ago in an ancient Eskimo grave on one of the Diomede Isles in Bering Strait, which he judged to be of Chinese origin from etchings on it.

U

URBANIZATION is the movement of the North American Indians from tribal or reservation lands to modern, Western cities. Although the largest movement of Indians to cities resulted from a governmental relocation policy inaugurated during the 1950s, Indians have lived in cities long before this. Since about the turn of the century, many Indians have moved to cities, either temporarily to earn money before returning to the reservation, or permanently, on their own initiative. The most usual reason for such a move is in fact the poverty that is so prevalent on many Indian reservations and the hope that a better livelihood may be earned in an urban setting. But Indians arriving in cities often find that they are no better off there than on the reservation, since they frequently lack the necessary training and education that would qualify them for well-paying jobs.

The Mohawk Indians include one group that have done relatively well in this regard. Their move to the city was preceded in 1886 by the establishment of a working relationship with the Dominion Bridge

Company. They agreed to permit the company to use reservation lands for operations on one of its projects in exchange for jobs. Over the years, more and more Mohawks entered the construction industry. Since many of their jobs were centered in New York City, they settled in a group within a few blocks area in Brooklyn. Since the 1920s and 1930s, in fact, at least one hundred Mohawk families have lived in this area. The transition to urban life for them has been relatively easy, largely because of the economic security that prompted their move in the first place. In addition, however, there were some fortuitous parallels between the nature of construction work—high risk and seasonal labor away from home—that continued in an altered form and context the older characteristics of Mohawk warfare- and hunting-oriented lives.

In the case of the Mohawks, the community has remained close-knit, and much of the native culture has been continued, as demonstrated in part by the Indian decorations that adorn the apartments in which they live. In other cases, however, Indians moving to cities find themselves isolated from their own people on the reservation, and after several generations in the city are transformed into true urban Indians, split from the native languages and customs of their past.

When an Indian arrives in the city for the first time, it may be easy to simply accept white culture and blend into it. On the other hand, though, the distinctiveness of what is truly Indian may stand out by contrast, encouraging the preservation of the old ways. The relocation policy of the United States government, inaugurated during the 1950s, in fact encouraged this trend by fostering the growth of large concentrations of Indians in urban areas. One result of the mixture and concentration of Indians with differing backgrounds has been the support of the growth of a pantribal movement that emphasizes Indian-ness in general, rather than the traditions of particular tribes, especially insofar as they relate to the white culture around them.

The problems Indians encounter in the city are essentially the same as those encountered by any minority group poor—inadequate education, lack of familiarity with the predominant culture of the city, and perhaps racial discrimination. The first two problems are difficult to overcome without some awareness on the part of the dominant, white culture of the significant cultural differences between their society and that of the Indians—including language, custom, work-habits, and kinship and other group-ties. The latter problem—racial discrimination—may vary significantly depending on region. Most severe discrimination occurs in those border towns and areas located near a reservation. As frequently occurs, the farther city dwellers are from the centers of Indian populations, the more tolerant they are of them.

VANILLA—No wonder vanilla has a delightful flavor. It is from an orchid, a fragrant climbing variety native to tropical America, but now cultivated extensively in Java, Tahiti, Mauritius, and other islands of the tropics. The word *vanilla* is from Spanish *vainilla*, referring to the long slender pod (*vaina*) containing the seeds.

The Indians originated the technique of obtaining vanilla extract by picking the pods before they were ripe, drying them, and then removing the crystals from outside the pods.

WAMPUM. Of the beads that were manufactured and used by the Iroquois those known as "wampum" are by far the most significant. Though the term wampum has been used in some places to include both the discoidal and the cylindrical beads, the true wampum is an Indian-made shell bead, cylindrical in form, averaging about one-quarter of an inch in diameter, perfectly straight on the sides, with a hole running through it the long way. Some of the wampum beads prepared for commercial trade were as long as half an inch but none of the long beads has been found in the wampum belts. Wampum was made from the quahaug or hard shell clam (Venus Mercenaria) which provides both white and purple beads. The central axis (columellae) of the great conch shell (pyrula Carica), was used for white wampum.

Colored wampum had a special significance for the Iroquois. Colors ranged from a pale pink and delicate lavender to a deep purple. The purple beads were generally known as black wampum and were especially prized for political purposes. White was the emblem of purity and faith. Both pink and white wampum were appropriate to peace.

The first use of wampum was probably for personal adornment. Wampum beads were used in necklaces, collars, head bands and armlets and were sewed on articles of clothing.

Up to 1693 the Iroquois also used wampum as money, either in strings or loose. It served as currency between the Indians and the Dutch and English colonists. Enormous quantities were used to pay the tribute demanded from the Iroquois by other Indian tribes.

The Iroquois strung wampum on cords for use in minor tribal transactions and wove it into belts to convey messages, record treaty stipulations, carry on condolence ceremonies and for other religious and social purposes.

Wampum is mentioned in the legends of the Iroquois, many stories having been told of a wampum bird with which the legendary hero Hiawatha seems to have had an obscure connection.

Wampum Strings or Strands. Both discoidal beads and the cylindrical or true wampum beads were strung on nettle fibers or sinew to form wampum strings, several of which were usually tied together at one end in a bunch, bundle, or sheaf. Sometimes a special color arrangement was observed in stringing the wampum in order to convey an inter-tribal message or to serve as a record in some minor tribal transaction. A string of invitation wampum was provided with small sticks or wooden handles at the ends, so notched as to indicate the number of days before the event. A wampum string was sometimes bestowed by the clan matron when announcing the permanent name of an adult.

Wampum belt. Probably nothing which the Iroquois made has been of such universal interest as the wampum belts used as seals of friendship when the treaties were ratified. It was said that "the Whites should never regard an Indian Council as serious, or regard it as a dangerous thing unless the national wampums were brought forth and displayed."

Wampum belts were woven of cylindrical beads with a special technique on long strands of sinew, leather, vegetable fiber, or string. The various vegetable fibers on which wampum was strung included slippery elm (Ulmus faiva) fiber, dogbane (Apocynum cannabimum. L.) or black "Indian hemp," sometimes called amyroot, swamp milkweed (Asclepias incarnata), and the hairy milkweed (A pulchra), also called white "Indian hemp," toad flax (Linaria linaria), and Indian mallow (Abutilon-avicennae) popularly known as velvet leaf.

When the belt was to be made, both ends of the strands were put through holes in a small piece of deer skin so spaced as to keep the strands at equal distances from one another in parallel lines. The extreme ends of the strands were then fastened to the ends of a piece of splint which had been sprung as a bow, and the strands were therby held in tension to serve as the warp. The beads that were to form the width of the belt where then strung on a weft thread (in the early days the weft thread was of sinew) which was passed under the fiber strands so that one bead was lengthwise between each two strands, at right angles to them. The thread was then passed back along the upper side of the strands and again through each bead so that it was firmly held in place by means of two threads, one passing over, and the other under the strands. When the belt had reached the desired length the ends of the warp and weft strands were tied and the ends of the belt finished off, usually with a leather fringe. The belt varied from 5 or 6 beads in width to as many as 50. The finished belts were usually from four to six inches wide and from one foot to six feet long. Old belts contain 1980 beads, on the average. There are 3000 beads in the William Penn belt. An old Onondaga belt contains nearly 10,000 beads.

Designs woven in the belts included hollow squares, hexagons, diamonds, overlapping triangles, crosses, diagonal lines or bars, circles, hearts, pipes, houses, and human and animal figures. The designs were arranged in symbolic patterns. Their meaning was given by the maker of the belt or was said to have been "talked into it" when a treaty was made. Thus stories told by the designs served as reminders of tribal events. The belts were shown on regular ceremonial occasions and the significance of the designs explained, a ceremony known as "reading of the archives."

Some of the wampum belts were made only for temporary use, after which they were dismantled. Important belts were preserved and were entrusted to a hereditary keeper, versed in their interpretation, and thus their significance was retained.

The oldest wampum belt, known as the Hiawatha belt, is thought to date back to almost the middle of the sixteenth cnetury when it served to record the formation of the League of the Iroquois (1570). With twenty-four other choice old belts the Hiawatha belt is today preserved in the State Museum at Albany, New York.

The Hiawatha belt was made up with a pattern showing four hollow squares outlined in white and one white, heart-shaped design in the center, all connected about midway by white lines. These designs represent the five nations with the great peace lodged in the heart. When reversed, the figure representing the heart assumes the appearance of a tree—the Great Tree of Light under which the nations meet in council. The white of the lines and the central heart are emblems of the peace, love, charity, and equity that surrounds and guards the Five Nations.

The Washington Covenant belt used during the presidency of George Washington as a convenant of peace between the 13 original colonies and the Six Nations of the Iroquois, shows symbolic figures of 15 men with outstretched arms and clasped hands extending along its length. In the center is the figure of a house. The two figures on each side of the house are the Keepers of the East and West Doors, the 13 figures clasping hands are the original colonies. The designs are woven in the dark or purple beads on a solid white beaded field which denotes peace and friendship.

The widest belt known, called the Wing or Dust Fan of Council President, shows a series of ten connecting purple, hexagon-shaped figures on a white background. Both the figures and background are edged with a white and a purple line of beads. The design is said to represent "The Evergrowing Tree" which by its repetition symbolizes the permanence and continuous growth of the Great League of the Iroquois. It was displayed whenever the League constitution was recited, to protect the Council and to keep the eyes of the 50 civil rulers free from dust.

Another wide belt, sometimes called the Presidentia, is made up with a design of overlapping purple triangles with a chain of 14 white, open diamond-shaped figures along the central axis. The background is of white beads. At one time the belt was longer and there were 16 diamonds. The chain of diamonds represented a covenant, or chain of friendship, always to be kept bright.

On an old wampum belt, known as the General Eli S. Parker belt, there are five dark purple, open hexagons outlined in white beads. Each hexagon symbolized the council of one of the nations of the league. The white beads were emblematic of purity, peace and integrity. The dark purple beads symbolized royalty, dignity, and determination. This belt was originally known as the "five council fires" or "death belt" of the Five Iroquois Nations and was long held by the Seneca Nation which guarded the west door of the Iroquois League of Confederacy. It signified death or war against some nation or nations and was sent from one tribe of the Confederacy to another when war was pending.

WATER RIGHTS, of North American Indians was derived from aboriginal ownership and and verified by treaty or by federal enactments. State law, which defines the rights of other Americans, does not ordinarily apply to the Indians. For example, the question of constructive use is not relevant to their ownership of water rights.

In fact, however, Indian water rights have been undermined in a variety of ways. For example, the question of constructive use is not relevant to their ownership of water rights.

In fact, however, Indian water rights have been undermined in a variety of ways. For example, when Indians of the Washington Territory ceded their lands to the United States in 1855, they reserved their fishing rights. Subsequently, however, their usual fishing holes were demolished with the construction of a number of dams. And, under current termination procedures, tribes become subject to state laws the stipulated constructive use as the test for retaining water rights. This is a profound reversal of the situation under federal jurisdictions, under which aboriginal rights are supposedly invoilable. For many Indian tribes, the result of such state measures is the loss of all, or a great majority, of their water rights, since they do not have the means to exploit their water reserves now, and their potential for developing these resources in the future is taken away after five years or so.

WEAPONS. The Bow and Arrow was a weapon of major importance and universal use among the Indians of North America. It was used primarily for hunting and warfare, but was also employed in religious ceremony and symbolism, sport, and children's games. North American chipped-stone points, similar in size and craftsmanship to historic arrowheads, have been found which date back as far as 500 AD. At the time of European arrival, the bow and arrow was used by all tribes except the Eskimos of Smith Sound and East Greenland. Prehistoric arrowheads found in both these areas, however, indicate its former presence. The many details of the Indian's construction and use of the bow and arrow show a wide range of variation.

A bow made from a single length of wood, called a self bow, was used nearly everywhere except in the central and eastern Arctic where long enough pieces of wood were scarce or unobtainable. The Eskimos there made compound bows of two to six pieces of wood, bone, or baleen lashed together, with wood being the preferred material. The compound bow was also made, often from mountain sheep horn, in parts of the northern Plains, Plateau, and Great Basin.

Many bows were given sinew reinforcement, and

compound bows usually required it. The usual method used for compound bows was sinew cord backing. Sinew was fashioned into cords which were run lengthwise along the back of the bow and secured with transverse lashing. This method was used throughout the Arctic, by a few tribes in adjacent areas, and in the Southwest. The primary method of reinforcing self bows, called sinew lining, was accomplished by gluing sinew fibers along the back of the bow. Sinew-lined bows were used in the northern Plains, the Plateau, Northwest Coast, California, and throughout most of the Great Basin and Southwest. Bowstrings were commonly of sinew cord or plant fiber. Wrist guards, generally of hide, were widely employed to soften the blow of the bowstring.

Arrows were made with wide variation in the design of their components according to their particular purpose and the natural materials available for their manufacture. Arrowheads were of two general types, barbed and unbarbed, the former designed to stay in the wound in order to hold game or increase injury. Some Eskimo arrowheads were barbed and removable from the shaft so as to remain in the wound harpoon-fashion.

Most stone arrowheads were of a triangular or pointed-oval shape, but some were slender and pointed with an expanded base. The most common were of chipped igneous stone and were used everywhere except in the central and eastern Arctic where igneous rock was rare or unobtainable. Ground slate was used there and to a lesser extend in the western Arctic, Subarctic, and Northwest Coast.

Horn, ivory, or bone arrowheads were used to some extent in all areas except the Southwest. Wood or cane points were used everywhere, but especially in the Southeast, Southwest, California, and the Great Basin. Copper arrowheads were used in the Great Lakes region, the Arctic, and on the Northwest Coast. Multiple-barbed arrowheads of wood, bone, or horn were used widely in the Arctic, western Subarctic,

bow *(Awashiri, Iquito, Zaparo, Okaina, Bora, Coto, Urarina, Ssabela, Yagua, Candoshi)*. These tribes preferred to fight and hunt with poisoned javelins. The bow was not used by the early Chimu people and was never a popular weapon along the Peruvian Coast. It was known, however, to the people of the Tiahuanaco culture and is often represented on textiles of that period. Stone arrowheads have been found in great quantities at Tiahuanaco. In the *Inca* army the bow was used by the auxiliary troops from the Tropical Forest, but not by the mountain Indians, who were armed with slings and clubs.

Among the *Araucanians* and *Tehuelche* the bow lost much of its usefulness after the adoption of the horse for, unlike North American Indians, the equestrian tribes of the Pampas did not modify their bow so that it could be used on horseback. Bow and arrows went out of use among the *Tehuelche* in the first half of the 19th century. The bow survived among Chaco horsemen, but they employed it only when they hunted or fought on foot. In *Yahgan* culture the bow and arrow occupied a very subordinate position.

South American Indians have known only the self-bow, that is, a bow made of a single piece of wood. Large powerful bows were, as a rule, characteristic of the forest tribes while smaller bows were found in the open steppes. Extreme lengths occur among the forest-dwelling *Siriono,* whose bows sometimes measure 12 feets, and among the *Guayaki* and *Caingang*, whose bows are almost as long. The shortest bows are those of the *Ona,* which average 4 feet 4 inches to 5 feet 5 inches. Other bow lengths are listed in table i.

Most South American bows are symmetrical and slightly curved. In some bows of the Montana area the bend is scarcely perceptible; it is, however, very pronounced in *Ona* and *Atacama* bows.

Bow stave.—In every region of South America the bow stave is made of a few specific woods which experience has shown to have adequate strength and resilience: *Ona* and *Yahgan*, of beech wood *(Nothofagus antartica); Chaco*, mainly palo mataco *(Achatocarpus praecox)* but also *Prosopis abbreviata*, quebracho *(Schinopsis lorentzii)*, and urundel *(Astronium juglandifolium);* eastern Brazil and along the upper Amazon, chonta palm *(Guilielma gasipaes)*. In eastern Brazil, *Astrocaryum ayri* was so widely used for bows that its common name is pao d'arco (bow wood). In the Xingu and Madeira *(Parintintin)* area, bows are made of aratazeiro (an Anonaceae) or of *Tecoma* wood (also called pao d'arco). The *Tupian*-speaking tribes of this area are the only ones who sometimes use palm wood. In Paraguay bows are carved of *Cocos romanzoffianum, mbocaya totai (Guayaki), Copernicia cerifera, Guilielma insignis (Caingua)*, or *Tabebuio chrystanha (Caingang)*.

The Guiana Indians use six different species of wood, of which only purple heart *(Copaifera pubiflora)*, letterwood or snakewood *(Brcsimum aublettii* or *Piratinera guianensis)*, and *Lecythis* sp. have been identified. Letterwood was in great demand and was traded back and forth. Trade in wood for bows occurred in Peru and in Northwest Argentina between the mountain and forest people. In 1637 the Spaniards met in the *Diaguita* region a party of 300 Indians who had just returned from the Chaco forests with 20 bow staves each.

The fabrication of a good bow requires much time and patience. The *Wapishana* allowed the letterwood to season for months in the shade, then split a rough stave from the heart, covered it with beeswax, and dried it slowly under the roof of the house so that it would never crack. The stave was worked into shape by scraping it with a piece of quartz and then it was smoothed with a shell, a stone, or a tooth. The final polish was given with curatella leaves *(Cecropia peltata)*, an effective abrasive. Some Indians *(Warrau, Arawak,* Barama *Carib, Machushi,* etc.) smeared their bows with rosin.

shaped'') cross section. The Chaco bows, which, in comparison to those of most tropical Indians, are crude, exhibit a wide range of variations in their cross sections. As a rule, they are somewhat flat with rounded edges and the outer side more or less convex, but as one goes from the southern to the northern Chaco the bow staves take a rounded shape. The bows of the ancient *Atacameno* had a semicircular cross section.

Guiana bows were generally convex on the belly while the back or outer surface was concave or flat. The frontal concavity sometimes deepened to a groove in which was held the unused portion of the bow string (Barama River *Carib*). The relation between the two sides of the bow stave were reversed in a few tribes *(Oyana* and tribes of the Icana-Caiari Basin).

The bows of a great many *Tupi, Carib,* and *Arawakan* tribes south of the Amazon *(Tupinamba, Guarani, Caingang, Puri-Coroado, Mashacali, Bacairi, Bororo, Apiaca, Parintintin, Maue,* etc.) are convex on the outer side and flat or concave on the string side.

Some significance has been also attached by Father W. Schmidt (1913) to the fastening of the bowstring. In his opinion bows without shoulders cut at each end to hold the string belong to an archaic culture type. Actually, bows without terminal shoulders occur among some primitive tribes of South America, such as the *Guayaki, Siriono, Guato, Caingang,* and *Ona.* The extremities of the Chaco bows are sharpened but are without clear cut shoulders to give a fast grip to the string *(Mataco, Toba, Chamacoco, Sapuki, Lengua).* According to Father W. Schmidt the bows of three tropical tribes also lack shoulders *(Mirana, Yauperi, Uashmiri).* The Andean bow also was without any shoulder or notch (Puna de Atacama). Since bows with or without shoulders serve their purpose equally well, it may be surmised that the general shape of the stave determines the presence or the lack of shoulders at the ends. On large bows with a round cross section, a firm grip for the string at both extremities is often provided by a ring and bulge made of creeper strings (*Guato, Caingang*). On *Sirono* bows, a few turns of a piece of string prevent the bow string slipping down the stave.

The bows of the forest tribes are of considerable length, averaging from 6½ feet to 8 feet (2 to 2.4 m.). The size of the bows fluctuates between these two figures within the same area and even within the same tribe. *Caingua* bows measure from 6 to 8 feet (1.8 to 2.4 m.). The longest bows in South America and perhaps in the whole world are those of the *Siriono*, which averages from 6 to 9 feet (1.8 to 2.7 m.) and may attain a length of 12 feet (3.6 m.). *Asurini* bows are short, 4 feet 6 inches (1.62 m.) but unusually wide, 2.3 to 2.7 inches (6 to 7 cm.).

In southern Brazil and Paraguay bows are often entirely or partially wrapped with strips of guembe bark, *Philodendron imbe (Guato, Guarani, Caingang, Botocudo)*. Some bows are covered with a basketry casing in the center *(Guarani, Tupinamba, Guarayu,* etc.). A great many Amazonian bows are wound with cotton threads at the center or near the ends. Bows are often trimmed with feathers.

The strength of the Indian bow seldom has been ascertained by experimentation. According to Ryden (1941), the *Siriono* could perforate a wooden board an inch (3 cm.) thick at a distance of about 80 feet (25 m.). The *Guayaki* are said to be capable of hitting the mark at a distance of 300 feet (91 m.).

Bow strings.—Throughout tropical South America and the Chaco, bow strings are made of vegetal fibers, generally from the tucum palm or from a Bromeliaceae. In the southern part of the continent, they are made of strips of skin or of sinew *(Tehuelche, Araucanian, Ona, Yahgan)*. In the intermediary region of the Chaco strings of both kinds occur, sometimes in the same tribe; the choice between them is entirely a matter of personal preference. *Guato* bows have a string made of skin strips.

The extra length of the string is usually carried back and wound around the stave (Guiana tribes, *Caraja, Bororo,* Chaco tribes, etc.). This arrangement does not reinforce the bow, but provides an additional string if the one in use should break. To tighten the bowstring, an Indian slips it off one end, gives it a few twists, and replaces it while he flexes the bow by pressure against his knee.

ARROWS

The type of head is the main basis for a functional classification of arrows because as a rule the head varies according to the special use to which the arrow is put (figs. 64, 65). In most tropical tribes a different kind of arrow is used for war, for fishing, for hunting different game animals, and even for ceremonial purposes. Feathering, on the other hand, may serve as a criterion only to establish a regional classification of arrows.

Distribution of arrowheads.—In the mountainous areas of western South America, along the Pacific Coast from Peru to Chile and in the plains of the southern part of the continent, arrows were, as a rule, tipped with stone heads; in the forested regions of the Orinoco, Amazon and Paraguay Basins, and among the tribes of eastern Brazil arrow points were made of wood, bamboo, bone, or sting-ray spikes. There are, however, a few exceptions. The ancient *Diaguita* of Northwest Argentina used both stone and wooden points. Stone arrowheads have been found archeologically in the sambaquis, or shell mounds, of southern Brazil, in the Guianas, and in the Xingu River basin. Im Thurn states that a *Carib* Indian assured him that "as a boy he used to see bone, shell, or stone pointed arrows in common use." The same author writes that he has seen "arrows, headed with stone, in the possession of some Arecunas." In Peru stone heads of arrows or of spear-thrower darts are found at the Ancon-Supe (early Ancon) level and then disappear. (More complete information on the

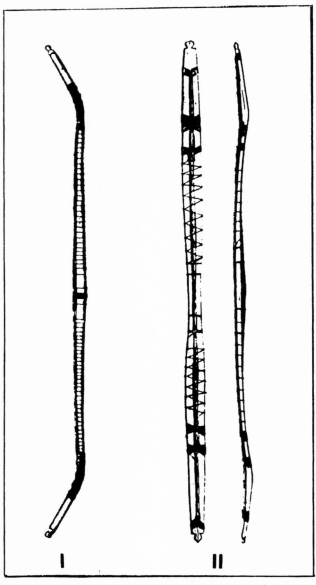

The four basic types of the Inuit bow; (I) with functional
siyahs, (II) with vestigial siyahs, (III) a confused pattern
where the siyahs are usually nonfunctional, and (IV) the

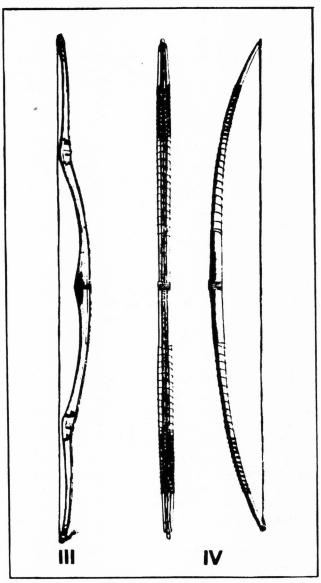

III   **IV**

final mature form, perfectly adapted to the arctic environment. Back views of II and III are also shown. In all side views, the back of the bow is to the left.

sequence and distribution of projectile points will be found in the archeological articles in the Handbook, especially vols. 1 and 2.)

Stone arrowheads.—No classification of stone heads has been made for South America but a map showing the regions where they have been found has been prepared by Linne. The main criteria which differentiate the various types of stone arrowheads are the size, the perfection of the chipping, and the presence or absence of a tang. The best arrowheads are those of the *Ona* and of the *Diaguita* region. The crudest specimens come from Patagonia. Stone arrowheads were chipped by a blunt rounded tool *(Ona)* or by percussion (Patagonia).

On the *Ona* arrows the tang of the head is fastened to the shaft with guanaco sinew. The ancient *Atacameno* fitted their stone points in a notch or pit at the end of a wooden foreshaft, a method used also in ancient Peru.

Flint arrowheads were used by the *Araucanians,* but bone heads seem to have been more common.

Arrowhead types in the Tropical Forests.—Five main types of arrowheads are distinguishable in the forested areas.

(1) The first has a lanceolate bamboo point with sharp edges and was used only in warfare and to kill large game animals. The point is fastened to a foreshaft of hardwood, which is laid in a groove at the tang of the point and is fastened with rosin, wax, and a tight binding (of peccary hair among the *Parintintin).* On *Bororo* arrows the bamboo blade is attached directly to the seriba reed *(Avicennia* sp.) shaft. A bamboo arrowhead was generally soaked or dried before being fixed to the arrow. The size of a lanceolate bamboo head varies from 20 to 70 cm. *(Caraja,* from 30 to 40 cm.; *Parintintin,* 40 cm.; *Paracana* of the lower Tocantins, 70 cm.). The shape may vary even within a single tribe. Some points are almost flat; some are semicircular in cross section; some have deep notches cut near the base produce

long, sharp barbs; and some have a continuous row of teeth almost to the point. Guiana bamboo heads often have a guard directly under the point that prevents too deep a penetration of the arrow and causes it to fall to the ground before the wounded animal breaks it when dashing into thick bush.

(2) The second type is a pencillike wooden rod inserted directly into the arrow shaft. Its cross section may be round, triangular, rectangular, or diamond-shaped. Some are carved in the shape of successive abutting cones *(Parintintin)*. Others may be smooth or jagged along one or both sides. Many specimens, especially fishing arrows, have a bone splinter or a string-ray spine fastened against the proximal extremity of the rod to form a sharp barb. In most cases, however, the needle-sharp splinter or spine is laid obliquely in a groove at the tip of the wooden head to serve both as point and barb. Some arrows, which are often classed in a special category, have a tubular bone—generally a monkey humerus—with a sharp point and a beveled, flaring base, fitted over the tapered end of the wooden shaft and cemented with wax *(Cayapo)*. All the arrows in this second category are used for hunting large and small mammals and birds, and also for fishing.

(3) The third type of head consists of two or three pointed rods inserted into the arrow shaft. This type is employed mainly for fishing *(Parintintin)*, but in some tribes *(Chiriguano)*, it is also used for shooting large birds. Generally, each rod is provided with a sharp lateral barb of bone or some other material. Triprong fishing arrows are common in the Guianas. The *Panoan Chama* of the Ucayali River use arrows armed with a bunch of seven points to shoot small fish, and the *Tupi-Cawahib,* arrows with four to seven points. The *Chane* fishing arrows which bristle with cactus thorns are a local variety of the same type.

(4) The fourth type has a harpoon head, and is used principally for fishing. The point has a hollow tang which is loosely fitted over the foreshaft and is con-

nected to the shaft by a recovery string. The shaft serves as a float. Arrows with heads of this kind are, in fact, small harpoons discharged with a bow. Some of the *Chama* harpoon arrows fall into three parts when they have struck their mark. In certain cases the recovery string is attached to the fisherman's wrist.

The harpoon head of the *Guato* was of bone with a single barb. It was fitted loosely into a funnel made by wrapping cipo around the end of the foreshaft and was attached to the shaft with a string.

Many Guiana Indians and the *Chake* of eastern Colombia employ harpoon arrows to shoot large game. The dragging shaft prevents the animal's escape into the thick bush.

(5) The fifth type is the blunt-headed arrow used to shoot birds. Instead of points, these arrows have knobs. The Indians give the following reasons for the advantages this type of arrow has over others for this purpose: A wide knob is more likely to kill or stun a bird than is a sharp point that might strike in a non-vital part or slide off; a blunt head does not draw blood and so does not spoil the plumage; birds hit by blunt arrows can be captured alive; when the arrow misses the mark, it does not stick in a branch.

The head of the bird arrow is ordinarily a conical or round piece of wood inserted into the shaft and often is provided with a protruding peg or point. Some Guiana bird arrows are elegantly carved and have flanges and sharp edges which enhance their appearance. The *Taulifpang* wedged the butt end of a deer horn into the split arrow point to form a knob for their bird arrows. For some bird arrows the Indians (*Botocudo, Paressi, Cayapo, Puri, Tupinamba, Guato*) use reed stems as the shaft and the bulging roots, carefully trimmed, as the round head.

The *Yuracare, Maue,* and several Guiana tribes tip their bird arrows with two or four short, cross sticks, lashed to a rod stem. Other tribes make the head of their bird arrows with a lump of wax. An ordinary arrow can also be transformed into a bird arrow by placing a piece of gourd over the point *(Mbaya)*.

Bird arrows seem to be rare or lacking altogether in northwestern Brazil and in the Purus River basin, where birds are shot with the blowgun.

Whistling arrows.—Many tribes place a perforated nut under the arrow head to produce a whistling noise when the arrow flies through the air *(Arara,* Tapajoz River, *Paracana, Yuruna, Shipbo, Amanaye,* Guarpore River, *Rucuyen, Guayaki,* etc.). Copper arrowheads with a hollow bulb in the middle have been found in Peru. (See Ryden, 1931.)

Arrowshafts.—In tropical South America, arrowshafts are made of uba stalks and taquara de frecha *(Gynerium sagittatum),* and camayuva reeds *Guadua* sp.). Cane for arrows is often cultivated. Many Chaco Indians cultivate the Cana de Castilla *(Arundo donax),* which was imported into South America at an early date and which in many places has supplanted the use of native reeds. Some *Bororo* war arrows had serib *(Avicennia* sp.) reed shafts. Even in the same tribe different materials might be used for the shafts of arrows used for different purposes. *Parintintin* fishing arrows, for example, have *Gynerium* shafts, while war and hunting arrows have shafts of *Guadua* sp.

The end of the forshaft is set directly into the shaft and is cemented with rosin or wax. Most Guiana Indians compress the section of the shaft which serves as a socket for the foreshaft with a special device which consists of a cord with two pieces of wood or two turtle bones attached at the ends. The operator holds one end between his toes, winds the cord a few times around the shaft and pulls the other end with his right hand, while with his left hand he rolls the shaft uniformly back and forward. A similar procedure is followed when a nock is inserted into the proximal end.

The end of the shaft is wound with a bark strip or cotton thread which extends to the lower part of the inserted wooden head; geometric designs are often produced by crossing the threads of the binding.

In Tierra del Fuego, arrow shafts were wrought of crooked wood which was heated and bent with the teeth until perfectly straight. The shaft was then scraped and polished with a grooved stone. The feathers were atttached to the shaft with the skin muscles of the guanaco lashed in spirals.

Feathering.—With the exception of the *Cuna, Chake, Macu,* and a few other tribes, all South American Indians attached feathers to the butt of their arrows to facilitate their flight through the air. Only fishing arrows are, for obvious reasons, without feathering.

The classification of types of feathering in South America estblished by H. Meyer (1898) has been so often quoted that it is necessary to reproduce here the definition of the six main types of feathering he found in Brazil, although it is open to criticism in several respects:

East Brazilian or Ge-Tupi feathering.—"Two feathers unchanged, seldom halved, are fastened at either upper and lower ends to the shaftment opposite each other with thread, fiber, or cipo bast. Frequently these wrappings are laid on in patterns or have an ornamention of little feathers added."

For this definition to be adequate, it should be added that the two feathers generally are twisted in a spiral so that they have a propellerlike appearance.

Guiana feathering.—The feather is cut at its base and tip and the barbs are removed from one side. The wrapping seizes the two halves at regular intervals and takes ornamental patterns.

Xingu sewed feathering.—Two half feathers are stitched to the shaft opposite each other through perforations. The ends are seized fast with plain or patterned lashing.

The "sewed" feathering had a very limited distribution. It was used by the tribes of the upper Xingu *(Bacairi, Aueto, Camayura, Trumai),* by the *Bororo, Cayabi, Huanyam* and *Paracana* (lower Tocantins), and *Asurini.*

Arara feathering—Two long half feathers, which, in addition to the end seizings, are held down by narrow wrappings of thread at short distances apart. At the nock the wrapping is done in beautiful patterns.

Peruvian or cemented feathering.—The two feathers of the

cemented feathering are separated from the midrib with only a thin portion of the quill remaining. They are bound fast to the shaftment in a close spiral with thread or yarn, and, to increase the hold on the shaft along the feather, the shaftment is covered with black or brown pitch.

The Maue feathering.—Like the east Brazilian feathering, this type has two entire feathers bound on above and below. At the base of the shaft, however, a nock piece or footing is set in.

Meyer's classification, which has been accepted by many specialists of South American ethnology, needs to be revised and established on a single principle, for the features that Meyer considers to be characteristic of his five main types have been selected arbitrarily and are sometimes entirely unrelated. In three cases he regards the nature of the binding as a distinctive trait; in one case, the presence of a nock; and in still another, the addition of a substance to the binding.

Our present classificaton will rest exclusively on the method of attachment of the feathers. If the position of the feathers is considered, two main types of feathering may be distinguished, as follows:

In the first type we have shaftment with two feathers tied at both ends and slightly arched and twisted propellerlike. This type corresponds to the "Eastern Brazilian" or "tangential feathering" of Meyer, and will be called "arched feathering" (stegfederung) *(Tupinamba, Caingua, Guarayu, Cayapo, Caraja, Parintintin, Apiaca, Mashachali, Yuruna, Bororo, Botocudo,* etc.).

In the second type the feathers, split along the quill, are applied flush to the shaft. This type of feathering will be called "flush." It may be divided into various subtypes according to the method of binding employed:

(*a*) The threads may be wound around the shaft from one end to the other or they may be wrapped at close or far intervals. This subtype is called "wrapped feathering" and corresponds to the "Arara" and "Guiana'" feathering of Meyer *(Apiaca, Mura, Maue, Parintintin).*

(*b*) The feathers may be sewed by threads passing through perforations across the shaftment. This is the "sewed feathering" and corresponds to Meyer's "sewed Xingu feathering."

(*c*) The binding may be smeared with wax or rosin. This is the "cemented feathering" and corresponds to Meyer's "Peruvian cemented feathering."

Further distinctions may be made in regard to the size or shape of the feathering. In the arched feathering, one vane is removed or is greatly reduced by burning; generally, the remaining strip presents a toothed edge. In flush feathering, the feathers are halved along the quill and the remaining vane is used either with its full length or cut up and down so that only the central portion is left.

Ona feathering belongs to the subvariety (*a*) of our second type, but many details mark it off from all other featherings. The two half-feathers are lashed radially to the shaft with spirally wound sinew or gut. Except in Tierra del Fuego, the feathers are usually fastened to the shaft with cotton threads, often of several colors, or with thin strips of guembe bark. In many tribes the threads are crossed or wound to produce ornamental effects. W. E. Roth, writing about the Guianas, describes four types of feather bindings which he names after their final appearance: diamond, claw, bar, and spiral. According to Ahlbrinck, the *Carib* of Guiana had 10 different feather bindings, called, scales of kariwaru *(Hoplosternum),* ananas, tracks of kotaka *(Aramides cayanea),* etc.

Oviedo y Valdes states that arrows of some Patagonian Indians carried three instead of the usual two feathers. Nordenskiold has made much of the fact that a *Caingua* arrow published by Ambrosettie likewise had three feathers; actually *Caingua* arrows had the typical "arched-feathering" so widespread in eastern Brazil. Arrows with more than two feathers occur now and then in tribes which otherwise conform to the classic types of feathering. The *More* for example, attached three or even four feathers to some of their arrows so that they would rotate faster in their trajectory. To single out these exceptions as survivals of a time when the feathering of South American arrows was more like that of North American ones is to take undue advantage of the historical methods. Moreover.

several types of featherings may be found in a single tribe. Thus, the *Tupi-Cawahib* have arrows with flush, sewn, and arched feathering. The *Apiaca* used arrows both of the arched and flush types. Krause explains the presence of several different kinds of arrows within a single tribe by the widespread Indian custom of exchanging arrows as signs of goodwill and friendship. However, such an explanation cannot apply to all cases. The feathering may also vary with the function of the arrow; for example, the large war arrows of the *Parintintin* and *Mura* have flush feathering, while their arrows for hunting small game have arched feathering.

Nocks.—The butt end of the arrow is generally notched to prevent its slipping from the string. If the shaft reed is a *Gynerium* and consequently likely to splinter, a grooved wooden plug is inserted into the shaft *(Shiriano, Choco, Palicur, Paracas,* etc.). The *Guato*, instead of notching the brittle uba reeds, insert three small wooden splinters in the butt of the arrow. The nock of the arrow is always reinforced by a tight wrapping, generally of cotton thread or of strips or bark, irrespective of the presence or absence of a peg.

Arrow release.—As there are few descriptions of the methods of South American arrow release, it is impossible to map their distribution satisfactorily. Moreover, in a single tribe, such as the *Ona*, the archer ordinarily may shoot with the primary release, but use the secondary or tertiary type if he wishes to shoot far. The three main types of release are as follows:

Primary release.—The butt of the arrow is held between the thumb and index finger. Used by Guiana tribes, Indians of the Xingu Basin, *Palicur, Siusi*, and *Ona*.

Secondary release.—The butt is held as above, but the string is pulled back with all the remaining fingers. Used by the *Caraja, Tupi-Cawahib, Shavaje, Ayonmano* of Venezuela, and Chaco Indians.

Tertiary release.—The butt is held between the index and middle fingers and the string is pulled with the remaining fingers. Used by *Tupi-Cawahib,* Xingu tribes, *Shavaje, More, Guato,* and *Chake.*

Wrist guards.—Usually the archer protected his wrist against the impact of the string by wrappings of strings of cotton or human hair *(Guato, Caingua, Guayaki, Parintintin, Caraja, Shavante),* with a leather bracelet *(Choroti, Mataco, Ashluslay, Goajiro),* with a strip of bark cloth *(More),* or with a wooden guard *(Abipon, Mocovi).*

Poisoned arrows.—Poisoned arrows were not so widely used by the Indians as is commonly assumed from the exaggerated accounts of the Spanish conquistadors. Curare, which is the most deadly poison known to the Indians, is prepared by relatively few tribes though it is traded throughout wide regions. The descriptions of the effects of poisoned arrows on wounded Spanish soldiers do not suggest the use of curare, and it is not improbable that this deadly substance spread in post-Columbian times to regions where is was formerly unknown. The Indians who in the 16th century lived along the coast of Venezuela and the Gulf of Uraba had the reputation of concocting terrible poisons. The basic material is said have been the juice of the manzanilla fruit (*Hippomane mancinella)* but the statement has been doubted by modern authorities. Rochefort also mentions manzanilla juice as the poison with which the *Island Carib* smeared their arrows. Orellana was convinced that the soldiers whom he lost at the mouth of the Amazon had been wounded by poison arrows.

The Indians of the Apaporis and the Cairari-Uaupes use curare to poison their arrows. The heads of these arrows consists of a round stem notched at the end to hold a piece of hardwood loosely fastened with rosin and strings. This point is smeared with curare and sometimes is provided with circular incisions.

The tribes that poison their war and hunting arrows are the *Macushi, Maku, Tucuna,* and, south of the Amazon, the *Kepkiriwat, Amniapa* and *Pawumwa* of the right side of the Guapore River, the *Nambicuara,* and the *Paressi.* In the 16th century, the *Chiquitos* were greatly feared by both their neighbors and by the Spaniards becuase of their poisoned arrows. It is probable that, like the modern tribes of the area, they extracted curare from a *Strychnos.* The *Araucanians* poisoned their arrows with the juice of the coligerey root *(Colliguaja odorifera).*

Tribes that use poisoned arows cover their arrowheads with a sheath as a precaution against accidents and also to prevent water from washing off the coating of poison.

Quivers.—A sharp distinction should be made between quivers for arrows shot from bows and those for blowgun darts. The latter have the same distinction as the blowgun and will be described below. Quivers for arrows have a limited distribution—mainly in the southern tip of the continent among the *Ona, Alacaluf, Chono, Tehuelche, Araucanians, Diaguita, Charrua, Abipon,* and *Mocovi.*

Ona quivers were made from the hide of the hair seal.

To manufacture them a hide was cut in a rectangular pattern of suitable size and shape. This was doubled and sewn up the side, while at the bottom a small oval piece of hide was inserted and stitched into place. Were it not for this flat bottom the delicate glass point [made in post-Columbian times] would have been jammed against one another and thus become broken. On the upper end of the quiver there is a small loop of hide by which it was hung out of reach of dogs when in camp.

Similar quivers were used by the *Yahgan* and *Alacaluf.* The *Tehuelche* seen by the early navigators did not have any quivers, but "inserted their arrows in a narrow woven fillet encircling the head so that they projected above like a crown". However, quivers are mentioned in more recent descriptions of these Indians. Hide quivers were used by the *Araucanians* and the ancient *Atacameno,* as is apparent from a skin quiver found at Rio Loa. Azara, states that the ancient *Charrua* carried their "small arrows in a quiver suspended from their shoulders." Quivers are not used by modern Chaco Indians and are reported only once for the *Abipon,* by Dobrizhoffer, who says, "The quiver is made of rushes and is adorned with woolen threads of various colors." A quiver of the same type was found by Baucke among the weapons of the *Mocovi.* A long strap attached to the quiver suggests that it was slung from the shoulder.

The arrows of the tropical Indians were too long to be comfortably carried in a quiver suspended from the shoulders. This probably explains the rare occurrence of quivers north of the Chaco. Quivers, however, were necessary as a protection against one's own poisoned arrows.

Nordenskiold lists the following tribes north of the Amazon who supposedly had quivers: *Motilones, Menimehe, Guahibo, Guypunavi, Corbago,* and the Indians of the Trinidad. The *Menimehe,* who poisoned their arrows, carried them in wicker quivers, in bamboos with the partitions scraped out, or in more elaborate containers made of bound bamboo strips. The quiver also is mentioned among the *Guahibo,* who used poisoned arrows, but is not described. The allusion to a quiver full of darts in Juan de Castellanos' poem hardly is valid evidence for the occurrence of quivers among the Trinidad Indians. The cylindrical baskets in which the *Motilones* stored their arrows at home cannot properly be called a quiver. The *Corbago* Indians, like the ancient *Tupinamba,* put their bows and arrows in casings, probably as a protection against worms or humidity.

THE PELLET BOW

The pellet-bow is aptly described by Nordenskiold as a combination of a sling and of a bow. Instead of arrows, it projects small clay pellets which are placed on a fabric cradle stretched between the two strings of the bow. A small forked stick keeps the strings apart. When shooting with the pellet-bow, the strings must be pulled aside from the stave.

The pellet-bow has a peculiar distribution in South America. It is found among all the Chaco tribes, among the *Chiriguano, Yuracare, Churapa, Guato, Mashacali, Caingua,* and *Caraja,* and among the Caboclos of eastern Brazil. Nordenskiold is inclined to consider the introduction of the pellet-bow as post-Columbian, because of the resemblance between Hindu and South American pellet-bows, both of which have a thick round grip. He surmises that it spread by means of Portuguese who had become acquainted with it in India. The pellet-bow, is in fact, a favorite toy among Mestizo children; Krause points out that the *Caraja* borrowed it from the Caboclo children. Moreover, our many and detailed authorities on the ancient Indians of the Brazilian coast never mention this weapon, which became so common among their acculturated descendants.

THE SPEAR THROWER

The spear thrower (fig. 67) is an old weapon in South America. It was found in Peru in several cultural horizons from Nazca to the *Inca* period. It was known to the builders of Tiahuanaco, and the dart is held between the thumb and middle finger and the two remaining fingers rest against the grip under the dart. The dart is supported by the left hand. The *Caraja* use the weapon to play the "game of the *Tapirape*"; it is probable that they received the spear thrower from the *Tapirape,* who in turn may have borrowed it from the Xingu tribes (Krause).

The spear thrower of the Purus River was a small board with a narrow handle and a hole for the forefinger. The spur was lashed at the distal end.

The Indians of the upper Amazon *(Mainas, Cocama, Omagua)* fought against the first Spanish explorers with spear throwers; 18th century *Omagua* and *Cocama* still used it, mainly to hunt turtles. A *Cocama* museum specimen closely resembles the descriptions of early travelers. It is a thick board, flat on the upper side and convex underneath, that widens toward the center, where it has a pit for the fore finger. The peg is lashed at the end of a groove running the full length of the shaft. The same type of spear thrower, characterized however by a bulging distal end, occurred among the Indians of the Cauca Valley, Antioquia, and the upper Magdalena. A spear thrower is also mentioned but not described among the *Panobo*.

The *Mojo* and *Canichana* used the spear thrower for hunting and warfare. Eder describes the spear thrower of Mojos as a tube (capsula), which must mean a halved section of bamboo; according to a picture in Eder, the *Mojo* spear thrower was a narrow board with a hook to engage the butt of the dart. The *Mojo* discarded this weapon soon after European contact.

In the 17th century, the *Caripuna* and *Quirina,* of the Purus River, had beautifully carved spear throwers which they traded to other nations.

The third category of spear thrower is represented by a single specimen in the Museum of Copenhagen, collected in the 17th century from the *Otschukayana*, a "*Tapuya*" tribe of eastern Brazil. It consists of a tapering piece of wood with a deep groove to receive the dart, which is engaged by a horizontal peg lashed to the proximal and narrower end of the instrument. It measures about 35 inches (88 cm.) in length and 1½ inches (4 cm.) in width. It is mentioned by Herckman and has been drawn by Eckout.

The spear thrower (varas tiraderas) has been attributed by Oviedo y Valdes to the *Chana* and *Timbu* of the Parana Delta, and a spear-thrower hook was found archeologically by Lothrop in a region formerly occupied by the *Querandi*. The mouth of the Rio de la Plata probably is the southernmost limit of the spear thrower in South America.

THE BLOWGUN

Distribution.—Although the blowgun has attracted wide attention among modern travelers, it is rarely mentioned by 16th- and 17th-century writers. There is a reference to its use in Colombia by Cieze de Leon and, according to a report of the Maldonado expedition to eastern Bolivia, it was used by an Indian tribe located approximately in the Beni Basin. Heriarte refers to the blowgun in the Province of Aguas, somewhere on the upper Amazon, and both Oviedo y Valdes and Simon speak of the "zerbatana" of the natives around Lake Maracaibo *(Bubure?).* According to Saabedra and Figueroa, who were among the first missionaries to visit the area of Mainas (eastern Ecuador and Peru) at the beginning of the 17th century, the *Mainas, Paranapura,* and *Muniche* of this region used the blowgun.

It was obviously an ancient weapon in Peru, for men shooting birds with a blowgun are represented on early Chimu vases and on a fabric discovered at Pachacamac. The Peabody Museum of Harvard recently has acquired a blowgun made of an 18-foot (about 5.4 m.) cane found near Trujillo. With it were discovered a bundle of darts from 4 to 5 inches (about 7.5 cm.) long. That it was of little importance or obsolete at the time of the Conquest may perhaps be surmised by the silence of our sources.

Early data on the occurrence of the blowgun are scarce mainly because the tribes that used it inhabited regions that were explored long after the more desirable parts of the continent had been subdued, but 17th-century conquistadors did not fail to allude to it when the tribes they visited used it. The *Jivaro,* however, constitute a remarkable exception, for although today they manufacture beautiful blowguns, the 16th-century Spaniards who fought against them never mention the weapon. A possible explanation is that the *Jivaro* acquired the blow gun sometime after the 16th century. Recently, it has been adopted by many tribes who formerly did not use it. Nordenskiold rightly observes that the efficiency of the blowgun depends on the use of curare poison, the preparation of which is the monopoly of a few tribes.

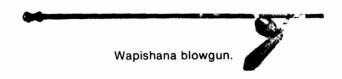

Wapishana blowgun.

Nordenskiold bases his hypothesis that the use of the blowgun is fairly recent in tropical America and that it spread mainly in post-Columbian times on the scarcity of references to curare in the early sources and on the distributuion of the weapon. The vagueness of our early sources on tropical South America does not jusify our accepting such purely negative evidence, but it is, nevertheless, striking that the blowgun is not found in eastern South America and in the Xingu region. In the Guianas the blowgun is found among the *Western Carib (Taulipang, Arecuna, Acawai)*, but is lacking among the more easterly groups (*Warrau* Barama *Carib*, Sirinam *Arawak*).

The blowgun reached it highest development in South America among the tribes of the upper Amazon and in the regions between the Orinoco and the Andes. It remained unknown to the tribes of the West Indies.

Manufacture of blowgun was formerly the specialty of some tribes that bartered them to their neighbors. In Brazilian Guiana, the *Yecuana* had the monopoly of their fabrication because the best bamboo for the purpose grew along the upper Marewari, Ventuari, and Orinoco Rivers. The *Iburuana* of the upper Ventuari imported the tucum nuts of which they made the mouthpieces of their blowguns. Likewise the *Macushi* imported their blowguns from the *Arecuna, Maiongkong,* and *Guianau,* who live in a region where the *Arundinaria* are abundant. The *Camaracoto* obtained their blowguns at high prices from the *Marikitare;* sometimes they bought only the inner tube and then encased it themselves, for they were well provided with suitable wood for the outer tube.

Certain tribes had a monopoly on the fabrication of

curare. The blowgun poison of the *Tucuna* was considered to be the most effective in the whole of Amazonia, but the knowledge of its preparation, which requires time and care, is being lost.

Types of blowguns.—There are four main types of blowguns:

(1) The most primitive type consists of a single bamboo tube. It is represented in South America by the *Majo* and *Huari* blowgun, which is a simple bamboo stem, straightened by heating it over a fire and with its inner partitions abraised by fire, sand, and water.

(2) The seond type, found among the tribes of the Guianas and of the Orinoco and Uaupes Rivers and also among the *Macu* and *Passe*, consists of two tubes, one placed within the other to prevent warping. The inner tube generally is of *Arundinaria schomburgkii*, which is cut to the desired length, rotated over a fire until dry, and then exposed to the sun until it becomes yellow. The outer protective tube is made of a straight stem of the paxiuba palm *(Socrates exorrhiza)* or more rarely of a palm of the Arecineae tribe, which is dried until the central pith can easily be removed with a rod. The bore often is rubbed clean and is polished by rubbing through it a little bunch of tree fern roots. A conical mouthpiece, often carved from an *Astrocaryum* kernel, is fitted to one end of the tube, while the other end is reinforced with a wooden ring. A peccary tusk stuck in wax is mounted on the tube to serve as a sight. The weapon often is wound spirally with the shining black bark of a creeper. Its length is 10 to 13 feet (3 to 4 m.).

(3) The third type also consists of two tubes. The inner reed is encased within the two halves of young stems that have been carefully scooped out. The whole in smeared with a layer of black wax and is wrapped with bark strips "in a somewhat overlapping spiral" *(Siusi, Tucano)*.

(4) The fourth type, found in the upper Amazon and the *Choco* region (*Chebero, Jivaro, Choco, Shipibo, Mirana, Pioje, Zaparo, Quijo, Coto, Colorado,*

Ticuna, Tucuna, Yamamadi), consisted of two sections of palmwood grooved longitudinally and fitted together to form a round bore. The manufacture of this type was observed and described by Stirling among the *Jivaro.*

The *Conibo* blowgun was wrapped first with maize leaves, then wound with bark strips and finally coated with rosin.

The *Cuna* blowgun, which is unlike any. other in South America, is composed of several tubes of slightly varying diameters joined together so as to obtain the correct length.

Missiles.—In Central America the most common missiles for blowguns are clay pellets, but in South America such projectiles are reported only among the *Cuna* and the *Colorado* Indians of western Ecuador. Ribeiro de Sampaio's statement about the use of clay pellets among the Indians of the Jurua River is not sufficiently specific to be included in a distribution map.

Everywhere else in South America, blowgun missiles are darts smeared with curare, a poison which made the blowgun into an efficient hunting weapon. The darts were thin splinters of the midrib of palm leaves (kokerit, *Astrocaryum,* inaja, bacaba, etc.). The technique used by the *Jivaro* for making these darts also has been described by Stirling.

A wadding of wild cotton that will receive the impact of the air puff is attached to the butt end of the dart. Since the wad is put on the dart when it is loaded, the Indians carry a supply of floss in a little calabash or in a basket tied to their quivers. Before shooting the dart, the hunter notches the curare-smeared point to facilitate its breaking off in the wound if the wounded animal tries to rid itself of it. Formerly, the notch was made with a piranha jawbone (*Pygocentrus),* which aslo was attached to the quiver.

Blowgun quivers and protection of darts.—Guiana quivers, which sometimes hold 150 to 200 darts, are twilled baskets made of strong strips of creepers. The

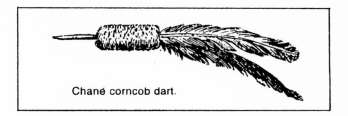

Chané corncob dart.

bottom is made of wood or a gourd, the lid of tapir skin. The outer surface is smeared with wax or pitch; sometimes (e. g., among the tribes of the Icana and Caiari Rivers) the quivers are partly covered with an additional layer of basketry with geometric designs. The *Jivaro, Chama, Aguano, Candoshi, Mayoruna, Chayawita,* and *Lamista* use bamboo quivers that sometimes are engraved in various patterns. Wooden quivers are reported among the *Buhagana* of the upper Apaporis and Tiquie. A palm spath serves as a quiver among the *Huanyam* and the *Yecuana.*

The darts must be stored with great care to avoid accidents. Many Guiana tribes *(Taulipang, Macushi,* etc.) twine their darts together with two pairs of cotton strings—one at each end—and then wrap the bundles so obtained around a stick of the length of the quiver. A hoop is attached at the end of the stick as a protection for the hand when the quiver is reversed in order to let the bundle of darts drop out. The Icana and Caiari River Indians place their darts point down in the quiver, where a layer of bast fibers prevents them from breaking. The *Buhagana* fold their darts in a grass mat. The *Jivaro* fill their quivers with a fibrous material which holds the darts in place.

Not all the darts in a quiver are poisoned, for the Indian smears with curare only those he intends for immediate use. The *Arecuna* sprinkle their darts with powdered stone to prevent the darts from sticking together.

Technique of shooting.—Shooting with a blowgun does not entail so much skill and strength as has often been claimed. When shooting, the Indian holds the tube with both hands, palm down, close to the mouth and with the sight uppermost. He sends the dart on its way with a slight puff. The maximum effective range is from 30 to 45 yards.

This weapon is especially useful for shooting birds or small mammals, but the amount of poison on the darts is not sufficient to cripple permanently a large animal and even less a man.

SLINGS

Distribution.—The sling (map 4) can be used to good advantage only in open country. It was the favorite weapon of mountain Indians from Colombia to Chile (Cauca River, *Quimbaya, Ica, Panche);* it was also used by the *Ona* and *Yahgan* of Tierra del Fuego and by the *Tehuelche.* In the forested areas of South America it occurs as a boy's toy, e. g., in the Chaco. It is found in eastern Bolivia among the *Mojo, Canichana, Itonama,* and *Baure,* who live partly in open savannas. Lacking stones, the *Mojo* are said to have cast with them clay pellets bristling with curare-poisoned thorns. The sling also is found among the *Chiriguano,* who have borrowed it from their *Quechua* neighbors.

Types of slings.—The Andean sling generally was made of wool or cotton; the broad central cradle which held the stone was woven in a tight fabric, often decorated with varicolored geometric designs. The slit in the middle of the cradle gave a certain elasticity to the textile so that stones of different sizes could be thrown. On some slings the cradle was a separate piece to which strings were tied. One of the strings ended in a loop which was slipped over a finger. Both strings were held in the same hand, the sling was whirled around the right shoulder, and the missile was thrown by releasing the loopless string.

The cradle of the *Ona* and *Yahgan* sling was a piece of Guanaco or seal skin. On *Ona* specimens it was suspended on braided whalegut lines, while on *Yahgan* slings it was attached to strips of guanaco hide. The method of discharge also differed in the two Fuegian tribes. The *Ona* wrapped the "long end around the fore finger, while the *Yahgan* inserted it between the fourth and little fingers so that it extended across the palm of the hand".

The Chaco sling is a flimsy implement made in a few minutes by looping a cord in the middle to form a rudimentary cradle or central net. The only missiles are fragments of hardened clay.

BOLAS

Distribution.—The distribution of bolas (Spanish: boleadoras) coincides, in part with that of the sling, a coincidence that is not entirely fortuitous, since both weapons are effective only in open country.

The occurrence of the bolas among the *Ona* of Tierra del Fuego is doubtful. Spherical stones that may have been for bolas have been found in the open country of the Isla Grande, but their actual use is not reported by our authorities on these Indians. Bolas were a favorite weapon among the *Tehuelche, Puelche, Querandi, Charrua,* and probably all tribes of the Pampa. They were known to both Chilean and Argentinian *Araucanians.* In ancient Peru, bolas were used mainly by the *Aymara,* but also by the *Quechua.* Bolas have been found in the chullpas of Bolivia, but they do not appear in archeological collections made on the coast and are not reproduced on the Chimu ceramics, an indication that they were not adopted by the coastal cultures. Bolas are also mentioned by the conquistadors who, at the the beginning of the 16th century, entered the plains of Mojos. In the 18th century, both the *Mocovi* and the *Abipon* used them. In modern times, the *Lengua* still employed them to catch rheas. Koenigswald assigns the use of the bolas to the *Shokleng (Aweikoma)* of Santa Catharina, but the statement needs confirmation. Stone for bolas were found archeologically in Uruguay and in southern Brazil, a distribution which coincides with historical data.

Types.—Typologically, bolas may consist of one, two, or three stone balls. The one-stone bolas, or "bola perdida," is described by the 16th-century Spaniards who saw it in the hands of the *Querandi* when they attacked the horsemen of the Adelantado Mendoza. The bola perdida was still used 100 years ago by the *Tehuelche,* who sometimes handled it as a mace to smash the skull of pumas. A text by Sarmiento referring to a *Quechua* weapon may be interpreted as a reference to the bola perdida. The *Uro* on the southern shore of Lake Titicaca still hunt ducks with a straw bola perdida.

Two-stone bolas are reported in Patagonia, and among the *Aymara* and the *Shokleng (Aweikoma)* of Santa Catharina.

The most common type of bolas consists of three stones; the one held in the hand is smaller and more · elongated than the others. This is the bolas used by the *Aymara,* the *Mojo,* and the Chaco Indians, and today by the gauchos of Argentina and Uruguay.

The weights of the Patagonian bolas were often beautifully polished spherical stones with a deep groove around the middle for fastening the cord. The stones of *Aymara* bolas (llivi) were smaller but also grooved; modern *Aymara* bolas are folded in raw leather, as were the stones of the *Mocovi* and *Abipon* bolas.

The bolas was principally a hunting weapon, but it became a war weapon that was used with some success against the Spaniards when the Indians observed how effectively it stopped their horses.

CLUBS

South American clubs fall into four main categories: (1) staff clubs or cudgels; (2) flat clubs or wooden swords, called in Spanish literature "macanas"; (3)

Tapuya man and spear thrower.

maces or clubs with a stone or metal head; and (4) throwing clubs.

Staff clubs or cudgels.—The crudest forms of this weapon are the ordinary sticks used by several tribes for hunting or warfare *(Botocudo, Yahgan, Alacaluf, Guayaki)*. The Indians of the Apaporis region used knotty branches to break their enemies' legs. Nimuendaju saw the *Parintintin* use simple sticks as cudgels.

Cudgels usually are carefully carved and given a conical shape *(Caraja, Shavaje, Cayapo, Caingang, Shipaya)*. The clubs of the Southern *Caingang* have prismatic cross section and sharp edges. Clubs with a square cross section occur only among the *Caingua*. The clubs of the Chaco tribes were heavy cudgels of palomataco wood with a bulging conical head or a wooden disk carved at the distal end of a cylindrical shaft. The latter type is reminiscent of the *Inca* maces. The *Shipaya* used short, cylindrical clubs with a suspension loop.

Flat clubs, or macanas.—"Macana," a *Taino* word, was applied by the Spanish conquistadors to all flat wooden swords or clubs used by the South American Indians. The original macana of the *Taino* was about 5 feet to 5 feet 4 inches (1.50 to 1.60 m.) long and 2 inches (5 cm.) wide. It was flat with two sharp edges and tapered from the handle to the straight distal end. The Indians handled it with both hands.

On the mainland the wooden sword is reported among the Indians of Darien, Uraba, the Cauca Valley, the region of Piritu (*Cumanagoto* and other tribes), among the *Piapoco, Guahibo, Pioje,* and *Achagua,* and, south of the Amazon, among the *Cayabi, Huari* and the *Nambicuara* (as a ceremonial weapon). It was also the weapon of the Panoan tribes of the Ucayali.

The wooden sword was also used by the *Inca* armies. Here it was made of hard chonta wood, was about 4 feet (1.2 m.) long, 4 inches (10 cm.) wide, and tapered toward the handgrip. The rounded hilt ended in a knob or pommel.

The Guiana macana had the appearance of a sharp-edged paddle. The short, flat clubs of the *Macushi, Acawoi, Carib,* and *Umaua,* which had the handle near the middle and a pointed shaft, served as a knife, a club, and a bayonet.

Typologically the famous *Tupinamba* tacape, or sword, with its round or oval flat head at the end of a long-flattened shaft, is related to the Guiana paddle club, though it must be regarded as a highly aberrant form. The spatulate club of the *Chiriguano* and *Guarayu* belongs to the same general type.

Besides their conical cudgels, the *Cayapo* had two types of flat clubs: the first with a round grip and a flat rounded end; the other flat from the tapering grip to the sharp flat blade. The latter type is covered with a basketry sheath.

our ancient sources make this distinction so that it is difficult to establish the respective distribution of these two weapons.

Lances and spears.—The distribution of the lance certainly is greater than would be apparent from a listing of the tribes mentioned in the available literature. Moreover, the iron spear heads traded to the Indians by the Spaniards contributed to the increased popularity of this weapon among many tribes that perhaps had not previously used it or had considered it of secondary importance.

The lance was one of the chief weapons of *Chibcha* and *Inca* warriors; it is still the chosen weapon of the *Jivaro*. The use of the thrusting spear or lance is reported among a great many tribes of the upper Amazon and its tributaries, including the *Yameo, Coto, Mayoruna, Cashibo, Chayvita, Iquito, Chamicuro,* and *Jivaro.* It is also found among the tribes of the Tapajoz River (*Apiaca* and *Mundurucu),* the Araguaya River *(Caraja, Shavaje),* the coast of Brazil *(Puri-Coroado),* southern Brazil *(Caingang),* and the Chaco, and among the *Guato.*

The thrusting power of a lance carried by a man on horseback made it the favorite weapon of the equestrian tribes (*Abipon, Mocovi, Mbaya, Araucanians, Charrua, Tehuelche).*

The chief weapon of the *Yahgan, Alacaluf,* and *Chono* was the spear. The *Yahgan* spear varied in type according to the purpose for which it was intended; fish and bird spears consisted of "a beechwood shaft tipped with a serrated whalebone head lashed in place with seal-hide or braided sinew". Sometimes an additional point was slashed against the shaft. Guanaco spears were equipped with large, single barbed bone point. *Ona* fishing and hunting spears had a unilaterally barbed bone shank. Throwing spears with a wooden serrated point, identical to those of the *Yahgan,* were used by the ancient *Macovi* to kill capivara and caimans.

Lances were often a simple pole with a sharpened

and fire-hardened end *(Tucuna, Charrua,* Indians of Darien, and, in certain cases, the *Inca).*

In some tribes the shaft and head were carved out of one piece of wood. *Jivaro* spears, for instance, have a head "either diamond shaped with a low ridge running down the center of each side and tapering to a cutting edge, or triangular in section without the cutting edge". Similarly, the *Yamamadi* spears, which were used both as lances and javelins, ended in a tip with four to six edges.

Lances were frequently tipped with heads, which may be classified as follows: (1) A sharp wooden or bamboo blade *(Apiaca, Mayoruna, Arara, Omurana, Tucuna, Pioje, Andoa):* (2) the sharpened portion of a tubular bone of a large animal—generally a jaguar—or occasionally of a man *(Shavaje, Caraja, Sherente, Ssabela, Encabellado, Guato);* (3) a socketed deer horn *(Mocovi, Abipon, Mataco, Toba);* (4) a stone point *(Araucanians)* or a copper or bronze head (ancient Peru). In the Colonial Period iron heads became very common among Chaco and Pampa Indians. The longest lances were those of the equestrian *Araucanians, Charrua,* and *Guaycuruan* tribes of the Chaco, averaging in these tribes from 12 to 18 feet (3.6 to 5.5 m.). Lances handled by footmen were generally from 6 to 7 feet (1.8 to 2 m.) long *(Paez, Latacunga, Apiaca, Caraja, Sherente).*

Lances were often trimmed with feather tufts *(Caraja, Sherente, Apiaca, Maina, Zaparo, Mocovi)* or were decorated with a black and white basketry cover with geometrical patterns *(Caraja, Shavaje).*

Javelins.—The use of the javelin in preference to the bow and arrow characterizes a great many tribes on the tributaries of the upper Amazon River *(Mayoruna, Candoshi, Zaparo, Gaye, Chebero, Maina, Ssabela, Menimehe, Muinane, Tsoloa, Coto, Bora, Witoto, Yameo).* Warriors and hunters generally carried several javelins which they hurled in rapid succession. The javelins of the *Yameo, Iquito, Gaye, Pioje,*

Menimehe, Muinave, Ocaina, Yagua, Tucuna, Bora, Witoto, Juri, Uainuma, and *Passe* were tipped with a poisoned palm spine. Simson describes this type:

Here, these weapons are scraped to taper gradually almost to a point at the hilt; and the head end of the spear, which by degrees thickens, has another thin, sharp dart of chonta, about 3 inches long, inserted into and bound to it. This dart is besmeared with poison; and when the lance is thrown at any animal it breaks off in the flesh, to facilitate which it is usually cut half through at the base.

The javelin was one of the weapons used by the *Querandi* and *Charrua* in their fights against the Spaniards.

The Chaco Indians, particularly those who adopted the horse, wore leather—generally jaguar skin—jackets that sometimes reached the knees. These served the double purpose of a protective and an ornamental garment. The ones made of jaguar skin communicated to their wearers the fierceness of the animal. The *Ocaina* were said to have tapir-hide armor.

The conquistadors of Chile mention that the *Araucanians* had hide armor, sometimes made of seal skin. In post-Columbian times long cowhide jackets were part of the regular outfit of *Araucanian* and *Tehuelche* warriors. In Gozalez de Majera, there is a reference to "whale bone armor," but unfortunately he gives no details.

The term "armor" also may be extended to the thick shirts of the *Mataco, Choroti,* and *Toba* Indians, which were made of a fabric of caraguata fibers and were donned for battle as they were not easily pierced by arrows.

Some of the huge complicated headdresses of the Chimu warriors were perhaps helmets that, besides being extremely ornamental, protected the wearers from the impact of clubs and sling stones. A helmet described by Montell consisted of a wooden frame covered with a layer of sticks wound with cotton. Both sides of such helmets have disks that covered the ears and generally have been interpreted as earplugs. Cobo lists among *Inca* defensive weapons helmets made of reed, wood, and cotton wool. The *Mapuche* had helmets made of sealskin.

WEAVING. Textile work is one of the most ancient of crafts. Fragments of cloth or imprints, dating from the first agricultural age, have been discovered in many archaeological explorations.

The ancient Mexicans wove their fabrics on the so-called waist loom. Proof of this is found in the codexes and recently, a figure representing a woman weaving on one of these looms was found on the island of Jaina.

The waist loom is of simple manufacture. The threads that form the warp are tied to two sticks, a bit longer than the width of the fabric to be woven. One of the sticks is tied at both ends with a rope which is then fastened to a tree or pillar. The stick at the other end of the warp is attached to a wide leather or cloth band which the weaver places on his back at waist level.

The main weaving implements are the "lanzaderas" or shuttles, small sticks wound with the various threads to be interwoven, and a wide ruler, called "tzotzopaxtli", made of hard wood, which is used to separate the threads of the weft as they are counted with the other hand; the tzotzopaxtli is first placed in a vertical position in order to separate the two groups of threads, the shuttle is introduced, then the tzotzopaxtli is again laid flat and knocked several times to tighten the weaving. This procedure is repeated each time a thread is interwoven. It is estimated that eighteen hours of work are needed to weave about a yard of fabric. The finished weave is rolled on the stick which is near the weaver and is secured with another similar piece of wood. A series of smaller sticks are placed among the warp to facilitate the counting and separating of the threads.

Usually the thread itself is also spun by the Indians. A small stick with a clay or stone wheel at one end is used. The thread is held in one hand and wound around the stick as it is turned with the other hand.

The waist loom is still used by most of the indigenous communities of Mesoamerica, among them, the Otomis of San Pallito, Puebla (see illustration) and of Santa Ana Hueytlaplan, Hidalgo, the Nahuas of Cosoleacaque, Veracruz, the Trique and Tzeltales of the highlands of Chiapas, the Tarascan and Huichol Indians.

The principal items woven are waist bands, bags, quechquemitles, white cotton cloth for various uses, embroidered muslin and fabric for wrap-around skirts.

Contrary to the waist loom which is handled by women, the pedal loom which was introduced into America by the Spaniards, is run only by men. This loom consists of a wooden frame upon which are mounted two large spools. The warp is rolled up on the front spool, and the sarape as it is woven is wound around the back spool. The pedals move two pulleys which in turn raise and lower two pairs of sticks. To each pair of sticks is attached a series of criss-crossing threads which separate the warp so that the "lanzaderas" or shuttles with multicolored yarn can be inserted to form the design. The frame which holds the vertical threads and which hangs from the top part of the loom is pulled by the weaver towards himself so as to tighten each thread of the weft. He moves the pedals alternately by standing on them, while one hand moves the frame and the other inserts the shuttles. He usually has the design memorized as most of the patterns are traditional and the weavers know them by heart. Innovations are not frequent.

A hundred years ago, in the haciendas near Saltillo, Coahuila, the exquisite sarapes of Saltillo were made, which were later imitated in San Miguel de Allende, Guanajuato. This type of sarape, greatly prized by the charros as a gala part of their attire, ceased to be made long ago. Among collectors, its price nowadays is over' five thousand pesos. San Miguel now only makes the thick sarape which nevertheless is still one of the best in quality. At present, Teocaltiche, Jalisco, Leon, Guanjuato, and the city of Aguascalientes produce sarapes which imitate the style of those of Saltillo and although not of such fine quality, are still very beautiful.

Many towns make sarapes of a characteristic or distinctive style: Teotitlan de Valle, Oaxaca, in red and black with a large edged circle in the center; San Luis de la Paz, Guanajuato (see illustration); Jocotepec, Jalisco, makes those with two basic colors and multicolored flecks across them; Coroneo, Guanajuato, with an open weave and small geometric designs. Other places, like San Cristobal de las Casas, Chiapas, the city of Peubla and Cholula, Valle de Bravo, Zinacantepec and Coatepec de Harinas in the State of Mexico; Zitacuaro, Patzcuaro, Carapan and Parcho, In Michoacan, as well as numerous other towns in the states if Jalisco, Michoacan, Zacatecas, Guanajuato, Mexico, Queretaro, Guerrero, Veracruz, Oaxaca and Chiapas, make sarapes of a local style which are sold only in the local areas. In the north-western part of Mexico, the Yaquis and Tarahumaras produce an unlimited amount of beautiful sarapes which rarely are sold outside of the tribe.

A great number of distinctive sarapes which have a large national and international distribution, come from the great textile centers of Santa Ana Chiauhtempan, Tlaxcala, and San Miguel Chiconcuac, State of Mexico.

WEAVING

True weaving, the interlacing of warp and weft elements at right angles to each other, usually with the aid of frame or loom, is known to many South American tribes. Some, however, fabricate hammocks, bags, etc., by plaiting, netting, twining, or other finger work; they do not weave, or their weaving is rudimentary. The *Yuraro*, northwest Amazon tribes, *Ge* peoples, *Bororo, Guato, Guayaki, Siriono,* and tribes on the southern coast and of Tierra del Fuego are representatives. Some tribes limit their weaving to narrow bands *(Yuracare, Huanyam, Chacobo, Huari,* etc.).

Investigators express doubt that developed weaving was ever done by the *Choco,* the *Chibchan* tribes, and the West Indian *Carib;* the *Taino* cottons may have been netted or otherwise fabricated. Evidence also points to the disappearance of weaving from some areas. What is known of *Huarpe* and *Lenca* weaving is gleaned from old writers, since there are no available textile specimens. The same may be true of the southern *Guaymi* in coming generations. *Arawak* in the Chaco were formerly great weavers; *Omagua* and *Cocama* wove cloth for barter in the mid-seventeenth century; textile impressions on potsherds are sole direct evidence of former *Comechingon* wool (?) weaving.

By contrast, there is the phenomenon of development in modern times. Modern *Quillacinga, Pasto,* and *Coaiquer* developed weaving after the Conquest, using sheep's wool in addition to cotton; *Caraja* women learned weaving in the late 18th century on a loom introduced by a white man; the *Puelche* did not begin their weaving until the 19th century.

SPINNING

Cotton.—Cotton was cultivated by pre-Columbian Indians, and apparently was spread to many tribes through *Carib* and *Guarani* migrations. Wild cotton was collected, ginned, and spun by the *Aymara, Conibo, Macheguenga, Piro, Caraja, Northern Cayapo, Bororo,* Pilcomayo River peoples, and *Talamanca.* Cultivated cotton trees bearing white bolls range in height from 6 feet *(Tupi)* to 12 feet *(Mosquito and Sumo)* and even 15 feet (Huallaga River tribes); trees from 8 to 10 feet tall are common. Some bear continuously for 3 years, others from 7 to 10 years. Both white and brown cotton are cultivated (Ecuador,

Peru); in Paraguay, yellow cotton is occasionally seen; among the *Chiquito* alternate rows of white and yellow cotton trees are planted. Small quantities of cotton are grown and spun by almost all Guiana Indians. The *Arecuna* are credited with teaching the *Macushi;* from them the *Wapishana* may have received their knowledge in recent times. Cotton bolls from planted shrubs or from those that come up perennially near the houses or in protected spots are collected in July and August, stored in leaf-lined baskets suspended from the rooftrees, and ginned by hand as needed.

Cotton is also cultivated by *Northwestern Ge, Caraja,* and eastern Bolivian tribes in some quantity; also, in the Chaco, not abundantly, and by Paraguayan tribes. Dobrizhoffer describes procedures among these last. Women collect ripe bolls daily and spread the cotton out on hides in the courtyard. If thoroughly sun dried, raw cotton may be safely stored for years. Women gin cotton in this area by passing it between close-set wooden cylinders; ordinarily, Indian spinners laboriously pick out the seeds with the fingers.

Mundurucu, Piro, and Central American women beat raw cotton with small sticks to clean and separate the fibers; a few who came in contact with White civilization use the cotton bow, a device that reached South America during mission times. The cotton is fluffed by snapping the bowstring repeatedly on a layer of fibers spread out on a mat. Nordenskiold's map shows the *Caraja, Guato, Churapa, Guarayu, Chacobo, Guarani,* and *Guana as bow-using tribes; the more and Kashiha* also use the bow. The *Paressi* card cotton with a wooden comb.

Prelimary preparation of cotton fibers results in the following forms, which can be conveniently manipulated by spinners: Soft bands to be wound loosely around the left wrist in a position from which fibers can be drawn *Arawak);* baskets full of fluffed cotton or loose masses mounted on sticks thrust in the

giving motion to insert twist in the strand of fibers attached to the short spindle section below the whorl. The strand is slowly elongated by the movement away of the left hand. When sufficient twist has been given the length, it is wound on the longer section of the shaft.

The *"Bacairi"* spindle is given a vigorous twirl with the fingers of the right hand or between the palms, then allowed to drop slowly to the ground, thus drawing out and twisting the strand of fibers attached to its upper tip. Highland spinners following this procedure make yarn while walking along the roads or going from one household task to another. Other spinners give motion to the spindle by rolling it against the thigh, then allowing it to whirl freely in the air as it drops *(Bacairi,* Guiana tribes, *Western Tucanoans, Tupinamba)*. The *Carib* woman stands or sits on a high seat and holds the strand of fibers high with her left hand to permit the spindle to revolve freely. Yarn accumulates on the short section of the shaft, above the whorl; she subsequently transfers it to the long section. Women sitting at their work may twirl the spindle in a special small pottery bowl *(Aymara)*, or gourd (Caribbean Lowland tribes of Central America, *Conibo, Piro, Macheguenga, Mosquito, Sumo)*, or on a small earthen plate made for the purpose *(Chane)*, or on a shell *(Pauserna)*. The *Piro* and *Conibo* dip their fingers into ashes in order to counteract perspiration. *Jivaro* methods require dexterity. The woman sits with a basket of raw cotton at her feet. She plunges the sharpened slit tip of the spindle into the mass and draws away the spindle, simultaneously twsiting it rapidly between her fingers. At arm's length she reverses the twisting motion to wind up the length of yarn. The movements are outward and back, in principle the same as those of the drop method; they continue until the ball of yarn becomes too heavy to permit rapid twisting.

All yarns are initially spun single-ply; to form stronger yarns it is necessary two, three, or multiple

singles. Some tribes make the larger yarn by twisting
two or more singles together on the thigh *(Piro,*
Guiana tribes, *Guato)*; other tribes combine the balls
on two spindles by twisting on a larger, third spindle
(Guiana tribes, *Carib, Arawak);* the *Guaymi* and
Wapishana use a bow drill and spindle combination.

One noteworthy spinning achievement of the an-
cients has to do with doubling and redoubling single-
plies an uncounted number of times. The *Inca* built
suspension bridges of bark or fiber ropes spun to the
thickness of a man's body. Several cables bound
together formed a foundation for the plank floor;
smaller cables formed hand rails. *Aymara* bridges of
the same type are in use today.

Ropes are spun in some areas *(Lenca)* on wooden
devices twirled in the hand. Two people stand at some
distance from each other in an open space. Similar
methods are used by maguey spinners in Central
America.

Qualities of yarn are noted by observers. Tribes
whose needs include cotton threads for binding heads
to arrow shafts, garment materials, and hammocks
obviously must consider yarn sizes and strengths.
Guiana Indians make fine threads and coarse twines;
Jivaro fine yarns compare favorably with our sewing
cottons; *Yaruna* women spinners have been famous
since Mission times for their spun yarns. As every
authority recognizes, the ancient Peruvian spinners
produced superlatively fine cottons.

Cotton strands are effectively reduce to desired sizes
by various procedures: preliminary to using the spindle, women of some Guiana tribes and the *Caraja*
form a loose sliver by rolling the strand along the
thigh; after the first spinning the yarn is respun onto a
second spindle. The Guiana woman may rest in her
hammock with one end of the spindle, which she turns
rapidly with her finger, placed between her toes. Successive spinnings make yarn thinner, stronger, and
more uniform. The amount of twist given to each
spindleful must be carefully regulated to allow for

are cut up for blankets. Wool from the guanaco, also undomesticated, is used today by Patagonian tribes. The *Tehuelche* tease out the coarse fibers with the fingers to use in felts and to spin yarn for ponchos.

Sheep were introduced by the Spaniards; today sheep's wool is a staple wherever warm clothing is necessary (Andean tribes, the *Araucanians, Abipon, Choroti, Ashluslay, Chiriguano, Chane,* and other Chaco tribes).

Operations preliminary to spinning wool fibers are few: sheared wool may be washed in cold water *(Araucanians);* or it may be spread out on platforms of palm leaves or bushes for rain to cleanse and sun to bleach (Pilcomayo River, *Lengua).* Usually women tease out the wool with their fingers or comb it with European hand cards. Wools are spun on drop spindles; the wooden shafts and the wooden, pottery, or stone whorls which give them balance are similar to corresponding parts of cotton spindles except for size. Prepared wool fibers are given one or another form: a band to wind loosely around the left wrist *(Quechua)* or arm *(Araucanians)* or a soft mass to mount on a wooden distaff stuck in the spinner's belt *(Quechua).* Old manuscripts show the same small wooden horseshoe above a short handle to be found in Highland markets today. A distaff formed of four sticks tied to make a standing rack is also used.

Highland spinners are almost always women and children. They make yarn incessantly, as they walk the roads or herd flocks of sheep on the pampas, as they sit in the market, or wait for their men. No matter how heavily burdened, the woman's two hands are usually busy with yarn and the falling spindle in front of her. If seated, she often rotates it on a small pottery plate.

Human and other hairs are treated as textile fibers: *Jivaro* men braid the long hair stripped from their enemies' heads, and tie the braid around their own waists to signify courage; the *Bacairi* spin the hair of their dead; the *Bororo* plait neck cords and wrist guards of hair taken from mourners during funeral ceremonies; the *Guayaki* make ropes of human or monkey hair sometimes mixed with palm or nettle fibers; and Southern Hunters use horsehair for ropes. *Ona* witch doctors sometimes make a cloak of human hair, to use in bullying the tribe. In the 16th century some *Chono* made short mantles from the hair of a breed of long-haired, shaggy dogs.

Wool fibers are felted to make men's and women's hats *(Canipa, Quechua, Aymara)*. Specialists in the craft meet a constant demand for their products; piles of hats appear in the open Highland markets. Styles and shapes differ with localities.

Palm fibers, grass, and barks.—Yarns, cordage of different sizes, and ropes are made of palm fibers: aeta *(Mauritia flexuosa)*, tucum *(Astrocaryum vulgare)*, buriti *(Mauritia vinifera, M. flexuosa)*. Aeta fibers are taken from the young leaf growing from the center of the tree; they are separated from the skin, boiled, and dried in the sun *(Wapishana, Mascushi, Tucano, etc.)*. Tucum fibers are taken from the outer covering of the long, thin pointed leaves; they are spun by the *Yagua*, Vaupes River tribes, *Tucano, Bacairi,* upper Xingu tribes, *Northwestern* and *Central Ge*, and *Nambicuara*. The buriti fiber is virtually unlimited in some areas; each long tonguelike leaf yields a band of fiber elements. Buriti fibers are spun by the *Guato, Timbira, Bororo, Caraja,* and many hammock-making tribes. The *Yaruro* strip the inner cortex of the moriche leaf, dry it, separate it into strands, and then moisten them to spin.

The method of producing a continuous strand by thigh-spinning is as follows: The spinner places a small flat band of fibers across the right leg *(Caingang* men and women) or the thigh, and rolls the band downward into a single ply under his right palm. By combining this ply with others he makes cordage of required strength for nets, fishing lines, bow strings, bag, hammocks, etc. A procedure requiring greater dexterity results in two- or three-ply cords: the spinner

ing of certain fibers requires strength: *Arawak* men pull out silk grass fiber, although women may help if other male assistance is lacking; or, •women *(Wapishana)* may be responsible for spinning ordinary hammock twines, but men make the heavy suspension ropes. *Jivaro* men do all the spinning when they have nothing else to do; *Tucano* and *Bororo* men make recreation of it. They bring prepared fibers to the communal center or clubhouse and work with others likewise employed. Both sexes spin among the *Aymara*, some Bolivian tribes, *Nambicuara* (thigh-spun tucum and buriti fibers), and *Lengua*.

Ancient Peruvians perfected cotton and wool spinning to an amazing degree. On their primitive looms they produced extraordinarily fine textures, and in addition, they had imagination, ingenuity, and technical proficiency to develop unknown numbers of simple and complex weave-variants. Designs and colors harmonies exhibit a confident sense of proportion which never fails to arouse admiration.

Weaving accomplishments of other South American Indians, taken as a whole, are less varied. The vastly superior civilation of the west is dimly relected in borrowings of nearby tribes north and south, by some in the Chaco, and in Bolivian areas. Some Chaco Indians adopted the backstrap loom, slit (Kilim) tapestry technique, and the greater technical achievement, the warp-patterning techniques. By means of the last, lengthwise bands of motifs are developed; many warp-pattern borders are found in *Inca* graves.

From any standpoint, South American looms and their few accessories are simple. Each of the common types has an accepted name: Peruvian, *"Arawak"* or Amazon, and Rio Ucayali. The principal weavings, may for convenience be divided into three groups: (1) narrow weavings, to include arm bands, tapes, fillets, garters, anklets, sashes, garments of apron and breechclout types; (2) wide weavings, to include materials for shirts, ponchos, the tipoy, blankets; (3)

hammock making. Each groups makes certain technical demands upon weavers, and each requires some specialized equipment. Weaving appliances without heddles for control of certain warps are, strictly speaking, frames, not loom, but the differentiations are not emphasized in this article.

The majority of South American weavings have one feature in common: each is individually woven to desired size. From ancient to Conquest times there is no evidence of cutting down a woven length, and even today only the *Quechua, Aymara,* and a few neighboring tribes alter the original size of the loomed rectangle or tailor it to shape.

Bands and narrow materials: looms.—The narrow fabrics woven on miniature looms may be technically identical with, and except for widths, may look like wider garment materials woven on big looms. Some tribes *(Chacobo, Huanyam, Huari, Nambicuara, Yuracare, Ona)* weave only bands; other tribes weave them in addition to wide fabrics but have special looms for bands. Warp lengths on these are relatively short and easily manipulated. Weaving can be done without tools if the warps are held at tension. Guiana Indians weave some of their indispensable arm and leg bands in place with only the fingers; such bands are from one to two inches wide. The *Caraja* follow the same practice, weaving in place broad bands on wooden forms.

Warps may run vertically or horizontally. The *Aueto, Guato,* and *Bororo* weave wide belts on warps held taut by winding them around wooden stakes driven into the ground. Weft is inserted with the fingers, driven down with a wooden sword. For simple belts and fillets the *Cayapa* drive two pegs into a plantain stem and wind the warps around them. The weft is a bell of pita put from side to side of the web through spaces made by the fingers; these also drive down the weft. Elemental weaving is slow but meets the demands.

The Peruvian type loom is very old. One proto-Chimu example without a heddle is shown in scenes painted on the flaring rim of a pottery bowl. A similar loom from a Paracas Cavernas site is equipped with heddle (Museo Nacional, Lima, specimen 8465a). Highland looms of today are like these ancient looms in all essential features.

The Peruvian or backstrap loom consists of two end-bars to hold the warp skein at tension. Shed-stick and heddle-rod with loops for opening sheds through which the weft passes, a slender bobbin, and a relatively heavy sword for battening weft and standard parts. A tenter for maintaining uniform fabric width and pattern sticks for developing design motives are accessories. The upper loom-bar is attached by an inverted Y-shaped rope to a house post, or the bar may be supported between two upright poles *(Jivaro)*.

WHALES AND WHALING is of general occurrence on the east Asiatic littoral from East Cape at Bering Strait at least as far south as Japan. It is commonly considered a general feature of Eskimo culture, though some groups, by reason of continental cultural orientation or environmental restrictions, do not indulge in it. It occurs from Point Barrow southward in Bering Sea and eastward to Greenland. Whaling spilled over in the east to the New England coast of Maine. Among the so-called Pacific Eskimo (Aleut, Kaniagmiut, or Koniag) whaling was a very important subsistence feature. Its southward extension was the west coast of Vancouver Island and the coast of northwestern Washington from Cape Flattery as far south as the Quinault River. The intervening stretch north of the Nootka to the Kenai Peninsula in commonly thought of as an area of non-whaling; the suspicion, for which there is some evidence, of the former existence of whaling in this coastal and offshore-island area of maritime peoples raises a separate problem.

On the Pacific littoral of northeast Asia there is a small, restricted area where whaling was accomplished by the relatively simple procedure of throwing a lance into the whale, the stone point of which was detachable and smeared with deadly aconite poison. The area is that of the Kurile Island and the Kamchatkan·coast. The Koryak to the north and Japanese to the south employed different methods.

Whale.—This is the polar, or bowhead, whale *(Balaena mysticetus* Linn.) which begins to swim up through the Bering Strait as soon as the ice permits free movement. Herds of these animals feed through the summer along the edges of the polar cap, returning southward in the fall when the ocean ice begins to thicken. Today as in the past, the baleen whales appear in the off-shore ice leads beginning in late April. They may still be sighted in early June. Whaling camps were set up on the edges of the leads and the crews pursued the whales in umiaks, each with several harpoons with two seal-bladder floats on each. The attempt was made to place as many harpoons as possible in the whale. When the animal tired and rose for air in the limited space of the ice lead, it was lanced, a special lance with a large stone head being used for this purpose. An attempt was made to spear the whale in the heart, lungs, or brain and so to kill it. The carcass was then towed back to the camp at the edge of the lead, tugged by communal effort on the ice, and divided. It is in respect to this whole activity that an extremely elaborate series of ceremonial usages arise and that a basis for extra-kin associations is seen.

The general term for the common baleen whale is aa vik. An especially large specimen—and it is worth noting that some exceed 60 feet in length and that a rough computation can be made of 1 ton per foot—is called qayrelik. Smaller specimens, the poggy whales, 20 to 30 feet in length, with 3 or 4 feet of baleen, and reflecting a varietal difference, are inutuk. A larger specimen of this type is inutuvak.

The northern villages engaged in whaling in the fall also, when the herds began to move south again. But this season cannot be considered important since it af-

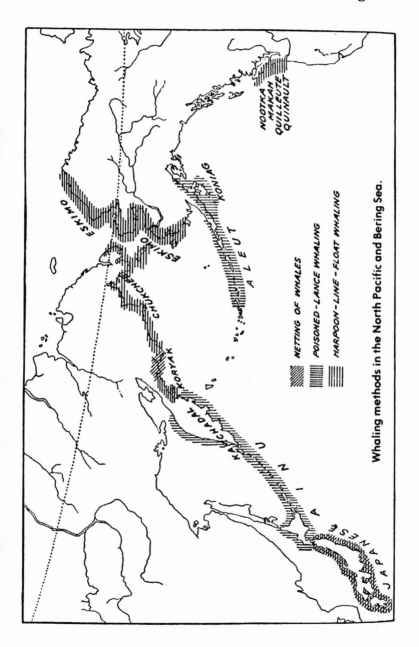

Whaling methods in the North Pacific and Bering Sea.

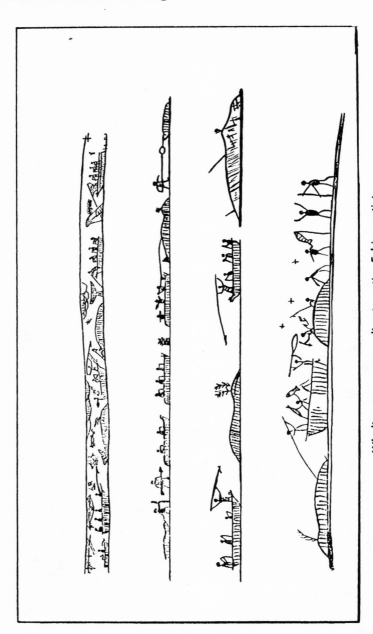

Whaling scenes according to native Eskimo artists.

fected only nuwuk and utkeaa vik. Even for these towns, no elaboration of ceremonial activity took place in the fall, this being reserved for the earlier season. At this time, whales were hunted in the open water, obviously a much more difficult undertaking in the fragile umiak. Two or three animals might be captured at this time, although this by no means compares with a successful spring season, when as many as 25 whales, representing hundreds of tons of meat, might be brought in.

The meat was divided in various ways between participating crews. It was carefully stored in ice cellars after being distributed according to well-defined regulation and ceremony. Use was made of virtually every part of the whale carcass. Apart from the especially prized skin—the delicate muktuk, eaten raw and boiled—and the blubber and meat, the bones were used much as wood, in making house beams, sleds, and many other artifacts, and the baleen, the long-fringed strainers in the mouth of the plankton-eating whales, was likewise used for many purposes, including the making of ornaments and amulets, of sledges, and of armor. Oil in great quantities, for use as food and fuel, was stored in seal bladders and skins. The upshot of the whaling, given an average year, made for considerable surplus of food and a basic ease of life. If, however, the herds changed their course for a year or two, the result was often starvation, or at least, limited rations. The population of a coastal community rose with a successful year, and declined markedly if few whales were taken, as the inhabitants struck out alone or in small groups to wrest a living from other sources.

WHISTLE, small musical instrument used ceremonially and to attract animals during a hunt, as a signal in war, as treatment for disease. The whistle was used throughout the continent, except perhaps in the arctic, and was a tube of bone, wood, pottery, reed, or metal. When blown, it produced one note.

In ceremonies and dances, the sound of the whistle may have represented the call of spirits, birds, or animals. In the Plains tribes' Sun Dance, whistles made of eagle bone and decorated with feathers were blown by the dancers, symbolizing breath and life, as well as the voice of the thunderbird who loosed the rain. In this instance, too, the eagle was the spirit of war, and by blowing eagle-bone whistles the dancing warriors invoked protection and success.

In the Peyote cult of the 19th and 20th centuries, the priest led the people outside at midnight and blew a bird-bone whistle to the east, south, west, and north to "call the winds," or "tell the birds about us."

INDEX